Steppingstones *to* Curriculum

A Biblical Path

Steppingstones *to* Curriculum

A Biblical Path
Second Edition

Harro Van Brummelen

purposeful design
p u b l i c a t i o n s

Colorado Springs, Colorado

Purposeful Design Publications is the publishing division of the Association of Christian Schools International (ACSI) and is committed to the ministry of Christian school education, to enable Christian educators and schools worldwide to effectively prepare students for life. As the publisher of textbooks, trade books, and other educational resources within ACSI, Purposeful Design Publications strives to produce biblically sound materials that reflect Christian scholarship and stewardship and that address the identified needs of Christian schools around the world.

Unless otherwise identified, all Scripture quotations are taken from the Holy Bible, NEW INTERNATIONAL VERSION® (NIV®), © 1973, 1978, 1984 by International Bible Society. All rights reserved worldwide.

Printed in the United States of America
16 15 14   8 9

Van Brummelen, Harro
    Steppingstones to curriculum: A biblical path
    Second edition
    ISBN 978-1-58331-023-6 Catalog #6255

Designer: Shelley Webb
Editorial team: Karen Friesen, Mary Endres

Purposeful Design Publications
A Division of ACSI
PO Box 65130 • Colorado Springs, CO 80962-5130
Customer Service: 800-367-0798 • www.acsi.org

Table of Contents

Preface

In this book I consider what a Christian worldview implies for curriculum theory and practice. I show how a biblical view of knowledge, of values, and of the person leads to distinctive curriculum approaches. The chapters that follow on school-based curriculum planning and planning classroom units are intended to help teachers and schools plan and implement distinctively Christian courses and units. The final chapter discusses how principals and other leaders (including teachers!) can bring about meaningful curriculum change.

I wrote this book because today's school curriculum, by and large, does not meaningfully address the superficiality of modern culture. Our curriculum can do much more than it does now to counter the self-centeredness and lack of commitment that plagues our society. I believe that God demands Christian educators to do so. I pray, then, that this book will help teachers and prospective teachers plan and implement programs that encourage their students to become responsive and responsible disciples of our Lord Christ Jesus.

The book has several intended audiences. It is a textbook for curriculum and instruction courses in Christian postsecondary institutions. It also serves as a guide for Christian teachers as they plan their day-to-day classroom units and school curricula. While the content will be useful particularly for teachers and leaders in Christian schools, a number of my Christian acquaintances in public education have told me that they found the content of the first edition of the book very helpful for thinking anew about the content and structure of programs and units that they design and implement.

A few explanations are in order. The first edition of this book was used in many different jurisdictions and countries. Rather than explaining age/grade equivalents each time, the term kindergarten is used to designate the first year of school for four- to six-year-olds. Primary grades include grades one, two, and three (five- to nine-year-olds); intermediate—grades four, five, and six (eight- to twelve-year-olds); middle school—grades six, seven, and eight (ten- to fourteen-year-olds); and high school—grades nine through twelve (thirteen- to eighteen-year-olds).

Discussion leaders and course instructors in schools may find that there are more questions and situations for discussion in the "footsteps" than can be used or analyzed; that allows for some choice. The footsteps not discussed will at least alert the reader to curriculum issues and situations that teachers and schools need to consider. When I use the book as a text with preservice teachers, I find that teaching chapters 5, 6, and 7 concurrently with the first four chapters helps students to integrate their own theory and practice.

This book would not have been possible without the cooperation of many classroom teachers in British Columbia and Alberta, Canada. The examples they provided and allowed me to observe give a unique flavor to the book. All examples with names are actual examples with actual names, and their schools are identified in appendix 3. Four persons gave me valuable feedback on either or both editions: Curtis Gesch, Albert E. Greene, Kim Franklin, and Robert Koole. Several classes of students at Trinity Western University who used the text also gave helpful responses. My thanks to all of them! The final product is, of course, my own responsibility.

The section on the experiential orientation and constructivism in chapter 2 is a revised excerpt of an article that was published in the September 1997 issue of *Pro Rege*, "Curriculum Development Is Dead—Or Is It?"

I thank Trinity Western University in Langley, British Columbia, for granting me sabbaticals in 1993–94 and the spring of 2001. These leaves enabled me to write, respectively, the first and second editions of the book. A grant from the Social Sciences and Humanities Research Council of Canada covered my expenses for the 1993–94 classroom visits.

I dedicate this book to my spouse Wilma. Our combined classroom experience ranges from teaching four-year-old kindergartners to postgraduate students in their sixties. Her constant example of unconditional love for children of all ages has added a much-needed dimension to my thinking. Her insights into teaching young children have complemented my experience at the secondary and university levels. Our discussions over the years and her sensitivities about children are reflected in the content of this book.

Harro Van Brummelen
Trinity Western University
Langley, British Columbia
vanbrumm@twu.ca

Steppingstone 1

Setting Out on the Curriculum Path

Over a ten-year period, English teacher Naomi White taught a future evangelist, a boxer who was to lose an eye in a brawl, two boys later convicted of theft and murder, and a student who now "beats his head against a padded wall in the state asylum." She reflected, "I must have been a great help to these pupils—I taught them the rhyming schemes of the Elizabethan sonnet and how to diagram a complex sentence" (White in Harmin and Gregory 1974, 84).

Despite this wry comment, White no doubt taught her students a great deal about life. Likely she had a significant effect on many of them.

Reflective teachers, however, know they fall short of their ideals. Like Naomi White, they mull over the effects of what they teach. They may feel caught between opposing curriculum forces. They want to teach a unit about their local community, but the topic is part of another grade level. They know that their students gain from hands-on science activities but can't find enough time to prepare them. They believe that the topic of statistics has great relevance for their students, but the district-wide tests omit it. They like to foster open-ended response, but arduous class dynamics call for a firm structure. They teach for commitment to a positive way of life, but peer influence undermines their attempts.

Even so, teachers do teach content and use strategies that enrich the lives of students. Their programs, when carefully planned, do help their students grow toward responsible maturity and commitment. They do nurture the insights and gifts of students so that those students learn to balance independence with personal and communal responsibility. True, some students' lives seem to display little of their influence. But they do affect the lives of many students positively, often more than they realize.

Let me give an example. Teacher Curt Gesch published excerpts from answers to essay questions in his exams. Sarah described how her tenth-grade short story unit taught her to be more sensitive to people around her. She pondered why teenagers, herself included, often act erratically: "We run on emotion most of the time, and sometimes the emotion is due to fear of what the family will think, our friends' reactions, and all-in-all, the people around us" (Gesch 1993).

Another student, Sheryl, recounted the five most important things she learned in twelfth grade. She became appalled at social injustice in society today by studying the biblical prophecy of Amos and the book *Black Like Me*. She learned how human sin demands discipline. She discovered that work is a gift from God, and that leisure time is time for recreation. Finally, Hemingway's *The Sun Also Rises* was her springboard for reviewing how others, and she herself, search for meaning in life. Sheryl concluded that "although there is always room for more knowledge, I am grateful for what I have learned so far."

I sometimes ask college students about teachers who affected their lives. Usually they first mention the types of persons those teachers were. They were the ones who loved their students unconditionally. They had a genuine desire to bring out the best in their students. They were always willing to help with both academic and personal concerns. And they were people of faith and integrity who walked their talk.

When I probe a little deeper, the students also begin to reflect on how those teachers planned content and structured classes to fit their beliefs about what was meaningful. They remember highlights of what they learned. They see how the curriculum implemented by those teachers shaped their own thinking.

Think back to your schooling. Recall cases where the content and structure of the curriculum made a difference in your life or in the lives of your classmates, either positively or negatively. What does this imply for planning curriculum? How can teachers shape curriculum? What is curriculum?

Footstep 1-1

In this first chapter we explore a number of preliminary questions:

- Can curriculum be neutral?
- Who makes curriculum decisions?
- What role does one's worldview play in making curriculum decisions?
- What does it mean to teach for commitment? What are the implications for teaching in Christian schools? in public schools?
- How do we define *curriculum*?
- Is a biblically grounded curriculum platform possible and desirable? What are its key elements?
- What are the overall aims of the curriculum?

Before you begin reading, think about your initial answers to some of these questions.

This book's starting point is that all school programs have a worldview foundation. Such a worldview may not always be stated openly. But every curriculum guide, every standards document, every textbook, and every course outline makes certain basic assumptions, for instance, about what is important for our society, which values we should promote, and the role of the learner as a human being.

This book, therefore, explores how worldviews affect school programs. In particular, it examines how a worldview based on the Bible, God's Word, provides a framework for school curriculum. At the same time, it considers how our cultural and educational context affects what and how we teach—and what and how students learn.

The book uses the metaphor of curriculum steppingstones. That is because there are certain stones that affect the nature and direction of a curriculum path. This book is intended to help you choose which stones are important for you and decide how you will make use of them as you plan learning in your classroom or your school. You need steppingstones to cross a stream. But it is up to you to pick your way across the stream, to plan how learning can be most beneficial for your students.

Footstep 1-2

"A curriculum must include a diversity of value positions without promoting any particular one." How do you react to this point of view? Is it possible to do what it says? desirable?

Is a Neutral Curriculum Possible?

An oft asked question is whether it is right for a curriculum to echo a teacher's own faith and values. Or should the curriculum be kept neutral? Philosopher Mary Warnock disputes the two reasons given by those who advocate neutrality in teaching:

- **You must avoid indoctrination**. Warnock shows that usually this term is applied only to ideas with which advocates of neutrality disagree. They themselves are not neutral! In fact, by aiming for a neutral curriculum, they indoctrinate students into thinking that values are either unimportant or can be chosen at will.

- **Students must draw their own conclusions from their own explorations and constructions.** But learning would be too complex if students were to investigate everything fully. Often they cannot understand—let alone assess—all evidence. If indoctrination means giving views without complete reasons, then most education of younger children involves indoctrination.

Warnock next shows that it is impossible to be neutral in teaching. Already our selection of content is biased by cultural assumptions and our view of what is important. Besides, she says, neutral teachers would seem remote to their students. They would also implicitly teach that any value position is as good as any other—a value position in itself. Teachers must present various positions fairly and leave students free to reach their own conclusions. However, since teachers will always go beyond teaching facts, they shirk their duty if they do not give their own views and opinions. They should show how they base their own conclusions on beliefs and evidence. That is the only way to be sincere and get students to think about what is right and wrong. Interpretation enters any meaningful argument. Good teachers hold, express, and defend moral and religious views (Warnock in Hare and Portelli 1988, 177–186).

To try to teach a valueless curriculum can have several results. With a supposedly objective curriculum students may:

- Accept society's dominant materialistic, self-centered values without much thought
- Learn to believe that objective concepts and skills are more important than values
- Take for granted that the structures and patterns of our culture are neutral

- Conclude that they may choose whatever values and commitments they prefer
- Adopt a dualistic view of the world where Christian faith is a private concern that has little to do with the warp and woof of life in society

What is clear is that even so-called neutral teaching involves initiation into distinct patterns of thought and behavior. Teaching cannot but encourage commitment of some kind even if it is to the idea that all worldviews are equally acceptable. Teachers live and nurture a way of life. That is why it is so important that their commitments be clear and defensible.

Making Curriculum Decisions

Teachers do not choose curriculum alone. Governments publish curriculum guides that are thought of as the formal or the prescribed curriculum. Authors use such guides, as well as what both educators and parents expect, to write textbooks. These texts may become the inherent curriculum. Professional associations may recommend a particular curriculum. School systems and schools use both guides and textbooks to construct grade-level and subject outlines that become the intended curriculum.

Still, teachers make the most vital curriculum decisions. They do not neglect the formal and intended curricula, but they decide which topics to emphasize. They determine unit themes and related values. They set suitable learning outcomes, either explicitly or implicitly. They create, choose, and organize activities. They select appropriate resources. They opt for ways to assess students. They constantly revise and adapt to meet the learning needs of their students. Above all, they plan so that their implemented curriculum becomes a meaningful experienced curriculum for their students.

Footstep 1-3

The previous two paragraphs mention a number of curriculum players at different levels:

- **Government departments of education**: the formal or prescribed curriculum
- **Textbook publishers**: the inherent or default curriculum when teachers allow texts to determine their curriculum
- **Professional associations**: the professionally recommended curriculum
- **School systems and schools**: the intended curriculum
- **Teachers**: the implemented curriculum
- **Students**: the experienced or attained curriculum

What other players have an impact on the curriculum? What worldviews and values might they bring to the curriculum path, and how might these affect curriculum decisions?

To plan a formal or intended curriculum, groups of educators usually involve themselves in a process of deliberation. Such deliberative groups may involve discipline and curriculum specialists, teachers, and others such as parent representatives. They seldom follow specific steps in a set order. However, their implicit starting point is often a set of commonly held beliefs about schools, students, teaching and learning, and content. Such planning groups, in the course of their deliberation:

- Pose and define the curriculum situation or problem

- Judge the best course of action in terms of their beliefs, weighing all the available evidence
- Apply theories, practical experience, and judgment to make recommendations

The resulting decisions and plans only inform the teacher's implemented curriculum, however. This is so because the experienced curriculum must be directly related to the needs, interests, experiences, and capabilities of the students. In the end, students must personally understand, interpret, and respond to knowledge. In other words, curriculum documents are no more than guides. Teachers who are reflective practitioners use their best judgment to do what is best for their students. They consider, choose, adapt—and reject—parts of guides, textbooks, and other resources.

Footstep 1-4

What curriculum content is meaningful and relevant? Teachers make such decisions on the basis of their worldview, their aims for education and learning, their students' social and economic backgrounds, their students' aptitudes and how they react to various types of learning activities, and the availability of resources.

Consider the following example. Suppose a tenth-grade mathematics teacher plans to teach a six-week geometry unit. She would like to explore the historical development of geometry, having her students weigh the effects of the Greek emphasis on theoretical reasoning. Some of her students are artistic, and she knows they would be excited if she based her unit on the use of geometry in art and architecture: the Golden Rectangle, perspective, geodesic domes, and so on. She also has available a computer program that shows how geometry is applied in drafting and in new car design. Developing the unit around such applications might encourage some students to become interested in technical design, an area with good job prospects. She does not have time to do justice to all three types of explorations, particularly if she purposed to teach all concepts in her curriculum guide. Her students have a wide range of abilities and interests. She wonders whether she should define a core that she teaches to all students, with optional modules for groups of students.

At the same time, three months from now her school board will evaluate basic mathematics skills for all tenth-grade students in the district. She knows that her students will do best on the geometry part of the tests if she carefully follows the curriculum guide and the textbook page by page. She would then teach the concepts sequentially and spend no time on the other approaches. How well her students do on the tests will affect her stature as a teacher—and how closely her teaching will be monitored. The local press is playing up the importance of the tests, and her principal is putting pressure on teachers to prepare the students well.

The teacher has to make some choices. In the allotted time, she cannot do everything she would like to do. What advice would you give her? In her situation, how would you decide on content that would be meaningful for the students and still take into account the intended curriculum?

The Underlying Basis for Making Curriculum Decisions

Planning groups need to ask several key questions throughout a curriculum development process:

- What are the overall aims of schooling?
- How can schooling help humanity work toward a more just and compassionate society?
- What ought to be done in the curriculum? What is the right thing to do?
- How can the curriculum lead students to discover meaning? How can it connect with their daily experiences? How can it link believing, thinking, and doing? How can it make them both more discerning and more committed to a principled way of life?

In this process, what soon becomes clear is that diverse views of the purpose and meaning of life and of education may make it difficult for a curriculum-planning group to arrive at specific decisions. Compromises are possible when basic outlooks on life and educational principles are similar. But to reconcile conflicting points of view about curriculum that involve matters of ultimate significance in life is an arduous task, if possible at all (Walker 1990, 206). Different recommendations for curriculum content and approaches are unavoidable among curriculum planners with different views on the meaning of life.

Some years ago the Ministry of Education in British Columbia launched an extensive process of deliberation in order to develop a new social studies curriculum. Several thousand people were involved and consulted. University faculty members, teachers, parents, and business people were all encouraged to give input and respond to draft documents. I recall one meeting of 300 or 400 educators that quickly deteriorated into a shouting match among factions with conflicting views of the aims of social studies—and of the meaning and purpose of life. After almost two years of wrangling among the various factions, the deputy minister of education cancelled the deliberative process and appointed a small committee of like-minded people. Within several months they had put together a new program.

The point here is that as educational leaders and teachers plan curriculum, they need a common vision of life to be able to reach consensus on major curriculum decisions. As T. S. Eliot said many years ago:

> To know what we want in education we must know what we know in general; we derive our theory of education from our philosophy of life. The problem turns out to be a religious problem. (Eliot 1952, 132)

In recent years, more educators express agreement with Eliot. They see that we cannot separate our deepest beliefs from our teaching:

> My vision of good teaching includes nurturing the moral and spiritual development, the civic engagement, and the socialization of students ... at the heart of my work on good teaching is the notion of a teacher as an enlightened, passionate intellectual. (Shulman 2001, 6)

> Everything that is done in schools, and in preparation for school activity, is already infused with the spiritual. All activity has moral consequences.... The problem of the schools is not that kids are not being taught moral and spiritual values, the problem is—the schools are not places where the moral and spiritual life is lived with any kind of intentionality. It is also quite clear to me that it is futile to hope that teachers can be aware of the spiritual in education unless they maintain some

kind of spiritual discipline. (Huebner 1999, 414–15)

An essential aspect of the project to understand curriculum is to understand that curriculum is also a moral and ethical project, grounded theologically … (Pinar et al. 1995, 637)

Critical theorists are one group of educators who recognize that all curricula promote a vision of life. They argue that many teachers just carry out prescribed curriculum directives. The result, they say, is that students become committed to the dominant cultural and economic values. Usually, they add, teachers serve up a superficial liberalism that leads to ethical and social starvation.

Some critical theorists go beyond critiquing formal curricula. They change them so that they become tools for social change. Barry Kanpol (1993, 203–11), for instance, describes teachers who stray from the official curriculum and teach the value commitments of critical theorists. Such planned curricula highlight race and gender rights, community life that resists individualism, and the social problems resulting from societal conflict and hierarchical authority.

Elsewhere Kanpol (1998, 117) praises a Christian teacher "who takes on the injustices he sees within the system such as teacher-proof curriculum, excessive competition, teacher apathy, and teacher oppression of others." Christians, he concludes, should practice curriculum in Christlike harmony that weds spirituality with social critique.

Footstep 1-5

The late Brazilian educator Paulo Freire can be said to be the father of the critical theory movement. He believed that curriculum should be used to liberate oppressed people. When he taught literacy to adults in third-world countries, for instance, he first taught that all people can have an impact on their surroundings and can create culture. The first words the adults read were about the terrible consequences of nuclear war. Some well-known educators who have tried to apply these ideas to North America include Michael Apple, Henry Giroux, Peter McLaren, and David Purpel. Find out more about the curriculum thinking of critical theorists. In what ways do you agree with their conclusions and recommendations about curriculum? disagree?

My view of rights, justice, and values agrees only in part with that of the critical theorists. I dispute their claim that political and economical equity will enable people to solve society's problems. But critical theorist Kanpol is right that a redemptive pedagogy and a curriculum of compassion obey the teachings of Jesus. He is also right that Christian faith and accepting the Christian narrative or story leads us to a covenant not only with Christ but also with our students.

If Christians in education take seriously the teachings of Jesus, they will, like the critical theorists, teach with and for commitment. Their belief in biblical love and justice will affect how they plan and implement their programs. They will plan units and courses that are framed by a biblical worldview. Their faith and their worldview will inform the key curriculum decisions they make each year, each month, and each day.

Footstep 1-6

Before reading the next section, describe how you interpret the idea that a teacher is a guide who teaches for commitment. Do you think that a school curriculum can promote commitment without undue indoctrination? Why or why not?

The Teacher as Guide

Christian teachers are more than facilitators. They are guides. They develop their teaching skills reflectively within a well-defined philosophical and religious framework. They then use these skills to guide young persons into knowledge and discernment that lead to service for God and fellow human beings. Teaching requires diverse competencies as well as a sense of direction and purpose that enables persons to be effective guides. (This section is based on Van Brummelen 1998, 40–50.)

The Bible calls Jesus our great Shepherd (Hebrews 13:20). A shepherd guides his sheep, using his rod and staff to nudge them in the right direction. The intent of such guidance is that the sheep go in the direction where they will have food and be safe from danger. As a result, they will be able to fulfill their intended role. Today, just as the Spirit of Truth guides us into all truth (John 16:13), God calls teachers to lead their students in the way of wisdom (Proverbs 4:11). They guide them to develop their gifts and take on life's calling in an ever deeper and fuller way. They help them become competent, discerning, responsible, and responsive disciples.

Such guidance requires unfolding meaningful content—especially making known the basis, contours, and implications of a biblical vision of life. Christian teachers are prophets in that their teaching proclaims God's handiwork in creation, the effects of sin, and the possibilities of reconciliation and restoration (Luke 1:76–79). This prophetic role requires them to have a thorough knowledge of what they teach and the ability to interpret such knowledge authentically and clearly.

The unfolding of meaningful content deepens students' insight into God's world and their place in it and leads them to take delight in God's creation as well as feel hurt by the effects of sin. An obstacle that Christian teacher-guides must overcome is the pervasive influence of our secular society on themselves and on their students. God calls teachers to help students develop the insights, abilities, and dispositions necessary to serve God and His Kingdom in all aspects of their lives in society. Teachers need to guide in the truth. Therefore, they search out the will of God for their content and how they go about teaching it. Jesus warns of the grave risk of leading children astray (Matthew 18:2–6).

Planning a curriculum that guides into truth does not mean that Christian teachers put children into narrow Christian straitjackets. Prejudice and intolerance contradict what Jesus stood for. Christian teachers want students to develop critical discernment. For this, students need a knowledge base that they apply to questions and issues. Then teachers can help and stimulate their students to make prudent commitments on which they will base personal and communal decisions and actions.

Philosopher Elmer Thiessen (1993, 141–43) has shown that nurturing children into critical reflection, open-mindedness, and normal rational autonomy is impossible without first initiating them into a stable and coherent tradition. All traditions inevitably include faith and commitment. These, indeed, form a necessary framework for developing critical faculties. Therefore, teachers need to teach for defensible commitment and "spare our children and students the hell of noncommitment" (p. 277).

Christians do not need to apologize for planning curricula that foster commitment to the self-sacrificing love, righteousness, and justice of the Christian faith. Christian faith has a great deal to say to society about compassion and respect, about justice and truth, about rights and responsibilities. Christian teachers cannot and do not demand that students commit themselves to specific beliefs and values. But their programs do show students that commitment to a set of coherent beliefs and values is crucial in their lives. And those programs also show that the Christian faith, despite the shortcomings of its followers, provides a sound basis for a just and compassionate society.

Teaching for Commitment in Christian Schools

This section will summarize Elmer Thiessen's views on Christian nurture (1993, 245–67) and then apply his conclusions to Christian school curricula.

Thiessen shows that every child is necessarily initiated into a particular religious (or irreligious) tradition. He argues that it is not only desirable but essential that schools deliberately initiate children into a stable, secure, and coherent tradition. In a society that increasingly excludes religion, Christian schools initiate children into their Christian inheritance. Early initiation through stories "provide[s] children with the necessary tools for further growth and development in the area of religion" (1993, 249).

But, Thiessen continues, Christian schools must do more than initiate. Their goal is also to guide students into normal rationality and autonomy. Students with a stable initiation base are most likely to

achieve personal identity and appropriate autonomy when they reach adolescence. Especially at that age teachers must respect the freedom of students to affirm or deny the Christian heritage and must avoid unwarranted indoctrination. Schools "should attempt to foster both growth in rational groundings of Christian convictions and honest and serious grappling with doubt, questions, and objections to Christian convictions" (1993, 263). They should therefore also discuss other religious and philosophical belief systems.

Teachers in Christian schools, especially in higher grades, may not find it easy to keep in balance initiation into a Christian tradition and growth toward normal autonomy. Students often crave the stability and coherence that tactful initiation can give. Also, many parents who enroll children in Christian schools like safe climates. Yet students need to develop their critical and creative faculties in order to make their own decisions. They also need to learn to deal with the consequences of such decisions.

The Christian school curriculum, therefore, needs to give students room to examine various views and to formulate their own. Teachers should challenge students not to give easy or pat answers to difficult issues. They should present non-Christian beliefs and positions honestly and fairly. They should acknowledge that Christians do not have all answers to social and moral problems. They should admit that they themselves have questions about, for instance, why God allows suffering to take place. They should show how God's common grace gives both Christians and non-Christians insights and abilities to create worthwhile books, economic theories, works of art and music, and technological breakthroughs. They should help students discern the strengths and weaknesses of positions taken by both Christians and non-Christians.

Christian schoolteachers need to remember three key points as they formulate their classroom curriculum:

- **They confidently initiate their students into their cultural and Christian heritage.** Using a supposedly neutral curriculum to which they add a course in religious studies and occasional value discussions is not sufficient.

- **They encourage their students to grow in normal rational responsibility.** That is, they help them to think critically and discerningly, and to recognize that such thinking always takes place within the bounds of faith commitments. Allowing for genuine and honest response is particularly important.

- **They teach with commitment since they want to teach for commitment.** Their commitment affects how they make decisions in the classroom, how they structure learning, how they assess learning—and how they plan their curriculum.

Teaching for Commitment in Public Schools

This book explores, in the first place, Christian school curriculum. However, as one public school leader said to me about its first edition, most of its content is also valid for Christian teachers in public schools. In this section, therefore, I look at how Christian teachers can teach for commitment in public schools.

Public schools, like Christian ones, cannot be neutral. However, since public schools serve all sectors of society, the curriculum is secular. As a Christian teacher you may not use the public school classroom as a forum for evangelism. Accepting a position in a public school means that you agree to teach a curriculum that is suitable for all children, no matter what their background. You may not promote or encourage commitment to a particular religion inside your classroom. You present different points of view, including religious ones, fairly and sensitively.

However, public school teachers do have an obligation to teach and encourage commitment to a set of basic values without which a democratic society cannot function. Most primary teachers, for instance, initiate their students into standards of behavior that reflect responsibility and compassion. At all grade levels teachers choose literary selections that illustrate or promote discussion of values important for a democratic society: respect for human dignity, empathy for others, integrity, perseverance, and fair-mindedness (ASCD 1988, 5; Paul 1988, 15).

Thomas Lickona's writings on character education in public education became popular in the 1990s. Lickona showed how religion has always been a crucial moral force in American life. American civil rights leaders, for example, were motivated by the religious belief that we are all equal in the sight of God, who calls us to live in harmony and justice (1991, 40). Lickona then built a case for teaching respect and responsibility in public schools. Respect, based on the Golden Rule ("Do unto others as you would have them do to you"), includes respect for other humans, for the whole complex of life, for authority, and for property. Responsibility means that we help rather than hurt others, that we are dependable, and that we keep our commitments. He showed how honesty, fairness, tolerance, prudence, self-discipline, helpfulness, compassion, cooperation, courage, and "a host of democratic values" stem from respect and responsibility. People may disagree about the application of these values in specific situations. But, Lickona added, almost all teachers and parents will agree with this basic moral ground (pp. 43–47).

Your curriculum, also in a public school classroom, will foster a certain view of life with certain values, dispositions, and commitments. For a Christian teacher, the basic common moral ground outlined by Lickona is a good starting point. Here are some other suggestions for planning a curriculum that is fair to all religious (and nonreligious) positions, and yet fits Christian beliefs:

- **Choose content that helps students to function well in society and contribute to it.** Such content should call for personal response suitable for the students' age and should encourage thinking about the nature and purpose of life. The content also should lead to discussions about what Kieran Egan calls "transcendent human values" (see chapter 5).
- **Ensure that your pedagogy reflects the implications of a biblical view of the person** (see chapter 5).
- **Acquaint students with the Christian heritage,** especially in social studies and literature. That faith has been one of the foundations of Western culture for many centuries. Also teach about other religions to demonstrate the importance of faith. Students should begin to realize how beliefs affect actions and historical developments, both positively and negatively. They also should learn that religion is the key to understanding a culture, whether that faith be Hinduism in India, Islam in Saudi Arabia, Roman

Catholicism in Quebec, or Calvinism in the Netherlands. Discuss the religious motives for the English Civil War, for riots in Indonesia, and for the humanitarian work of World Vision.
- **Be balanced in your approach.** You may show how in the eighteenth century the influence of the Roman Catholic Church brought about a more stable and peaceful community in Quebec than existed anywhere else in North America. Or you may discuss how love and compassion motivated Christian missionaries to aboriginal people. But you may not neglect how churches have sparked bitter religious strife, and how missionaries in their attempts to convert people also often imposed Western cultural imperatives, sometimes with negative effects.
- **Use the templates in chapter 7 for planning units.** The only values on the brainstorming template that you cannot promote in a public school situation are ones in the spiritual dimension. But you would be remiss not to discuss godliness and faith, for instance, in connection with the pilgrims coming to America or theologian Bonhoeffer being involved in an attempt to kill Adolph Hitler.
- **Adapt the unit examples in chapter 7 to public school classrooms.** For the unit "How does my garden grow?" drop the "God makes it so!" (figure 7.5). Also delete references to the Fall and to praise response to God—but most activities can remain the same. Similarly, for the nutrition unit (figure 7.7) intended learning outcomes K4 and V10 would be removed, but most of the rest of the unit can stay intact. Public school teachers can also use a novel such as *The Outsiders* (figure 7.9) to have students explore their values in

relation to those portrayed, and point students to the importance of committing oneself to a coherent and defensible set of guiding principles in life.

As a Christian teacher in public schools, you must be careful that your curriculum presents a diversity of views on crucial and controversial issues. You should present diverse views fairly and equitably, giving students full freedom to consider and adopt points of view that differ from yours. However, you should not sell your students short by not indicating your beliefs and your reasons for them at appropriate points.

I recognize that teachers who take their beliefs seriously may face problems. Usually you will be able to follow the prescribed curriculum. You can plan meaningful units on topics within the curriculum. You could design those units to meet, for instance, most of the criteria for justifying curriculum decisions found later in this chapter. At the same time, a standard intended curriculum becomes increasingly problematic as society becomes more pluralistic. A curriculum that satisfies people with opposing views on such issues as the nature and purpose of life, the concept of progress, or the role and task of governments may be unachievable. Attempts to create such a curriculum often are superficial and bland.

Regrettably, the structure of schooling in most jurisdictions in the English-speaking world ignores the diversity of our pluralistic society. Both the Bible and the United Nations Charter of Rights make clear that the education of children is primarily the responsibility of parents. Yet the trend has been to centralize schools and their curricula under state control. By avoiding central value questions, such curricula alienate especially those students and parents who reject dominant worldviews and values. The only long-term solution that recognizes diverse faith commitments is that governments allow the operation of tax-maintained alternative schools whose curricula reflect the views of their supporters. True democracy not only tolerates but welcomes diversity, in school curricula as well as other areas.

Public school teachers need to remember:

- **Your beliefs implicitly color your teaching.** It is, therefore, only fair that students, especially adolescents, are aware of your personal views.
- **Your students need models in life** that will show that beliefs are important and have consequences.
- **Many questions students ask can be discussed honestly only if teachers relate the issues to what they believe.**

Footstep 1-7

If you teach or plan to teach in a Christian school, discuss how you can teach for commitment while allowing students to express and hold other points of view. Give some specific examples in social studies or science.

If you teach or plan to teach in a public school, discuss whether you can allow your worldview to influence your planned curriculum while ensuring that your curriculum is suitable for students of all backgrounds.

In my jurisdiction the public school curriculum must be secular by law. Yet Huebner claims that everything in education is infused with spirituality. Can you reconcile these two apparently opposing views?

What Is Curriculum?

Footstep 1-8

How do you use the word *curriculum*? I have used the word several dozen times in this chapter already, but I have not yet explained what I mean by the term. Before reading this section, formulate and write down your own definition of *curriculum*. Even better, work with a small group and design a poster that illustrates what *curriculum* means for you. After reading what follows, compare your definition and/or portrayal with the four definitions given in this section. Then revise your own so that you feel comfortable with it.

In medieval times, *curriculum* meant the length of time needed to complete a program of learning. Gradually, its meaning shifted to the content that was to be taught. This shift was likely due to Protestant church reformers who wanted to bolster the knowledge of the common person. Today, dictionaries define *curriculum* as it is most commonly used: the course of study in a school. Most people assume that such a course of studies outlines the content to be taught.

In the last 100 years, however, educators like Montessori and Dewey expanded this definition by including not only course content but also teaching methods. In other words, how questions became as much part of curriculum discussions as what questions.

Most educators today favor a broader definition for *curriculum* than that found in dictionaries. Such definitions often reflect the authors' beliefs about education in general and about planning for learning in particular.

Many different definitions of *curriculum* are possible. Here are four common ones:

- **Curriculum is what is taught, particularly the subject matter contained in a school's course of study.** This definition parallels the dictionary one. The curriculum is a box from which we draw subject content. Academic traditionalists and most of the general public use or assume a definition similar to this. Academic traditionalists plan curriculum by dividing the program of study into subjects. Then they list the content to be taught by topics and subtopics. Implicit in the definition is the belief that the overall aim of education is to transmit a body of knowledge.

- **Curriculum is an organized set of documented, formal educational plans intended to attain preconceived goals.** This definition embraces a more technical conception of curriculum. Curriculum is a blueprint from which we build and then assess how well we have followed the plan. This view holds that curriculum planners must first decide goals or objectives. They use these to develop a series of precise prescriptions for teaching and learning. Teachers use the resulting detailed, sequenced documents to plan day-to-day teaching and learning activities. They then carefully monitor whether they have attained the prespecified learning outcomes. One value implicit in this model is the benefit of efficiency. With this definition, a basic curriculum question becomes, How can we reach our objectives in an efficient manner? Detailed ends and means are specified. Curriculum planners intend to take full control of all learning situations. Teachers are considered technicians who carefully implement prescribed learning activities.

- *Curriculum* **is a dynamic, ever-changing series of planned learning experiences.** The curriculum is a path that sets out a general direction, but teachers and students modify the path as they go along and may even decide to explore side trails—or sometimes stop in their tracks. This definition holds that teachers plan learning activities, but then adapt them as they see fit. Even as teachers implement activities, they (or the learners) may change them because of new circumstances. Persons who hold to this definition do not consider learners to be objects to whom they apply the curriculum. For them, learners are subjects. Teachers must carefully consider their background and reactions as they implement their intended curriculum. The formal and intended curricula may suggest topics and methods, but they are not rigid blueprints. Each particular learning situation will affect how learning proceeds. Teachers always deliberate and then adjust their intended curriculum in order to meet the needs of their learners.

- *Curriculum* **is everything learners experience in school.** This definition considers the curriculum to be like a playground where teachers give some suggestions for using the equipment, but where students also learn a great deal through all kinds of activities in which teachers are not involved. The curriculum encompasses everything that happens in the school. The implication of this definition is that the school influences students both formally and informally. Students, it is held, construct their own personal knowledge and meaning as a result of both planned and unplanned learning experiences. Most persons who endorse this definition do not want to define curriculum content too precisely. They delineate some general guidelines and some skills that need to be taught. They leave much latitude for teachers to decide what works best in their particular circumstances. A few even argue that developing a documented curriculum plan undermines their belief that pupils should be totally involved in planning their learning experiences (McLaren 1986, 229). Persons favoring a definition such as this are sometimes called experientialists.

Note that even how you define *curriculum* is rooted in your worldview! Not all teachers have drafted an explicit, clearly defined worldview—or a particular definition for *curriculum*. Yet what teachers believe, perhaps implicitly, about the nature of the learner, their role as teacher, meaningful content, and worthwhile learning strategies affects how they define and implement their curriculum. Chapter 2 outlines how different worldviews lead to distinctive curriculum orientations.

Aims of the Curriculum

Curriculum aims are general goals that provide a framework for action. So a key question for curriculum planners at all levels is, What are our aims for curriculum? Christian schools want their aims to reflect a biblical worldview. They want them to be clear and attainable, influencing curriculum and lesson planning. They want them to be accepted and used. To avoid creating a statement of aims that will simply be filed and forgotten, the statement should be the result of community consensus, and it should always be visible in the school (Greene 1984).

The aims or general goals for a Christian curriculum have been articulated in many different ways. Here is one of them:

1. To unfold the basis, framework, and implications of a Christian vision of life
2. To learn about God's world and how humans have responded to God's mandate to take care of the earth
3. To develop and apply the concepts, abilities, and creative gifts that enable students to contribute positively to God's Kingdom and have a transformational impact on culture
4. To discern and confront idols of our time such as materialism, hedonism, technicism, relativism, and other "isms" in which faith is placed in something other than God
5. To become committed to Christ and to a Christian way of life, able and willing to serve God and neighbor

Footstep 1-9

Are there any aims that you would add? delete? For instance, Newfoundland's Pentecostal Education Council in 1991, when it was still part of the publicly funded denominational system, included the following "pervasive goals":

To apply Christian principles to life issues:
- To develop the critical, creative, reflective thinking and decision-making skills necessary to resolving societal issues
- To recognize that career decisions are an integral part of students' Christian commitment to God and service to society

Do these aims meet the criteria for effective aims? That is, do they reflect a biblical worldview, are they clear and understandable, and are they attainable? Why or why not?

For aims 1–5 mentioned at the beginning of this section, list some more specific objectives. For instance, for the second aim, you might have an objective such as: To examine the essential role of government and law in human affairs, and what it means to be a responsible citizen.

If you teach or may teach in a public school, develop a suitable statement of curriculum aims for that context.

Curriculum planning for Christian schools needs to be based on clear aims and intents that relate to a biblical worldview. A key question is, How do we tackle this topic in faithfulness to Scripture? Designers and implementers also continually ask about the effects of curriculum plans and their implementation on teachers and students. They do not forget about the overall aims but implement their curriculum plans flexibly. Schools, teachers, and students revise curriculum plans constantly as particular needs become clear—but do so while keeping their aims in mind.

Justifying Curriculum Choices

If we do not justify curriculum decisions and choices explicitly, we allow others to make such decisions for us. We may, for instance, let a government curriculum outline or a textbook determine what we teach and how we teach it. Sometimes using such material may be legitimate. A curriculum guide may stipulate knowledge and skills that you agree are necessary or desirable for students to function in society. A textbook may match the aims you have set for a course. You may disagree with the content of a curriculum guide but still decide to include much of it in your implemented curriculum because an external examination based on it will affect your students' university entrance.

Using such materials, however, may also undermine your basic educational beliefs and aims. The likelihood of this happening decreases when you use some clear criteria for curriculum decisions, criteria that reflect your beliefs about education. To do so, your criteria should be stated in terms of your overall curriculum aims.

This book's guiding principle for justifying curriculum decisions is whether the curriculum enhances the possibility of students' becoming responsible and responsive disciples of Jesus Christ. Disciples are not blind followers but persons who take the principles of the Teacher and make them operational in their own setting. To justify our overall curriculum choices, we therefore ask the questions given below. You will note that they parallel the five curriculum aims of the last section.

- Do students become familiar with and experience a Christian worldview and its implications for life in society?
- Do students investigate and build on their experiences with the world around them? Do they learn about and respond to what for them is new and significant knowledge? Do they learn how humans have developed culture and how they have taken care of the earth, both in positive and negative ways?
- Are students given opportunities to develop their diverse abilities? Do they create products, procedures, and theories that unfold God's reality and develop their own gifts? Do they use their learn-

ing to contribute to life both inside and outside of school? Does the curriculum encourage them to be and become servant leaders.

- Do students become aware of and critique the shared meanings of our culture? Do students begin to understand the key trends in society and develop their personal responses? Do they learn to discern and confront the negative aspects of our culture?
- Do they respond to and have the opportunity to choose and commit themselves to a biblical way of life?

Not all of these questions apply to all curriculum topics. But it is important to check and justify curriculum decisions. You can use these questions or an alternative set of fundamental questions that you have developed on the basis of your overall curriculum aims, and you can do so whether you are working at a regional, school, or classroom level.

Footstep 1-10

A few years ago in one of my courses, a small group of teachers, led by Paul Still, developed a set of questions to guide them in making curriculum decisions for developing units in the middle grades. With minor changes, you could use them at any grade level:

1. **Does the curriculum enhance understandings needed for exercising responsive discipleship?**
   a. Does it contribute to an understanding of some aspect of a Christian worldview, especially the importance of biblical shalom?
   b. Does it help students to consider biblically based values and encourage them

to form dispositions and commitments based on such values?

c. Does it help familiarize students with our Christian as well as our Western cultural heritage?

2. **Is the curriculum relevant for students?**

a. Does it connect with and expand students' previous backgrounds, experiences, and knowledge?

b. Does it address meaningful and significant current issues in the world and encourage response in personal ways?

c. Does it foster students seeing and investigating interrelations with different subject disciplines where this contributes to understanding issues and their applications?

3. **Does the curriculum meet students' pedagogical needs?**

a. Is it imaginative enough to maintain student interest?

b. Does it provide for active response suitable for the learners' stage of development?

c. Does it support diverse learning activities appropriate for diverse learning styles and other individual differences?

d. Does it encourage the development of different modes of knowing?

Consider a curriculum topic such as nutrition, government, or measurement. Choose a specific grade level. Indicate what you would have to do to teach the unit on the basis of the foregoing criteria. Is it possible to take any topic and teach it according to these criteria? Why or why not? Give some examples.

An Example of Curriculum Planning

What does a curriculum unit look like that takes into account the aims outlined in this chapter? Let's look at an eighth-grade humanities unit developed by Wendy Pattison, Rita Bot, and Darleen Kifiak, teachers from three neighboring Christian schools. Humanities is an integrated study of past and present human relationships and actions. Students learn to see the connections between themselves and the world around them by exploring and examining their relationship with God, each other, the past, their own and other cultures, and creation. The content comprises themes and issues from biblical studies, English, and social studies.

The unit described below is "Kingdom Building" (Society of Christian Schools in British Columbia 1996). The three teachers got together one summer to pool their ideas. They then piloted their initial draft in order to refine the unit. They defined the unit's thematic statement, learning outcomes, and focus questions as follows:

> Jesus Christ left his throne in glory, humbled himself, and came to Earth to restore the Kingdom of God. His sacrificial death on the cross destroys the power of sin and establishes the eternal Kingdom. Christ uses the Church to demonstrate his Kingdom on Earth.

> Human forms of the Church on Earth both reflect and distort God's intent for his people. At the same time, following Jesus on Earth frequently runs counter to the current culture's expression of greatness.

The unit is intended to help students:

- Understand the historical unfolding of God's plan for salvation and redemption through Jesus Christ

- Understand that the Kingdom of God, as revealed through Jesus' life, ministry, death, and resurrection, runs contrary to the patterns of this world, and brings freedom from oppression and healing from brokenness
- Compare the Kingdom of God to kingdoms of this world by examining the sovereignty and consistency of God with the rise and fall of civilizations (e.g., Rome, Germanic tribes, medieval feudal system)
- Discover truths in stories as revealed in the struggles of mythical characters between the forces of darkness and light

Four focus questions were to guide the unit's development and implementation: What makes a kingdom great? How did people in the Middle Ages try to establish the Kingdom of God on Earth? Why do human kingdoms rise and fall? What is the role of the Church?

The unit consists of four main parts:

- **The Beginning of the Kingdom of God:** In a study of the Gospel of Mark, students explore the meaning of the phrase "Kingdom of God." For instance, the students select a parable and make a poster that explains in their own words and art what it teaches about the Kingdom of God. They then study the relationship of the Roman Empire and Christianity, including case studies of early church martyrs, the ideas of Augustine, and the fall of the Roman Empire.
- **The Kingdom Grows—Early Europe:** The students consider the Germanic tribal culture in Europe. They also study northern European myths to help them understand the cultural values of the tribes and how Christians interpreted the

myths. They answer questions such as, Why do you think there are different stories about creation, evil, and the afterlife that come to us from centuries ago? What purposes do myths serve? Christianity is not just another myth. How do we know? The class discusses elements of the King Arthur legend to show how they were used to present Christianity within a pagan context, with a follow-up discussion about how we present the gospel cross-culturally today.

- **The Kingdom of God—the Middle Ages:** Besides doing several projects on feudalism, the students study ballads, including ones about Robin Hood with a written response to questions like, Why was the legend of Robin Hood necessary during the time period in which it was told? Who are the Robin Hoods of today? The students also consider passages from Scripture in order to contrast medieval, contemporary, and biblical justice and use of power with students answering at the end, What would a perfect justice system be like?
- **The Kingdoms in Conflict:** The students investigate the religion of Islam. They read excerpts from the Koran. They then explore the Crusades through, for instance, a writing assignment in which a Muslim scholar writes a letter to his cousin in Turkey about the Crusades.

A concluding activity asks students to compare the characteristics of medieval kingdoms with Christ's Kingdom. What kind of a King was Christ? What is His Kingdom like?

The unit keeps before the students the concept of the Kingdom of God while studying content from various subject areas.

The unit incorporates the study of history (human response to God's mandates), literature (myths and ballads), drama (a play about Charlemagne), art (a study of medieval artists), and geography (maps of Europe). The wide range of learning activities goes much beyond memorization or simple interpretation. The unit calls for personal response and action: What are our responsibilities as citizens of Christ's Kingdom?

The development and use of the whole humanities program is also instructive. First, teachers in each school worked on school-based programs. The principals gave pairs of teachers some joint planning time a couple of times a week. Once teachers had tried various approaches in their classrooms, three of them saw the benefit of getting together for several weeks during the summer to pool insights and experiences. They drew up a joint program with the help of a curriculum specialist. The resulting program was superior to any of the three original parts. At the same time, the teachers did maintain their individuality. For instance, in the community and culture unit, they included units both on Judaism and on Chinese culture, with teachers choosing one of the two. For the unit entitled Taking a Stand, one school added an extensive service project as an integral part of the unit.

Footstep 1-11

In what ways does the foregoing Kingdom Building unit meet (or not meet) the aims of the curriculum described in this chapter?

The teachers who planned the unit did meet the basic requirements of the government curriculum guides for English and social studies, but took liberties in interpreting the documents. If a state or province mandates curriculum content and performance standards (e.g., for accreditation), to what extent should teachers follow them? Give some examples of what you consider to be appropriate and inappropriate deviations.

Reviewing the Main Points

1.   **A neutral curriculum is not achievable**. Curricula inevitably promote certain values, even if it is the value that values are relative and can be personally determined. Christian teachers plan units and courses that are informed by a biblical worldview. They teach for commitment but allow different points of view to be explored and expressed.

2.   **There are several levels of curriculum.** Government agencies develop the formal or prescribed curriculum. Publishers make textbooks available that often form an inherent curriculum. School systems and schools develop grade level and subject outlines (the intended curriculum). Teachers develop specific plans (the implemented curriculum). These specific learning activities, as adapted, result in the students' experienced or attained curriculum.

3.   **Curriculum decisions are difficult to make** unless planners share a common vision about the purpose and meaning of life, and about the nature and role of education. Basic beliefs always inform key curriculum decisions.

4.   **Teachers are guides who unfold content while helping students develop normal rationality and autonomy.** In a Christian school, teachers explore the significance of the Christian tradition and heritage, and encourage students to consider and commit themselves to a Christian worldview. The worldview of Christian teachers in public schools will also influence their curriculum—as is true for members of other religious groups, agnostics, and atheists. However, while teaching how worldviews shape society as well as the importance of students' choosing and implementing a worldview and a coherent and defensible set of values, public school teachers may not promote their own worldview over any others.

5.   **Curriculum can be defined in different ways**: as content, as a set of specific educational plans, as a changing series of planned learning experiences, or as everything that learners experience in school. Definitions reflect certain worldview perspectives.

6.   **The curriculum of a Christian school aims to prepare students for responsible and responsive discipleship**. To do so, teachers unfold a Christian vision of life as it applies to all aspects of life in our culture. They also encourage students to develop and use their gifts to have a transformational impact on individuals and on society. It is important to justify curriculum decisions and choices on the basis of an adopted set of overall curriculum aims.

References

ASCD Panel on Moral Education (ASCD). 1988. Moral education in the life of the school. *Educational Leadership* 45 (8): 5–7.

Eliot, T. S. 1952. Modern education and the class. In *Social Criticism*. London: Penguin.

Gesch, C. 1993. Selections and highlights from English 10 and Bible 12 examinations. Distributed, respectively, as *Powerful stories, Sensitive readers*, and *Studying God's Word: Light for our path*. Smithers, BC: Bulkley Valley Christian School.

Greene, A. 1984. Helps for preparing a statement of educational objectives for schools. Seven-page paper. Seattle: Alta Vista.

Hare, W., and J. Portelli. 1988. *Philosophy of education: Introductory readings*. Calgary: Detselig.

Harmin, M., and T. Gregory. 1974. *Teaching is ...* Chicago: Science Research Associates.

Huebner, D. 1999. *The lure of the transcendent*. Mahwah, NJ: Lawrence Erlbaum.

Kanpol, B. 1993. The pragmatic curriculum: Teacher reskilling as cultural politics. *The Journal of Educational Thought* 27 (2): 200–215.

———. 1998. *Teachers talking back and breaking bread*. Cresskill, NJ: Hampton Press.

Lickona, T. 1991. *Educating for character: How our schools can teach respect and responsibility*. New York: Bantam.

McLaren, P. 1986. *Schooling as a ritual performance*. New York: Random House.

Paul, R. 1988. Ethics without indoctrination. *Educational Leadership* 45 (8): 10–19.

Pinar, W. et al. 1995. *Understanding curriculum: An introduction to the study of historical and contemporary curriculum discourses*. New York: Peter Lang.

Shulman, L. 2001. Appreciating good teaching: A conversation with Lee Shulman. *Educational Leadership* 58 (5): 6.

Society of Christian Schools in British Columbia. 1996. *Humanities 8: A resource guide*. Langley, BC.

Thiessen, E. 1993. *Teaching for commitment: Liberal education, indoctrination, and Christian nurture*. Montreal: McGill-Queen's University Press.

Van Brummelen, H. 1998. *Walking with God in the classroom*. 2d ed. Seattle: Alta Vista College Press.

Walker, D. 1990. *Fundamentals of curriculum*. San Diego: Harcourt Brace Jovanovich.

$\mathcal{S}$teppingstone ~2~

Choosing a Curriculum Orientation

Followers of Jesus Christ share a common faith. They believe that God created people in His own image but that humanity fell into sin. They know they need Christ's redemption for personal salvation. They also believe that the Bible is God's authoritative Word for life. It provides their framework not only for the spiritual dimension of life, but also for the ethical, aesthetic, economic, social, intellectual, psychological, and physical aspects of life. They share the belief that God calls them to live in society according to His purposes. The basic norms of Scripture guide their thoughts, words, and deeds.

Christians are not always united, however, on how to apply those biblical principles in a complex society. Think, for instance, about capital punishment or about whether women ought to be appointed to leadership positions in the church. Christians also differ with respect to the type of schooling they want for their children. Some feel that their children should attend public schools so that they will interact with students of different backgrounds and will thus become salt and light in our society (Matthew 5:13–16). Others feel just as strongly that God's injunction to impress His commandments on the hearts of children also applies to the school (Deuteronomy 6:6–9), and that therefore we need Christian schools with curricula that proclaim God's glorious deeds (Psalm 78:4). Even within Christian schools, supporters differ about the aims of schooling and how Christians ought to interact with their surrounding culture.

Let me give four examples of schools with different curriculum orientations. All four may well involve Christian parents and teachers. Each of the first three could be an alternative within a public system or a charter school. The last one is an independent Christian school, although in the Canadian province of Alberta it could also be a faith-based alternative within the public system. As you read, think about what you see as positive and negative features of each school.

The *Glendale Traditional School* emphasizes the teaching of basic skills and the accumulated wisdom of civilization. The school puts most of its time and effort into imparting knowledge in basic subject areas such as language, mathematics, history, and science. Students develop their abilities and powers of reason using the information they have memorized and the skills they have practiced. Most lessons feature teacher presentations followed by individual practice and assignments. The teachers structure their lessons carefully and give regular quizzes and tests. The school also emphasizes character education. Each week the curriculum highlights a personal virtue such as honesty, helpfulness, or respect.

The *Valley Achievement School* has a tightly structured curriculum. Teacher-taught classes follow precise steps of direct instruction or mastery learning. Teachers have specific, measurable objectives for each lesson. They give students frequent positive reinforcement. They use pre-specified standards to assess student achievement. Students spend substantial time learning the language arts and mathematics curriculum from computer software supplied by a large corporation. The company promises that this interactive, reiterative, and skill-focused program will substantially increase students' scores on standardized tests.

The *Coulee Discovery School* wants its students to be agents of their own learning. It believes in their essential goodness and limitless potential. Through open-ended investigations, students construct their own knowledge. Teachers are facilitators who suggest activities and strategies. They pose questions to help students draw defensible conclusions. Skills, the school believes, will be learned within the context of such exploratory learning. Learning must originate with students' own experiences and interests to have lasting effects. The curriculum is project-oriented, with students often working in small groups. They are encouraged to interpret what they learn so that they develop their personal sense of meaning, direction, and values.

Canyon Christian School bases its curriculum on the conviction that biblical guidelines apply to all of life. Therefore, such principles are relevant for all school subjects. The school also holds that biblical faith directs the Christian community to work at influencing all aspects of culture, including science, politics, the media, health care, and the arts. The school therefore designs its curriculum around units that emphasize biblical themes. These include, for instance, responsible stewardship of creation's resources, the promotion of justice as a task of government, and the importance of serving society with moral integrity and compassion. The teachers use both Christian and secular resources. They discuss with students the relevance of faith for the issues addressed. The teachers acquaint students with their Christian and cultural traditions but also allow them to respond in personal and creative ways.

I have not described a typical neighborhood public school. The reason is that in most of such schools, there will be teachers who lean toward each of the first three orientations. Many will also be eclectic. That is, they will use what for them are comfortable parts of several orientations, going back and forth among them in response to their subject and their class. Here I wanted to describe schools with distinct curriculum orientations since that makes clear how different worldviews lead to diverse approaches to curriculum. In this chapter, we will discuss and evaluate the key elements of the curricula of each of these four schools.

Footstep 2-1

A worldview is a set of basic beliefs and assumptions about life and reality. It answers what a person believes about the nature and purpose of life in our world. It provides meaning, and it guides and directs the thought and action of its adherents.

The persons involved with each of the four schools described above share a common vision. That does not mean that board members and teachers do not have lively discussions or that they always agree! For instance, some teachers in the middle grades of the Traditional School may emphasize the three Rs, while others dwell on the great ideas that recur in history and literature. In the Discovery School some teachers may stress learning for personal meaning. Others, however, may want learning to lead to social transformation. As well, in the Christian school some teachers may skip literature selections that do not promote godly living, while others choose them in order to contrast their views with Christian ones.

In spite of such internal differences, each school's vision is rooted in a particular worldview.

Use the (short) descriptions to list a few of the key features of the worldview that you believe to be at the basis of each school. Consider how each looks at knowledge, learning, and the meaning of life. Which approach do you prefer? Why?

Four Curriculum Orientations

In this chapter you will learn about four different orientations to curriculum. The four schools described above reflect these orientations. They are the traditional, the process/mastery, the experiential, and a Christian orientation. **A curriculum orientation** (sometimes called a curriculum platform) sets out:

- Basic worldview assumptions and how these suggest an overall vision for education
- A view of knowledge and of the person, and how these affect classroom learning and teaching, and how we go about planning programs
- The general aims of the curriculum

The purpose of a curriculum orientation is to provide a school, a department, or a teacher with a clear sense of direction for an educational program. The four orientations described in this chapter are not the only possible ones. But most curriculum planners, including teachers, either adopt the essence of one of these orientations, or combine elements of two or more of them.

As we saw in chapter 1, proponents of each orientation may already begin with different definitions of the concept of curriculum. Also, distinctive questions may be foremost in their minds as they develop curriculum:

- **Traditionalists** ask, What content do students need most? What have thinkers found out about our world that we want students to know?
- **Process/mastery supporters** ask, How can we achieve our objectives efficiently? How do we specify and assess learning outcomes?

- **Experientialists** ask, How can we best help students construct knowledge and meaning from their experiences?
- **Proponents of a Christian curriculum orientation** ask, How do we foster students' positive response and responsibility toward God, their fellow creatures, society, and themselves?

These four orientations will lead you in four distinct curriculum directions. For each orientation, we will examine and analyze how its proponents view knowledge and content as well as the role of the teacher and learner. As you read, consider your own basic beliefs in the light of how you have experienced the practice of teaching. You can then decide the contours of an orientation that you want to follow in your teaching.

This chapter introduces a Christian curriculum orientation. The remainder of the book develops this in much more depth. Keep in mind, as the apostle Paul said in 1 Corinthians 13:12, that all we know in this life is partial and incomplete. That also applies to my portrayal of a biblically based curriculum orientation. Therefore, read critically and take time to develop and justify your own curriculum framework.

The Traditional Orientation

Traditional schools may also be called essential or fundamental schools. You probably envision a school like the following:

- The curriculum consists of prescribed and carefully structured subject matter in disciplines such as literature, history, science, and mathematics.
- Teachers impart a great deal of content and emphasize basic literacy and numeracy skills.
- Teachers check the level of content and

skill assimilation with frequent tests.
- Schools stress hard work and discipline.

Traditionalists look at knowledge as an organized collection of facts, concepts, and theories. Schools exist to transmit this body of knowledge. Such knowledge provides a basis for learning to reason. Rational thought, more than experience, is central in generating and validating knowledge. When art is included as a subject, it emphasizes content and reasoning: art history, critical appreciation of art, definitions of art terms, and the meaning and function of art (Council for Basic Education 1991).

Teachers in traditional schools carefully sequence, present, and transmit knowledge to their students. Students are expected to store knowledge and use it as a fund for rational thought. They will have few guidelines for action or experiences in applying their learning to real-life situations. For instance, learning how humans have classified plants in biology is more important than observing how plants grow.

There are two main types of traditional schools, essentialist and perennialist. **Essentialists** hold that:

- **Schools systematically teach basic facts, concepts, and skills.** These are mastered through memorization and drill. By learning many facts about plants, for instance, students will develop schemas and generalizations that will enable them to apply their knowledge. Similarly, learning the elements of phonics is the best way for students to become fluent readers.
- **Teachers generally know what knowledge is significant for living and working in society. Therefore, they decide what to teach.** They use lists of topics and skills in curriculum documents and

textbooks to guide them. They use direct, well-sequenced, large-group instruction in order to help students grasp subject matter.

- **Teachers tell students and parents how well students achieve on tests.** They report whether students have reached defined academic standards. They also report how well they do in comparison with their classmates. Students need to get used to living in a competitive world in which some do better than others.

Traditionalists can also be **perennialists**. A network of perennialist schools known as *Paideia* schools exists in the United States, mainly at the secondary level. Perennialists believe that:

- **The basic feature of humans is their ability to reason. The main thrust of education therefore becomes cultivating reason.** Through reason students can discover and explore knowledge including truth, beauty, goodness, and justice.
- **There should be a general core curriculum for all students that emphasizes our common cultural heritage.** Great writings of the past transmit shared cultural ideals and values. They are also important as examples of reasoned thought about universally valid truth. Students need to read, study, and analyze primary source materials written by great intellects.
- **In school, thinking is more important than doing.** Therefore, there is little emphasis on vocational skills. Students have few electives.

Both essentialists and perennialists are traditionalists. As they plan curriculum, they first focus on the subjects they want taught in school. Usually these include language and literature, math, science, history, geography, and a foreign language. They then establish lists of content and skills for different grade levels. Until the 1970s, most curriculum guides were based on this approach.

Let's consider the two basic components of the traditionalist orientation: knowledge of content and skills, and proficiency in the ability to reason. Are traditional basic knowledge and skills also considered basic in the Bible? All of us agree that students need literacy and numeracy knowledge and skills to function in society. We can also agree with the perennialists that if we do not inculcate their heritage in students, both they and our society will be impoverished. But the Bible also makes clear that basic knowledge does not primarily mean knowing how to read or having insight into the history of Western democracy. Rather, it holds that a lack of basic knowledge means not acting justly and not loving mercy—that is, ignoring biblical norms (Hosea 4:6, Micah 6:8). Knowledge is not just intellectual, but it is also an affair of the heart, something that traditionalists often overlook.

Perennialists have correctly pointed out that the ability to think critically about life's issues is an aptitude that too few students develop. But perennialists go one step further. The faith assumption of many of them is that reason stands outside of faith and is itself the ultimate human value. It needs no justification and can answer all of life's basic questions.

It is this stance that has resulted, for one, in the failure of such moral education initiatives as values clarification and Kohlberg's moral reasoning approach. Yet while reasoning is important, it does not lead to ultimate answers in life. Reasoning always takes place within the bounds of religious beliefs, whether Christian or otherwise (Wolterstorff 1976, 72). Reason always functions within a framework of faith assumptions that determine one's stance toward life. In biblical terms, it is our heart knowledge and commitment that govern our minds and our rationality.

Footstep 2-2

At the elementary level, the curriculum favored by essentialists and perennialists may not differ much, since perennialists look at those years as ones in which students learn the basic tools. At the secondary level, however, there would be some significant differences. List some of the similarities and differences. Which of these two approaches do you prefer? Why?

Footstep 2-3

Summarize the strengths and weaknesses of the traditional curriculum orientation. If you work in a small group, you may want to use chart paper as you brainstorm and then come to a consensus about the points to be listed. To get started, discuss the last two paragraphs in this section. Complete the chart for the three other orientations as you finish reading each section that follows. The charts will help you later to develop your personal curriculum orientation.

The Process/Mastery Orientation

The process/mastery orientation (also called the cognitive process, the social behaviorist, or the technological approach to curriculum) has the following characteristics:

- **The curriculum uses efficient means to reach predetermined, detailed, and measurable ends.** Its proponents use the results of empirical research about the effects of certain methods on learning outcomes (L. Darling-Hammond and J. Snyder in Jackson 1992, 41). They want to control and manage the curriculum, the teacher, the learner, and the learning environment. They emphasize the question, "How can we most productively accomplish what we want to do?"
- **The key to efficient learning is carefully structured inquiry based on observations and guided thought.** For example, a detailed set of sequential questions guides students to observe the characteristics of plants. Using their conclusions, they then classify plants according to the standard classification system.
- **Knowledge is viewed as an objective, impersonal, value-free commodity to be grasped.**

Process/mastery advocates begin with specific objectives for which they can measure student attainment. They then develop and sequence learning experiences that will achieve the objectives. If evaluation shows a less than satisfactory degree of student success, they revise the learning experiences (and possibly the objectives). This linear process of planning curriculum has been popular since the efficiency movement championed by Franklin Bobbitt early in the twentieth century. It is also at the basis of the most popular twentieth-century curriculum publication, Ralph Tyler's *Basic Principles of Curriculum and Instruction* (1950).

In 1854, Herbert Spencer asked what arguably has become the most famous curriculum question, "What knowledge is of most worth?" Spencer answered his own question by stating that directly useful information and skills take precedence. Learning should focus on self-preservation, securing life's necessities, the rearing of offspring, maintaining proper social and political relations, and filling up the leisure part of life. Practical science and health are also important. History as usually taught, on the other hand, has not the "remotest bearing" on any of our actions and is therefore of little value (1911, 3–44).

Process/mastery supporters often pose Spencer's question—and then also answer it by pointing to everyday living skills that will help students find a productive job. They emphasize content and skills that prepare students directly for the world of work. Basic reading, writing, communication, and computer skills are essential. The social sciences are also important to help students function as citizens in society. The humanities and the arts, however, are not as directly applicable, and therefore, are given less emphasis.

Let me give two examples of the process/mastery approach. In the 1970s behavioral objectives became popular. Such objectives, also referred to as performance objectives, are precise statements of purpose whose specific outcomes are measured. For example, "The student will demonstrate knowledge of multiplying three-digit numbers by two-digit ones by successfully completing eight of ten such problems within ten minutes." Such objectives, process/mastery proponents believe, give a clear focus to teaching and learning, and enhance accountability. For each lesson, they construct a set of

objectives and then carefully design activities to maximize student mastery. Some designers have even used the term "teacher-proof curriculum," since teachers were to be technicians whose task was solely to follow the step-by-step instructions in their manuals.

In the 1980s several large corporations jumped into the educational fray in the United States. They promised school districts that they would raise average standardized testing results by a certain number of points if the school districts would sign a time-limited contract. The corporations would use scientifically designed curricula as well as computer technology to improve learning and raise standards. These ventures have not had notable long-term success. However, corporations continue to provide process-oriented software for teaching specific content and skills.

The process/mastery approach to curriculum has been a popular one. It gives careful consideration to performance objectives or detailed standards, and how such outcomes can be effectively attained. Some educators find it attractive to follow uniform steps in planning and implementing a program, and to have well-defined procedures to assess its effectiveness.

Many questions remain unanswered about this orientation, however. Can all learning be listed in terms of specific objectives? Is this orientation so focused on efficiency and narrowly defined conceptual and skill knowledge that it neglects more important but less easily measurable goals? In concentrating on specific objectives, does it overlook other long-term significant effects? Does it neglect the spiritual, ethical, and aesthetic dimensions of education? Isn't learning so complex and aren't learners so different that a formula-like approach to lesson design is not likely to work for all students?

To give an example, process/mastery proponents may apply Rosenshine's exact and defined steps for direct instruction. This method may well improve students' short-term long division skills. But there are doubts that those effects can be maintained for a long period. Also, its narrow emphasis on individual students solving the algorithm in isolation may inhibit other abilities or applications such as creative problem solving.

Many proponents of the process/mastery orientation are empirical positivists. That is, they gain knowledge primarily from sensory observations. Statements are meaningful only if they can be validated from experience or are logically self-evident. There are several problems with this position:

- **Sensory experience is incomplete and misleading.** Even scientists usually interpret their data to fit preconceived theories. Those theories are not unbiased; they are based on certain assumptions.
- **The theory that knowledge certainty results only from sense perception cannot be validated by sense perception itself.** This is therefore a faith assumption. Yet process/mastery proponents instill the impression that sensory-based knowledge is more valid and compelling than any other kind.
- **For empirical positivists, religious statements and beliefs are not knowledge.** They are not logically self-evident, nor can we verify them from observed data.

Process/mastery advocates may teach some knowledge and skills efficiently—this is their main curriculum aim. But they gloss over their tendency to neglect long-term aims and deeper value considerations. Indeed, by default they often accept and, therefore, promote the values that dominate our Western society. In the name of efficiency, they tend to treat students as less-than-human objects. As a result, they may train technically competent persons who lack the commitments needed to foster a just and compassionate society.

Footstep 2-4

We usually consider technological processes to be a positive feature of our society. Being able to make flight reservations by computer and to withdraw money from bank machines all over the world is convenient. In schools, the use of word processing programs improves writing.

Yet, there is another side to technology. The French Christian philosopher Jacques Ellul has said that "technology has two consequences which strike me as the most profound in our time. I call them the suppression of the subject and the suppression of meaning" (1981, 49). Ellul is particularly concerned about the techniques imposed by a technological mind-set.

A process/mastery orientation emphasizes efficiency in planning and implementing teaching and learning. Ellul's ideas suggest that in education such a technological approach is so concerned with specific objectives and step-by-step methods of how we teach and learn that we lose sight of why we live and what we want our students to become. It also treats persons as objects to be processed rather than as responsible subjects. Moreover, knowledge cannot be objective and value-free. If God made the creation with the specific intention of revealing Himself (Romans 1:20; Job 42:5–6), is not all knowledge filled with meaning and value? In short, the process/mastery orientation suppresses goals and values of ultimate significance.

Is Ellul right? Or is he overstating his case? First, list the advantages of a process/mastery orientation to curriculum. Then, reflecting on Ellul's claims, assess the disadvantages of this approach. Add your results to the chart you began in footstep 2-2.

Footstep 2-5

Consider Herbert Spencer's famous curriculum question, "What knowledge is of most worth?" Think back to your schooling. What are the three or four things you learned that have benefited you most? If you had designed an ideal curriculum for the schools you attended, what changes would you have made? Why? What does that say about what knowledge you consider to be of most worth?

The Experiential Orientation

The **experiential orientation** to curriculum stands in the Western humanistic tradition exemplified by John Dewey's progressivism. Experientialists believe that:

- **Students are innately good.** They are self-directing, autonomous individuals, themselves the source of their own truth and freedom.
- **Students learn through active involvement in personally meaningful learning experiences.** In this way they develop their abilities and assign personal

meaning to what they learn.
- **Teachers facilitate learning by providing positive learning environments that stimulate active, self-directed learning.**

Today, there are various branches of this orientation. The critical theorists described in chapter 1 favor an experiential curriculum, for instance. The experiential ideology of *constructivism* is the most influential movement in curriculum today, however. It is rooted in the work of the late Swiss psychologist Jean Piaget and the Russian Lev Vygotsky. Constructivism is the rallying cry for those who oppose the traditional and the process/mastery orientations. Terms like *constructing knowledge* and *socially constructed reality* are mentioned so often that we do not even notice that constructivist values and metaphors have changed the way we think about knowledge and education.

Before I describe the constructivist approach to curriculum, consider an example of a constructivist unit, Greenprints for Changing Schools (Greig, Pike, and Selby 1989). The unit stresses ecological stewardship and is used in some public schools in my area. One of its themes is that change is a personal process through which individuals discover personal meaning. The unit does not want teachers to be tour guides. Instead, they involve students in negotiating the learning process in an open and participatory setting. This is done so that students "realize that one creates one's own reality" (p. 24). Students are told, "You are the center of the world. You are a free, immensely powerful source of life and goodness. Affirm it. Spread it. Radiate it. Think day and night about it. And you will see a miracle happen: the greatness of your own life" (p. 26). The unit emphasizes that students make their own choices (also about their learning), construct their own reality, and create their own meaning. They need only to look inward into themselves for meaning. Teachers suggest various activities and explorations and encourage self-reflection. The unit promotes "the great, simple and so effective concepts of love, peace, compassion, truth, purity, goodness, humility, faith, divinity, the heart, the soul, resurrection, infinity and eternity" (p. 32). However, one wonders whether and how, with students creating their own reality, there can be any common perception of such values.

This is, of course, just one example, and there is a wide spectrum of constructivists. (For a thorough overview, see Phillips 2000, *Constructivism in Education.*) The most influential constructivists are the radical and the social constructivists. Both believe humans make or construct knowledge. For them, knowledge is not acquired or discovered and does not reflect or copy an external reality. Radical constructivists believe that knowledge is created in the minds of individuals in their cultural context. Social constructivists hold that knowledge can be entirely accounted for through social interaction. What you need to remember is that many teachers who think of themselves as constructivists have adopted some of the teaching and learning strategies that constructivists promote, but have not consciously accepted these constructivist theories.

Constructivism often contrasts itself with traditional education. It opposes passive learning, thoughtless regurgitation, and rigid classroom structures. For constructivists, learning is an active process. Students do not just absorb information, nor do they just become acquainted with worthwhile works of the past and think about them. Classrooms are communities of learning engaged in activity, reflection, and creative

experiences. Teachers no longer supply information but facilitate autonomous learning. They coordinate and critique student constructions. Challenging, open-ended investigations lead learners to dialogue, explore, and generate many possibilities (Fosnot 1996, 20). Many of these constructivist strategies are ones that teachers used successfully long before constructivism was identified as a theory.

Few teachers realize the theoretical basis of constructivism, even when they openly use constructivist strategies. The theory breaks radically with the Western—and Christian—tradition that knowledge can be gained through the senses and thus leads to a picture of the real world. Constructivism holds that humans do not discover knowledge or read the book of nature. Rather, it claims that humans construct all knowledge either individually or through social interaction. Knowledge does not discover or reflect a world that exists out there. Instead, humans make knowledge and impose it to help them cope with their experience. Order in reality is arbitrary, imposed on the world by humanly constructed knowledge in order to create personal meaning and significance. No ultimate, true, objective knowledge exists. Knowledge is strictly subjective. That is why constructivists assert that "others have realities that are independent of ours ... we can never take any of these realities as fixed" (Paul Ernest in Steffe and Gale 1995, 485).

In the classroom, therefore, learning begins with children's own ideas, hypotheses, and explorations. Students do not discover knowledge but create their own understandings and meaning by reflecting on their physical, social, and mental activity. Teachers pose problems and encourage students to set personal goals. Learners play an active role in selecting and defining curriculum activities, with teachers being willing to follow children's pursuits even when those seem naive or immature (June Gould in Fosnot 1996, 93). Teachers seek and value learners' constructions, viewpoints, and solutions. They ask whether their work is coherent and useful, and help them open their windows further.

Constructivists value meaningful activity over right answers. Indeed, there are no single right answers or misconceptions. There are only discrepancies that students may analyze and resolve in a variety of ways (Ackermann in Steffe and Gale 1995, 342). Thus, they hold that "right answers are not possible in a constructivist textbook. It goes against the philosophy" (Baker and Piburn 1997, p. xv). Even mathematical laws and procedures are viewed as social conventions that, like the rules of chess, could be changed (Ernest in Steffe and Gale 1995, 477). There are no external standards of right or wrong: "As long as a student's solution to a problem achieves a viable goal, it has to be credited" (Luise McCarty and Thomas Schwandt in Phillips 2000, 49).

Moreover, there cannot be an all-encompassing curriculum model because both teachers and students create and transform knowledge and meaning as learning takes place. Course outlines and unit plans are therefore loose and indeterminate. After all, there is no one truth, no one right way to view phenomena and situations. That explains why, for the intellectual domain, one constructivist curriculum document lists twenty-eight process objectives (e.g., uses effective strategies, locates, organizes, applies, communicates, demonstrates). However, it gives only a single content objective, and even that has a process component: "acquires information through reading, listening, and observing" (British

Columbia Ministry of Education 1990, 135).

When we read literature, according to radical constructivists, everyone's interpretation is equally valid. Its study becomes important not so much because it helps us understand important issues in life, but because it helps us develop the tools of meaning-making and effective writing. Thus, we can create our own reality, our own answers, and our own values. Language, as leading radical constructivist Ernst von Glaserfeld put it, is an important tool, "but it does not transport meanings or concepts" (Fosnot 1996, 7).

Similarly, history is not learned to understand the roots of our culture but to be able to see how change comes about and to write personal interpretations of events. Mathematics is a human way of thinking and solving problems that helps us make sense of the world. Science confronts students with evidence that contradicts their nonscientific conceptions so that by changing their conceptions they may bring order to their world.

The basic problem with constructivism is that, since people construct their own knowledge and meanings, many viable realities exist. Ultimately, then, we no longer share important commonalities. We no longer have to recognize common bonds and values. The most we can say is that for individuals or groups, some constructions may be more viable than others at a particular time and in a particular context. All personal choices become legitimate. In the end, one model of reality and one set of values is as good as any other. If personal meaning justifies constructions of knowledge and meaning, then rampant individualism and self-centered relativism results (Airasian and Walsh 1997, 448). Personal voice supplants authority and community. Many constructivists duck this issue by claiming that some constructions are obviously better than others. But as soon as teachers apply certain standards to show that some are superior, they compromise the basic tenet of constructivism. They no longer give students full freedom to construct meaning themselves. This, it seems to me, is the inevitable Achilles' heel of constructivism.

In some ways constructivism is a manifestation of postmodernism. If there is one postmodern notion that has become as pervasive in our culture as the air we breathe, it is that there are no universal standards that exist independently of human choice. Therefore, values, including moral ones, are constructions that vary from culture to culture and change over time. In the classroom, children must have a completely open mind on value matters as they construct their own defensible value framework. However, to allow students to choose their values freely means that we may have to sanction lack of respect or cruelty or dishonesty. In the end, constructivism undermines any sense of common ethical responsibility and accountability. It is doubtful that its narrow focus on individual construction of meaning can nurture students to become responsible and responsive contributors to a compassionate and just society (Hytten 1994).

For the radical constructivist there is little point in developing curricula at all since students should be the main determiners of learning activities. That is why books and articles on constructivism generally limit themselves to examples of how teachers have implemented constructivist strategies in the classroom, or discussion of topics such as Science and Affect; Styles and Students; or Time, Talk, and Teachers (Baker and Piburn 1997). The curriculum, in other words, consists mainly of processes, not content.

A student-initiated constructivist curriculum may be rich in student-generated topics that are immediately relevant for them. However, it is easy for such a curriculum to neglect curriculum topics that are not as immediately of interest to them but are nevertheless important for their overall development. The latter may also result from the immense amount of classroom time required. Imagine initiating activities by stimulating new constructions but giving no specific directions, and then responding to all the different and complex student constructions in open-minded and enriching ways (Airasian and Walsh 1997). Asking students to construct their own long division algorithms or effective forms of government in this way may lead to worthwhile creative thinking, but also to frustrations and drawn-out investigations that prevent other important topics from being considered.

Finally, despite constructivists' claims, there is a created reality governed by God-given absolute laws. The bedrock of all knowledge is God's creation. Our theories and conclusions may be constructions that fall short of revealing God's truth, and that may have to be modified or even rejected. However, there are interpretations and constructions that are more right than others—and some that are wrong. Schools of necessity introduce students to knowledge based on investigations of reality. Humans interpret, critique, validate, and sometimes reject knowledge, but knowledge does not consist solely of personal constructions. Radical constructivism undermines the certainty and relevance of a common knowledge base and, beyond that, a common faith and ethic. Yet it does not admit that its view that all knowledge is relative leads to a logical problem since the statement itself must therefore be relative and not always true.

Footstep 2-6

Constructivists claim that:

- What students already know, their attitudes, and their interests provide a basis for meaningful learning.
- Curriculum encompasses pedagogical processes as much as it does content.
- Learning, to be meaningful, requires students to be actively involved and take responsibility.
- Knowledge is either personally or socially constructed.
- There are no right or wrong answers, but only discrepancies that we help children to resolve.

Critics of constructivists claim that:

- Besides active explorations and constructions, students also need instruction about basic concepts, skills, and, especially, universal laws and values. Students benefit from presentations, explanations, and drill.
- To construct all knowledge would be too complex and time-consuming: "If knowledge cannot be imparted ... then how can children come to the knowledge of complex conceptual schemes that have taken the best minds hundreds of years to build up" (Matthews 1997, 12)? Children inevitably must take a good deal of knowledge on faith (for example, that water molecules consist of two atoms of hydrogen and one of oxygen, or that the Magna Carta was sealed in 1215).

Which of the claims made by constructivists and their critics do you agree

with? Which aspects of constructivism could you use in your classroom? Which would you reject?

Orientations Are Not "Fixed"

We have seen that each of the three curriculum orientations described thus far has strengths as well as weaknesses. Their proponents have grasped something about education that can benefit student learning. But, at the same time, their basic assumptions result at best in a one-sided approach to teaching and learning.

That is why units used by classroom teachers often do not fit any one specific orientation. When planning an eighth-grade science unit, for instance, teachers may well have a whole section of investigations that encourage students to reexamine their previously held beliefs about everyday phenomena (experiential orientation). They may also have some tightly controlled step-by-step instruction in basic concepts, with daily quizzes and feedback (process/mastery). Then they may conclude the unit with readings and presentations that give a historical overview that the students analyze and summarize (traditional).

My division of the curriculum field into these three orientations is not the only one possible. Other educators have given different classifications, with as few as two and as many as six categories (Pinar et al. 1995, 21–22). Yet, despite the difficulties and dangers of pigeonholing individuals too precisely, we need to be aware of different ways of approaching curriculum. Our presuppositions do influence what happens in classrooms. If we are not aware of the basic thinking behind different orientations, we tend to be eclectic in our approach. That is, we use every new idea that seems attractive without recognizing that it may not fit our own beliefs about the nature, purpose, and practice of education.

👣 Footstep 2-7

All curriculum planners develop programs based on value presuppositions. In the next chapter we will consider how biblical values affect the curriculum. Here let's look at the values promoted by each curriculum orientation described thus far:

- **Traditionalists** foster faith in absolute truths, hard work, respect for authority, and the power and ultimate authority of reason.
- **Process/mastery proponents** teach students the value of efficiency and that humans can master their world as long as they provide the right environment and procedures.
- **Experientialists** promote human worth, autonomy, and the capacity to create not only knowledge and meaning, but also a world of love and justice.

These values differ significantly. Yet, as C. A. Bowers points out, the underlying theories share some common values:

- Faith in rationality is the sole arbiter of the affairs of everyday life.
- Human nature is good or at least can become so through education.
- Persons, therefore, are autonomous and self-directing.

The Russian author Solzhenitsyn already concluded in the 1970s that the dominant emphasis on individual autonomy left little sensitivity to the idea that freedom requires restriction of the self for the sake of others. Strangely, rights and freedom are held to be independent of goodness and responsibility. Individual selfishness has replaced mutual servanthood. The resulting focus on the pursuit of material self-interest and self-realization has undermined responsible mutual concern, weakened social commitments, and made the outlook for maintaining wholesome community and civic life "increasingly problematic" (Bowers 1988, 23; Lickona 1993, 6).

Do you agree with this analysis? Why or why not? Define and justify the values you believe the school curriculum should nurture. Suggest how you could promote these values for a specific curriculum topic.

Toward a Christian Curriculum Orientation

A Christian worldview and therefore a Christian curriculum orientation, takes as its starting point that the Bible is God's authoritative Word for life. Scripture is God's inspired self-disclosure that calls for obedience and response. That does not mean that the Bible gives us detailed formulas whose applications solve all current issues. God created us as human beings. As such, He calls us to think through and act on the principles for life that He reveals to us in Scripture, in His creation, and in the person of Jesus Christ. As we respond, we continue to work out our salvation with fear and trembling (Philippians 2:12). In other words, God calls believers to continue to understand His Word and apply it in increasingly responsible ways.

God's written Word, the Bible, provides guidelines and wisdom for answers to basic questions about the sort of world we live in and our role in it (Psalm 119:105, Romans 16:25–27). Our culture has privatized Christian faith. Consequently, a Christian voice in society has become marginalized. Society around us assumes that Christian faith has little to say about life in a pluralistic society. Yet, the Bible takes a very different approach, claiming that the Christian faith is all-encompassing. It calls not just individuals but whole nations to obedience. We are called to be imitators of God, full of love and sacrifice, not just in church, but everywhere in life (Ephesians 5:1).

If the Bible is relevant for all of life, then it is also relevant for curriculum. If the Bible makes clear that God demands a life of love and sacrifice, then classrooms should be places where teachers encourage and help students to be responsive disciples of Jesus Christ. If the Bible says that people are created in God's image, then classrooms should encourage students and teachers to unwrap their talents and gifts to God's honor and to the well-being of other humans. If Scripture expects Christians to share each other's joys and bear each other's burdens, then classrooms should stimulate teachers to seek *shalom*—God's peace and righteousness—for and with their students, their communities, their nation, and their world. If teachers believe that a Christian worldview is relevant, then they should strive each day for a curriculum that promotes such ideals as they prayerfully plan and guide learning activities for their students. They will do so even when sin thwarts their best efforts to have their students think and behave as responsive disciples.

The next chapter describes more fully the nature of a Christian worldview as it affects curriculum. In chapter 1 appropriate aims for a biblically based curriculum have been suggested. The following is a brief glimpse of the content and the nature of learning that results from a Christian orientation to curriculum.

The Content of the Curriculum

Knowledge depends on God's revelation in His creation and in His Word. The knowledge we develop is rooted in and reflects God's truth, sometimes more accurately, sometimes less so. Knowledge is not just arbitrary human construction. All knowledge depends on God's faithfulness in creating and sustaining the universe.

Curriculum content thus advances a Christian worldview. However, teachers do not indoctrinate students by demanding unthinking regurgitation or uncritical compliance with specific views. Rather, they help students attain a knowledge and skill background that allows them to grapple with important issues and concerns. Teachers advance views based on biblical truth and its implications. However, they accept their own fallibility and the fact that none of us have a full understanding of God's creation or His will for our lives. They do not attempt to force adherence to particular interpretations. Rather, they allow students to develop their personal response, always pointing them to the importance of considering basic principles. Thus they encourage them to take on life's tasks capably and responsibly.

The content of the curriculum is rooted in students' experiences of God's created reality. Teachers choose content related to students' experience in the past, or they allow students to consider and explore an aspect of God's creation at the beginning of a unit or topic. Teachers then help their students analyze, develop, and respond to the concepts and issues in more formal and abstract ways, at a level appropriate to their age.

At least five criteria govern the choice of curriculum content. Curriculum content should:

1. Be significant for students' lives; students must recognize that it is meaningful
2. Explore questions of importance for our nation and culture
3. Acquaint students with the strengths and weaknesses of their cultural heritage
4. Help students develop the skills necessary for functioning effectively in society, including the ability to assess various viewpoints and interpretations
5. Develop attitudes, values, dispositions, and commitments based on a careful consideration of the worldviews affecting culture

Curriculum content based on these criteria will encourage students to consider and adopt a Christian vision of life. It will also affect their decisions about personal and social phenomena and issues.

A Framework for Learning

To guide students into paths of wisdom requires much more than disclosing content. Teachers provide classroom structures that let students experience the meaning of living out a biblical worldview. They create classroom structures permeated with righteousness, justice, compassion, and respect. Without these values, teaching reaches the minds but not the hearts of students, and thus is ineffective in guiding them to become persons who understand and do the will of the Lord.

Learning strategies need to take into account that students are unique images of God, called to serve and love God and other humans. Teachers allow for diverse learning styles and modes of knowing. Providing for a rhythm of preparing, presenting, practicing, and responding in learning enables all students to exercise and extend their unique gifts. A mixture of individual, whole-group, and small-group learning also helps students develop their diverse abilities, and they learn to contribute their gifts to the classroom community for the good of the whole. Teachers evaluate students in terms of desired outcomes and standards, not just for intellectual progress, but also for spiritual, moral, aesthetic, social, emotional, and physical growth. Chapter 5 considers in more detail how teachers may implement a pedagogically and biblically responsible framework for learning.

Responsibility Teaching

Stephen Holtrop sums up a Christian curriculum orientation by calling for "responsibility teaching":

> Responsibility teaching views the person as unique, made in the image of God, redeemable in Christ, creative, a little less than the angels—but fallen, flawed and floundering. Further, the responsibility frame of reference says that not only are teachers and schools called to act responsibly and promote responsibility but also that students are responsible agents, called to the task of maximizing their learning.

> ...As the crown of creation, people have a special responsibility toward the world. Students can act most responsibly when they have not only intimate knowledge of many facets of God's world but also specific training in thinking responsibly about it. That means critical thinking about the issues, not just memorizing facts or someone else's response.

> ...A responsible curriculum is not just a personal choice or a legal safety net. It is

neither anything-goes nor back-to-basics. It involves careful planning of ways to engage students' minds and inspire their action in real issues. (Holtrop in Van Brummelen and Elliott 1997, 57–58)

Footstep 2-8

All humans live and work in God's world. Therefore, they may reach some similar conclusions about education despite differing philosophical and religious perspectives. Can you see some points of agreement between the Christian curriculum orientation described here and each of the three others, even though each upholds a different worldview and related values?

Christian educators do not always agree on their approach to curriculum. Some have favored a traditional orientation, fearing that others contribute to cultural impoverishment and ethical relativism. Other Christian educators hold that only constructivist strategies do justice to students' uniqueness as God's images.

Consider the teaching of Jesus in the Gospels. What aspects of each orientation come out in His teaching? Are there any implications for the way in which Christians should plan and implement school curriculum today?

Steps in Curriculum Planning

I conclude this chapter by considering how the steps in curriculum planning anticipate the steppingstones in the next chapters of this book.

The Tyler Rationale

The late Ralph Tyler proposed a model, or rationale, for the steps in curriculum planning that has influenced the North American curriculum field more than any other. Tyler's model pulled together a set of questions that until 1950 had seldom been addressed systematically (1950, 1–2):

1. What educational purposes should the school seek to attain?
2. What educational experiences can be provided that are likely to attain these purposes?
3. How can these educational experiences be effectively organized?
4. How can we determine whether these purposes are being attained?

Tyler's followers used his model as a linear, technical process for curriculum planning. They split teaching into small, manageable, and measurable behavioral objectives. They focused on the most efficient means to attain these prespecified objectives. These objectives spelled out narrow concepts and skills but often neglected important overall goals. Tyler himself became critical of his followers' objectives, saying they were too specific, they stressed behavior but neglected content, and they were not chosen with what he called "philosophical and psychological screens" in mind (Lauren Sosniak in Anderson and Sosniak 1994, 118).

Fig. 2.1   The Tyler Rationale

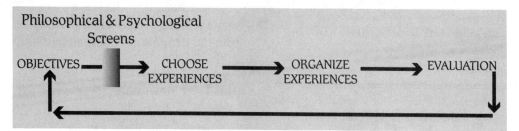

Tyler's rationale does indicate some of the curriculum steppingstones that curriculum planners must use. However, the way Tyler's followers have used the process shortchanges how curriculum planning actually proceeds. They have neglected the complex realities of making curriculum decisions. For instance, curriculum planners seldom follow Tyler's steps in exact order. Moreover, the rationale itself has no room for affirmation of basic beliefs, for reverence for life, or for compassion or justice (Macdonald and Purpel 1987, 183). The rationale has no place for considering overall aims rooted in a worldview. It only allows some objectives from a list suggested by subject specialists and others to be filtered out by philosophical and psychological discrepancies. It also assumes that teachers are technicians who are to follow instructions for processing students efficiently. The result is that the way the rationale has been used fits especially the process/mastery orientation to curriculum. However, it falls short in providing a model for implementing other orientations.

Components of Program Design

I now describe a model that more closely reflects how curriculum develops in practice. I see curriculum as a dynamic series of planned learning experiences. Teachers continually assess, revise, and adapt their curriculum plans as they work with their students.

This model for the process of curriculum has three concentric wheels: the foundational frame factors on the outside, the program components in the center, and, in the middle, the deliberative process that connects the two (see figure 2.2).

The lines of the model are broken ones because of the many interactions within and between the circles. Let me give some examples:

- How planners view knowledge affects their pedagogical approaches.
- Evaluation needs to take place while planning is going on, as well as during implementation.
- Activities depend to some extent on resources within reach. Those, in turn, may affect objectives or intents.
- The social, economic, and political contexts of schooling will influence plans for learning.
- Beliefs about the purpose of schooling affect how planners implement and evaluate their work.

In these and other ways, various process elements interact in a fluid and dynamic manner.

Note two points: First, there is no one proper starting point for curriculum planning. You cannot plan curriculum in a neat, step-by-step way. Intents, for instance, arise from groundings and contextual frame factors. But they also develop from potential activities and resources. Goals, activities, and resources often emerge together.

Second, all those involved in planning will not directly consider every aspect of the model. A curriculum specialist cannot take into account the features of a specific class. Teachers will seldom ask explicit questions about, say, the nature of knowledge. But they should know, be able to influence, and agree with the basic thrust of a program. Otherwise, plans will quickly founder when used in their classrooms.

Fig. 2.2   Components of Curriculum Planning

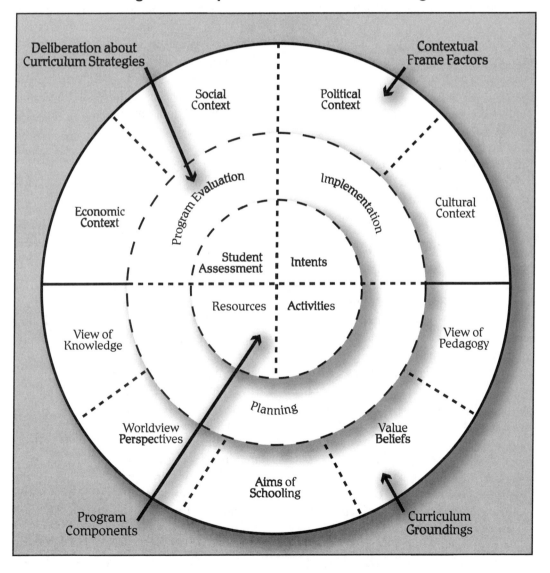

The model's outer circle shows the factors that frame curriculum planning. All who make curriculum decisions, from state officials to students, have beliefs about life and about education. They also work in a certain context. Answers to key questions frame their work. What is their guiding vision of life? What values do they hold to be important in education? What are schools for? What is the nature of knowledge? How should they choose and structure subject matter? How do they view persons, and what does that imply for the curriculum planning? What are the economic, political, social, and cultural contexts that will affect what is possible? The next three chapters examine the biblical groundings for curriculum. Chapter 6 also briefly considers some of the contextual frame factors.

Curriculum planning teams seldom outline their views on groundings in an orderly way. Often their members are chosen to represent special expertise or different interest groups. No matter how appointed, they will have disagreements that will become clear as they develop program components. Some diversity can lead to healthy discussions and deeper insights. But unresolved fundamental clashes can stymie a project or lead to a curriculum that lacks a clear focus.

The innermost part of the model lists program components, i.e., the intents, activities, resources, and student assessment (Werner and Aoki 1979, 7). Planners at some point must address the intents of their project. What should the proposed curriculum accomplish or achieve? What ends or outcomes should be defined and selected? Intents are broader than objectives. They include both written and unwritten ones. An unwritten intent may be to raise the level of public confidence in a school. Written intents include thematic statements and objectives or intended learning outcomes. Planners usually consider intents, learning activities, resources, and, more recently, student assessment of learning, in concert. Even if they first formulate goals, they will clarify and often alter them as they plan, implement, and evaluate learning activities and resources. The content, activities, and resources of final plans should be in accord with the project's intents.

Planners ask a number of questions that help them develop and choose activities and resources. How can we achieve our intents? Which content, skills, and expressive activities do we include? How do we structure, balance, and sequence them? Which resources do we choose, and how should they be put to use? Are the connections among intents, activities, and resources logical and clear? Does the proposed program have a clear and unified focus? Answers to these questions will depend a great deal on the planners' views of curriculum groundings.

The middle circle represents the deliberative process that links groundings and context with program components. Curriculum making involves three interrelated but distinct acts: planning, implementation, and program evaluation. Here planners ask how they can coordinate and monitor curriculum planning. What factors do they need to consider and act on for successful implementation? How can they best meet their intents? What do they assess and evaluate? How? Planning is never finished. Implementation and evaluation lead to more planning. Even the prescribed government guidelines, once published, are interpreted, adapted, and evaluated before, during, and after implementation. Teachers invariably modify them for their own use.

In short, when planning curriculum at any level, developers thoughtfully or inadvertently take into account their groundings and the project's probable or actual context. They derive their intents, learning activities, and resources from a process of deliberation that includes planning, implementation, and evaluation. To be effective, planners, including teachers, need to consider carefully their views of the foundational frame factors before or while nailing down intents and learning experiences. The next three chapters are intended to help you do so.

Footstep 2-9

Suppose you are asked to chair a committee to assess and make recommendations for a new science program in your school. Discuss how each of the elements in figure 2.2 would affect how you would go about your task.

Footstep 2-10

Make a one-page outline of points you would include in a statement that describes your personal curriculum orientation. Save this outline and update it after you have read the next three chapters.

Reviewing the Main Points

ORIENTATION with curriculum metaphor	BASIC QUESTIONS	KNOWLEDGE AND LEARNING EMPHASIS
TRADITIONAL Curriculum as conveyor of information and ideas	What have thinkers found out about our world that we want students to know? What content do students need most? (transmission)	Basic skills and reasoning ability; gaining knowledge in the subject disciplines
PROCESS/MASTERY Curriculum as a controlled and efficient process	How can we achieve our objectives efficiently? How do we specify and assess learning outcomes? (control)	Investigating, mastering, and applying data in small, defined, manageable steps
EXPERIENTIAL Curriculum as a quest for personal meaning	How can we best help students construct knowledge and meaning from their experiences? (personal meaning)	Autonomous creation and negotiation of knowledge and meaning
CHRISTIAN Curriculum as reflective interpretation of God's truth	How do we foster students' positive responses toward God, their fellow creatures, society, and themselves? (responsibility)	Understanding and unfolding God's revelation through experience, observation, conceptualization, and application

Planning curriculum is a complex task. Tyler's four-step rationale oversimplifies the process. Teachers and other curriculum planners generally do not use a linear process. Rather, throughout their deliberation they move back and forth among intended outcomes, learning activities, and choice of resources, keeping in mind both their view of curriculum groundings and their societal context.

References

Airasian, P., and M. Walsh. 1997. Constructivist cautions. *Phi Delta Kappan* 78 (6): 444–49.

Anderson, L., and L. Sosniak. 1994. *Bloom's taxonomy: A forty-year retrospective*. Ninety-third yearbook of the National Society for the Study of Education, Part II. Chicago: NSSE.

Baker, D., and M. Piburn. 1997. *Constructing science in middle and secondary school classrooms*. Boston: Allyn and Bacon.

Bowers, C. 1988. *The cultural dimensions of educational computing*. New York: Teachers College Press.

British Columbia Ministry of Education. 1990. *Intermediate program: Learning in British Columbia: Response draft*. Victoria, BC: BCME.

Council for Basic Education. 1991. Standards: A vision for learning. *Perspective* 4 (1): 1–5 and enclosed chart.

Ellul, J. 1981. *Perspectives on our age*. Toronto: Canadian Broadcasting Corporation.

Fosnot, C. 1996. *Constructivism: Theory, perspectives, and practice*. New York: Teachers College Press.

Greig, S., G. Pike, and D. Selby. 1989. *Greenprints for changing schools*. London: The World Wide Fund for Nature, and Kogan Page.

Hytten, K. 1994. Pragmatism, postmodernism, and education. Paper presented at the American Educational Studies Association, November 1994. ERIC document ED378181.

Jackson, P., ed. 1992. *Handbook of research on curriculum*. New York: Macmillan.

Lickona, T. 1993. The return of character education. *Educational Leadership* 51 (3): 6–11.

Macdonald, J., and D. Purpel. 1987. Curriculum and planning: Visions and metaphors. *Journal of Curriculum and Supervision* 2 (2): 178–92.

Matthews, M. 1997. Introductory comments on philosophy and constructivism in science education. *Science and Education* 6: 5–14.

McNeil, J. 1995. *Curriculum: The teacher's initiative*. Englewood Cliffs, NJ: Merrill.

Phillips, D. 2000. *Constructivism in education: Opinions and second opinions on controversial issues*. Ninety-ninth yearbook of the National Society for the Study of Education. Chicago: NSSE.

Pinar, W., W. Reynolds, P. Slattery, and P. Taubman. 1995. *Understanding curriculum: An introduction to the study of historical and contemporary curriculum discourses*. New York: Peter Lang.

Spencer, H. 1911. *Essays on education*. London: J. M. Dent and Sons.

Steffe, L., and J. Gale, eds. 1995. *Constructivism in education*. Hillsdale, NJ: Lawrence Erlbaum.

Tyler, R. 1950. *Basic principles of curriculum and instruction*. Chicago: University of Chicago Press.

Van Brummelen, H., and D. Elliott, eds. 1997. *Nurturing Christians as reflective educators*. San Dimas, CA: Learning Light Publishing.

Werner, W., and T. Aoki. 1979. *Programs for people: Introducing program development, implementation, and evaluation*. Vancouver: Centre for the Study of Curriculum and Instruction (University of British Columbia).

Wolterstorff, N. 1976. *Reason within the bounds of religion*. Grand Rapids: Eerdmans.

Steppingstone 3

A Christian Worldview as a Basis for Curriculum

There's a fascinating story in modern physics that affirms a biblically based worldview and, in turn, also shows how such a worldview affects the teaching of physics.

The story deals with the history of the theories of relativity and quantum mechanics. Unlike what quantum mechanics claimed in the 1930s, Einstein showed that the element of chance was not inescapable in a physical description of the universe. He also discovered that there was some form of communication that was faster than light, a result that contradicted his own theory of relativity. Einstein called it telepathy. In 1964 John S. Bell proved Einstein's discovery mathematically. In 1972 Bell's proof was verified experimentally.

Why was this so important? Well, Einstein and Bell gave back to physics the correlation between cause and effect at a deep and awesome level. Information between subatomic particles somehow gets around faster than the fleetest photon. There is something beyond light. Just as an onion has many layers that we can peel off one by one, there appear to be multiple levels of reality (Owens 1983, 106ff).

The story reminds us, first of all, that human knowledge is limited. What humans discover is but a pale, superficial reflection of God's infinitely rich creation. This discovery and others in physics have once again sparked the flames of awe and wonder. "The impression of design is overwhelming," says physicist Paul Davies (*Time*, 28 Dec 1992, 39). That design, many physicists agree, reveals God's power and faithfulness (Romans 1:20).

This story undercuts the positivist view of knowledge that underlies most school science programs. This view asserts that the only knowledge—and therefore, the only reality—is what we can observe. We arrive at truth only through the observation-based scientific method. The existence of God and of God-given absolute norms for life is relegated to beliefs that do not have the weight of actual knowledge. This story from modern physics, however, makes clear that much exists beyond what we can observe. Indeed, Einstein developed his theories long before they were verified through observation. He realized that they uncovered only one small layer of God's design of the universe.

The story also rejects the constructivist view of knowledge (that is, that the only reality is the meaning that you construct). Even non-Christian physicists agree that "the universe seems calibrated for life's existence" (*Time*, 34). Yet many educators today claim that as autonomous beings, students must construct their own reality and meaning, and choose their own values. There is no absolute truth, they say. Modern physics, on the other hand, shows that we *discover* and *interpret* reality and meaning; we do not just *construct* it. We live in a well-designed universe.

Moreover, the story contradicts fatalist views that everything depends on chance and there is no meaning in reality. Physicists have concluded that the overarching pattern of twentieth-century science suggests that there is "something authentically divine about how it all fits together" (*Time*, 36).

By pointing out the flaws in the foregoing views of knowledge, this story from physics affirms a biblical one. The starting point of this view is that God governs all things in His sovereignty and faithfulness. Further, all knowledge depends on God's revelation. God reveals Himself in creation, in Scripture, and in Jesus Christ. In the classroom we may peel away layer upon layer of meaning in God's revelation. Yet our conclusions will always be imperfect. As Agur already said in Proverbs 30, we never understand fully; we never reach the core of the onion. Yet we may use the knowledge we gain to God's glory and in obedience to His norms for human life. This view gives us comfort and hope as well as a sound basis for our approach to science education. It is also the basis for the first injunction God gave to humans, the Creation Mandate.

A second mandate that God assigned to humans was the Great Commandment: *Love God above all and your neighbor as yourself.* Therefore, in physics class we discuss, for instance, how the subject has led to a technology that provides new opportunities but can also enslave us. Consumption rather than stewardship has become the norm in industrial nations. Our Western technological genius, combined with greed for profit, arms nations around the world, contributing to untold agony. Do our physics courses investigate how we can use technology to help people live more with less? provide a respectable living for people across the world? be less self-centered in our personal and societal use of technology?

The structure of physics classrooms, like all classrooms, should also reflect biblical *agape* love for God and neighbor. Physics is a practical science that we can teach in a way that can excite a wide spectrum of students. Do we structure physics courses so that students with a theoretical and practical bent learn to help each other in the classroom? Do theoretically oriented students explain basic concepts and ideas to small groups of students? Do other students take leadership in doing experiments, building models, and exhibiting their work to the class? In this way, do we help students to appreciate each other's diverse gifts and learn to support and care for each other?

A third mandate that God gave us was the Great Commission. It bids Christians to preach the gospel and to teach nations everything that Christ commanded. Physics classes should not just unfold theories and applications of physics. They might discuss, for instance, how technology can help us spread the gospel. But there's more. Jesus also taught us, "Blessed are the peacemakers, for they will be called sons of God" (Matthew 5:9). How can we use physics to promote peace? What are the ethical dimensions of how we use physics?

Sometimes there are no easy answers. The jet that contributes to the deterioration of the ozone layer also sends Bible translators to Papua New Guinea. Yet our students should grapple with issues of stewardship, compassion, peace, and justice. That is part of what it means to obey everything that Christ commanded us. Only then can they live as God's images who, as they grow in their relationship with Him, are granted the grace to erect signposts here on Earth that lead to the Kingdom of Heaven.

I've mentioned three of God's injunctions to humankind in this section: the Creation Mandate, the Great Commandment, and the Great Commission. Can you suggest how these three mandates might affect how you teach a topic in another subject area?

A worldview is a comprehensive framework of basic convictions about life. Worldviews embrace what we believe about the nature and purpose of reality, human beings, knowledge, and life in society. Our professed worldview may not always be our actual operative one; our actions may speak louder than our words. However, our framework of ultimate beliefs (even if we hold them implicitly) plays a decisive role in how we view and live our lives.

Worldviews are the often-unseen rules within which society operates. Worldviews also shape how we view and conduct schooling. Today, the dominant worldview in Western society is secular. It has effectively made God and Christian faith irrelevant. If Christians are to respond, they must, therefore, understand, be able to defend, and put into practice a biblical worldview. The Christian heritage is fading but is still real. We must, therefore, seize the opportunity we have in schooling to promote a Christian vision of the world (Jones 1998, 10–12).

A Christian worldview is shaped by God's revelation in His Word: His Word in creation, His Word in the Bible, and His Word Incarnate, Jesus Christ. The Bible makes clear that reality is God's creation. God created, upholds, and rules His world. He sustains the laws of nature. He also provides us with the norms or values for human culture and society that enable and call us to be His coworkers in carrying on His work. God's norms for human life include love, faithfulness, compassion, righteousness, integrity, justice, responsible stewardship, and peace.

Humankind's fall into sin, however, perverted God's good creation. Sin distorts all of human life—personal morality, marriage and family life, political systems, economic and environmental practices, the use of technology, the fine arts, agriculture, and health. Sin is foreign to God's order for creation, and it is only through Christ's death that redemption and restoration have become possible.

The task of Christians in society is to proclaim the good news of Jesus Christ. They do so by discipling others and by calling and working for a restoration of all aspects of culture according to God's creation norms. Christians recognize, at the same time, that God's creation will be restored fully only when Christ returns. Until that time, nevertheless, God calls us to erect signposts for His Kingdom.

The details of a responsible biblical worldview are beyond the scope of this book. (For a more complete description than is possible in this book, see, for example, Noebel 1991; Walsh and Middleton 1984; and Wolters 1985.) This chapter considers the relevance for education of three biblical charges or injunctions that are essential to a biblical worldview. These are the *Creation (or Cultural) Mandate, the Great Commandment, and the Great Commission.* Then discussed are the values God wants us to uphold that flow out of these mandates.

Keep in mind, as each mandate is described, that they are interrelated. God gave the Creation Mandate to humans when He created them and placed them on the earth. After humankind's fall into sin, God added precepts that Jesus summarized as the Great Commandment. God needed to instruct us in what it meant to serve Him in obedience. And after His death and resurrection, when the outpouring of the Holy Spirit was imminent, Jesus supplemented the Creation Mandate and the Great Commandment with the Great Commission. The Great Commission gave us the privilege of becoming God's coworkers through Christ's redemption and reconciliation.

All three mandates require us to seek first God's Kingdom and its justice and righteousness. All call us to conform to the image of Christ in all of life. All instruct us to reach out to others and to this world with the power of the gospel. And all challenge us to understand, evaluate, and transform the world from the foundation of God's unchanging values.

Worldview Questions for Curriculum Planning

Here are four basic worldview questions with the related biblical concepts enclosed in brackets:

- **Who and where am I?** What are the nature, task, and purpose of human beings? What is the nature of the world and universe I live in? [**creation**]
- **What has gone wrong?** Why do we personally and as a society fall far short of perfection? Where do pain

and evil come from? [**fall**]
- **What is the remedy?** Where do we find answers to the human plight? [**redemption** that enables us to work toward restoration]
- **What does the future hold?** Where do we find our hope? [**fulfillment** in a new heaven and a new earth] (adapted from Walsh and Middleton 1984, 35)

For planning many curriculum topics, we can rephrase these questions as shown below:

1. **What is God's intention** for the particular area of creation or culture that we will investigate?
2. **How has this purpose been distorted** by the effects of human disobedience and sin? How have humans deviated from God's original intent?
3. **How does God want us to respond?** Are there ways in which we can, through Christ's work of redemption, restore, at least in part, the love, righteousness, and justice God intended for the world?
4. **How can we help our students develop a deeper understanding of, experience in, and commitment to a Christian way of life?** How can we instill in them a sense of hope, strength, and courage despite the many problems and struggles we face? (revised from Blomberg 1991, 9)

Footstep 3-1

Choose a curriculum topic, theme, or issue. Discuss how your answers to the four numbered questions above would affect your teaching. Are there other questions that you would add to the four given here?

The Creation Mandate

Psalm 19 says a great deal about God's creation and our place in it:

The heavens declare the glory of God; the skies proclaim the work of his hands. Day after day they pour forth speech; night after night they display knowledge.... The precepts of the Lord are right, giving joy to the heart. (Psalm 19:1–2, 8)

Created reality reflects God's handiwork. We gain awe, understanding, and insight from the way God speaks to us in His creation order. We may not leave God at home when we do an experiment in a science class or discuss a pattern in mathematics.

But God's laws go beyond the physical laws that He created. God also gave us trustworthy laws to govern our everyday lives. These precepts provide strength, comfort, and discernment (Psalm 19:7–8). While we have no choice but to obey physical laws, the impact of God's statutes for obedient living depends on whether and how people apply them (Wolters 1985, 36).

What we need to remember is that all truth is God's truth. There are no separate secular and sacred realms, with God having little to do with the former. Rather, God calls us to use His marvelous physical gifts within the guidelines He gives us for religious, ethical, political, social, economic, and aesthetic life. The fear of the Lord, including submission to all His commands, is the beginning of wisdom, discernment, and knowledge (Psalm 111).

Before the fall into sin, God told Adam and Eve to be fruitful, to rule over the earth, and to work and take care of the God's garden (Genesis 1:28, 2:15). These verses have been called the **Creation Mandate** or the **Cultural Mandate.** God thus calls humans to develop and unfold the earth's possibilities, to be his co-regents as they form cul-

ture. In Scripture, ruling and leadership always involved service. To rule over the earth therefore meant to serve for the benefit of others. "Taking care" denoted that humans as responsible stewards should enable everything in God's world to fulfill its intended function. God entrusts us with His creation in all its complexity so that all creatures will benefit.

The fall into sin has not negated that call, even though sin will continue to undermine our efforts until Christ's return. God still calls us to be salt and light in our society. We beam the gospel's message and illuminate a manner of life worthy of the gospel. We boldly advocate what is true, worthy, and upright. We preserve family, government, and social structures insofar as, by God's grace, they restrain evil and promote virtue, justice, security, compassion, and human dignity. We also try to change anti-biblical behavior and structures such as those that cause discrimination, inequity, and abuse (Stott 1978, 57–68).

What does that mean for our classrooms? We help our students sense that God calls them to be His servants in His world. We invite them to be stewards of the God-given gifts within and around them. Our students learn about, use, and value mathematical, physical, and biological entities and theories. They also experience how God-given norms can promote love, integrity, and justice in communication, economics, social interaction, the arts, government and law, and family life. We encourage students to be and become committed to and involved in Kingdom service.

The story of creation as well as Psalm 19 make clear that we do not personally construct all knowledge and meaning. A biblical view of knowledge allows us to recognize that our observations, theories, and applications are limited and imperfect. They do not necessarily lead to truth, yet they enrich our lives. Our interpretations, extrapolations, and applications take place within the bounds of our faith parameters. God calls us to explore scientific phenomena so that we can understand and use His creation. We also depend, however, on the framework of Scripture, God's special revelation to us for interpretation and application. We need these in order to use our results in service to God and to each other, even when we recognize that our knowledge is tentative.

The Creation Mandate calls Christians to be involved in forming culture. We therefore plan a curriculum that challenges students to explore how they may work at and call for more biblical direction in the structures and practices of society. They study how God has given us basic guidelines, for instance, for business, law, and the use of technology. We encourage them to be part of networks of Christian businessmen, doctors, lawyers, musicians, and artists who communally explore what it means to reclaim important areas of life and re-form them strategically. They also learn that, while the Bible is a guide to Kingdom living, Christians must remain humble. They do not have all the answers, and their thinking and action are also tainted with sin.

Footstep 3-2

Teacher Clayton Chalfour switched from teaching mathematics to teaching media because he believes that Christians should become more active in the media. He hopes that those students who enter careers in the media do not end up just producing stereotypical Christian movies but will have a Christian impact on mainstream film productions. He teaches the basics of scriptwriting, acting, and camera techniques. With his students he explores the worldviews and values at the basis of advertising, television programs, and films. This is important, he believes, since his students, for instance, blithely accept television soap operas because "they're not real."

During the course of the year, Chalfour's students produce programs of news and commentary about life in the school. Other students in the school can see these once every three weeks. Toward the end of the course, Chalfour's students produce a three to five minute dramatic documentary on a relevant issue in the community, such as homelessness. The class members consider what they try to portray as they produce their documentaries—and why. The teacher also discusses how, in the future, students can get into larger productions and begin to influence such production on the basis of a Christian worldview.

In what ways does this teacher help his students exercise the Creation Mandate?

The Great Commandment

"Love the Lord your God with all your heart and with all your soul and with all your mind." This is the first and greatest commandment. And the second is like it: "Love your neighbor as yourself." (Matthew 22:37–39)

In this Great Commandment Jesus brings together two separate passages of the Old Testament Scripture (Deuteronomy 6:5 and Leviticus 19:18). Thus He underscores that love for neighbor flows naturally out of love for God. Love is the key to being transformed by the renewing of our minds so that we no longer conform to the pattern of this world (Romans 12:2, 9ff). We cannot carry out the Creation Mandate responsibly without also obeying the Great Commandment.

The word Jesus used for love, *agape,* does not mean friendly or sentimental affection. Rather, it is self-sacrificial love, love even for the unlovable. Agape love embodies a total commitment, a deliberately chosen, faith-based devotion. It consumes all our strength: strength of conviction, strength of character, and strength of will (Mark 12:30). And it includes our whole mind: to love God, we need to have the mind of Christ.

We face obstacles as we try to implement the demands of the Great Commandment. Even the second part of the Great Commandment—which, in one form or another, is found in all major religious traditions—often no longer serves as a basis for living in today's society. An arrogant faith in individual achievement and in intellectual certainty and reason undermines values such as care, compassion, and humility. David Purpel (1989) claims that schools may contribute to this malaise. How and what we teach, he shows, may foster self-gratifying individuality.

The Great Commandment means that teachers strive for a classroom that is a loving community based on shared values, one where we bear with each other in love and use our unique gifts for building up the whole community (Ephesians 4). Jesus Himself exemplified what this meant. He spoke the truth in love. He treated all those with whom He came in contact as important. He encouraged and allowed them to use and develop their diverse gifts for the benefit of God's Kingdom. His love and gifts reached out to children, the sick, the poor, and, yes, to the leaders of society.

Lesslie Newbigin (1989, 227–33) described how a community true to its Christian calling understands and displays a gospel framework for life. It is a community of praise and thanksgiving that lives by the amazing grace of a boundless kindness. It is a community of truth that is modest and realistic but also skeptical of modern propaganda. It is a community that has deep concern for its neighborhood rather than living for and focusing on itself. It is a community that offers sacrifices of love and obedience as it exercises its diverse gifts in the public life of our society. It is a community of mutual responsibility. It is a community that provides a foretaste of a social order based on God's peace and justice. Finally, it is a community of hope, one that rejects not only the false technological optimism of Western culture but also the nihilism and despair of modern Western literature.

Here are some marks of classrooms that strive to obey the Great Commandment:

- Teachers care and pray for their students and help them be and become what God wants them to be.
- Teachers encourage students to use their minds to the best of their ability in service to and love for God and neighbor, and to develop the mind of Christ (1 Corinthians 2:16).
- Teachers promote constructive and fair relationships. They implement strategies for conflict resolution based on repentance, recompense, forgiveness, and mutual respect.
- Rather than insisting on personal rights, teachers and students together observe personal and communal gratitude for God's gift of grace.

- Praise and thankfulness are built into the curriculum. The school celebrates students' diverse gifts.
- Students engage in learning activities in which they help and support classmates.
- Teachers set high but realistic expectations for all members of the school community. Assessment practices treat students fairly and help them improve their learning.
- Teachers trust their students with meaningful responsibilities while holding them accountable for agreed-upon commitments.
- Curriculum content deals with issues in our society in which agape love can make a difference. It deals with the effects of sin in society, but it also proclaims hope in the future because God is faithful forever (Psalm 146).
- The school arranges for service projects through which students practice love for neighbor.

In school, a vital part of the Great Commandment is that the curriculum helps students unfold their gifts for service to others. Students and teachers share each other's joys and bear each other's burdens. Together they celebrate and bring about God's *shalom* when it is possible to do so, and lament its absence when the power of sin prevails. Such a curriculum is most likely to succeed in a school that functions as a Christlike community.

Footstep 3-3

How does an elementary school of more than 400 students enable them to understand and experience the Great Commandment? Most important, says principal Henry Contant, is that his school provides opportunities for service. His school gives the seventh-graders (the highest grade level in the school) meaningful areas of responsibility. In a full-day September retreat, the students (joined by their parents in the evening) brainstorm possible areas of service and choose ones in which they will serve.

One year the students identified sixteen areas. These included refereeing and keeping records for the school's intramural program, supervising the computer room at noon, setting up and taking down audiovisual equipment, organizing the school's recycling program, and "adopting a block" in the neighborhood for litter pickup. Each teacher trained students in one or two areas, and maintained contact with them during the year. Each student signed a service pledge. The school also held regular team-building events such as pizza and swimming parties.

The program has affirmed students, especially those not academically inclined, who usually serve more responsibly than the teachers anticipate. Teachers appreciate students' willingness to help the school function smoothly. They have gained more faith and trust in their students. The seventh-graders also interact frequently with students in other grades. As a result, overall interpersonal relationships in the school are more respectful and caring.

Henry Contant considers this program a significant and strategic part of the seventh-grade curriculum. In what ways does the program realize both parts of the Great Commandment? Is this a legitimate part of the curriculum? Why or why not?

Footstep 3-4

Teacher Curt Gesch (1993) designed an eleventh-grade course called Conservation and Outdoor Recreation Education. The course focuses on what it means to live in community with other humans and with animals in recreation activities such as hiking, fishing, and hunting. Students explore issues that go beyond outdoor recreation: how laws and regulations protect the community; what it means that something dies in order for other things to live; the moral standards upheld by most civilizations; why it is important to be courteous, considerate, and cooperative; and how people go about reaching a compromise when they have conflicting goals, preferences, or ethics.

In what ways can a course such as this contribute to students' understanding and applying the Great Commandment? Because of the issues raised, is such a course as important as, say, a mathematics course? Why or why not? What are some other concrete ways in which a curriculum can help students to love God above all and their neighbors as themselves?

The Great Commission

God first assigned humans the Creation Mandate. He added the Great Commandment after the fall into sin. Today, God still calls us to tend His earth and relate to God and others in loving and responsible ways (Romans 8:17, 1 Corinthians 3:9). After His resurrection, Jesus added the Great Commission:

All authority in heaven and on earth has been given to me. Therefore go and make disciples of all nations, baptizing them in the name of the Father and of the Son and of the Holy Spirit, and teaching them to obey everything I have commanded you. And surely I am with you always, to the very end of the age. (Matthew 28:18–20)

Now Christians usually think of the Great Commission in terms of witnessing to those who do not believe in Christ, and that is an important aspect of it. But read the verses once more with fresh eyes. Jesus enjoins us to make disciples (not just converts) of all nations (not just individuals). Disciples are people who base their thinking, words, and deeds on the principles Jesus taught us. If an entire nation recognizes what it means to serve God, the resulting conditions will set the stage for a more loving, just, and joyful implementation of God's mandates.

Jesus then adds the far-reaching command that is particularly significant for curriculum. He says that we must teach people "to obey everything I have commanded you." Jesus here makes us, as Paul puts it, God's fellow workers in teaching all nations—and all our students—what Christ has commanded us.

What are Christ's decrees that we ought to teach? The Gospel of Matthew, the gospel of the Kingdom of Heaven in which we find the Great Commission, is clear. Be meek and humble, merciful, peacemaking, seeking justice and righteousness. Be persons of integrity, with compassion and forgiveness even for those who oppose you. Be faithful to your marriage partner. Don't put value in earthly riches. Be thankful for and enjoy God's blessings. Give generously to the needy. Be responsible in your business ventures. Use your God-given gifts in meaningful ways. Avoid legalism and hypocrisy. Believe that the Kingdom of Heaven is ever-renewing and all-powerful, but remember that its current manifestations are beset by sin until Christ returns.

The late Lesslie Newbigin sums up such discipleship as follows:

> Christian discipleship is a following of Jesus in the power of his risen life on the way which he went. That way is neither the way of purely interior spiritual pilgrimage, nor is it the way of realpolitik for the creation of a new social order. It goes the way Jesus went, right into the heart of the world's business and politics, with a claim that is both promising and vulnerable. It looks for a world of justice and peace, not as a product of its own action but as the gift of God.... Such discipleship will be concerned equally in the private and in the public spheres.... It will provide occasions for the creation of visible signs of the invisible kingship of God. (1983, 37)

Thus, the Great Commission requires Christians to tell the story of salvation and at the same time act on its demands. A community enabled by the Spirit to live in Christ will challenge both individuals and the powers and principalities (e.g., the structures of society such as global consumerism). Both our words and our deeds can then promote justice and peace, though we need to remember that no human endeavor is free from the corrupting power of sin. Our words are empty unless our daily activities reflect them in all our involvements (Newbigin 1989, 119–39).

Since Christ's resurrection, the Great Commission, the Great Commandment, and the Creation Mandate have been closely intertwined. The first letter of Peter is instructive. Because of a new life and hope through the resurrection of Jesus Christ (1 Peter 1:3), we may prepare our minds for action (1:13) and live holy lives (1:15, 2:1). In everything we do, Peter continues, God calls us to be His servants (2:16), living such good lives that our good deeds teach others to glorify God (2:12). If we live in harmony, compassion, and humility, repaying insult with blessing and doing good (3:8–9, 14), then we can in good conscience and with gentleness give an answer to everyone who asks us to give a reason for the hope that we have (3:15). We should use whatever gifts we have received to serve others (4:10). In short, God's three great injunctions form three legs of a tripod, and all three are needed in the Christian life.

Let me again give a number of classroom implications (to which you may want to add your own). Teachers are to:

- Make clear that our whole life and being depend on our relationship with God (Acts 17:28). Teachers are to take opportunities to lead students to a personal relationship with God when students ask questions about the source of hope and peace.
- Model lives of joyful obedience so that their students, too, will begin to understand what it means to put their lives into God's hands.
- Recognize Christ's authority and presence in the classroom, and therefore cherish and promote the fruit of the Spirit—compassion, self-sacrifice, justice, righteousness, and truthfulness.
- Choose curriculum content that reveals how people have responded obediently and disobediently to God's mandates. To understand the influence of sin and explore Christian responses, teachers sometimes discuss controversial, anti-Christian materials, such as modern rock music videos. This helps students avoid

blithely accepting what they read, hear, and see; and apply Christian principles to personal and societal life issues.

- Examine with students the Kingdom norms that Christ taught us together with their implications for our society. They help their students investigate, at an appropriate level, what it means to be ambassadors of Christ wherever God puts us.

All this is a tall order in a society drenched in secularism. Nevertheless, teachers who realize the importance of the Great Commission will model a lifestyle, design units, choose resources and literary selections, and structure their assignments so that students will learn "everything I have commanded you." Their goal is that their students, in turn, as part of the Christ-community, will "go and make disciples of all nations."

Footstep 3-5

As one element of a theme on communities, Inge Maier's second-grade class has discussed what it means to be part of the Body of Christ. She has a large cutout of a person on the bulletin board made up of segments of different colors, each piece with the name of one of her students. After a discussion about the role of the church in the community, the children write a story about their church with an accompanying drawing. The stories have included such sentences as these: "We go to church and prays God. My church looks better than my house. In my church I usually go to Sunday boring. My grampa does the offering. I sing in choir. We have communion."

Discuss how the teacher could continue this unit so that her students begin to understand the scope of the Great Commission, taking into account that her students are from many different church and ethnic backgrounds.

Worldviews, Values, and Schooling

Values are an integral part of all worldviews. Values are ideals or desirable guides for living that are deemed to be important. They set direction in life, giving it meaning and purpose.

Today, three major influences in Western society have coalesced to convey a value mind-set that undermines a just, civil, dependable, and peaceful society. First, technology has led to an economy that requires humans to consume at an ever-increasing rate. At the same time, it gives the false impression that persons can control their own lives and their own destinies. Second, the media promote individualistic pleasure, often as dictated by large corporations seeking to maximize profit. Third, postmodernism (including constructivism in education) advances the idea that values are relative to each individual. Together, these three influences have produced the following commonly held value framework:

- Since persons are autonomous and good, they deserve a comfortable, exciting, and happy life. Happiness results from material things.
- There are no transcendent values based on a source outside of self. Persons have the right and freedom to do as they please.
- A common ethos formed by one's heritage and community is unimportant.

- Authority is to be tolerated only when convenient. Violence may be used to resolve conflict.
- Families with a mother and a father are unusual, and family relationships are superficial at best.

I need to make clear here that not all public school teachers promote these values. Indeed, speakers at public educational conferences today speak more openly about the need to heal our society on the basis of Judeo-Christian values, and to help students to become moral agents who respect truth and live responsibly in community. Also encouraging is a greater emphasis on implementing character education programs in schools. Nevertheless, surveys have shown that a substantial majority of American teachers, contrary to the wishes of parents, hold that schools should not teach values overtly—and therefore, by default, teach individualistic value relativism.

My intent in describing society's commonly held value footing here is threefold:

- First, **we strive to foster values that help students become loving and principled persons,** able to contribute positively to society by following Jesus. But we need to recognize that this is not an easy task. Our society adheres by and large to the opposite of Jesus' values: hyper-individualism, aggression, sexual exploitation, and materialism. Postmodernism compounds this state of affairs by supporting the right to choose and adopt values individually.
- Second, since values permeate all aspects of life and of schooling, **we need to carefully define the broad spectrum of values embedded in a Christian worldview.** It is not enough to oppose a few selected values with which we disagree. Christians have sometimes been justly accused of emphasizing certain biblical values while neglecting other important ones. That is why this chapter describes a biblically based value framework in some detail.
- Third, **we need to oppose the notion that values are to be pursued just for our own betterment or self-interest.** Rather, we seek and follow the values established by God as creation's Lawgiver. Without them, His creation and creatures cannot function in the way He intended. Because values are often caught rather than taught, schools should carefully consider how they affect students' values, both implicitly and explicitly.

Education always involves initiation and socialization into a way of life. Both the planned and the hidden curricula develop attitudes, foster the acceptance of certain values, instill dispositions, and encourage certain commitments. If this is labeled indoctrination, then all schools indoctrinate. Kindergarten classes, for instance, cannot function without teachers' initially insisting that some behavior is desirable and some is unacceptable. Kindergarten teachers may instruct their five-year-old students in how to resolve interpersonal conflicts. They then "indoctrinate" them to value the principle that conflicts ought to be dealt with in open, caring, and peaceful ways.

Of course, withholding or skewing evidence or deterring students from examining all sides of a controversial issue has no place in education. Such improper indoctrination takes place when sex education programs fail to present the physical, emotional, and social benefits of abstinence before marriage, for instance, or when literature selections implicitly promote gender bias. Wise teachers encourage students, as they mature, to examine and analyze the validity of value positions, including those of both the explicit and the implicit curricula.

The Greek philosopher Aristotle already said that children develop rationality best only after families and schools have habituated them to life's important values. Critics of values-based education have yet to disprove that claim. At a young age students learn a great deal about life from observing adult role models, reacting to values embedded in stories, and experiencing and practicing virtues. They have an intuitive sense of what is right and wrong. Only gradually, however, do they learn to develop full-fledged arguments for the value positions they hold or reject.

School programs today often imply that students (or communities) may choose whatever values they deem best. In other words, truth is what works for you at a particular time; there are no absolutes. Yet, as Thomas Lickona points out, to survive and thrive, society needs basic values such as justice, honesty, civility, dependability, democratic process, and a respect for truth. He adds that schools must help students face two important questions: How can we live with each other? and How can we live with nature (1991, 20–21)? Schools that do not base their structures and programs on well-defined values will hinder children from becoming loving, principled, and contributing members of society.

Values and the Curriculum

The values embedded in the curriculum are rooted in particular worldviews. Therefore, school communities need to consider which values their programs ought to foster.

God makes clear in both the Old and New Testaments that true freedom exists for those who uphold biblical values (Deuteronomy 6, Galatians 5). Such biblical values are rooted in the three great injunctions described above. For instance, the Creation Mandate underscores the importance of responsible stewardship. The Great Commandment values unselfish love and service for God and neighbor, and enjoins us to respect the dignity and worth of all persons as images of God. The Great Commission encourages personal and communal discipleship based on righteousness and justice. All these are desirable ideals and qualities for Christians and for society at large.

People often use the terms *values* and *morals* interchangeably. Values, however, include but are broader than morals, as shown below:

Some Key Biblically Based Values

- **Spiritual**: faith, devotion, piety, holiness
- **Moral**: honesty, integrity, respect for truth, responsibility
- **Political/legal**: respect for authority, lawfulness, justice, peace, balance of personal and communal rights and responsibilities
- **Economic**: responsible stewardship, compassion for the poor and disadvantaged
- **Social**: respect for others, cooperation, trusting and unselfish relations, kindness, trustworthiness, upholding marriage and family as sacred covenants
- **Language/communication**: authenticity, meaningfulness, clarity
- **Analytic/logical**: validity, discernment, respect for the life of the mind

- **Aesthetic**: creativity, expressiveness, beauty
- **Psychological**: emotional balance, sensitivity to others, self-control, perseverance, prudential courage
- **Physical health**: physical wellness, vitality, coordination
- **Biological and physical**: respect and thankfulness for life and physical things; precision in observation, good judgment in interpretation
- **Mathematical**: accuracy, precision, responsible use of numbers and space

It is not easy to teach students how to be followers of Jesus while functioning in a society that adheres to few of His values. The media often oppose or even scoff at biblical values. Our society glorifies individualism, aggression, and consumerism. Within this context, most students accept and act on Christian values only if their general environment supports such values. Research since the 1920s consistently shows that, by themselves, neither didactic methods nor learning to reason about value questions has much lasting effect on students' value dispositions. Analyzing and considering values formally must be accompanied with creating a positive school ethos and moral climate (Kilpatrick 1992, 226). The values that operate in the students' home and church communities also need to be consistent with what the school teaches. If a wide gap exists, a school's planned curriculum will have little effect on students' behavior, values, and commitments.

To be effective, schools need to plan moral and values education comprehensively. Content alone has little long-lasting effect. Schools should implement a total program of nurture that goes beyond the direct instruction of values. The whole school milieu should lend itself to recognizing and addressing ethical and unethical thought and behavior. Teachers should help students develop wholesome and operative commitments. A trust relationship between teachers and students is also essential.

Thomas Lickona gives the following curriculum suggestions for teaching values (Lickona in Molnar 1997, 52–60):

- Implement explicit plans for developing students' sense of responsibility, including planned homeroom discussions and service projects.
- Encourage thoughtfulness and ethical sensitivity (e.g., During an egg incubation project, is it right to open an egg each week to monitor the embryonic developments of the chicks, even though that kills the embryo?).
- As a teacher, combine high expectations with high support for your students.
- In literature have students analyze moral strengths and weaknesses of the characters. Choose selections that promote respect and responsibility.
- In social studies discuss questions of social justice, ways to better one's community or country, as well as actual moral dilemmas faced by historical figures.
- Design science lessons on the need for precise and truthful reporting of data.
- In mathematics have students research and plot morally significant social trends.
- Involve parents in the curriculum through home activities in which families discuss stories that involve moral situations or in which children interview parents about value-related issues.

Some educators, and particularly the critical theorists, disapprove of what they believe to be Lickona's too narrow approach to character and moral education:

Our task as educators is not limited to striving for morally sound schools and to improving the character of students; it also involves participation in the broader task of creating a just and loving society and a culture of joy and fulfillment for all. (Purpel in Molnar 1997, 152)

These educators appreciate Lickona's reminder that value-free education is impossible. They also agree that we need to strive for a just and moral society. However, they believe that Lickona applies individual solutions to social problems, and that his solutions do not address growing economic inequality, ecological devastation, and the continuing dangers of international conflicts (Purpel in Molnar 1997, 149–50).

True, Lickona's values are not comprehensive. In the rest of this chapter, I will discuss a wide range of values for inclusion in the curriculum—a wider range than has been suggested by character educators like Lickona. However, Lickona has not only identified but has also given workable suggestions for fostering personal values without which a democratic, compassionate, and just society cannot function. Indeed, the focus of critical theorists and others on the self-realization of the individual will only continue to undermine responsible mutual concern, weaken social commitments, and make the outlook for maintaining wholesome community life increasingly problematic (Bowers 1987, 23; Lickona 1991, 6).

Fostering and living according to biblical values has, as David Noebel put it, regenerative power for both the individual and society. These values enable ordinary people to lead extraordinary lives. The willingness to live according to God-given values is crucial for serving God (1991, 258). Schools and teachers do well, therefore, to plan

curricula that encourage students to consider, probe, and adopt such values.

Footstep 3-6

"What makes your junior high school unique?" I asked Doug Monsma, assistant principal of the west campus of the Edmonton Christian School.

"It has to do with our fundamental convictions," he answered. "We constantly ask why we do things. The notion of servanthood is the basis of everything that goes on. At a staff retreat we pledged to help our students experience discipleship as a lifelong calling. This includes teaching thematic units that make students critically aware of God's complex world. It also means building a school community that heals brokenness through frequent acts of restoration, also in our discipline. As a school community we constantly stress 'us' over 'me.' It helps that all homeroom teachers spend at least half the school day with their class.

"We try to develop spirituality and involve our students in service projects. We encourage them to speak up about their faith. We set up cross-grade prayer families. Students lead our biweekly assemblies. The other day they role-played and discussed how some classmates get hurt when others form a tight-knit clique. Our students also volunteer in a thrift store and arrange food hampers for needy families. Older students help younger ones with reading or supervision. We try to foster a servant attitude throughout the school. We stress that servanthood puts the needs of others first without looking for recognition.

"At least once per year we have a theme week that includes all students and teachers. We've chosen the topics carefully to tie in with servanthood: world hunger, our environment, celebrating our creativity. But other classroom units also provide real-life settings where learning is done as part of discipleship training. We emphasize their responsibility to discover and share their gifts, and relate this to a Christian lifestyle.

"For any subject matter to be meaningful, it must be taught and learned in a community that is inclusive, accepting, and celebrative. Our peer support program has become an integral part of our curriculum. The program involves sixteen girls and five boys this year (one out of five students). There's good sampling from different social groups and types of students. The applicants we accept go on a two-day team-building and training retreat. They then have weekly sessions on biblical servant leadership in a school setting. The students themselves decide their goals and activities each year.

"Last year's peer support group set up a student-run tutoring system during lunch hours. They also became daily 'hallway walkers' who modeled and encouraged positive talk and behavior, and resolved conflicts. They did so without other students realizing that this was part of the program. Finally, they were available for friendship and informal conversation about situations fellow students faced. We train them to be 'listening ears' but to refer rather than solve problems. Significantly, theme units such as Taking Care of God's Earth take on additional meaning as students learn to care for each other."

List the values that this school set out to teach. How do these relate to the Creation Mandate, the Great Commandment, and the Great Commission? Is Monsma right when he claims that schools should plan programs like peer support as part of the curriculum just as they do regular subjects? Are initiatives like this necessary only in an age of weak family nurture? Or should this type of emphasis be part of any school? Why or why not?

Biblical Values and the Curriculum

My starting point in considering values is that the Bible as God's revelation is the ultimate source of values for Christians. Of course, that does not take away our human responsibility to define and explore the implications of those guidelines for our present-day society. In the remainder of this chapter I will present some biblically based values that ought to govern life and, therefore, to permeate the curriculum. Following is a description of the notion of *shalom* found throughout Scripture with discussion of specific values in various dimensions of life.

Schools ought to nurture shalom, the biblical peace, justice, and righteousness that heals and restores broken relations with God, with other humans, with self, with other creatures, and with nature. To experience shalom, schools seek to replace abuse, racism, sexism, and bullying with love and justice. They honor all students and teachers for their gifts and roles. They replace selfishness and faith in the autonomy of the individual with self-sacrifice, humility, and servanthood.

Schools need strategies that promote such shalom. For instance, they can introduce a consistent program of conflict resolution, starting at the kindergarten level. They can use collaborative learning through which students learn to support each other. They can give students service opportunities to reach out to and help others within and outside the school. They can choose unit themes and literature selections that encourage students to deal with shalom-related issues. They can celebrate the presence of shalom and deplore its absence in the school and in the community.

While schools foster the love and justice undergirding shalom, nevertheless, they should also provide room for students to explore and develop their own value framework and its implications. Trying to impose values unilaterally on students is counterproductive and leads to hypocrisy. Students, at the same time, may not undermine the type of community the school tries to establish, even when they disagree with the school's basic values.

Spiritual Values

All of life is religious in nature. All that God has given us is to be consecrated to His service. Secularization is the attempt to push religious faith out of the public domain. Where successful, a nonreligious faith commitment replaces faith in the God of the Bible. Nonreligious idols of our times include faith in economic growth and material prosperity, faith in the power of technology to bring about a better world, and faith in security guaranteed by the government (Goudzwaard 1984). Such idols are the driving force of our society today. Schools must therefore counter the effects of these influences that distort the true meaning and purpose of life.

Christian schools acknowledge their dependence on God through devotions, praise, and prayer. Also, teachers model the importance of godliness and piety in their own lives, praying regularly for and with their students as needs arise. But the academic work of the school day is itself also a form of worship and a channel through which students come to know the Lord. By studying God's creation, they consider the praiseworthy deeds of the Lord, and learn to praise Him and put their trust in Him (Psalm 78:4–7). The academic work of the school can also provide an atmosphere that nurtures spiritual commitment and maturity.

Life-affirming faith and commitment provide a sense of personal meaning and purpose, something sorely lacking in today's generation. Many Christians, for instance, bring qualities such as mercy and humility to our political system (Holmes 1992, 103–4). Curricula should at least explore how people's faith commitments have affected their personal lives and the society they live in. How did the Protestant Reformation shape Western culture? How were the founding fathers of the United States influenced by their faith? To what extent did a Christian ethos undergird life in pioneer communities? How did their faith move Dutch Calvinists to risk their lives by hiding Jews during the Holocaust in World War II? What is the role of Islam in countries like Saudi Arabia and Nigeria? Why are many world conflicts rooted in religious strife? Such curriculum content will demonstrate the crucial role of religious faith and spirituality in people's lives and culture.

Footstep 3-7

Do you agree with the following quotation? If so, suggest some curriculum implications. If not, formulate your own alternative position.

Exclusion of religious perspectives is anything but neutral or fair. Students need to learn that religious and philosophical beliefs and practices are central to the lives of many people. Omission of discussion about the religious and philosophical roots of developments in history, economics, literature, and other subjects gives the student the false impression that only nonreligious ways of seeing the world are valid. (Haynes 1993, 32)

Ethical Values

During the last generation, many schools have been reluctant to deal directly with not only the spiritual but also the ethical dimension of life. This is partly the result of society's belief that moral guidelines are nothing more than individual expressions of taste, with no need for communal acceptance (Lasch 1984, 255). Faith in the moral autonomy of individuals has resulted in a society that has lost its moral moorings.

Schools should, therefore, help students see and experience the importance of the ethical foundations of life: love and compassion for others, honesty and integrity, righteousness and forgiveness, faithfulness in marriage and family life, and respect for others' property. Such morality, of course, is not for Christians only. Nor does upholding these moral laws make a person a Christian. But it is what God expects. Support for moral laws allows society to function in a human and humane way. That is why an organization such as the Association for Supervision and Curriculum Development can publish a set of universal moral guidelines for schools, guidelines that bear a striking resemblance to some (though not all) biblical moral principles (ASCD 1988).

The two major approaches to moral values education since the 1970s have both fallen short. Sidney Simon's values clarification introduces students to complex moral dilemmas when they are not yet equipped with basic values and are unable to recognize all the consequences of their decisions. They are then left with the belief that they can choose values for themselves, with the result that they embrace ethical relativism (Simon, Howe, and Kirschenbaum 1972).

Lawrence Kohlberg's moral reasoning approach (1971) is based on the ability of the autonomous individual to reason out and apply universal standards of justice. However, there is little evidence that the ability to reason will lead to action based on such reasoning. Moreover, reasoning in itself will not lead to the values espoused by Jesus if a person starts with wrong basic assumptions.

Teachers who effectively foster responsible moral action and commitment act as models and help students care about each other—something Simon and Kohlberg ignore. Such teachers use discipline and conflict resolution techniques to habituate students to respect others and their property, and to obey legitimate authority. If moral tendencies are to be internalized, teachers must accompany modeling and discipline with reasons. Those reasons must point students back to basic principles as well as pointing out how others would feel about the consequences of a particular attitude or act (Wolterstorff 1980, 67). Teachers can also encourage moral reflection and application "through reading, writing, discussion, decision-making exercises, and debate" (Lickona 1991, 70).

Some claim that children in kindergarten or first grade as yet have little moral knowledge. Piaget and Kohlberg's stage theories have nurtured that notion. Those theories, however, focus on abstract, out-of-context reasoning. But children can react to and deal with moral values that are presented in story or narrative forms. Children benefit, for instance, from Bible stories and other carefully chosen selections in which they can identify with characters who face moral dilemmas. Good stories are memorable because all details contribute to the dramatic tension that usually centers on clearly defined moral values such as compassion or fairness. Such narratives are effective in raising ethical questions and helping children consider what human life ought to be.

Footstep 3-8

Multinational corporations like Calvin Klein control advertising trends. Indirectly, they also control the media that are vehicles for such advertising. The advertising aimed at teenagers—and more and more at children too—often models youth who appear to be morally and socially unconcerned. It promotes self-centered consumerism and hedonism that undermine human dignity, positive approaches to sexuality, respect for others, and responsibility. In the end, the media can leave children and young adults empty, disillusioned, and void of purpose and meaning. What is the role of the school in countering such influences?

Political, Legal, and Economic Values

If there is one sin that God condemns in the Old Testament, it is injustice: "Administer true justice; show mercy and compassion to one another. Do not oppress the widow or the fatherless, the alien or the poor" (Zechariah 7:9–10). The command to administer justice has particular relevance for political and economic institutions and leaders.

Humans have certain basic, God-given rights: the right to life, the right of respect, the right of equality under the law, and the right to property. As soon as these rights are violated, governments must protect their citizens (e.g., from cruelty, from false accusations, or from theft). Governments should therefore prohibit and punish injustice. At the same time, citizens must respect and obey the government's authority and help it to preserve order (Noebel 1991, 625ff).

Society's social and economic problems are complex. We don't have all the answers. Yet school programs can foster sensitivity to social justice. For instance, all persons and communities have the right to full participation in society, with access to basic services. And yet, unemployment prevents certain persons from making their rightful contribution to society's well-being. In high school, students need to examine government taxation and investment policies that favor capital-intensive projects and look at alternate worker-intensive ones. Curricula also need to address issues involving justice for disadvantaged groups in society, the physically or mentally or socially handicapped, and those who have been abused.

Students should be given opportunities to reach out with love and grace in situations resulting from personal or societal injustice. A twelfth-grade class organizes biweekly recreation activities for jailed young offenders. An eleventh-grade class helps a youth emergency shelter with maintenance work. A tenth-grade class volunteers in a drop-in center for troubled youth. A school annually visits an aboriginal settlement, forming long-term relationships that foster mutual appreciation of each other's culture. Eleventh-grade students spend time working in a third-world setting while continuing their own courses by correspondence. Such ventures are important. Students experience circumstances resulting, in part, from injustice. They also leave their own comfort zone and ask themselves how they can bring healing to broken situations in society.

Bong-Ho Son (1993, 97–107) and Calvin Beisner (1993, 21) argue that biblical economic justice means that societies provide persons with basic needs such as adequate food, clothes, health care, and education simply because they are human beings. Luxuries, on the other hand, can be awarded according to one's contributions and achievements. The Bible demands that where the needy suffer because of injustice, they need justice, and, if that is not attainable, charity. Even where they suffer because of their own actions, they still need our compassion and mercy.

Today, the economic sphere of life dominates all others. Progress is defined in terms of increases in the gross domestic product. Corporations use the media to glorify materialism and self-gratification. The underlying value is that economic growth is an autonomous and ultimate good. Wolterstorff argues that the "fundamental worth in our modern world-system ... [is] increased mastery of nature and society so as to satisfy our desires" (1980, 65). Increased mastery can be beneficial, as advances in medicine show. But when the main aim of mastery is self-satisfaction, we view work as a means to satisfy material needs rather than as a way to fulfill our calling. We lose values that matter a great deal: personal craftsmanship and skill, a reflective lifestyle, acting justly and caringly, and living with joy and hope without needing all modern technological gadgets and toys.

Again, schools ought to show a different way. Taking care of God's garden means being stewards. Stewards hold economic resources in trust so that they can distribute benefits and liabilities equitably. Students should investigate how we can use resources to sustain an economy that provides a basic living for all. The curriculum should uphold the values of individual responsibility, simple and thankful lifestyles, fair wages and working conditions, and a caring and sharing attitude.

Footstep 3-9

For the example that follows, decide which values the students are learning. Consider to what extent these reflect a biblical value perspective. Would you make any changes? Why or why not?

Wayne Lennea teaches tenth-grade consumer education. His textbook holds that consumers must make rational decisions based on their favored style and quality of life. Students, it suggests, must choose their own values, basing them on their experiences, and they must remain flexible to explore and modify their values. They can exercise their voice in the marketplace by comparing the quality and price of various brands. They also increase their self-esteem by how and what they buy (Woods 1982, 1–13).

Lennea disagrees with this approach. He first discusses with his class what the Bible says about wealth and financial freedom. He shares his own definition of *wealth*: not what you accumulate but how your life has made a difference. Wealth, in other words, consists of the positive effects your life has had on others. Similarly, he asks students to react to his view that financial freedom is not the ability to purchase all kinds of things, but to be able to meet your basic needs in thankfulness to God. He discusses, for instance, how in North America today, we squander resources by buying homes much larger than needed for comfortable living. The students explore what it means to use credit cards and make loans in a responsible way. They discuss whether prosperity is a blessing of God or the result of an unjust system where some go without basic needs. They discuss what it means to make a fair profit and still love your customer as yourself. Only afterward do students read and react to the textbook and its themes.

Values Relating to Social Interaction and Personhood

In our society individualism and freedom of self-direction have led to self-centeredness. This is often expressed through competition and aggression as well as prejudice and intolerance. Schools try to counter this by teaching students to value kindness, loyalty, trust, and unselfish relations with others. They uphold marriage and family relationships as sacred covenants. They also help students develop positive psychological values: balance and self-control, realistic recognition of one's own gifts, sensitivity to others, perseverance, prudential risk-taking, and responsibility. Schools may plan carefully structured programs to nurture values such as responsibility throughout the school.

Specific units and topics can also address these issues. Many kindergarten and first-grade teachers plan units on God Made Me Special. At higher levels, units may focus on friendship, family life, personal development, and courtship and marriage. Units on multi-

culturalism explore what it means to live in a pluralist society where, on the one hand, the right of minority groups to live by their ideals is celebrated and, on the other, common social and psychological values are recognized as necessary for a community to function. Carefully chosen literary selections and works of art also may encourage students to consider what it means to live in families and communities that promote social and psychological shalom.

Footstep 3-10

Rick Binder and the other fifth- and sixth-grade teachers plan a unit for the last five weeks of the school year. They are concerned about some of the racist attitudes that students display, especially toward the large number of Indo-Canadians in their community. The theme of the unit becomes that loving your neighbor as yourself means celebrating cultural differences and building bridges.

The teachers begin the unit with two activities. First, they ask students to complete a survey of their attitudes (e.g., I think Punjabi clothing is beautiful). Then they act out a skit that includes all the racial remarks, slurs, and jokes that the teachers have heard over the last year or two. The teachers regroup the fifth- and sixth-grade classes into five groups that rotate among the five classrooms, three days a week from 10:30 to 12:00. The students all study five strands: the history of Indo-Canadians in their community, the Sikh religion, contemporary issues facing Indo-Canadian families, food and clothing, and language and music. The strands include concrete experiences: Indo-Canadian speakers, visits to a Sikh temple and the local Sikh market, preparing and eating Sikh food, music performances, and so on. Each student makes a personal scrapbook. At the end the teachers act out the skit again, but now they react to comments on the basis of what happened during the unit.

What were the results of the unit? First, the students addressed an issue affecting the whole community. A concluding survey revealed that their positive experiences with a different culture had resulted in startlingly more positive attitudes. The next school year almost all comments about East Indian culture among the students were positive ones. The unit also stimulated parents to talk and think about their own attitudes. Most responded positively and said they had gained some knowledge and understanding.

What are the values nurtured in this unit? What other social values need to be addressed by schools, particularly in the middle grades?

Values in Communication and Aesthetics

A society driven by a faith in economic growth distorts values in the communication and aesthetic aspects of life. The media, especially through advertising, have legitimized deception to serve the end of profitability. The school curriculum should therefore help to restore effectiveness, meaningfulness, authenticity, and integrity to communication. This requires an emphasis on honest and forthright oral and written communication skills—including listening skills—throughout the curriculum.

The technical-economic basis of our cul-

ture has sidelined aesthetic values. Few of us consider aesthetics central to a meaningful life. Fewer still take time to create, playfully probe and pursue, understand, appreciate, and find joy in the suggestion-rich beauty, concord, and coherence of aesthetic works. Yet the Bible values beauty and harmony, as created both by God and by human artists and artisans. God enjoins us to take delight in the radiant wonder of His handiwork (Psalms 19 and 104). God values expressiveness, imagination, and originality. He delights, for instance, in our worship of Him through music, poetry, and dance (Psalm 149). But He also calls us to use our creativity to unfold other aspects of His creation. Without imagination and creative insight into the design of the universe, Einstein would not have developed his theory of relativity, for instance. Similarly, students never fail to be surprised and intrigued by the aesthetic wonders of the Fibonacci sequence in mathematics. An appreciation for aesthetic values enriches our lives.

Analytic Values

Rationality, despite claims to the contrary, is not the highest human aptitude or value. It is not the essence of selfhood. It does not answer the basic questions about the purpose and meaning of life.

Yet rationality is important. All intellectual work in schools should foster a respect for truth and the ability to develop coherent, lucid, and convincing arguments. Students should be encouraged to exercise intellectual curiosity and respond to what they experience and learn, not only with wonder and awe but also with effective reasoning. Critical thinking exercised within a framework of overarching values can help develop biblical discernment and wisdom.

Teachers can use case studies about familiar experiences to promote critical thinking. They first describe the situation as accurately and completely as possible. (For young children a story format serves best.) They solicit different possible courses of action from the students. They then help students establish the basic value principles that have a bearing on the case and ask them to reconsider the options in terms of these basic values. The students may immediately rule out some possibilities and perhaps add others. They decide how the values lead them to favor certain options, and they try to predict the consequences of their choices.

Sometimes, of course, several basic values may conflict (e.g., the needs to protect the environment and to provide work in mining). Then the students have to decide which value(s) ought to receive priority, or whether there is another solution by which both values can be upheld. The key differences between this approach and values clarification are (1) the reasoning is based on universal biblical values, not on students' choosing their own values, and (2) teachers model bibical values and encourage students to commit themselves to such values.

Biological and Physical Values

The Bible rejects two conflicting views of nature. First, it does not value nature for its own sake, nor does it seek divinity in nature, as pantheism does. The physical creation exists so that creatures can honor God by fulfilling their God-given calling. On the other hand, Scripture also opposes the mastery of nature just to satisfy human desires. Such a view leads to unacceptable exploitation. The curriculum, therefore, should emphasize nature's splendor, abundance, and potential to provide for all our needs. Concurrently, it should foster the need for the preservation and responsible stewardship of the resources God has given to sustain and enrich life. Respect for plant and animal life complements the respect we should show for our own physical lives through healthy lifestyles. We also encourage careful observation of phenomena in science. And in mathematics we value accuracy and responsible use of numbers and space.

Footstep 3-11

For this example, decide which values the students learn, both directly and indirectly. To what extent do these reflect a biblical value perspective? How could you use this unit to nurture communication, and aesthetic, analytic, and scientific values?

Teachers Bruce Hildebrandt and Paul Smith plan an election simulation for their school's seven classes in grades four through seven. Each class represents one electoral district and has candidates for three parties with predetermined platforms on public works, the environment, curriculum content, criminal justice, arts and entertainment, social services, and taxes. The Leafy Green Party, for instance, will give all students jobs to do at lunch or recess, allow them to choose their assignments, let the girls choose physical education activities for the whole class, insist on reusable lunch containers (with offenders doing several hours of public service work), have a subsidized canteen for everyone, and provide a free entertainment video—but also have a high tax levy on all students. The party that forms the government is to carry out the policies for one school day.

Each student writes a short essay to support the policies of one party. The teachers use the essays to select a candidate for each party in each class. All students choose roles in the campaign. The roles reflect their own abilities and interests: campaign worker, debater, poster designer, maker of radio commercials, pollster, returning officer, and so forth. The class discusses how to conduct a fair, ethically responsible campaign. The teachers encourage the students to foster care and concern for other candidates. That leads the students to conduct a campaign without slander or personal attacks. Supporters of one party even help other parties with posters and speeches. The students also compare their campaign with the nationwide election taking place at the same time. They pray for God's guidance and for personal integrity in both campaigns. They also investigate how they can be a constructive influence in the political process.

The Implicit and Null Curricula

Schools have a planned curriculum. Many things happen in the classroom, however, that teachers do not formally plan. Students learn through the everyday goings-on in the school. For instance, teachers' expectations with respect to behavior, how teachers relate to students, and the values teachers project will influence student learning. Some researchers say that the **implicit** or **hidden curriculum** affects students more than the explicit one.

The implicit curriculum has both positive and negative effects. Students may learn to treat each other with respect, to work hard to accomplish both short- and long-term goals, and to resolve conflicts with fellow students in peaceful ways. But they may also give up on learning when they are labeled negatively by a strongly competitive grading system. Their history lessons may glorify heroes of war rather than peacemakers. Having art only on Friday afternoons may leave the impression that art is unimportant relative to math or language. School rules may be so arbitrary that students learn to see authority as a power game that they try to undermine. Bullying on the playground may teach students a great deal about where they are pegged in the pecking order, often to their detriment.

Teachers need to reflect on the effects of the implicit curriculum on their students. Such reflection may well lead to changes in structures and approaches. Further, it may mean that teachers explicitly include topics in the curriculum that deal with aspects of the implicit curriculum (e.g., bullying and peer power struggles).

What is left out of the curriculum also affects students. This is sometimes called the **null curriculum**. When we plan a curriculum, we need to ask why we leave out certain topics and issues. Why do few students study economics when it is the driving force of Western society? Why do the fine arts become part of the null curriculum for many students in high school when mathematics is compulsory for all? Why do some readers exclude selections about wholesome family situations? Why do textbooks neglect Christian contributions to society? The exclusion of each of these topics will affect what students believe to be important in life, and, therefore, will affect their values.

When planning curriculum, ask, On what basis do we include or exclude certain curriculum content and approaches? We need to justify our choices by referring to our worldview and the values we hold to be important. At the same time, ask, Does our implicit curriculum contribute to or detract from our curriculum intentions? Without serious attention to these questions, the general thrust of a school's program will be to promote mainly the technical-economic direction of our secular culture.

Footstep 3-12

Give some examples of the implicit and null curricula from your experience. Then discuss the values nurtured by the implicit curriculum in the example below.

Two schools plan for Thanksgiving. In the first school the main activity in the primary grades is to color photocopied line drawings of Thanksgiving dinners in pilgrim and modern times. The teachers display the differently colored but otherwise identical pictures on the bulletin boards and windows, and ask the students what they are thankful for. In the second school the main activity consists of small groups of students designing costumes and planning and putting on a pilgrim Thanksgiving celebration, and the students go around the school in their costumes to collect food for the local food bank.

the values that you chose. Consider how the implicit curriculum might affect these values. For instance, a third-grade unit on spiders and *Charlotte's Web* might foster compassion, respect for living things, and the importance of self-sacrifice. A teacher might also implement collaborative center activities that promote sensitivity to others and their feelings, and that develop a sense of community in the classroom. At the same time, the teacher who shows an instinctive fear of spiders (or of a garter snake brought in by a student) may implicitly undo the teaching about respect for living things.

Footstep 3-13

Choose a fairly general curriculum topic at a suitable grade level (e.g., your local community, trees and forests, weather, the history of your state or province, government, modern music). Choose some values that you would want to promote in teaching the unit. Then suggest learning activities that would foster

Reviewing the Main Points

Fig. 3.1   Elements of a Christian Worldview

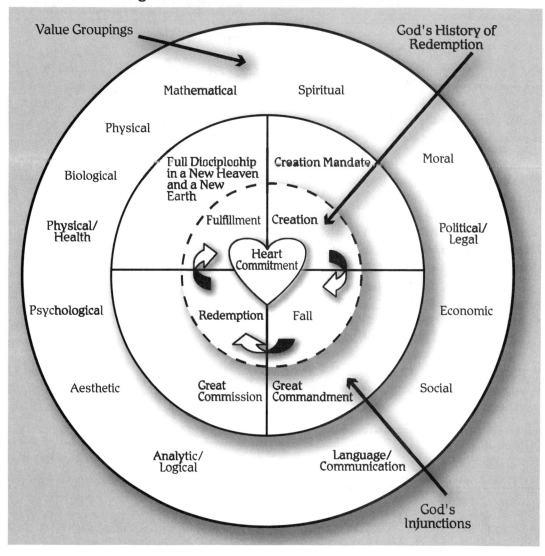

- **A worldview is a comprehensive framework of convictions about life. All curricula are based on a worldview perspective.** Curricula must help students answer who they are as human beings in the world, what has gone wrong, where they can find answers, and the source of their hope. A curriculum based on a Christian worldview will take into account the biblical themes of creation, the Fall, redemption, and fulfillment. It will also embrace the implications of God's Creation Mandate, His Great Commandment, and the Great Commission, as well as values for Kingdom living put forward by the Bible.

- **Whether intentionally or not, schools and teachers teach values through both the planned and the implicit curriculum.** Values fostered by educators reflect their worldview and their curriculum orientation. Biblical values do not include moral values only, but also spiritual, political, economic, cultural, social, psychological, communicative, analytic, aesthetic, biological, and physical ones. Christian teachers model such values, use discipline to uphold them, give reasons for them, and introduce stories and cases that lead students to consider how such values apply in particular circumstances. Teachers should ensure that their teaching does not become manipulative indoctrination that prevents normal rational growth and independence.

References

ASCD Panel on Moral Education (ASCD). 1988. Moral education in the life of the school. *Educational Leadership* 45 (8): 5–7.

Beisner, E. C. 1993. Justice and poverty: Two views contrasted. *Transformation* 10 (1): 16–22.

Blomberg, D. 1991. The integral curriculum. *Christian Educators Journal* 31 (2): 6–13.

Bowers, C. 1987. *Toward a post-liberal theory of education*. New York: Teachers College Press.

Gesch, C. 1993. *Teaching aids for the conservation and outdoor recreation education course*. Telkwa, BC: Eskerhazy Publications.

Goudzwaard, B. 1984. *Idols of our time*. Downers Grove, IL: InterVarsity.

Haynes, C. 1993. Beyond the culture wars. *Educational Leadership* 51 (4): 30–34.

Holmes, M. 1992. *Educational policy for a pluralist democracy: The common school, choice, and diversity*. New York: Falmer.

Jones, A., ed. 1998. *Science in faith: A Christian perspective on teaching science*. Romford, UK: Christian Schools' Trust.

Kilpatrick, W. 1992. *Why Johnny can't tell right from wrong*. New York: Simon and Schuster.

Kohlberg, L. 1971. Stages of moral development as a basis for moral education. In Beck, C., B. Crittenden, and E. Sullivan, *Moral education: Interdisciplinary approaches*. Toronto: University of Toronto.

Lasch, C. 1984. *The minimal self: Psychic survival in troubled times*. New York: Norton.

Lickona, T. 1991. *Educating for character: How our schools can teach respect and responsibility*. New York: Bantam.

Molnar, A. 1997. *The construction of children's character*. Ninety-sixth yearbook of the National Society for the Study of Education. Chicago: NSSE.

Newbigin, L. 1983. *The other side of 1984*. Geneva: World Council of Churches.

———. 1989. *The gospel in a pluralist society*. Grand Rapids: Eerdmans.

Noebel, D. 1991. *Understanding the times: The religious worldviews of our day and the search for truth*. Eugene, OR: Harvest House.

Owens, V. 1983. *God spy: Faith, perception, and the new physics*. Seattle: Alta Vista College.

Purpel, D. 1989. *The moral and spiritual crisis in education*. Granby, MA: Bergin and Garvey.

Simon, S., L. Howe, and H. Kirschenbaum. 1972. *Values clarification: A handbook of practical strategies for teachers and students*. New York: A & W Publishers.

Son, B. 1993. Uniqueness of Christ and social justice. *Evangelical Review of Theology* 17 (1): 93–109.

Stott, J. 1978. *Christian counter-culture: The message of the Sermon on the Mount*. Downers Grove, IL: InterVarsity.

Walsh, B., and J. Middleton. 1984. *The transforming vision: Shaping a Christian world view*. Downers Grove, IL: InterVarsity.

Wolters, A. 1985. *Creation regained: Biblical basics for a reformational worldview*. Grand Rapids: Eerdmans.

Wolterstorff, N. 1980. *Educating for responsible action*. Grand Rapids: Eerdmans.

Woods, J. 1982. *Looking at the consumer*. Toronto: Gage.

Steppingstone 4

Knowledge and the Curriculum

Teacher Derk Van Eerden uses September to set the stage for his year-long twelfth-grade biology course. The month has two complementary components. The first is a four-day biology wilderness field trip and retreat in which students experience relating to God, each other, animals, plants, and physical things. They do a number of group tasks that deepen their knowledge in biology, ecology, and geology. They also learn a great deal about responsible stewardship.

The retreat is also important for students to get to know each other as persons in a different setting, to draw them together into a community. They work together on chores like preparing meals. They sing and pray. They learn to appreciate each other for who they are rather than just for their intellectual strengths. They contribute their specific gifts to the whole community in collaborative activities. Van Eerden encourages all students to take on certain roles as servant leaders. Later in school, far more students are willing to interact and do their share of assigned work.

The second component of this course is an introductory unit that looks at human interaction with nature. Students examine scientific, aboriginal, and Christian views of such relationships. They view and analyze films and articles on wildlife and forest management issues. They discuss biblical passages that reveal the relationship of humans with God, each other, and nature. They react to articles written by aboriginal people who regard the earth as our mother and describe people conversing with animals. How do those insights compare with biblical and Western technological views? Students reflect on how we all act on beliefs. They consider the importance of values such as economic, social, and biological justice, as well as respect for the views of other cultures. Van Eerden then shows that often we say one thing but do another in how we relate to and use the physical world. He discusses why this is so. He then invites students to examine, redefine, and act on their convictions and commitments.

Van Eerden makes education an affair of the heart as well as the mind. He actively and intentionally engages his students in discussions about real issues. He believes that his students will not know what it means to love God and neighbor as stewards of the earth unless they experience positive relationships with each other as well as with the physical world. He holds that the more abstract learning in the course will have long-term meaning only when students learn within a framework of basic values and a supportive classroom environment.

From this description, can you deduce the beliefs about knowledge that guide this teacher's curriculum planning?

The dominant Western view of knowledge in the 1900s has seen it as an objective body of facts, skills, concepts, and theories. The more knowledge people acquire, the better chance they have to do well in life. Four hundred years ago Francis Bacon said, "Knowledge itself is power." By knowledge, he meant collections of facts. For Bacon, values were speculation and personal prejudice. In the nineteenth century, poet Arthur Clough likewise separated faith and values from knowledge when he wrote, "Grace is given by God, but knowledge is bought in the market."

Persons holding a biblical view of knowledge do not identify knowledge with an objective body of information. All knowledge exists within a framework of beliefs. Faith itself is not only knowledge but the basis of all knowledge. The Bible teaches not only that the fear of the Lord is the beginning of knowledge, but also that true knowledge involves committed action. In other words, for Christians the basic point of departure in gaining and applying knowledge is reverential trust in God and an acknowledgment of and submission to His laws. True knowledge includes an active response to God and neighbor. Truth must be done to be known (1 John 1:6). Human knowledge is not neutral: people's development, interpretation, and response is part of knowledge.

While constructivists agree that knowledge is not neutral, they go one step further. They hold that all knowledge is personally constructed, provisional, and open-ended. Knowledge is therefore subjective, based solely on people's own insights, values, and cultural context. Universal truth does not exist (Luke and Gore 1992, 7). They therefore cannot accept the biblical starting point that God's laws for the physical world and for human interaction are the basis for human knowledge.

This chapter posits a biblical view of knowledge and truth. It then explains how we can categorize knowledge into different aspects or disciplines, and how that affects the organization of the curriculum. Finally, it considers how these aspects lead to different modes or ways of knowing (also referred to as *multiple intelligences*). Throughout, ask yourself, What are the implications for planning and implementing curricula?

Footstep 4-1

The dominant view of knowledge in our culture influences us so much that we find it difficult to accept that knowledge is not an objective body of information to be used to control our world. Think back to your own schooling. What view of knowledge was implicit in most of what you learned? Can you suggest what attitudes to life you learned in subjects like social studies? science? mathematics? art? Could the school have taken a different approach? a better one?

A Biblical View of Truth and Knowledge

Since a biblical view of truth and knowledge affects our approach to education and curriculum, I will briefly discuss some relevant scriptural touchstones of truth and knowledge.

My starting point is that the Bible is God's inspired Word. Believing the truth of Scripture means not so much believing *that* as it does believing *in*. Jesus said, "I am the way, the truth, and the life" (John 14:6). Truth came in Jesus Christ. He is the meaning of the world. We know truth in personal relationship to Christ, not just in objective statements of that truth but in subjective meaning discovered by the individual self.

Every created thing points beyond itself to Christ, who holds the world together (Colossians 1:17, Hebrews 1:3). Jesus testifies to the truth and thus gives us understanding (John 1:17, 18:37; 1 John 5:20). If you hold to Christ's teaching, you will know the truth, and the truth will set you free (John 8:31–32). Whoever lives by the truth that is Christ, comes into the light (John 3:21). Such truth leads to love with actions (1 John 3:18). God's love demands that we walk in His truth; love and truth may never be separated (Psalm 26:3, 40:10–11). When "truth has stumbled in the streets," so have justice, righteousness, and honesty (Isaiah 59:14–15). Truth, in other words, is not just a correct statement but a right deed.

Fig. 4.1   Views of Knowledge

A MODERN VIEW OF KNOWLEDGE	A POSTMODERN VIEW OF KNOWLEDGE	A BIBLICAL VIEW OF KNOWLEDGE
• Objective reality exists. Valid knowledge is therefore the same for everyone. • Knowledge and truth may be discovered through a combination of empirical evidence and reason. • There are absolutes, although we may not always know them. • Belief is not knowledge since it is not based on empirical or analytic verification. • In the curriculum, students acquire facts, concepts, and abilities based on the accumulated knowledge of previous generations.	• Knowledge is neither static nor abstracted from experience. It does not reflect an external reality. Knowledge is made, or constructed, not acquired. • Knowledge and truth are relative. They vary across cultures, across time, and across persons. Knowledge is not correct or incorrect. If knowledge serves viable goals, it must be accepted. • In the curriculum, the students' individual search for meaning and truth become all-important. Inquiry and process rather than content are emphasized in the classroom.	• Knowledge is grounded in God's revelation of Himself in His created reality and in the Bible. • Knowledge points to God as the ultimate source of truth. Human theories and laws reflect God's laws imperfectly. • Knowledge goes beyond one's intellect and involves personal response, commitment, and service. • In the curriculum, students learn about God's creation and how humans have unfolded it, investigating and personally responding to interpretations and issues.

Recognizing the truth that is Christ leads people to respond with responsibility and compassion. Faith is in the doing. Truth is in the doing. Knowledge is in the doing. Lived Christian faith, truth, and knowledge arise from and lead to obedient response to God's intentions for the world (Groome 1980, 65). We seldom live up to God's intentions. That is precisely why our relationship with Christ is so crucial. Only if we live in the truth that is Christ can we live with our failure and yet continue to receive the power to follow His mandates within a biblical framework of values. Education in the truth treats humans as subjects, images of God, who participate fully and responsibly in unfolding reality.

Truth is a call to rigorous and demanding love in communion with God, other humans, animals, plants, and the physical world. Education involves listening and submitting oneself to truth in community. In school, relations between teachers and students are crucial. Even the best curriculum will not lead to truth unless teachers themselves walk in the truth and allow students to search out truth and experience it personally and communally.

Knowledge is rooted in God's revelation. We gain knowledge through God's revealing Himself in creation, in the Bible, in Jesus Christ, and through His Spirit. Christians recognize, first of all, that God established all of creation and its inherent meaning. God is the ultimate source of knowledge. He is the creator and sustainer of reality. The world, His creation, is real and orderly. All laws, beings, events, and ideas find their meaning in God. He reveals His greatness and purposes in both His natural revelation in the universe and in His written Word, the Bible. God calls humans to be coworkers, but as His creatures we nevertheless must work within His law structures. In science, for instance, we make clear that we explore the laws God created. Human theories reflect God's laws imperfectly. Yet because of God's faithfulness, we can use them to exercise His calling to unfold and develop our culture, helping it to function as a loving and just society.

The Old Testament word for knowing, *yada*, always refers to active and intentional engagement in lived experience (Groome 1980, 141). We do not have knowledge until we exercise it by living our commitment in all of life. Knowledge involves the heart, not just the mind. Paul says that knowledge without love is empty (1 Corinthians 8:1). Knowing, being, loving, and acting are all tied together in a biblical view of knowledge. God Himself says that to know Him means to do what is right and just, and to defend the cause of the poor and needy (Jeremiah 22:15–16). Conversely, to lack knowledge means to ignore the law of God (Hosea 4:1, 6). Rejecting true knowledge means breaking our relationship with God.

School knowledge may therefore never be just head knowledge. We design units and learning situations so that the knowledge students acquire is a means to an end. The end we have in mind is students' personal response to their learning. This response does not have to be something society considers practical. It may just be delighting in God's marvelous world or grieving the pain caused by sin. Biblical knowledge leads students to act on deepened or new commitments, and to exercise biblical norms and values. Growing in knowledge means growing in wisdom and understanding, doing good, and walking worthy (Colossians 1:9–10). It leads to loving, obedient service (1 John 2:3–5).

In the Bible knowledge is relational. It originates with our relating to God with awe and wonder (Proverbs 1:7). Conversely, a lack of knowledge involves breaking a loving and faithful relationship (Hosea 4:1, 6). When Adam "knew" Eve (Genesis 4:1, KJV), they had formed a sexual covenant of faithfulness with each other. When the Israelites knew God, they covenanted to walk a life of obedience and trust with Him. Similarly, the rigidity and hypocrisy of the Pharisees prevented them from knowing God, despite their thorough intellectual knowledge (John 8:19). Knowledge of Christ is not just factual; it is based on a living, experiential relationship that transforms a person (Philippians 3:8–10). Our relationship with God affects how we interpret and use knowledge. Also, relationships between and among teachers and students affect the willingness to accept and gain knowledge.

In the Bible, knowledge is never objective and "out there." Knowledge, discernment, and wisdom form a unified triad. The discerning heart seeks knowledge, and knowledge comes to the discerning (Proverbs 15:14, 14:6). Knowledge and good judgment form a team (Psalm 119:66). Prudence, knowledge, and discretion accompany wisdom. All these lead to righteousness and justice (Proverbs 8:12, 20). But biblical wisdom does not depend just on intellectual knowledge or rationality. Wisdom ultimately rests in our relationship with Jesus Christ, in having the mind of Christ (1 Corinthians 1–2). Biblical knowledge embodies a love for the Author of wisdom and thus applies knowledge with compassion and justice. In school, students must have opportunities to transcend intellectual knowledge by applying it in what for them are new situations. If they apply their knowledge according to biblical values and mandates, they will be gaining wisdom and discernment in the process.

Even knowledge of the physical world involves listening and responding to the daily outpouring of God's creation-speech (Psalm 19:1–2). Significantly, God presented Job with many facts about reality to help him gain true knowledge, but that knowledge was hollow until Job acknowledged a personal God as the source of those facts (Job 38–42). True knowledge of the physical world cannot be separated from knowing the Creator. Science promotes awareness of God and His call to respond obediently to Him with our knowledge.

Of course, sin taints all of life, including how we gain and apply knowledge. Our society uses knowledge to control our physical world, plant and animal life, and human life. We display much arrogance about the little we do know. We often cannot see beyond our own lives in our own communities. Misapplied knowledge, whether wielded by Christians or others, leads to the exercise of illegitimate power in family life, business, politics, schools, and churches. When the need to dominate drives the search for knowledge, an ethical basis for its use and the desire to do what is right are missing (Palmer 1983, 8).

A biblical approach to knowledge keeps us humble. The Bible reminds us that "we see but a poor reflection [of knowledge] as in a mirror [of polished metal]" (1 Corinthians 13:12). Thus, in our teaching, we guard against arrogance about our expertise. We admit our tendencies to fall short, misread situations, and make mistakes. We also show how humans often use technical knowledge that brings short-term profit but long-term catastrophe or anguish. We show how both our scientific and economic knowledge are often much more limited than experts will admit, and that our lack of insight into the consequences of decisions often comes back to haunt us.

Footstep 4-2

Alisa Ketchum teaches an eight-week unit in eleventh-grade English in which small groups of students write, act, direct, and produce one-act plays. Students choose a problem in society that is real for them and their parents. They are to deal with the problem in the light of the gospel without being pedantic or offering easy answers. Before they begin, the students are taught certain standards for good drama, and examples from well-known plays are given to illustrate how a character changes as a result of conflict resolution.

The unit teaches students much about writing and producing effective plays. How do you use dialogue to develop character? Do the theme and the plot weld together into a believable unit? What about blocking, sets and props, sound and lighting, or quality of the acting? Ketchum supplies lists of criteria to ensure frequent self-evaluation. Throughout, questions are asked, such as, Does this play cause you to question your life or look at things differently? Are you commenting on what teens believe about themselves, about adults, about their faith? Are you proposing how difficult issues might be resolved or bad situations changed? The plays must pertain to students' own life experience and reveal their personal response.

To be successful, the students have to exercise and experience servant leadership. They work through frustrations, take risks, and support each other. Eventually, they carry out a team consensus. Students reflect in their journals after each group meeting, answering questions such as, How does your group work best? They assess other group members according to specific criteria for servant leadership. They also adjudicate all other plays at a dress rehearsal. They write a detailed critique of one play. Before producing their own play for a parent audience, they revise it on the basis of feedback from fellow students.

State ways this unit reflects a biblical view of truth and knowledge. How would traditionalist and constructivist teachers react to this unit? What changes would you make if you taught the unit? Give reasons.

Footstep 4-3

Throughout the rest of this book we will consider the implications of a biblical view of truth and knowledge. But here is a preliminary list of some strategies for implementing one:

- Ground learning in students' own experiences, and God's revelation in the physical and social world as well as in Scripture.
- Foster a sense of awe and wonder about God's creation; make the familiar seem uncommon and amazing.
- Have students investigate issues and situations of real significance for them and for society. As they do so, help them examine how biblical truth and biblical values affect how we deal with the issue or situation.

- Integrate content, where meaningful, so that students see the interconnectedness of God's creation order.
- Give opportunities for and encourage diverse personal response. Allow students to exhibit and explain their learning products.

What are the curriculum implications of these suggested strategies? What other strategies can you suggest?

Classifying the Aspects of Reality

Schools usually organize their curriculum in terms of a fairly standard set of subjects. Most often, language arts and mathematics form the nucleus. Subjects like art and health wane and wax in importance in cyclical fashion. At the primary level many teachers use interdisciplinary units, but even those often focus on a social studies or science theme. School subjects may deal with one particular aspect of reality (e.g., chemistry) or a combination of several disciplines (e.g., social studies may include geography, history, economics, sociology, political science, and anthropology). How did these subjects originate? And how should we use subjects to organize the curriculum?

The Bible does not provide a formula for organizing the curriculum. Such organization changes as culture unfolds. The Bible does convey, however, that all of education must be used to nurture obedient living. Curriculum organization, therefore, must allow students to examine God's call for the place and task of humans in the world. That means that schools should acquaint students with the diversity of God's created reality and also prepare them to participate in modern society. Students should become familiar with the range of aspects of reality from the numerical to the ethical and spiritual, as well as with, for instance, using modern modes of communication and computers. This section shows how we can categorize the various aspects of reality. The next discusses what that means for curriculum organization.

We experience reality holistically. At the same time, we recognize that we deal with facets of phenomena and knowledge in what seem to be natural categories. For instance, when you spend a day on the beach, you use arithmetic to pay for an ice cream cone. Marking off a volleyball court in the sand requires geometry. Someone who explains why it will get foggy before nightfall uses her science knowledge. A mother uses psychology to discipline her child. The book you enjoy is an example of literature. You may, however, be bothered by the loud music that blasts from a nearby car. You (gently) discuss with the culprits the noise bylaw and the ethics of inflicting loud music on others. Later, around a campfire, you use theology to explain God's providence. Economics is a factor in deciding whether to make the long drive home in the fog or to stay overnight in a local motel.

Usually, we do not think in subject categories when we experience or use, for instance, geometry or economics in real life. But these and other subjects are embedded in all situations. To gain deeper insight, we focus on particular aspects in a more formal way. For instance, you may want to analyze how the mother disciplined her child and review alternate ways on the basis of psychological theories. Or you may study the literary merits of a book you enjoyed. Psychology and literature and the other subjects mentioned are different realms of knowledge that relate to diverse aspects of reality.

For many centuries philosophers have debated how to categorize the whole realm of knowledge into its various aspects. Christian scholar Roy Clouser uses the work of Dutch philosopher Herman Dooyeweerd to propose a list of fifteen aspects of reality, each of which has created orderly structures consisting of unique and irreducible meanings, concepts, and laws. Clouser does not claim that his list is definitive, since further reflection may lead to revisions. He adds that all aspects function together in human situations, but we may focus on one or two to gain deeper understanding (1991, 202–15).

I show a revised version of Clouser's list of aspects of reality with their irreducible key meanings and related subject disciplines in figure 4.2 (see also Fowler 1991, 210–25; and Greene 1998, 179–210). From the bottom to the top of the list, the aspects show increasing complexity. The laws unique to each of the lowest four aspects (biological to quantitative) govern how things are in a predetermined way. Humans cannot change the fact that mammals need oxygen to function, or that 2+2=4. But the laws in the upper eight aspects are normative. That is, humans can decide whether or not to live according to God's laws for those aspects. A basic law for social life is that we must love our neighbor as ourselves. Obeying this law leads to shalom; defying this law, to hurt and brokenness. Each day again, we choose whether or not to follow such laws. (The psychological aspect includes both types of laws.) In school, students experience, consider, and apply both types of laws. What is important is that they see both types as God's laws for life, and that we help them explore the implications of accepting or rejecting God's norms in the first nine aspects, both personally and as a society.

Human thinking about aspects of reality corresponds to subject content, that is, to distinct ways of organizing knowledge in one or more aspects. I have indicated examples of such disciplines in the third column of figure 4.2. Knowledge in the disciplines results from the work of specialists. Schools plan their curriculum so that their students become familiar with the key meanings, concepts, laws, and methods of inquiry in each category. What needs to be remembered is that the knowledge of specialists is also affected by their beliefs about reality, about humans, and about the purpose of life. Therefore, Christian educators should discern the spirit behind the knowledge offered in terms of biblical norms and directives (Steensma and Van Brummelen 1977, 17–18).

My list is open to modification. Clouser himself splits the physical into two, adding a kinematic aspect with motion as the key meaning. Subjects like geography and physical education do not correspond to a particular aspect. Philosophy is also missing; Clouser argues that philosophy is an overarching discipline that relates to and interprets all aspects of reality (for example, we speak of the philosophy of science). I removed "cultural formation" from Clouser's list and put it at the bottom, since it seems to me that cultural formation also overarches all aspects. It is in each aspect as well as in the totality of aspects.

Other philosophers, using their own criteria, have arrived at hierarchical categorizations of knowledge similar to this list. They may use terms such as *realms* or *forms of knowledge*. The exact categorization of the aspects is not as important as it is for the curriculum to cover a wide scope so that learners become familiar with the breadth of human life.

Footstep 4-4

Even in its organization the school curriculum is far from neutral. There are reasons why, for instance, some schools teach history and geography separately while others teach social studies. Some make consumer education compulsory, while others do not deem it a worthy subject. In the United States many students graduate without studying a foreign language; in Europe, students may study as many as four languages. Sometimes teachers delete geometry and statistics from mathematics courses, yet elsewhere these are separate subjects. Schools may require art and music only in the lower grades but mathematics up to eleventh or twelfth grade. Can you suggest reasons for such arrangements? Can you give other examples to show that subject arrangements reflect certain beliefs about the purpose of education?

One question that arises here is the extent to which certain subjects should be compulsory. We are all stronger in some modes of knowing than in others. For instance, to do well in high school physics, you need to have some aptitude for numerical, spatial, scientific, and logical knowing. But since physics is an important aspect of life in a technological society, should not all students take at least some physics, even those whose strengths are in verbal or aesthetic knowing? Or should we make aspects of physics compulsory only as part of interdisciplinary units on technology in society? What do you think?

List the subjects that you think should be compulsory in the school curriculum. Suggest the grade levels at which you think they should be required. Give reasons for your choices. Then compare your list with the

Fig. 4.2   Aspects of Reality

ASPECTS OF REALITY	KEY MEANING	RELATED SUBJECT DISCIPLINES
Confessional	Faith	Theology, religious studies
Ethical	Integrity	Ethics
Political/legal	Justice	Law, political science, civics
Economic	Stewardship	Economics
Social	Personal interaction	Sociology
Linguistic	Symbolic meaning	Language
Logical	Rational analysis	Logic, computing science
Aesthetic	Creative allusiveness	Visual art, music, drama, dance
Psychological/emotional	Feeling	Psychology
Biological	Life	Biology, physiology
Physical	Energy	Chemistry, physics
Spatial	Space	Geometry, topology
Quantitative	Number	Arithmetic, number theory
Cultural formation	Formative power	History, cultural studies

aspects of reality outlined in this section. Does your list cover all the aspects? Should it? Why or why not?

Curriculum Subjects and the Aspects of Reality

Suppose we agree with the categorization of a list such as the one given in the previous section. The question remains whether we should plan to organize our curriculum on the basis of the subject disciplines shown. We can argue that when they graduate, students should have some knowledge of each aspect of reality, especially since each has its own key meaning, concepts, and laws. If we teach all of the aspects explicitly in the curriculum, and explore how to use them in modern society, students will receive a balanced view of reality. The difficulty with this argument is that it is not clear that the key meanings and laws of the thirteen aspects are best taught in thirteen separate subjects. Indeed, five facts militate against this position:

1. **Situations in real life never fall neatly into a specific category**. We can learn in science all about the physics of a television set, but television exists in and affects social situations. To study only the electronics of a television set denies students the opportunity to consider its impact on language, aesthetics, economics, ethics, and faith. A more meaningful unit about television might be one that integrates the study of all these aspects, allowing students to experience and respond to the pervasive effect television has on our daily lives.

2. **The separation of academic disciplines into independent pigeonholes contributes to a fragmentation of knowledge.** It overlooks the fact that many interrelations exist among the disciplines. You cannot go very far in physics without knowing some mathematics, or in biology without knowing some chemistry. Some knowledge of the history of science and the economic impact of science and technology gives science a more meaningful context. The difficult decisions that have to be made today with respect to reproductive technologies and ecological questions demand that the study of ethics be an integral part of biology.

3. **Some school subjects combine or cut across several aspects of reality.** New subjects arise as we use our cultural power to unfold God's creation. For instance, we usually combine the quantitative and spatial aspects of reality in mathematics. Social studies embraces cultural formation in at least the confessional, ethical, political/legal, economic, and social aspects. Literature and drama involve cultural formation as it finds expression in the linguistic and aesthetic dimensions. Practical subjects such as physical education, home economics, business management, and industrial education do not fit into any one category. Yet these subjects have a legitimate place in the curriculum.

4. **Some modes of knowing and some aspects of reality can be learned well in the context of subjects that focus on other aspects.** For instance, ethics is best taught to young children through stories and literature. Visual arts and writing skills are best practiced in the context of units with relevant cross-disciplinary themes (although we do need to teach the specific skills). Logical reasoning is

best taught within all subjects, especially since the methods taught in logic as a subject seldom transfer to other situations.

5. **Students' own developmental levels affect how we organize the curriculum**. As people unfolded reality over the course of history, they gradually developed more specialized disciplines. Psychology became a separate discipline only late in the nineteenth century; computing science, only in the last fifty years. Similarly, when children enter school, they have experienced reality holistically. Integrated thematic approaches allow them to build on and relate to their early experiences. As they grow older, they gradually take more interest in specific aspects of reality.

For example, younger children learn about the psychological aspect of reality in school, but not in the subject of psychology. They study units such as God Made Me Special, and Friendship. Sensitive teachers consciously and continually address their students' emotional growth in a community setting. But psychology as a subject is not taught until the senior high school or college level. The same is true for sociology, economics, law, and ethics. In North America, most schools teach social studies in the lower grades. Gradually, at higher levels they teach geography, history, and economics separately, while sociology, anthropology, and criminology represent further specialization at the college level.

In short, identifying the aspects of reality or the forms of knowledge still does not give us easy answers for the organization of the curriculum. But there are at least four guidelines we can follow:

- **Does the curriculum include all aspects of reality and deal with their key mean-** ings? Is that true even when the curriculum does not include particular disciplines corresponding to some aspects of reality?

- **Does the curriculum organization take into account students' developmental levels?** Does the organization allow content to be rooted in students' own experience, and does it pose problems that are relevant for students at their level of understanding?

- **Does the unity and interrelatedness of knowledge become clear to the students?** Is there sufficient opportunity to experience how the aspects of reality are interconnected?

- **Does the organization enable students to live faithfully according to God's will?** Will the organization lend itself to helping students to reconcile what is harmed by sin, and to understand and proclaim love and justice?

One implication of these guidelines is that we teach a core curriculum—but one that differs from the way core curricula are usually defined. Another implication is that students benefit from integrating some content. However, in-depth considerations of the key meanings, concepts, and laws of each aspect of reality are probably best done in subjects that highlight one or two particular aspects. There also are subjects, especially more practical ones, that do not correspond to a particular aspect of reality and yet enable students to serve society and help reform it.

Footstep 4-5

Neil Postman, in his book *Technopoly* (1993), makes the point that a curriculum not only organizes information but also serves as a mechanism for information control. What the curriculum includes and excludes, he continues, reflects a theory about the purpose and meaning of education. Most North American schools teach astronomy but not astrology, and evolutionism but not creationism. The curriculum thus gives expression to what is considered legitimate knowledge. He then goes on to decry that cultural literacy in the curriculum often means mastering thousands of names, places, dates, and aphorisms, but excludes learning that is more valuable for life. Postman concludes that cultural literacy is a case of calling the disease the cure (1993, 74–75).

Respond to Postman's claims on the basis of what this section says about curriculum organization.

Footstep 4-6

Go back to the list of compulsory subjects that you made earlier. Would you now make any revisions? Why or why not? Do you agree that a core curriculum is desirable? If so, what should it include?

Planning a Core Curriculum

A core curriculum is that part of the curriculum required for all students. What should be included in the core has been debated vigorously ever since, in 1860, Herbert Spencer asked in his famous essay, "What knowledge is of most worth?"

Over the years there has been a notable shift in how educators view the core curriculum. In the 1940s, the core was usually defined in terms of personal and social life situations encountered by youth, and the behavior competencies considered necessary for effective living in a democratic society. Since the mid-1980s, the core has been described more and more in terms of basic subject content and skills in English, mathematics, science, and social studies—often as tested by external standardized tests (Pinar et al. 1995, 698).

It is instructive to look at some examples of core curricula. What educators define as core depends, like other curriculum choices, on their basic aims for schooling and their matching curriculum orientation. Academic traditionalists, for example, influenced British Columbia's 1977 core curriculum. It included the "essential skills and knowledge" students should acquire in reading, writing, listening, speaking, arithmetic, geometry, science, social studies, health and research, and critical thinking skills (British Columbia Ministry of Education 1977). The Minister of Education introduced this core curriculum to certify that schools taught the "basics." For several years, the Ministry used the document to plan more detailed curriculum guides and to evaluate whether schools met the curriculum criteria.

Twelve years later, a government task force and subsequent commission led to a so-called Year 2000 core curriculum. Unlike the earlier core, the documents did not list content to be covered. Instead, they reflected the influence of both the process/mastery and the experiential orientations. Process/mastery proponents, for instance, provided almost 250 focused, precise, measurable, process-oriented learning outcomes for primary mathematics (e.g., "Use the correct notation for dates: 1991-09-25"). On the other hand, the program was to be one "that you, the teacher, envision, create and, together with your students, call into being" (BCME 1990, 356). The experientialist's influence was seen in instances such as the stipulation that teachers should report only what students had accomplished, and not what they could not yet do nor where they stood in relation to their classmates (pp. 279–309). The resulting inner contradiction and lack of comparative standards led to so much parental turmoil that the province's premier abruptly canceled the program in 1993.

In recent years many North American jurisdictions have defined the core curriculum not so much in official curriculum guides as they have through standardized tests that all students must take at various grade levels. The results of these tests, which are widely available, are used in ranking the schools. School board members, administrators, and parents consider the test results to be important. Consequently, many teachers have begun to teach to these external high-stakes tests, especially in the core areas of mathematics, reading and writing, science, and social studies. Both the content and the form of the tests, in effect, define the core curriculum. Christian schools face a dilemma. While they support high standards in "basics," their curriculum is at least to a certain extent imposed by a public agency that sets the exams—and that by law promotes a secular worldview.

Different contexts and social demands mean that core curricula are never static. However, a core curriculum should be based on what is considered fundamental and indispensable. For Christian schools, unfolding a Christian vision of life is fundamental. That goal includes understanding and being able to apply the three basic biblical injunctions: the Creation Mandate, the Great Commandment, and the Great Commission. Also, students cannot function as responsible disciples unless they know the important ideologies, theories, concepts, and skills of our culture and can use and respond to them with integrity, competence, and creativity. They must be able to discern and critique the issues of our time. The core must nurture values, dispositions, and commitments in harmony with biblical norms and values such as love, responsibility, peace, justice, righteousness, and truth.

The scope of a core curriculum based on these principles will be all of human culture, and goes much beyond what standardized tests assess. Basic skills such as sequential numerical ones must be taught and reinforced, of course. But at the elementary level, the core should also teach the importance of love and responsibility in units on friendship and community, of peace and justice in units on civics and national history, of righteousness and truth in units on the environment and economics. Often teachers can develop skills in communication, research, and art as part of such units.

In middle schools, the core might include units that focus on cross-disciplinary situations that students face in their everyday life. For instance, units on understanding ourselves, life in community, communication, work and leisure, and economics can be taught in the humanities strand; units on technology and the role of computers, in the sciences strand. Alternatively, schools could design a two- or three-year core course that includes all such units. At the senior high school level, some schools offer a core course for eleventh or twelfth grade called *Living in Hope* that includes units on marriage and family, government and justice, work and the job, and education (De Moor 1992). Others at that level require a core course called *Understanding the Times* that examines worldviews as they affect Western culture (Noebel 1991). Especially in these courses it is important to ask questions like the ones I posed in chapter 3 immediately preceding footstep 3-1 (De Moor 1992, 6):

- What does the Bible teach us about this issue or aspect of society?
- How have history and tradition shaped people's ideas about the issue? How have they developed this aspect of society?
- What is the present state or condition of this issue or social institution in society?
- What changes and alternatives can Christians propose and implement, at least in part, to be God's instruments of justice, peace, and reconciliation?

If students are to receive and experience a balanced overview of key issues facing society, the core curriculum should include elements of all thirteen aspects of reality: How does faith affect our stance in life? What does the Bible have to say about sexuality and the marriage relationship? What is the government's and our personal role in promoting justice? How do we address economic problems as Christians? What is the nature of a healthy community, and what do we do to overcome prejudice? How do we respond to communication through advertising? How has technology shaped our lives, both positively and negatively? How does modern music affect our attitudes and values? Why does rational argument often fail to sway people in their voting decisions? What is a biblical view of self-esteem? How do Christians respond to the ethical issues of genetic engineering and ecology? Are we being good stewards of space as we plan our suburbs? Is it right for governments to make decisions on the basis of statistical polls?

Many of these questions are complex ones. At the kindergarten and primary levels,

we introduce the topics piecemeal, usually in story contexts. A kindergarten unit on transportation may have the teacher read a book on the pollution problems caused by cars and trucks, then conduct a field trip allowing the children to experience public transit alternatives. A fourth-grade unit on aboriginal people or Native Americans may show students some positive features of their culture and the problems resulting from dependence on paternalistic governments. Only in higher grades will students be able to analyze some of these problems in depth.

In short, the core curriculum in Christian schools should touch on all aspects of life. Of course, basic literacy and numeracy skills, as well as a basic store of conceptual knowledge, are an important part of that core. Without these, students cannot begin to understand the core issues, nor can they function as responsive disciples in society. For Christians, however, the ultimate basics deal with how we respond in our everyday lives to God's call to obedience. For this, students need the ability to identify, analyze, and respond to the issues of our time in the context of a biblical worldview.

Footstep 4-7

At the end of the last section, you considered what a core curriculum might include. What, in your view, are the basics that we should include in the required core curriculum? On the basis of this section, what changes would you make in your list? Share your list with another person and discuss the pros and cons of each of your approaches. If you worked together in one school, could you reach a consensus? Why or why not? To what extent should external standardized tests affect a school's core curriculum?

Factors That Affect Curriculum Organization

There is no one right way to organize knowledge in the curriculum. A host of factors influence how schools and teachers structure the curriculum. Also, teachers who know their aims and values will achieve a great deal with any curriculum organization. Yet, the way we organize the curriculum does affect learning.

Society—and therefore parents—have certain general expectations about the curriculum. For instance, it is expected that all schools will:

- Teach students to read and write their first language
- Make mathematics compulsory at least up to the ninth- or tenth-grade level
- Use a grade-level curriculum structure
- Give grades in well-defined subjects starting in at least fourth grade

Except for a few schools maintained by unique parent communities, most schools uphold such conventions. That is not to say that the curriculum organization cannot or does not change. National and regional commissions may be instrumental in adding courses or topics to the curriculum. Government officials may impose rigid time requirements for individual subjects if they are academic traditionalists, or encourage timetable flexibility if constructivists. Politicians responsible for departments of education may introduce tests that determine a core curriculum, or introduce information technology as a required subject. Parental pressures may force school boards to insist

that teachers plan separate time slots for spelling, reading, and writing. While changes do occur, the reality at the classroom level changes much less than public rhetoric implies.

School-level factors also affect curriculum organization. The school sets certain expectations, often adapted from state or school board guidelines. Christian schools usually organize their curriculum within some broad parameters, although their curriculum topics and organization often resemble those of public schools. School principals usually insist that teachers adhere to time constraints and other guidelines for specific subject areas. Together with the staff, they specify topics and themes at each level. The teachers' own inclinations, as well as their planning time, the availability of resources, student interest, and class dynamics affect the actual curriculum organization.

At the K–5 levels, teachers typically teach one class for most of the day. As a result, they have much leeway in their curriculum organization. Longer blocks of time used for interdisciplinary themes or significant topics related to social studies and science enhance the possibility of meaningful investigation and experience of what it means to live as a Christian in society. Within such a learning context, students recognize the usefulness of the skills and can apply them better in various settings.

For these reasons, many elementary teachers, instead of planning separate social studies and science time slots, plan larger blocks of time each day for integrated units. Such blocks may focus in turn on science, social studies, or interdisciplinary topics. Skills in language arts and research are practiced during the units. A fourth-grade teacher may plan a series of consecutive units on insects, the local state or province, trees and forests, aboriginal culture, and electricity. The study of novels might be integrated into several of these units.

In middle schools, one teacher often guides learning for a fairly long time block each day. This practice is appropriate for the middle-school level, especially as it affects students' attitudes. At this level more specialization occurs. The humanities teacher may not feel comfortable teaching science, and a specialist may need to teach a foreign language or music. Nevertheless, a rigid subject-centered timetable would hinder the implementation of units that are particularly relevant for these students.

Students at this level may not yet have reached what Piaget calls the formal reasoning stage. Yet their interests have broadened significantly since the elementary grades. Interdisciplinary topics relevant to their lives can maintain the interest of seventh- and eighth-graders. Units in these topics can capitalize on the students' increased awareness of what is happening in society and on their need to take on increased responsibilities. Thus a large variety of short exploratory electives and other minicourses is particularly effective.

Courses in the secondary-level curriculum center more on one or two aspects of reality. Teachers are specialists in one or two subjects. Colleges and universities or external examination agencies demand the completion of specific subject sequences, especially in the eleventh and twelfth grades. Students are at a developmental level in which they appreciate investigating discipline-based issues in more depth. To accommodate a range of electives, the timetable must be more rigid. Yet schools do well to provide time for a core (as described in this chapter) while allowing organizational flexibility for meaningfully integrated experiences.

Finally, schools at all levels should check whether their curriculum content and organization take into account all aspects of reality. Many schools today fail to do justice to the confessional, ethical, political/legal, and economic dimensions of reality. Yet students who become skilled mathematicians, scientists, musicians, or writers need to understand how their faith, morals, and political and economic values frame and direct how they use their abilities. Otherwise, they will ultimately lead empty lives. The separation of facts and skills from values has wreaked havoc with our civilization and does not do justice to a biblical view of knowledge.

Schools can make a difference if they base their curriculum and its organization on a clear vision of their aims, their values, and the different aspects of reality that need to be investigated in order for their graduates to lead holistic, balanced, and God-honoring lives in society.

Footstep 4-8

A sixth- through eighth-grade middle school appointed a committee of parents and teachers to develop a list of topics considered of prime importance but currently not taught:

1. Different religions and moral values represented in the community
2. Crime and justice in the local community
3. War and peace in the world
4. The operation of small businesses
5. The influence of modern music on culture
6. Teenage gender relations
7. The impact of technology on society
8. How statistics are used and misused in society

While there was general agreement about the topics, there was little agreement as to how the topics should be included in the curriculum.

- Some teachers wanted to insert all topics in current subjects in the timetable.
- Some proposed a timetable with longer blocks and more time assigned to humanities so that teachers could include most topics in humanities over a three-year period.
- Some suggested teaching the topics as part of a core course, with English, social studies, and science each losing one period per eight-day cycle to make room for the new course.
- Several urged that each year the school dispense with the regular timetable for two weeks and tackle two topics in depth with all grades. The topic of war and peace in the world would be included in social studies, and how statistics are used and misused in society would be included in math.

The debate was heated. The English teachers did not want to give up any periods, nor did they want a general humanities course to subsume English. The mathematics teachers favored the core course option but did not want to teach it. The social studies teachers liked the idea of a new humanities block that they would plan and implement jointly with the English teachers.

What are the strengths and weaknesses of each organizational approach? Which do you favor? Why? If your board instructed you as principal to include the topics in next year's curriculum, how would you go about coming to a decision?

Integrating Curriculum Content

Dictionaries define the term *integration* as "combining different parts into a unified whole." In education, such combining is done in many different ways. Here are three:

- **Schools integrate racial minorities or children with handicaps in "regular" classrooms** (the latter is now more commonly called "inclusion").
- **Schools integrate faith and learning.** That is, the curriculum shows how our beliefs affect how we look at and use our learning. Learning, as we have seen, is always rooted in certain beliefs. As such, we do not combine faith and learning. Yet this is called *integration* since the harmony of faith-based learning results in an integrated whole.
- **Schools integrate content from different subject disciplines** in courses or units.

In this section, we will consider the last definition. That is, we will look at how teachers in a course or a unit include content from several aspects of reality. Students experience real-life situations integrally. For the sake of in-depth analysis, we often focus on a particular subject-related aspect of a phenomenon. For broader insight, it may be useful to integrate two or three related subjects. As an alternative, we can study situations as holistic ones from the start, without differentiating and reintegrating. If so, it would be more accurate to speak of an *integral* rather than an *integrated* curriculum. For now the term *integration* will be used since it is the one commonly used. Later in the book the term *integral unit* will be used.

The following chart shows examples of four types of curriculum content integration. To make this clear, food metaphors are used.

Each type is compared to a turkey dinner, pizza, soup, and potluck dinner approach to integration.

First, when teachers align curriculum content so that they deal with similar themes in different subject areas, the result can be thought of as a turkey dinner. The plate may contain turkey, potatoes, and two vegetables—all separately identifiable but together forming one meal. In the Egypt example, the teacher taught social studies, language, and Bible separately, but the content in each complemented the others. An example in

which I was involved some years ago was a tenth-grade ecology unit. The biology teacher provided scientific content. The mathematics teacher taught a unit on statistics highlighting ecological data. The English teacher taught a novel dealing with an ecological issue and how to write a research paper on such a topic. Such concurrent teaching on a common general topic is fairly easy to arrange, but students do not experience the topic as a unity.

The gardening unit is an example of what we might call the "pizza approach." There is

Fig. 4.3   Examples of Four Types of Curriculum Integration

Turkey Dinner–Type Content Integration

Berta Den Haan taught a seventh-grade unit on ancient Egypt. The students first brainstormed all they knew about Egypt and categorized their knowledge. Students' resulting questions and areas of interest gave focus to the unit (this is sometimes called the K-W-L strategy: I know, I wonder, I learned). In social studies the students examined ancient Egyptian culture in depth.

Simultaneous with social studies, Den Haan discussed a novel about ancient Egypt, Bert Williams' *Sword of Egypt*, for language arts. The novel dealt with a boy asking Egyptian gods to help him get his father a proper burial and join his mother in the hereafter. Thus the novel showed the students how religion dominated the life of the ancient Egyptians. During the Bible period in the morning, the teacher followed up students' responses to the novel by talking about their personal faith and its implications. In art, the students examined Egyptian art and made models of Egyptian pyramids and sphinxes.

Pizza-Type Content Integration

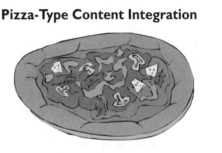

Glenda MacPhee taught her second/third-grade class a science unit on gardening. A widow next to the school allowed the class to use her backyard. The students planted two large beds, one for flowers and one for produce. Small groups of students took on specific tasks: rototilling, building frames for the beds, spreading topsoil, and so on. They learned much about gardening (e.g., how mulching helps preservation of water and how some products turn out either more or less desirable than those in stores). The students also learned a great deal about science in an experiential setting: the parts of plants, conditions needed for successful growth, and types of flowers and vegetables.

The children also did activities that related to subjects other than science. They practiced math skills as they calculated how much lumber they needed to build the beds. They discussed the ethics of respecting their neighbors' property. They drew pictures of their garden at different stages. They wrote thank-you notes to all those who helped with supplies and advice. Later, they analyzed why some things worked and some didn't. They planned a closing chapel for the whole student body that became a time of praise for God's provision of food and the beauty of plants and flowers. Throughout the unit, children learned a great deal about cooperating, about being responsible, and about taking on leadership roles.

Fig. 4.3 continued

Soup-Type Content Integration	Potluck Dinner–Type Content Integration

Emma Johnstone taught an integrated unit about a small Scottish village, Chapel Hill, close to her school. Throughout the study she allocated special times for fieldwork and class lessons, but she integrated most of the work into daily programs. She divided her seven- and eight-year-olds into three mixed-ability groups. She gave each child a kit with eight assignments on topics such as the village in the past, designing and building a house, and the village within the surrounding area. Specific skills that were built into the assignments were observing, describing, using reference books, making models, making rough maps and updating older topographical maps, interpreting change from old newspapers and photographs, writing stories, displaying and reporting on work, and so on.

Though the unit was taught as an integral whole, the students learned about many aspects of reality. For mathematics, they made plans and charts, read bus timetables, and priced items in the store. For science, they tested materials used in building and did some pollution experiments. For geography, they did map work. For history, they created a picture of what life was like in the village 50–100 years ago. For art, the children took some photographs of the village and used them to make paintings of village scenes. For language, they recorded written work from observation, conducted interviews, and wrote poems, stories, and letters. For religious education, they considered how religion and morality have changed over the last 50–100 years. Johnstone emphasized, however, that while she could identify these aspects "for convenience," her approach was an integrated one.

Anna-May Taekema worked with a group of seven other primary teachers on a two-week unit on the jungle. Its theme was that the jungle is part of God's intricate design; God calls humans to care for, develop, and enjoy the jungle. An important unit theme was how humans must and can help to protect the jungle ecosystem from mismanagement. The teachers completed large charts with spokes from the center showing objectives and activities in six developmental areas: faith, intellectual, aesthetic, social and emotional, physical, and social responsibility. They then each chose one jungle topic (e.g., reptiles of the jungle, rafts, or going on a jungle hunt).

The teachers divided the eight classes into eight cross-grade groups, and these groups rotated from class to class each morning from 10:30–12:00. Each teacher provided several centers. Small mixed-age groups worked at the centers, with the older children helping the younger ones. Activities included writing a short story about the adventures on a trip to the jungle, making rafts, creating indigenous jewelry, making reptiles from play dough, building an Amazon village, writing a three-day diary of tenting in the jungle, and painting pictures of themselves in the jungle. Classes did grade-specific activities at other times. The third-graders, for instance, made posters on the "save the jungle" theme. All students shared initial and culminating activities.

a subject discipline "crust." In this unit the crust is science. But the teacher brings in different kinds of "toppings" from other subject areas that enrich the unit in two ways. First, the students experience and see the interrelatedness of knowledge. Second, the students reinforce and exercise skills from other areas in the curriculum. While the subject crust remains evident, the unit is a far more interesting and meaningful whole with

the additions. This unit focuses on science but incorporates language arts, mathematics, and visual arts activities. It also includes social studies when students investigate the community people involved in gardening and garden marketing.

The pizza type of integration is probably most common in schools. Kindergarten and primary teachers frequently teach thematic units of this type. Teachers at higher grade levels often teach units with a social studies or science theme in which students also use their language arts and mathematics insights and skills. With clear goals and careful planning, such units often provide stimulating and comprehensive learning experiences. Teachers need to ensure that the topics chosen are meaningful ones and that balanced concept and skill development takes place.

Emma Johnstone's community study is the "soup approach." Soup is made from various ingredients, but even when we can identify some of the ingredients, what makes it special is the overall taste of the blend. We focus on the whole effect, not on individual ingredients. This approach uses large blocks of classroom time, possibly even a fully integrated day. If carefully planned, the unit provides students with a meaningful experience of a real-life phenomenon or issue. They can become very excited about their learning.

The soup approach, though worthwhile, is used much less than the pizza approach. Put together and effectively implementing this type of unit is time-consuming and takes sophisticated organization. Also, most teachers prefer to teach skill-oriented subjects, such as reading, mathematics, and physical education, in separate time slots. They find that otherwise, they cannot teach and reinforce necessary skills and keep track of each student's progress.

Finally, for the "potluck dinner approach," teachers put together, perhaps once a year, a cross-grade thematic unit in which groups of students move from classroom to classroom. Together, the teachers design an overall plan to ensure that the whole unit has integrity and coherence. They then all contribute some personal "dishes" to the potluck dinner. Teachers may plan some activities in a particular subject area, or interdisciplinary ones.

An example of a potluck unit is a culture study with each homeroom class studying a particular country. They then develop center-based activities to highlight the country for other classes. On successive days, the other classes rotate through each classroom to learn about the different countries. In this way, students get the chance to learn about several countries and also exhibit what they learned in their own in-depth study. Schools have also used this type of integration to study current events such as the Olympic Games. While planning is time-consuming, schools find that cross-grade units of this type can forge teachers and students into teams in which they learn from and support each other.

Before asking what type and how much curriculum content integration should occur, I want to consider more fully the advantages and disadvantages of the pizza and soup types of integration. Advantages include:

- **Integration allows students to consider and develop their experiences and interests as a unity.** Students often cannot see the relevance of the narrowly focused content of separate subjects.
- **Integrated units can deal with issues, problems, and experiences that cut across disciplines.** Themes can relate to practical living and responsible decision making. Spiritual and moral questions are not set aside.
- **Integration can make clear the unity of knowledge.** Teachers can show the links between various aspects of reality.
- **Teachers can more easily include diverse modes of knowing in the curriculum** (see the next section).
- **The longer time blocks often used for integrated learning allow students to**

focus on investigations for sustained time periods.
- **When several teachers plan units jointly, integration can lead to renewed enthusiasm for teaching.** The more creative teaching approaches that often result also lead to increased student interest and motivation (Jacobs 1989, 51).

However, integration also has some disadvantages:

- **A curriculum with much integration may pay little attention to the structure of the separate disciplines.** That may result in inadequate or unbalanced development of concepts and theories. An integrated curriculum may also neglect sequential skill development.
- **High school teachers with in-depth knowledge in one or two fields may feel uncomfortable with topics that go beyond their expertise.** They may prefer to deal with important interdisciplinary issues within their subjects.
- **Planning integrated units with teacher teams is time-consuming.** One grade-level planning team estimated that it took 164 hours to brainstorm, research the subject matter, develop and sequence activities, find resources and materials, set up speakers and field trips, plan each day, monitor student and teacher progress, and keep parents informed (Jacobs 1989, 51).
- **Integrated units may lack focus or significance.** (This can be overcome!) Topics may be vague, narrow, or trivial.
  - Topics such as Change, Equilibrium, or Evidence are too indefinite. The resulting units may lack unity, especially if teachers do not write a clear

thematic focus statement. A topic more focused than Change, for instance, is How Change That Occurred in the 1960s Affected Western Culture.
  - A topic like The Microscope is too limiting. This could be subsumed under a topic such as Cells as the Building Blocks of Life.
  - Units on The Circus, Balloons, or Dinosaurs may include a wealth of fascinating activities, but the topics are superficial or secondary in importance. While teachers can do valuable things with each, there are more socially meaningful topics to investigate. A topic such as Communities of Living Things has more significance, for instance, than Dinosaurs (although dinosaurs could be studied within this broader unit as a historical community that died out).

The main conclusion we can draw from these advantages and disadvantages of integration is that *no single plan is best for all situations or at all times.* Students benefit from both integrated content and individual subject disciplines. Integration is particularly desirable for investigating cross-disciplinary experiences, issues, and problems relating to student interests and practical living concerns. Organizing curriculum content by subject is especially useful when developing more abstract conceptual schemas or sequential skills. Schools and teachers need to stay flexible.

The amount of integration in the curriculum usually decreases as students progress through the grades. At the kindergarten and first-grade levels, the study of themes through class activity and learning centers may take more than half of the available time.

Skill development becomes part of the integrated theme. Teachers may offer only biblical studies, mathematics, and physical education in separate time slots. At the fourth- and fifth-grade levels, teachers may have an 80–105 minute block each day for integrated unit study. The theme may be interdisciplinary. It may also focus on a science or social studies "crust," with learning activities added that relate to other aspects of reality. Middle schools may integrate on the basis of curriculum strands such as the humanities or the sciences. High schools may integrate a core block. They may also encourage, for example, social studies and English teachers to work together by scheduling simultaneous classes adjacent to each other.

Some integration can also take place within blocks set aside for individual subjects. The thirteen aspects of reality are interrelated. Physics makes use of mathematics, biology of chemistry, history of geography, and so on. Further, issues that arise in one aspect of reality affect and are affected by considerations of other aspects. For example, studying trees or forestry in science in a responsible way will include reflection on:

- Economic stewardship and sustainable harvesting
- The historical background to the claims and needs of earlier cultures
- The biological, aesthetic, and social concerns of clear-cutting
- The ethical dilemma of providing jobs or preserving a species of a particular bird

Thus the pizza approach, while focusing on a particular subject, lends itself well to content integration. For individual teachers, that means that even with a timetable arranged strictly by subjects, they can provide integration if they plan what I call integral units. Such units will be discussed in chapters 6 and 7.

Footstep 4-9

From the short description of the following unit, infer its theme. What type of integration does the unit illustrate? Suggest how you might structure the unit using other types of integration. Which type of integration would you prefer for this unit? Why?

Glenda MacPhee began a unit on garbage by discussing the diversity of things in creation and how all things have a place in reality. Her students considered various natural cycles, such as the food cycle, as well as cycles resulting from human activity. They then explored how garbage results particularly from human activity. The students visited a garbage dump to experience how much our society throws away, and investigated how much of what is wasted could be recycled. In the classroom they decided how they themselves could reduce consumption and reuse products. They implemented an appropriate plan of action. Meanwhile, the students read and discussed a book about an empty lot that its owner planned to sell for a gas station development. The owner discovered, however, that the lot was not just a place where people dump litter, but that its every nook and cranny contained much life. This story led the students to look for garbage and for life on an empty lot close to the school. The students also began composting their classroom garbage, opening it up two months later to see what had happened (the students planted and later harvested some cherry tomato seeds that had sprouted). Throughout the unit, the students used their journals to respond to issues as they arose.

Modes of Knowing

As we saw earlier in this chapter, there are different aspects or forms of knowledge, as shown by the different subject disciplines. There are also different modes or ways of knowing. Howard Gardner (1993) refers to these as *multiple intelligences*. Whatever we call them, clearly all human beings possess and have the potential to develop each way of knowing to some degree. All have a potential for a unique constellation of various modes of knowing. Also, our ability in one mode to some extent is independent of our ability in other modes.

Schools have, by and large, emphasized the numerical, logical, scientific, and verbal modes of knowing. Regrettably, that means they have often neglected other modes such as the interpersonal and aesthetic. Some students who are not strong in the numerical way of knowing may be strong, for example, in solving problems that they encounter in everyday life, or in providing a specialized service valued in society. We need to change the question How smart are you? to How are you smart?

Classifications of aspects of reality (or knowledge disciplines) and modes of knowledge are similar, and they parallel the types of values discussed in chapter 3. These similarities and parallels reflect the fact that God's creation forms a unity. Still, we use different modes of knowing to learn about specific disciplines. For example, learning about mathematics involves numerical and logical knowing in arithmetic and algebra, and spatial knowing in geometry and topology. But mathematicians also use scientific, intuitive, and aesthetic knowing (Nel Noddings in Eisner 1985, 117). Mathematicians often arrive at new conclusions through observing and classifying patterns, through intuition, or through aesthetic visualization. They may use deductive reasoning to prove their results later.

Why is it important to take into account the different modes of knowing? If students are to internalize knowledge and respond in personal ways, they will benefit from the opportunity to learn and react using the modes of knowing to which they are naturally inclined. They should also use other modes of knowing so that they learn to appreciate and become somewhat comfortable with them. While not everyone can excel in all modes, growth in areas such as emotive, interpersonal, and aesthetic knowing is important for all. Sensitivity to the diverse modes of knowing helps us design a balanced curriculum.

We do not know precisely how many different modes of knowing exist. Howard Gardner lists eight kinds of intelligence:

- visual/spatial
- logical/mathematical
- verbal/linguistic
- musical/rhythmic
- bodily/kinesthetic
- interpersonal/social
- intrapersonal/introspective
- scientific/naturalist

Gardner has admitted that his list may not be complete. He added the naturalist intelligence in the late 1990s and has considered the possibility of moral and spiritual intelligence (Silver, Strong, and Perini 2000, 9). At the same time, it is doubtful that the logical/mathematical intelligence should be just one category since analytic thought goes far beyond mathematical reasoning.

Nevertheless, Gardner's work in showing how people use, prefer, and have dispositions for particular modes of knowing has been invaluable. Learning, he has demonstrated, can be more effective if we deliberately allow students to employ different ways of knowing. The following is a discussion of a number of modes of knowing that generally parallel the aspects of reality: numerical, spatial, physical, scientific, emotive, intuitive, aesthetic (musical, visual, and dramatic), logical, verbal/linguistic, interpersonal/social, economic, political/legal, ethical, and spiritual.

Footstep 4-10

Students in Paul Smith's fourth-grade biblical studies class learn about the forty-year desert trek of the Israelites. Paul's theme for the unit is that God provides for His people, and that, therefore, we can trust God and accept His blessings, especially salvation in Jesus Christ. The teacher recognizes that for knowing to be meaningful, it must involve personal response. He also realizes that students prefer different ways to consider and deepen their knowledge.

Smith therefore provides opportunities for learning and responding that involve diverse modes of knowing. Students work in groups to review parts of the story by dramatizing it. Some construct models of the tabernacle or of an Israelite encampment. Some write and perform music that the Israelites might have sung. Others create poems. Small groups make a booklet about the forty-year journey. All write personal responses to issues that arise, and make a personal dictionary with the new words they learn.

Note that the teacher is aware of different ways students deepen their knowledge: verbal (oral and written), aesthetic (musical), and interpersonal. He might also encourage his students to use and expand their spiritual mode of knowing by putting together a meaningful worship experience. Other students might use and foster their logical mode of knowing by developing a detailed time line and map of the journey. Can you suggest other modes of knowing that might be incorporated to enhance students' learning?

Numerical Knowing

Some students are strong in numerical knowing. They quickly sense relationships and patterns among numbers. They have a knack for calculating and estimating with numbers. Some students who are strong in numerical knowing may become good bookkeepers but not be disposed to become mathematicians because they are less strong in logical knowing.

Spatial Knowing

Some students shine in the spatial mode of knowing. They are sensitive to lines and shapes in space. They easily recognize relationships of objects in space, can form mental images and transformations, and can make graphic representations. They have a keen sense of location and direction.

Physical Knowing

The physical, or kinesthetic, is also a separate mode of knowing. Persons as diverse as athletes, surgeons, dancers, television camera operators, and sculptors can solve problems involving movement in space or make products using physical coordination. Such coordination depends on mind-body connection that allows one to make and carry out successfully two or more almost instantaneous decisions. Learners who lean toward this way of knowing learn best by doing, moving, and acting things out (Silver, Strong, and Perini 2000, 8).

Scientific Knowing

Until very recently, the dominant view of logical positivism tended to equate knowledge with scientific knowing. When seen as the main or only mode, scientific knowing becomes stifling. When viewed as one among many ways of knowing, however, the scientific mode of generalizing from investigations of physical phenomenon is a useful one to foster in students. The scientific mode of knowing involves identifying patterns and generating concepts and theories from observation and sensory evidence. Persons strong in this way of knowing have particular insight into the intricacies of the interconnectedness of God's creation in nature.

Emotive Knowing

Daniel Goleman (1995) has shown that the emotive mode of knowing has a powerful impact on the way humans perceive, respond to, and are able to solve problems—indeed, he claims, likely more so than cognition (Goleman calls it emotional intelligence). This way of knowing helps persons to have an accurate picture of their strengths and weaknesses, to persist in the face of frustrations, to overcome their own anxiety and help others to do so, and to approach issues with an apt depth and sincerity of feeling (Lambert and Mitchell 1997, 154–67). They are sensitive to the moods and feelings of others, and discern underlying motives.

Intuitive Knowing

I do not know of an adequate description of the intuitive mode of knowing, or even whether we can help students cultivate this mode. Yet the intuitive mode of knowing exists. It is the ability to perceive directly or apprehend immediately the dynamics of a situation or the solution of a problem—without applying formal reasoning power. Intuitive knowledge has to do with feeling and perception. It can include having an accurate perception of oneself and how one fits into a new social situation (thinking, for instance, "I'll have to be careful here," even before any words are spoken or formal analysis has taken place). It may also be quickly sensing the undesirability or immorality of a situation (thinking, "There's something not kosher here"). It may be reacting instantaneously and successfully to an unexpected traffic situation when driving, without any awareness of intervening mental processes.

Henri Poincaré (1956), one of the world's foremost mathematicians around 1900, could not add simple numbers. His spatial mode of knowing was equally abysmal: his geometric diagrams were undecipherable. What modes of knowing, then, allowed him to be a great mathematician? First, his analytical prowess was astounding. But he also had what he himself and others have called intuitive power, the ability to perceive at a glance the situation as a whole. Poincaré has described how he often found solutions to difficult problems suddenly and with immediate certainty. He had, as he put it, sudden inspirations or revelations, often unexpectedly after putting the problem aside following several days of fruitless work on it. After such an intuitive grasp of the situation, he would use logical reasoning to verify his earlier conclusion. Poincaré added that the feeling of absolute certainty usually proved valid. Sometimes, however, his intuition deceived him without being any less vivid.

Psychologist Rudolf Arnheim argues that both the intuitive and rational share in every cognitive act. The intuitive mode of knowledge allows us to grasp the structure and function of a situation and its components. We need reasoning, however, to validate initial conclusions and draw conclusions. Thus, intuition and reasoning complement each other, with each having a legitimate place in classroom learning. Not knowing how to improve students' abilities in the intuitive mode of knowing should not prevent us from recognizing it as legitimate and valuable in learning.

Aesthetic Knowing

The aesthetic mode of knowing allows us to create and experience products that imaginatively capture a slice of life. To know aesthetically means to portray or understand a work that has an allusive or referential meaning. Such a meaning could not be captured in the same way by words or cognitive analysis. Aesthetic modes of knowing point to certain aspects of life and help us experience them in imaginative and often playful ways. Aesthetic knowing allows persons to make new mental connections, providing them with insights and understandings not available through other modes (Shapiro 1993, 27).

Aesthetic knowing comes to the fore particularly in the visual arts, music, dance, poetry, and drama. However, social and physical scientists also work imaginatively, for instance, with metaphors. The most effective theories often are aesthetically attractive ones (Eisner 1985, 26–28). The visual arts require more than the spatial mode of knowing. They also require persons to create and re-create pictures, images, and sculptures in such a way that they allude to or symbolize meaning while imaginatively capturing an aspect of life.

Persons gifted in music can produce melody and rhythm. They also are sensitive to sound and its structure, and can create music to set a mood or impression (the referential function). The musical way of knowing is likely a separate one from the other aes-

thetic ones (Fowler in Lambert and Mitchell 1997, 144).

Logical/Analytic Knowing

Schools have long stressed logical, or analytic, knowing. This emphasis began with the ancient Greeks. For Plato, a sign of a good education was the ability to manipulate abstract concepts. For many centuries Euclidean geometry, consisting of logical proofs of geometrical propositions, was a required study for any educated person.

Today, Piaget's followers continue to assume that the logical is the foremost mode of knowing (e.g., Kohlberg's emphasis on moral reasoning). The logical mode of knowledge enables persons to discern relationships, connections, and patterns, and to reason both inductively and deductively. Students who are strong in this mode of knowing have the ability to handle long chains of reasoning (if-then, cause-effect). They love to question and put ideas to the test.

Verbal/Linguistic Knowing

Students strong in the linguistic mode of knowing have verbal facility and learn well by communicating orally or in writing. They use words and language effectively, both for their own learning and to explain things to others or convince them of a position or course of action. They are sensitive to the meanings of words and the different uses of language.

Students who do well in the logical and linguistic modes of learning generally do well on so-called IQ tests. Yet the other ways of knowing are just as much ingredients of overall intelligence (Gardner 1993, 8).

Interpersonal/Social Knowing

Howard Gardner shows that the interpersonal or social mode of knowing is independent of the linguistic mode (1993, 22–23).

Until teachers began to use collaborative learning, they often neglected the interpersonal mode of knowing inside the classroom. Students have graduated from high school knowing little about interacting positively with others. Yet this mode of knowing is a crucial one for the welfare of persons and for society. Interpersonal sensitivity and competence is crucial for society's well-being.

Many students learn through interaction with others. They are able to discriminate among many different kinds of interpersonal cues and are able to respond to and work effectively with others. All students can benefit from classroom structures that regularly encourage them to nurture positive interpersonal interaction. It is, therefore, important to help students work cooperatively in groups, where they learn to build on each other's strengths.

Economic, Political/Legal, Ethical, and Spiritual Knowing

The foregoing are ten separate modes of knowing that schools need to incorporate in their curriculum. A social studies teacher dealing with the structure of government can, for instance, make use of the numerical, spatial, intuitive, logical, verbal, and interpersonal modes of knowing. For a topic such as Communities of Plants and Animals, a teacher could help students use and develop their numerical, spatial, physical, scientific, aesthetic, logical, verbal, and social ways of knowing, especially if the unit involves a field trip and other project work that would enhance the learning process.

There are still other modes of knowing that have not as yet been examined in depth. We do speak, for instance, of persons having economic know-how, political savvy, ethical or moral discrimination, and spiritual insight. Do these also reflect distinctive ways

of knowing, or do such abilities represent combinations of other modes? I suspect that these are separate modes of knowing, though Gardner claims that this has not yet been established scientifically or rationally. Yet some people, without being known for deep logical thinking, are recognized for keen moral sagacity. Others, by taking leaps of faith, develop spiritual discernment. The importance of spirituality as a way of knowing, long neglected by positivists, is beginning to be recognized more widely once again.

Some Unanswered Questions

Admittedly, we are still left with many questions about the various modes of knowing. We still have difficulty defining the intuitive and aesthetic ways of knowing, and recognizing how to nurture these in school. Also, while we can show that all modes of knowing are important in life, are some more important or more suited for school curriculum? Is certain curriculum content or are certain structures particularly appropriate for teaching specific modes of knowing? Do different ways of knowing develop best at different ages? Should mastery of various ways of knowing be an explicit curriculum goal? Do some modes of knowing require more active involvement in posing, analyzing, and solving problems than others? (See Elizabeth Vallance in Early and Rehage 1999, 66–67.)

While answers to such questions may be unclear, we do know that in the past, schools have focused too narrowly on numerical, logical, scientific, and verbal modes of knowledge. The curriculum needs to take into account the other modes as well. The chart in figure 4.4 gives some suggestions for classroom strategies appropriate for learners who are strong in particular modes of knowing—and for helping other students develop in those modes.

As a teacher you do not have to include each mode of knowing in each lesson. That would become stilted and artificial. What is important is that you try to include strategies for all appropriate modes of knowing in each of your units. You can use the planning chart in figure 7.4 (chapter 7) for brainstorming learning activities for both the modes of knowing and the values that you want to emphasize in a unit.

Footstep 4-11

In this section it was suggested that there are fourteen or fifteen modes of knowing,

most paralleling an aspect of reality. Suppose you are about to teach a unit on communities of living things and a unit on government. For each of these units, make a chart like figure 4.4, listing appropriate modes of knowing that students could experience and develop, together with classroom activities for each mode listed.

This chapter claims that knowledge, to be meaningful, needs to involve active engagement and response. Can you suggest ways of encouraging vibrant involvement and response for these units?

Fig. 4.4 Some Appropriate Learning Activities for Various Modes of Knowing

Numerical	Calculations; number games; working abilities, fractions, formulas, and equations
Spatial	Visual presentations; drawings and models; use of symbols; interpretation and construction of maps
Physical	Hands-on manipulation and experimentation; dramatization; creative movement; role-playing
Scientific	Field observation; stargazing; plant identification; rock categorization; weather forecasting
Emotive	Allowing expression of feelings through teaching and through student responses; making learning personally meaningful
Intuitive	Using intelligent guessing to tackle problems and situations; encouraging students' conjectures
Aesthetic	Expressing oneself through one of the arts; performance of music; painting
Logical/analytic	Problem solving; critical thinking; analysis of paradoxes, cause and effect, etc.
Linguistic/verbal	Discussions; storytelling; presentations; research; writing journals, reports, essays, and poetry
Interpersonal/social	Collaborative learning; group assignments; peer tutoring; debates; building of classroom community
Economic	Cultivating and upholding resource and time stewardship in all classroom activities
Political/legal	Conveying a sense of fairness and justice about issues inside and outside the classroom
Ethical	Examining moral dilemmas in terms of ethical principles; building an ethical classroom community
Spiritual	Exploring how faith affects life and culture; experiencing the classroom as God's "sacred space"

Reviewing the Main Points

- **A biblical view of knowledge holds that God has created the world, and that humans are able to uncover layer upon layer of reality as they gain deeper understanding of God's truth.** Knowledge involves unfolding and shaping reality, but humans based their knowledge on God's revelation, using their faith presuppositions and their personal and cultural interpretations. Therefore, knowledge involves personal and communal response and commitment. Knowledge is not just an objective, organized body of concepts; however, neither is knowledge just personally constructed and totally subjective.

- **We can identify different aspects of reality in our approach to knowledge, beginning with the quantitative aspect and ending with the confessional.** As a student progresses through the grades, the curriculum gradually becomes more specialized by subject disciplines. Subjects at higher grade levels often (but not always) focus on one or several aspects of reality. If they do, students can investigate the key meanings of the aspect(s) in some degree of depth.

- **We experience everyday situations in holistic ways, not as isolated aspects of reality.** To make learning meaningful for students, schools should allow for the exploration of phenomena in their contexts. Integration of subject content is possible in different ways. For younger children integration often takes place through integral units with activities that involve many aspects of reality. What is important at all grade levels is to provide a core curriculum as well as integrated approaches through which students explore interdisciplinary topics and issues crucial for being and becoming responsive disciples of Christ.

- **Different modes or ways of knowing (also called *multiple intelligences*) roughly parallel the aspects of reality.** Humans use diverse ways of knowing to learn, and have dispositions for different combinations of those ways of knowing. Therefore, we plan curriculum to include the various ways of knowing, including, for instance, the interpersonal and aesthetic ones. In this way we help students develop and feel more comfortable with a spectrum of ways of knowing, and thus nurture them to be and become more versatile and resourceful disciples of Jesus Christ.

References

British Columbia Ministry of Education (BCME). 1977. *Guide to the core curriculum*. Victoria, BC: BCME.

———. 1990. *Primary program: Foundation document*. Victoria, BC: BCME.

Clouser, R. 1991. *The myth of religious neutrality*. Notre Dame: University of Notre Dame Press.

De Moor, A., ed. 1992. *Living in hope: Teacher resource manual*. Grand Rapids: Christian Schools International.

Early, M., and K. Rehage, eds. 1999. *Issues in curriculum*. Ninety-eighth yearbook of the National Society for the Study of Education. Chicago: University of Chicago Press.

Eisner, E., ed. 1985. *Learning and teaching the ways of knowing*. Eighty-fourth yearbook of the National Society for the Study of Education. Chicago: University of Chicago Press.

Fowler, S. 1991. *A Christian voice among students and scholars*. Potchefstroom, South Africa: Potchefstroom University for Christian Higher Education.

Gardner, H. 1993. *Multiple intelligences: The theory in practice*. New York: Basic Books.

Goleman, D. 1995. *Emotional intelligence*. New York: Bantam.

Greene, A. 1998. *Reclaiming the future of Christian education: A transforming vision*. Colorado Springs: Association of Christian Schools International.

Groome, T. 1980. *Christian religious education*. San Francisco: Harper & Row.

Jacobs, H. 1989. *Interdisciplinary curriculum: Design and implementation*. Alexandria, VA: Association for Supervision and Curriculum Development.

Lambert, I., and S. Mitchell, eds. 1997. *The crumbling walls of certainty: Toward a Christian critique of postmodernity and education*. Sydney, Australia: Centre for the Study of Australian Christianity.

Luke, C., and J. Gore, eds. 1992. *Feminisms and critical pedagogy*. New York: Routledge, Chapman and Hall.

Noebel, D. 1991. *Understanding the times: The religious worldviews of our day and the search for truth*. Eugene, OR: Harvest House.

Palmer, P. 1983. *To know as we are known: A spirituality of education*. San Francisco: Harper & Row.

Pinar, W., W. Reynolds, P. Slattery, and P. Taubman. 1995. *Understanding curriculum: An introduction to the study of historical and contemporary curriculum discourses*. New York: Peter Lang.

Poincaré, H. 1956. Mathematical creation. In James R. Newman, *The World of Mathematics*, Vol. 4, pp. 2041–50. New York: Simon and Schuster.

Postman, N. 1993. *Technopoly: The surrender of culture to technology*. New York: Vintage.

Shapiro, B. 1993. Interpreting the world: Artistic and scientific ways of knowing. *English Quarterly* 26 (1): 26–29.

Silver, H., R. Strong, and M. Perini. 2000. *So each may learn: Integrating learning styles and multiple intelligences*. Alexandria, VA: Association for Supervision and Curriculum Development.

Steensma, G., and H. Van Brummelen, eds. 1977. *Shaping school curriculum: A biblical view*. Terre Haute, IN: Signal.

Steppingstone 5

Learning and the Curriculum

When I ask Susan Dick about her primary curriculum, she says little about content. Instead, she talks about how she arranges learning. Although she carefully considers her unit themes and the concepts that her students need to learn, she knows that her pedagogy affects her children at least as much.

She plans her program so that her children develop and celebrate their diverse and unique gifts. They are challenged to cultivate and use their abilities, even if at first they may fail. She applauds their successes and uses mistakes as a launching pad for further learning.

At the same time, she emphasizes that she consistently makes her children accountable for their learning and actions. She often gives them choices about their tasks and where they sit, stepping in only when the children cannot handle their responsibility. She may ask, "Do you think you should move to get your work done?" Disruptive children must apologize to the whole class. On specific days children complete their own daily time schedules. They plan their work for one or two open time slots for the day. They are responsible for their own progress. They regularly evaluate their progress through simple checklists and completions (I think I can do better in ...). They also give each other feedback. The teacher incorporates some cooperative tasks that encourage servanthood. They work with new mixed ability groups each month.

Susan Dick goes further than finding methods that teach content effectively. She thinks of her class in terms of her overall pedagogy. That is, she considers how she can best meet the needs of all children in her care. As she plans her curriculum, she thinks of herself as a mentor who guides and enables her children to take on life's tasks with knowledge, insight, skill, and commitment.

Why is it important to take into account how we shape and arrange learning when developing courses and units? How will a consideration of pedagogy affect the curriculum?

The Christian educator Comenius (1592–1670) already recognized that pedagogy and curriculum were closely intertwined. His concern for experiential learning led him, for instance, to be the first to use pictures in textbooks and ask questions about them. But 350 years later many curriculum planners still overlook pedagogy. Instead, they set down mainly the content or the cognitive skills that students must learn or the standards they must achieve. They leave it to learning theorists and teachers to determine how this is best done. What they forget is that pedagogy is not just a neutral funnel for dispensing content. Learning theorists frame and interpret their research on the basis of their beliefs about the nature of knowledge and human beings. Their research deals only with a small and possibly one-sided slice of the total complex of learning. Moreover, they may give some general guidelines for learning, but they cannot be prescriptive for specific classrooms, which always have distinctive dynamics.

Let me give two examples. Much more is known today than a generation ago about neuroscience and how the brain learns. We now know that the brain is a very complex collection of systems with different abilities. Neuroscience shows that there are sensitive age periods for developing specific abilities. It also indicates that our emotions play a large role in directing what we learn and remember. As Ronald Brandt and David Perkins conclude, "The findings help explain why students learn best from purposeful, meaningful experiences that engage their imagination and arouse their emotions" (Brandt 2000, 176). Long before he knew about brain research results, Brandt had already given similar advice to teachers. So this general result validates something that good teachers have always done. In fact,

research results are so limited and so complex that "we have little understanding of what [neuroscience] research might mean for education" (Bruer 1998, 18).

A second example is the use of computers as a learning tool in the classroom. Companies that have an interest in selling their products have funded much of the research. Of the objective research that does exist, "much of it documents no significant improvements in learning, and some actually shows a decline" (Healy 2000, 10). That is not to say that computers cannot be used meaningfully in the classroom. However, much of the available software does not lead to analysis and deep understanding. A program like PowerPoint used in conjunction with searches on the Internet may result in beautifully presented reports. But how much synthesis and evaluation have actually taken place? Too often we adopt technology without asking whether its use will reflect our view of knowing and learning. We may well conclude, as Jane Healy has put it, that with the way we currently use computers in schools children become "the tool of the tool" (p. 13).

Examples like these emphasize the importance of defining, understanding, and applying our own pedagogical framework as we plan our curriculum. Good teachers recognize that their pedagogy profoundly affects their curriculum-in-use. They take into consideration their knowledge of their children's backgrounds, emotional needs, learning styles, and developmental stages, as well as their classroom dynamics. Also, their perception of classroom interactions and situations (e.g., the nuances of verbal and body language) causes them to revise their plans constantly. Pedagogy involves much more than processing content efficiently (Max van Manen in Pinar 1988, 444).

Learning involves the whole person, the heart and the emotions as well as the mind. A biblical view of knowledge combined with a view of the person leads to conclusions that parallel what most researchers have concluded about the context of effective learning:

- An atmosphere of openness, trust, security, and warmth fosters successful learning. Students learn best from teachers who communicate care, acceptance, and a love for learning.
- Teachers who engage their class in coherent, purposeful, relevant, challenging, and imaginative learning affect students' attitudes and their quality of knowing positively—including what knowledge they are willing to consider, endorse, value, and apply.
- Initial personal exploration and meaningful personal response often lead to better motivation, retention, and meaningfulness.
- Students transfer their knowledge to new situations most frequently when teachers help them generalize and apply knowledge.

This chapter will consider how biblical views of the person and of knowledge affect how we look at learning and plan curriculum. After discussing a biblical view of the person, the chapter considers three broad topics:

- Learning styles and phases of learning
- Developmental layers and the importance of story
- Some implications of a Christian view of knowledge and the learner

Footstep 5-1

Two publications, published within two years of each other by the Association for Supervision and Curriculum Development, analyzed in detail what research shows about effective classroom pedagogy. They are Cotton's *Research You Can Use to Improve Results* (1999); and Marzano, Pickering, and Pollock's *Classroom Instruction That Works: Research-Based Strategies for Increasing Student Achievement* (2001). Below is a selection of conclusions and research results:

Results of Meta-Analyses of Research on Effective Pedagogy	
Cotton	**Marzano, Pickering, and Pollock**
• Use a preplanned curriculum with clear goals. • Provide strong leadership to guide the instructional program. • Interact with students in respectful and caring ways. • Emphasize the importance of learning and hold high expectations for student learning.	• Set clear but flexible goals (not too specific). • Have students generate and test hypotheses, and then explain their reasoning, preferably in writing. • Ask students to identify similarities and differences in things they learn (e.g., comparing, contrasting, classifying, suggesting metaphors, forming analogies).

Cotton	Marzano, Pickering, and Pollock
• Provide clear and focused instruction. • Integrate skills into content-area instruction. • Establish efficient classroom routines and clear discipline policies. • Monitor student progress closely and give frequent feedback about learning progress. • Use whole-group instruction when introducing new concepts and skills; use small groups as needed for short-term reinforcement and use of higher-level thinking skills. • Involve parents and community members in supporting children's learning.	• Encourage and help students to summarize and take notes. • Give students cues and advance organizers, ask relevant questions, and complement linguistic with nonlinguistic representations. • Provide adequate practice and homework with a clearly articulated purpose. • Reinforce student effort and provide recognition in terms of preset standards. • Use a reasonable amount of cooperative learning.

What are the similarities between the two lists? the differences? Why do you think there are substantial differences when both books claim they surveyed all the relevant research? Who appears to take a broader view of education? in what ways? Which vision do you prefer? Why? Note that both visions of education affect not only their interpretation of research results, but also which research results they consider to be relevant and significant. Even the sources quoted and used show only a limited amount of overlap! List some implications of this research for curriculum planning. (For a Christian analysis of how we learn, see Issler and Habermas 1994.)

A Biblical View of the Person As It Relates to Learning

As teachers we strive to be trustworthy guides and mentors for our students. We want to be present to our students in sensitive yet influential ways. We plan courses, units, and lessons so that students find learning meaningful. For this, we need to understand the implications of the nature of human beings for the classroom. (For more detail, see Van Brummelen 1998, 96–100.)

A biblical view of the person holds, first of all, that students are images of God. They stand in relationship to God as they reflect His image. A Christ-transformed relationship will lead them to live lives of loving service to God and their neighbors. They then image God as they carry out His injunctions. Students' heart commitments, whether to God or to other gods such as materialism or hedonism, affect their imaging, including their learning, attitudes, and values.

Thus a biblical view means that Christian teachers aim to foster commitment to God through both personal modeling and planned learning experiences. Students, like all of us, are sinful and will try to be independent of God and those in authority. Sometimes we cannot reach students no matter what we do; to do so would require a change of heart. However, the learning experiences we design can nurture mutual respect by showing that we recognize students' inherent dignity and worth. If we do this, most students will try to fulfill their tasks lovingly, responsively, and responsibly. In this way they will image God.

The Bible also makes clear that all people have unique gifts. All students are special, created with singular traits, gifts, and abilities that they unwrap in the classroom. We therefore plan diverse learning activities and encourage students to respond in unique ways. Thus learning becomes a personal occasion. It is rooted in students' own experiences. It involves telling stories, molding stories, transforming stories, and creating stories. It does so through thoughtfulness, playfulness, and creativity. Students develop their giftedness through different ways of knowing. Meaningful learning allows students to transcend content transmission and skill dexterity and to respond by developing, giving, and finding themselves.

God created all persons with unique gifts so that they can contribute to the welfare of those around them and enrich their communities. Classrooms must therefore be places where students learn to bear each other's burdens and share each other's joys, and where they learn to work together for the common good.

Teachers do need to stress personal relationships and opportunities for meaningful responsibilities. School can be a frustrating experience for students, especially adolescents. We ask them to learn things that do not seem relevant to them. We trust them with few meaningful tasks other than their own learning. Often the adults in their lives (including parents!) are too busy to develop meaningful relationships with them. A key principle is that our curriculum encourages

students to function as unique, responsive, and responsible images of God in a nurturing context.

👣 Footstep 5-2

Below, Margaret Barlow describes her experience of teaching *Pilgrim's Progress*. Explain how she has grasped what it means to regard her students as "images of God."

Frequently my teaching merely reflects the craftsmanship of my students, God's images. Our study of John Bunyan's *Pilgrim's Progress* exemplified this playful dynamic of our teaching-learning. I approached the work from an experiential framework, and from the onset, my students intervened lovingly and creatively.

After photocopying engravings from my personal copy of *Pilgrim's Progress*, my students were to interpret what they saw and to write in their response journals. Predictably, when students started to share what they had written, something happened. One moment they were reading, and the next they were up in front of the class using the transparency and explaining and pointing. The only directive I gave was that they had to support their ideas by showing us details in the picture and from the book. They were doing that anyway! The students commented readily on each other's responses. I watched, delighted, but no longer surprised. It is an honor to teach these precious beings.

The finale [of the unit] was an exam, which I said they were going to enjoy. Incredulous, they tried to extract its contents. I gave them only one hint: "Here are some giveaway marks. Make sure you know at least eight characters and eight places in the allegory." "That's easy," they smiled. I smiled.

The test was writing a short story about a student and a teacher meeting in a café to discuss *Pilgrim's Progress*. I indicated some topics to be discussed, but it was up to the students to create the story and the interpretations of the allegorical aspects of specific places and characters.

The test took just over two periods [over a matter of two days], which meant that by the second class, they would have been able to study further: "Oh, we know what's on the test!" Did it matter? Using a narrative format with expository overtones as they wrote their interpretations precluded the possibility of cheating. Quality of thinking when it exists transcends quantity of information. A well-crafted insight exudes intellectual integrity.

In the transcendence of storytelling, these students sit transfixed by their own knowledge and imagination, [using] both sides of the brain. They lose track of time. Affective, psychomotor, and cognitive aspects meld. Creativity reflects perhaps the quintessence of our former unfallenness, for, as God's images, we still create. God, our Creator, grants us merciful art.

This, then, is my cathedral. I sit and watch the students write. Ideas, like Impressionist tints, blur past, flowers of my garden.

Learning Styles and the Phases of Learning

After introducing the Renaissance, Leigh Bradfield gives his eighth-grade students three periods to complete an assignment on art and the Renaissance. They first study, either individually or in small groups, an untitled pre-Renaissance art picture. They answer ten questions (e.g., Is the person male or female? What expression is shown in the face? How would you improve this picture?). They then answer the same questions for a post-Renaissance painting that most have seen before, the Mona Lisa. *Next, the students use their answers and further research to draw three generalizations about art and the Renaissance. Afterwards, the teacher leads a class discussion and at the end tells students that the title of the first painting was* The Virgin at Prayer. *The class discusses whether there is anything specifically Christian about the* Mona Lisa, *and whether Christian artists necessarily paint Christian subjects.*

The students' initial exploration and the teacher's disclosure lead to students using vocabulary words in sentences that relate to their study. They then apply what they have learned by drawing a picture of a praying girl that shows characteristics of post-Renaissance art.

Bradfield gives several reasons why this learning activity is effective. It starts with an intriguing puzzle: What does that first picture portray? Students do much of the work themselves. There are no right and wrong interpretations. At the end, they respond personally and have a sense of accomplishment.

Note how the teacher deliberately plans for four phases of learning, each suitable for different types of learners. He sets the stage with open-ended exploration. The students' findings provide background for more formal disclosure through readings and class discussion. To show that they grasp the key ideas, the students reformulate them in writing using related vocabulary. Finally, they apply their learning in a personal way by drawing a picture that extends their learning.

To be a meaningful pedagogical presence to your students, you must care about them, and thus you will want to provide them with learning activities suitable for their various favored learning styles. It would not be practical to plan learning experiences for all styles in every lesson, nor would that be desirable. While all students should regularly have the opportunity to learn through their preferred style, at the same time, we need to stretch their learning style preferences so that they gradually become more flexible. We should be aware of our own learning style leanings so that we do not overemphasize those.

There are many ways to categorize learning styles. There are the left brain/right brain, sequential/random, and abstract/concrete distinctions. We also know that students may favor either visual, auditory, or kinesthetic means of learning. Some learners like to learn by themselves; others, in small groups. Some favor a certain temperature, a degree of sound and light, or a time of day. All show strengths in certain intelligences, or ways of knowing, with some authors melding these with learning styles (Silver, Strong, and Perini 2000). Learning styles are also affected by age, cultural background, and home environment. (For an overview of how to accommodate learning styles in the classroom, see, for instance, Guild and Garger 1998.)

You could choose one schema and apply it rigidly, neglecting all others. Or you could throw up your arms in despair at the complexity of it all. But a better alternative would be to relate learning styles based on psychological attributes to the natural rhythm of learning. Alfred North Whitehead (1929) described that rhythm in terms of romance, precision, and generalization. Doug Blomberg used the terms *immersion*, *withdrawal*, and *return* (Stronks and Blomberg 1993, 172ff). Maria Harris (1987, 43) preferred concrete experience, reflective observation, abstract conceptualization, and active experimentation.

Following is a summary of the four-phase model developed in *Walking with God in the Classroom* (Van Brummelen 1998, 109–20). This model takes into account the rhythm of learning and students' different learning styles, as well as a biblical view of the person and of knowledge. The summary incorporates the learning style categorization developed by Bernice McCarthy (1996, 1997). The model involves four phases of learning: setting the stage, disclosure, reformulation, and transcendence. Each phase is well suited (though not exclusively) to learners with a personality-based learning-style preference.

The four-phase model of learning intends to help you plan a balanced curriculum, one that acknowledges that both you and your students are responsible and responsive images of God. There is a natural rhythm as students grow in knowledge. Students need all four phases of learning for insightful, reflective, and committed response and action:

- **Setting the stage** or preparing, preferably based in real-life experience
- **Disclosure** or presenting a situation, problem, concept, or skill in a more formal way
- **Reformulation** or reinforcement through rephrasing, systematizing, representation, or practice
- **Transcendence** or responding to or applying learning in new, creative, and divergent ways and making personal choices and commitments

Each phase of learning lends itself to active involvement and response. The last one is called *transcendence* because there students go beyond what they have learned in earlier phases. During this phase students solve more complex and open-ended problems. They use their imagination and creativity, and develop discernment and wisdom.

112

Fig. 5.1 The Four Phases of Learning

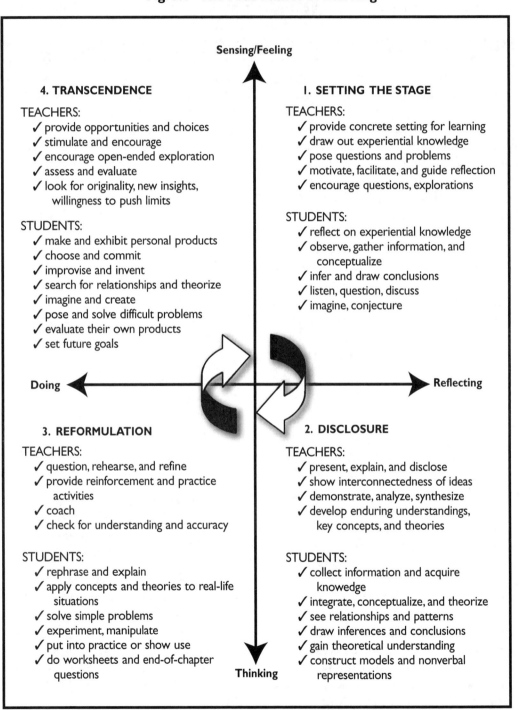

Sensing/Feeling

4. TRANSCENDENCE

TEACHERS:
- ✓ provide opportunities and choices
- ✓ stimulate and encourage
- ✓ encourage open-ended exploration
- ✓ assess and evaluate
- ✓ look for originality, new insights, willingness to push limits

STUDENTS:
- ✓ make and exhibit personal products
- ✓ choose and commit
- ✓ improvise and invent
- ✓ search for relationships and theorize
- ✓ imagine and create
- ✓ pose and solve difficult problems
- ✓ evaluate their own products
- ✓ set future goals

1. SETTING THE STAGE

TEACHERS:
- ✓ provide concrete setting for learning
- ✓ draw out experiential knowledge
- ✓ pose questions and problems
- ✓ motivate, facilitate, and guide reflection
- ✓ encourage questions, explorations

STUDENTS:
- ✓ reflect on experiential knowledge
- ✓ observe, gather information, and conceptualize
- ✓ infer and draw conclusions
- ✓ listen, question, discuss
- ✓ imagine, conjecture

Doing ← → **Reflecting**

3. REFORMULATION

TEACHERS:
- ✓ question, rehearse, and refine
- ✓ provide reinforcement and practice activities
- ✓ coach
- ✓ check for understanding and accuracy

STUDENTS:
- ✓ rephrase and explain
- ✓ apply concepts and theories to real-life situations
- ✓ solve simple problems
- ✓ experiment, manipulate
- ✓ put into practice or show use
- ✓ do worksheets and end-of-chapter questions

2. DISCLOSURE

TEACHERS:
- ✓ present, explain, and disclose
- ✓ show interconnectedness of ideas
- ✓ demonstrate, analyze, synthesize
- ✓ develop enduring understandings, key concepts, and theories

STUDENTS:
- ✓ collect information and acquire knowedge
- ✓ integrate, conceptualize, and theorize
- ✓ see relationships and patterns
- ✓ draw inferences and conclusions
- ✓ gain theoretical understanding
- ✓ construct models and nonverbal representations

Thinking

The transcendence phase may lead to new stage-setting situations or problems.

Despite a natural rhythm, the phases do not always follow each other sequentially. At the beginning of a unit, you may spend much time on stage-setting activities; at the end, on transcendence. In the middle of the unit, you may use just a few minutes to set the stage, with disclosure or reformulation making up the rest of the lesson. A tenth-grade geometry unit may contain more transcendence-type learning than one on simplifying polynomials. What is important is that each unit and most major activities include all four phases of learning.

The first phase of learning, **setting the stage,** makes use of students' experiential knowledge. It encourages students to enjoy, discover, imagine, brainstorm, ask questions, pose problems, search for relationships, and draw tentative conclusions. This phase of learning is a time for experiencing, exploring, and responding to immersion in real-life phenomena and imaginative cultural products. Students learn best when their own experience serves as a lead-in to more abstract knowledge. Sometimes that can be done by referring to students' own background and experience (asking, What do you know about ...?). At other times, a real-life situation may be used to give students the opportunity to experience a phenomenon and informally explore it. Teachers may pose a problem or ask students to pose problems about familiar situations. They then encourage students either to look at the situation in a fresh way as they extend the knowledge they already have, or to find solutions to the problems posed. This phase stimulates and prepares students to become involved in the more formal and abstract disclosure phase. It is important (particularly, but not solely) at the start of a unit.

Learners who are "intuitors" feel comfortable in this phase. They are the ones who need to experience a situation concretely. They examine and reflect on its aspects and related perspectives in order to seek meaning and draw conclusions. They benefit from personal involvement and social interaction as they go about their tasks. They learn by asking and answering why questions about their experiences and by reasoning inductively. They need their learning to be based on personal experience and on issues relevant for them.

The second phase of learning, **disclosure,** consists of precise, well-organized instruction. Teachers use the first phase of learning as a base for considering phenomena in a more focused and structured manner. They help students gain distance from everyday experience so that they can deepen their understanding and insight. Here teachers help students assimilate concepts, theories, and issues in structured ways. These can be oral and audiovisual presentations, penetrating questions, demonstrations, class discussions, small-group tutoring by the teacher or fellow students, or focused readings. Disclosure-type learning is sometimes difficult and even onerous, particularly when it is cumulative or requires deeper analysis. What makes it worthwhile for students is that they can see that the knowledge they gain is grounded in and useful for everyday situations and that it also expands their horizons.

Analytic learners delight and excel in the disclosure phase of learning. They prefer to perceive information abstractly and process it reflectively. They relish detailed, precise knowledge. They learn by asking information questions (what?) and by reasoning things out. They are interested in gathering, classifying, analyzing, and critiquing concepts, theories, and ideas. They find satisfaction in thinking through problems and issues, and determining the validity of hypotheses and conclusions.

In the third phase of learning, **reformulation**, students demonstrate that they can understand, interpret, and use what they learned in the disclosure phase. In this phase, teachers ask interpretation and inference questions. They ask students to explain what they have learned and to use it in simple applications. They use textbook questions, worksheets, journal responses, and various assignments to reinforce and sharpen what has been learned. Often teachers intersperse reformulation questions and activities with their disclosure.

Students who are implementers appreciate this phase of learning. They perceive information abstractly and process it actively. They are the ones who like to do well-defined, focused tasks, including drill and hands-on activities. They want to try ways of using the concepts they have learned. They want to be actively engaged individually or in small groups. They learn by asking, How do I do this? and by using step-by-step procedures to solve problems. They make the material their own through reformulation activities, adding something of their own and using the concepts in personal ways. If something works, they want to apply it, particularly in situations that they deem useful.

In the final phase, **transcendence**, students move beyond reformulation. Here conceptual knowledge and practical application lead to reflective and innovative response. Students apply concepts and principles in unique and, for them, original ways. They develop personally meaningful products and choose responses that affect their lives. They commit themselves to certain values and courses of action. They explore questions about the personal meaning of what

they have learned. They share in choosing, planning, and exhibiting their responses. Expressive representations and creative investigations may create new ways of seeing and responding to God's world.

Learners who are innovators do well in this phase. They perceive information concretely and process it dynamically. They like to make things happen, seeking out possibilities for themselves. They use and apply what they have learned in creative and imaginative ways. They learn by asking and answering, What if I try this? and finding out by trial and error. They enrich reality by animatedly trying out new possibilities. They take initiatives and risks, developing ideas on their own.

No learners, of course, fit any one learning-style category precisely, but most are stronger in one or two than in the others. Using the rhythm of the phases helps you maintain curricular balance. You will over-emphasize neither narrow academic content nor personal meaning-making. Students gain knowledge and respond by generalizing and applying it. Pedagogically it is wise, therefore, to plan activities for all four types of learners, in all four phases of learning.

Footstep 5-3

The following are two examples of lessons that used the foregoing model. What are the strengths and possible pitfalls of each?

"I Am a Canadian, Grade 7–8" (Arden Post, unpublished): The focus of this lesson is that being a citizen of Canada secures freedoms and demands responsibilities. For setting the stage, small groups brainstorm the meanings of *citizen, citizenship, responsibility,* and *privilege.* For disclosure, group members read handouts entitled "The Rights and Privileges of Citizenship" and "The Responsibilities of Citizenship." For reformulation, the groups discuss and list on a worksheet four rights and privileges, and then four responsibilities. The group leader assigns one right and one responsibility to each group member. They take a few minutes to write individually what that particular right means and how they can carry out the responsibility. After sharing what they have written, the group selects one responsibility and makes a plan to carry it out or to help others carry it out (transcendence).

"Key Themes in the Scriptures, Grade 9–10" (Ontario Alliance of Christian Schools 1994, 31–35): The focus of these two lessons is to identify and explore four key themes running through Scripture, [namely], the Kingdom of God, the covenant by which God relates to His people, the antithesis between the Kingdom of God and that of Satan, and the history of redemption focusing on the cross of Jesus Christ. For setting the stage, teachers ask how students would envision an ideal world. They ask them to compare their responses with the first and last two chapters of the Bible. They then discuss the reality of our world, why bad and good things happen in our lives, and why tension exists. For disclosure, the teacher presents information about the four key themes, discussing how these apply to everyday situations. For reformulation, the students complete a chart on an activity sheet outlining different types of covenants. For transcendence, students create a collage, design a symbol, draw a picture, or write a play or poem to show how they as adolescents experience the antithesis between the Kingdom of God and the kingdom of Satan at home, school, work, and play.

Layers of Development

Footstep 5-4

You may be able to teach some unit topics successfully at various grade levels as long as you consider students' developmental levels. Discuss how you could teach a unit on China (or another culture) at the first-, sixth-, and eleventh-grade levels. How would the units differ? Are there any themes or objectives that would be the same? If so, how would your learning activities differ? Can any science or social studies topic be taught effectively at any grade level as long as you adapt the learning to that level? Why or why not?

Persons move through different developmental stages as they mature. Some of the learning strategies that my spouse uses with five-year-old kindergartners would not be appropriate for a course I teach at the master's level—and vice versa. Psychologists and educators have described different developmental phases and their implications for learning.

Psychologist Erik Erikson, for instance, describes eight psychosocial stages, each of which builds on the previous one (Parkay and Hass 2000, 122ff). Erikson's stages do not follow a fixed formula. Maturation differs from one person to the next. Nevertheless, Erikson's stages give a general psychosocial backdrop for school curriculum. Three of Erikson's stages suggest several broad curriculum guidelines (see figure 5.2).

You may be more familiar with Piaget's stages than you are with Erikson's. Piaget's preoperational (1.5–7 years), concrete operational (7–11), and formal operational (12+) stages focus narrowly on the development of rational thought. Piaget's followers address mainly the development of logical thinking in the curriculum. Often they neglect the fact that nonanalytic types of learning are not only meaningful and enriching but also prepare students for more formal deductive thinking later (Egan 1986, 22–23). Young children can understand abstract concepts when we present them in concrete settings such as stories. Piaget's work is important in understanding how children develop their rational thought processes. But its application to school learning is limited mainly to the rational or logical mode of knowing.

Egan's Primary Layer of Understanding

More helpful for school curriculum planning than Piaget's stages are three of Kieran Egan's *layers of understanding* (Egan 1988, 1990, 1997; see figure 5.3):

- **Primary** (or mythic) understanding (up to nine years old)
- **Romantic** understanding (ages 8–15)
- **Philosophic** understanding (ages 14–19)

Egan uses the term "layers" rather than "stages," since students accumulate one layer on top of the previous one. The new layer does not replace the previous one but coalesces with it, giving deepened understanding and insight.

Fig. 5.2 Erikson's Stages of Psychosocial Development		
Stage (age range)	**Basic Characteristic**	**Curriculum Implications**
Initiative (3 to 6 years)	Children become more assertive and take more initiative, but their forcefulness may have to be channeled.	When children enter school, they are in a period of vigor, enterprise, and imagination. They need to explore and discover, to open up their world, to learn from structured play. They benefit from varied and stimulating learning centers.
Industry and Accomplishment (6 to 12 years)	Children learn knowledge and skills rapidly but may be bothered by a sense of inferiority or incompetence if they fail.	Students enter a stage of industry in which they appreciate executing and completing tasks. In this stage, securing real achievement is important. Learning should help them develop a sense of accomplishment. This is the time when students are ready and often eager to learn many basic skills and concepts.
Identity (11 to 17 years)	Teenagers achieve personal identity in gender relations, sports, intellectual success, occupation, religion, and others.	When students reach adolescence, what becomes particularly important is that classrooms allow students to establish and maintain a sense of identity. Often this is not an easy time. Here teachers continually try to balance the personal identity needs of teens with the need to keep their classroom functioning as a unit.

In early childhood, Egan (1988) argues, students take their surroundings for granted. It is difficult for them to "take enough distance" to deal intellectually with topics such as their families or neighbor-hoods. While their learning should focus on basic concepts that make life meaningful, they do so most effectively through knowledge that expands their horizons. What intrigues them at this age is the distant, the remote, and the imagined.

Moreover, education for young children is a serious adventure. Too often we trivialize it. When we design curriculum, meaning must be foremost in our minds. Children already know about joy and fear, hope and disappointment, and love and cruelty before they can perform concrete skills like riding a bicycle or skating. We need to teach fundamental meanings that help children make sense of their world. Children discover themselves, paradoxically, by focusing outward on the world and others.

The medium that allows this to happen is the story, Egan continues. Children can understand abstract concepts and causality within the context of stories. The story is the best tool we have to communicate meaning and values. It blends events into a powerful unit that evokes children's affective as well as intellectual responses. The story carries forward real and imaginative possibilities that develop a sense of wonder and awe. It can give children intellectual and emotional security. Within the context of the story, children can understand the role in life of abstract concepts like power, ambition, greed, and punishment. The curriculum at this level is more a set of great stories to be told than objectives to be attained, according to Egan. The story needs prominence because it is fundamental to our thinking. It precedes literal reflection and the development of theories.

What does this mean for curriculum in the early grades? It means that teachers need to be the principal storytellers of our culture, for instance, telling the great stories of history and science. They tell (not just read to) children the powerful, dramatic, and great stories, including the Bible stories that recount the story of God's dealing with His people. But more than that, teachers are to make units and lessons accessible and meaningful to children by using the main features of the story in their planning. In other words, teachers should design all units at this level so that they tell a meaningful story (Egan 1986, 1988, 1997).

To do so effectively requires five steps (Egan 1988; 1997, 245–51; see also Egan's website at <www.educ.sfu.ca/people/faculty/kegan> for his planning frameworks):

1. **Identify what is important and affectively engaging about a topic.** Don't underestimate or patronize children. A first-grade unit on Mexican culture may be more significant—and fascinating—than one on children's own neighborhoods.

2. **Find binary opposites that best express and articulate the importance of the topic.** Egan points out that children see issues in terms of opposites such as good and bad, love and hate, courage and cowardice, security and fear, and so on. (From a strictly logical point of view, the opposites contrast but may not be antonyms.) Egan (1988, 118, 234ff) gives many examples of binary opposites that will add dramatic tension to a topic: destroyer/helper (unit on heat); survival/destruction (North American Indians); practical visionary/conventionalist (flight); dominance/submission (our city); ingenuity/conventional dullness

(subtraction); and freedom/tyranny (the Greeks and Persians). For a unit on Mexico, the opposites might be scarcity/plenty. Units can also embody the basic antithesis of the Bible: the Kingdom of God (good) versus the kingdom of Satan (evil).

3. **Use the binary opposites to develop a story that reflects human hopes, fears, motives, dispositions, and beliefs.** Choose content that dramatically develops the opposites in story form, with a conflict or problem that is fleshed out as the unit progresses.

4. **Resolve the dramatic conflict inherent in the opposites at the end of the unit.** Such a conclusion reveals something that deepens children's insight into the topic.

5. **Evaluate whether the children grasped the unit's importance and learned its content.** Egan suggests looking at the amount of continuous time children spend engaged in a project, the kinds of questions and comments they make, the competence and originality of their representations, and so on (Egan 1997, 250).

Developing curriculum for primary children in this way helps us not to sell them short. We can teach children much about the meaning and purpose of life as long as we do so within a concrete story setting. We may question whether it is always possible or even desirable to teach all topics at this level as a story that resolves binary opposites. True, some topics do not easily fit this pattern. Nevertheless, Egan's approach is a powerful one that we can often use effectively. Thomas Groome (1980) and John Bolt (1993) also describe the importance of the shared story in passing on our cultural memory, wisdom, and vision.

Egan's Romantic Layer of Understanding

Egan's next layer of understanding is the romantic one (ages eight to fifteen). He uses the term *romantic* because now a desire for adventure, imagination, and idealism often governs students. They enthusiastically explore the world and their experience in it. They are fervent in their quest for knowing about the extreme, the exotic, and the distant. Detailed factuality and explanations of how things happen fascinate them. They like lists, tables, and formulas. They want to know about other ways of living, both past and present, about the technology of familiar things, and about animal and plant life—especially if these involve the dramatic and unexpected. Teachers continue to stimulate wonder and awe, but now more by making the familiar strange (Egan 1990, 1997).

Gradually a more technical, nonnarrative form of teaching becomes possible. But narrative involving a powerful affective component is still important. The central role of the binary opposite story gives way, however, to broader narratives that deepen students' understanding of the meaning and purpose of life. Students develop a rational grasp of details and particulars within a narrative context. Transcendent human values such as goodness, vigor, resilience, and ingenuity replace binary opposites as the unifying threads for teaching topics. Units now focus on human motives, intentions, and emotions. Through concrete and disparate examples of ideas, students learn about justice, love, courage, grief, patience, authority, beauty, and altruism. During this layer we stimulate both imaginative and literal thinking (Egan 1990).

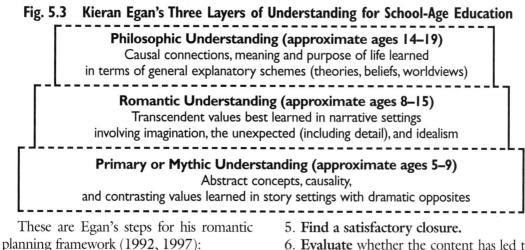

Fig. 5.3   Kieran Egan's Three Layers of Understanding for School-Age Education

Philosophic Understanding (approximate ages 14–19)
Causal connections, meaning and purpose of life learned
in terms of general explanatory schemes (theories, beliefs, worldviews)

Romantic Understanding (approximate ages 8–15)
Transcendent values best learned in narrative settings
involving imagination, the unexpected (including detail), and idealism

Primary or Mythic Understanding (approximate ages 5–9)
Abstract concepts, causality,
and contrasting values learned in story settings with dramatic opposites

These are Egan's steps for his romantic planning framework (1992, 1997):

1. **Consider which transcendent human values are central to a topic** and can evoke emotional engagement and imagination. Egan (1992, 120ff) suggests, for instance, teaching about geometry in terms of practical ingenuity; trees in terms of their faithful support of civilizations; government in terms of courage and generosity of spirit. Choose values that reflect what you believe to be important. For instance, you may prefer to study trees in terms of God's faithful provision for life on Earth.

2. **Choose content that stimulates romance, wonder, and awe about reality.** Seek out something that embodies the chosen transcendent values and is wonderful, vivid, strange, or extreme.

3. **Organize content into a narrative structure that shows human intentions, hopes, fears, and other emotions.** The human interest angle is important at this age.

4. **Ensure that students can pursue some aspect of the topic in exhaustive detail.** Stimulate their imaginations and encourage them to see the topic in a wider context.

5. **Find a satisfactory closure.**

6. **Evaluate** whether the content has led to students' understanding of the topic and the transcendent values, and whether it has stimulated students' imagination.

When using Egan's romantic unit planning framework, remember his two main points:

• The detail and skill learning of the romantic layer needs to support learning about significant values.

• Units can often be developed best through a narrative approach, although the role of narrative is now less central than the story form was for younger children.

Egan's Philosophic Layer of Understanding

The third layer of understanding Egan calls "philosophic understanding" (ages 14–19). Here students realize that all knowledge of the world and our experience is connected and that they are part of a historical process. They want to understand and develop causal chains and networks. They redirect their intellectual attention from detail to general concepts in culture. They become interested in general questions of religion, anthropology, politics, economics, and psychology. They search for truth about how society functions and their role within the world. They are now ready to focus much more on general schemas and ideologies (Egan 1990, 176 ff; 1997, 104–36).

Again, this layer does not replace the previous two. Students are still interested in the story. Reaching philosophic understanding does not negate the fact that the story of the holocaust or the discovery of non-Euclidean geometry still captivates students' interest. Narrative is powerful in all layers. But at the philosophic layer, students move beyond narrative for the sake of the story, move beyond detail into drawing general conclusions. They want to explore and understand what caused these happenings. As teachers we now focus our planning on underlying questions and issues. We help students explore and draw conclusions about the meaning of knowledge for their personal lives and life in society.

Egan's planning framework for this layer has six steps (1997, 264–75):

1. **Identify relevant general schemes.** Choose schemes that organize the topic into a unified whole using relevant theories and ideologies.
2. **Organize the content into a general scheme.** Choose content that shows the power of the general scheme.
3. **Introduce anomalies to the general scheme.** Challenge the students to deepen their discernment and both question and sharpen their own general interpretive framework.
4. **Present alternative general schemes.** For example, present not only Christian but also Marxist and liberal interpretations of history.

5. **Conclude** by leading students to recognize how defensible general schemes can lead to a sophisticated understanding of a topic.
6. **Evaluate** whether students have understood the content and have developed a defensible general scheme.

A Curriculum Example

Egan's insights show that it is possible for students of all ages to gain insight into important values and worldviews—as long as we take into consideration the different approaches appropriate for different age groups. The conclusion of this section will briefly show how this can be done for the topic of transportation.

For the primary level of understanding (say, six-year-olds), first ask what is important about transportation. In our world, we cannot be self-sufficient. Therefore, we need ways to move ourselves and our resources from one place to another. Without practical, effective transport, we would have far fewer conveniences and would lead lonelier lives. Several possible binary opposite pairs come to mind: slow-fast, fear-hope, tradition-change, constraint-freedom, and immobility-mobility.

If you choose the immobility-mobility contrast, construct the unit around the story of people searching for more mobility as they looked for food and other resources. The story of Abraham shows how animals at first helped people move from one location to another. Ships and wagons made settlement possible for the pioneers. Trains, cars, and airplanes allow us to get from one place to another very quickly and use products from around the world. At the same time, such mobility has created problems: pollution, less neighborliness, and more crime. Use books and stories that tell parts of this story. In your learning centers, let children experience and explore various means of transportation. Conclude the unit by considering how people can use transportation to build community in responsible ways.

For the romantic layer of understanding (say, age eleven), first identify the transcendent values central to transportation. Again, several come to mind: human curiosity and inventiveness, economic stewardship, and the need for governments to maintain peace and order and a sense of national identity. A unit could have economic stewardship (and its lack) as its main focus, with the other values playing a supporting role. In Canadian schools, the building of the first transcontinental railroad could provide the central narrative structure. A story of high drama, it involved the clash of native, Western, and Chinese ways of life, human ingenuity in overcoming the obstacles of muskeg and mountain, the development of rich farmland (but not without questionable land accumulation and speculation), and governments wanting to prevent an American takeover as well as to quash rebellions. The railroad can be shown as Prime Minister Macdonald's "national dream," culminating with his wife riding on the locomotive's cowcatcher through the Rocky Mountains soon after the railroad's completion in 1886.

While the main narrative of the unit is the building of the Canadian Pacific Railway, the unit would be broader in scope. Some students could investigate the building of other famous railroads. Others may want to trace the development and impact of the automobile or airplane. The focus of such investigations could continue to be how such inventions and innovations originated in human curiosity and ingenuity, with their development spurred by both positive and negative economic factors. At the end, students could draw conclusions about the positive and negative impact of today's transportation on our communities and on the world.

Transportation taught at the philosophic level would take a different approach. Now the students may consider the transportation infrastructure of their nation or compare that of their nation with a very different region of the world. Students could still investigate the specifics of transportation systems, but would use them to consider the underlying issues: In what ways do our lives depend on our transportation systems? What is the impact of the car on our communities and on our way of life? Transportation and communication have led to a "global village." What are the positive and negative effects? Which modes of transportation will become less or more important in the future? Why? A theme needs to give focus to such explorations. One possible theme is the use of transportation expertise to build more humane, caring, responsible communities. At the same time, students should explore different interpretative schemes about transportation and develop their own. For instance, airline executives, business people, ecological proponents, and groups like the Amish look at today's transportation systems very differently.

Note that learning in all three layers of understanding helps students consider and understand worldview and value questions. But the way we go about this changes as students mature. In the early years, we may juxtapose value-related binary opposites within stories and within units that have a strong story line. From ages eight or nine to fourteen or fifteen, we consider what Egan calls transcendent human values. We may build our units around such values, using narrative structures as a context for factual, technical, and imaginative explorations. During the philosophic years, we emphasize how causal relationships and interpretive frameworks inform the meaning and purpose of life. What Egan's work shows is that when our curriculum planning takes into account his three developmental layers, our teaching and learning can help students become committed to a meaningful and principled way of life, no matter what their level of maturity.

Footstep 5-5

Go back to the unit you discussed at the beginning of this section (footstep 5-4). In view of Erikson's and Egan's claims about developmental levels, what changes, if any, would you make in your plans for the unit at each of the three grade levels?

Knowledge, the Learner, and Curriculum Planning

If there were just one conclusion for curriculum planning that we draw from a biblical view of knowledge and people, it would be this: **The curriculum must take into account that students, as unique images of God, need opportunities to learn and respond to what they learn in personally meaningful ways.** This section discusses some practical ways to make this statement a classroom reality.

Differentiating Learning

The strategy of differentiated instruction is not a new one; teachers of one-room schools practiced it all the time. A differentiated curriculum allows for tasks of varying complexity and different learning rates. Teachers, of course, ensure that all students learn key concepts and skills. However, they push students

to maximize their capacities, especially in the reformulation and transcendence phases of learning. Differentiation is a refinement of a well-planned curriculum. It enables some students to reinforce knowledge or skills, while others expand their insights, interests, and experiences. It is also a way in which teachers can help students to assume more responsibility for their learning by providing learning activity options—and asking students to reflect on and justify their choices.

If you have little experience with differentiating learning, start small and gradually increase the learning options you provide. Be clear about the essence of what students must learn about a topic. Then adjust content, learning activities, and expected products in response to student readiness, learning styles, and preferred ways of knowing. Here are some examples of differentiating the curriculum:

- During their center time, kindergartners are free to choose the center at which they work. They must work at the writing center at least once a week, with a variety of other activities provided that suit personal readiness.

- As part of a fourth-grade poetry unit, students have to complete twelve items on one of two contract sheets. The headings of each item are identical, but the activities on the second sheet are for students ready for more advanced work. For instance, under the heading "Interpret," both sheets list titles of poems about poetry, but the poem on the first sheet is more concrete. Three of the items are left blank for students' own choice of activity. At the end, each student selects two of the twelve products to become part of a class book on poetry (Tomlinson 1999, 87–91).

- For two weeks during a seventh-grade unit on ancient Greece, students rotate among five learning centers. At some centers they work in small groups. At others, however, they work on individual tasks, choosing from three or four possibilities. On a sheet available at the center, the students first justify their choice of activity and set specific goals for completing it. At the end of the two days at the center, they use the same sheet to assess how and to what extent they have met their goals.

- In an eleventh-grade mathematics unit on conic sections, the more advanced students in the class substitute solving more difficult problems for some of the reinforcement ones done by the rest of the class. The unit ends with a collection of application problems in topics such as space orbits and architecture. Students work in ability-based small groups. Depending on their level of proficiency, they may tackle all problems or choose to do only two and use the rest of the time for structured peer tutoring that reviews basic unit concepts.

Learning Through Personal Response

A biblical view of knowledge calls for personal response. In the classroom, all four phases of learning elicit response from students. But the transcendence phase especially animates unique, formative response. Here students use their knowledge, thought, skills, and creativity to extend what they have learned. They make personal choices and act on personal values and commitments.

To do so requires, however, that we engage students through all four phases of learning. In particular, meaningful response demands that students have had precise, structured conceptual and skill instruction as well as adequate reinforcement and drill in phases two and three of learning. Students need to know how to calculate percentages, how to use a microscope, how to construct a logical argument, how to write a coherent paragraph, and so on. Only then will they be able to respond competently, discerningly, and creatively as they apply their knowledge in what for them are new settings.

How can you plan curriculum to foster meaningful response? Here are some suggestions:

- **Address the needs and understandings of your students in their particular context and allow honest response.** Jesus lovingly, but with conviction, addressed the needs of people. He did not force His views on His listeners; their response had to be genuine. He sought to influence but not to coerce or manipulate.

- **Demonstrate that each unit's learning is relevant for your students.** Encourage them to relate learning to their lives by thinking critically or creatively in application contexts and by solving related problems (Good and Brophy 1994, 425–26).

- **Include class activities that evoke wonder and surprise. Support different, open-ended, original forms of expression and products,** particularly during the transcendence phase of learning.

- **Involve the students in reflecting on and then choosing at least some unit content.** For this, you can use the K-W-L strategy: what I **K**now or think I know; what I **W**ant to learn; and, at the end, what I **L**earned (some teachers add **H**— **H**ow shall we find out?). If done in a teacher-led group activity, you can help your students categorize what they know and address misconceptions. You can also make the students' prior and experiential knowledge a springboard for further learning.

- **Plan the activities so that students have some choice and alternatives**, especially with respect to their responses. You can do this, for example, through learning centers, and through individual and group assignments and projects that allow options.

Footstep 5-6

Marian Piekema gives all her first-grade children specific tasks and expects all to make a contribution. In her introductory unit on the school, her class interviews all members of the school's support staff, asking, "In what way can we help you?" After telling Bible stories she asks, "Is there anything you wonder about?" Her children often bring up and talk about issues of life and death, heaven and hell, and so on.

In a unit on seeds, the teacher emphasizes the theme that the cycle of life is God's plan, a plan that gives us a task. She includes many open-ended personal response activities: art and painting, making models of flowers and bees and posters for recycle boxes, journal writing about observation of seeds or reaction to music, and so on. She also capitalizes on teachable moments. For instance, one time her class wrote a letter to the school custodian about sand that they had tracked into the classroom.

While the children's personal response nurtures their growth in attitudes and values, one question still troubles Piekema. Genuine personal response, she believes, is

important. Yet particularly at this level, she finds it difficult not to impose the response that she would like to see as a teacher. How do you strike a balance between eliciting genuine personal response and guiding students to responding as contributing members of the classroom learning community? Discuss this question for the age levels you teach or plan to teach.

Strategies for Intentional Knowing

The fact that knowledge involves active engagement and response is validated by the superior learning that students show when they use **metacognition**. This means that they are aware of and control their own thinking behavior. Students use purposeful strategies rather than just completing tasks. They analyze how they engage in learning, and they use problem-solving strategies deliberately. To foster metacognition, we lead students to ask themselves how they learn:

- What did you do to get started?
- How did you find what you needed to solve the problem?
- What steps did you take to make progress?
- How did you cope when you got stuck or became frustrated?
- What are some of the things you are doing to help you be successful in doing science activities? in learning social studies?
- How do you know you're correct?

To encourage such reflection, you should:

- **Teach students to set their own objectives and evaluate their own understanding and progress.** Robin Fogarty

(1994, 19) suggests giving students a two-column sheet entitled "My Reflection." In the first column students explain what they actually did, and in the second they reflect on the pluses and minuses of how they went about the activity.

- **Spur students to judge what is important and to identify their strengths and weaknesses**. Avoid the tendency to do these things for them.
- **Suggest strategies for self-regulation in learning**. Together with your students, develop lists of criteria to help them assess their own progress in integrated units as well as in reading, writing, and mathematics problem-solving skills. In writing, for instance, help students develop strategies and criteria for planning, actual writing, reviewing, and revising.
- **Give students opportunities to pose and solve problems in specific subjects** (problem-solving abilities seldom transfer from one subject area to another). Encourage them to pay attention to general strategies, not just to find the answer. Help students develop the ability and tendency to set goals, ask thought-provoking questions, evaluate their own approaches and understanding, and learn from both their successes and failures (Bereiter and Scardamalia in Jackson 1992, 533; Good and Brophy 1994, 245–47).

Let me give an example that high school teacher Janet Hitchcock related to me. She had seen a teacher explain how to find the area of the figure shown. The teacher divided the figure into two rectangles (see broken line), and then worked out the area as follows:

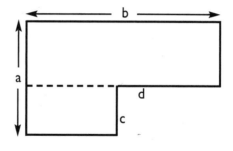

$$\begin{aligned} \text{Area} &= b(a - c) + c(b - d) \\ &= ba - bc + cb - cd \\ &= ba - cd \end{aligned}$$

The teacher had shown how to get the correct answer. A more productive approach, said Hitchcock, would be to ask the students to discover as many different ways of finding the solution as they could. At least the teacher should have asked why the answer turned out to be an unexpectedly simple one. What is the explanation? Could we have found the answer in a different way? How can you apply what you have learned? Solving knowledge problems becomes more meaningful when students learn to ask questions that go beyond finding a mechanical procedure that quickly yields the answer.

Exhibiting Learning

If students do not use their knowledge, it is inert. Theodore Sizer (1992, 24–27) therefore suggests that students regularly exhibit the products of their learning. Such exhibitions give students an incentive. They enable students to use their learning to convince others. They provide a focus for the school's program and purpose. They help students develop habits of thoughtfulness and responsibility. They also serve as affirmations for students and the school community that the learning has paid off. Audiences may include classmates, other classes, and parents. Exhibits may include:

- Presentations about personal yet universal issues that cut across traditional subject lines. At the middle and high school levels, these would include projects that demonstrate distinctively Christian approaches to a topic.
- Portfolio or poster displays with written or oral explanations, demonstrations, and performances.
- Subject-centered exhibits such as science fairs, art exhibits, music performances, creative-writing presentations, gymnastic displays, or three-dimensional geometry models.

Learning Through Service

Service learning can be a valuable part of the curriculum. Here students respond to knowledge by applying what they have learned. Service learning opportunities can be authentic experiences in which students develop communication, problem-solving, and leadership skills. Students who may not do well in the classroom show and develop surprising ingenuity, motivation, and responsibility (Diamond 1993; Willis 1993; Woehrle 1993).

To plan effective service learning opportunities, you should include four components: preparation, action, reflection, and celebration. Coordinate service learning with your curriculum units. Encourage students to pose questions that they want to answer. At higher grade levels ask students to research the context in which they will find themselves. The service experience itself then leads students to reflect on their questions and their initial findings. They discuss and write about how society deals with related issues. They consider their role in promoting compassion, justice, and integrity. They develop a sense of responsibility. They begin to ask what they can do to make a difference.

Examples of service learning include:

- Being peer tutors or buddies to younger children. For example, fifth-graders can help kindergartners complete learning logs (answering such questions as, What I enjoyed doing this week, and What I would like to do next week). The kindergartners can dictate descriptions about their drawings while their buddies write them down.
- In science, setting up recycling projects, maintaining a bird sanctuary, planting bulbs or trees, or raising salmon fry for release into a river while monitoring the river's water quality.
- In social studies, advocating certain political decisions or actions, or participating in hunger awareness events.
- In physical education, supervising games, or organizing activities for the physically or mentally challenged.
- Volunteering in hospitals and homes for the elderly. Young children can "adopt" a grandparent and read to him or her, sing songs, and share what's happening in their lives.
- Making art for a homeless shelter or senior citizens home.
- Writing letters to editors or leaders in society.
- Holding clothing and food drives for the disadvantaged or helping in a food kitchen for an integrated unit, such as Am I My Neighbor's Keeper?
- Volunteering service in a developing country. High school students can help build homes or schools as well as be involved in storytelling and drama outreach projects.

Learning in Community

Loving and faithful relationships are a pre-requisite for meaningful learning. Children need to be trusted and feel accepted. They need to know that people around them care for them, give them meaningful responsibilities, and at the same time hold them accountable. They need to sense that they are part of a community where people have pledged themselves to each other as they work toward a common goal. Below are two examples of how a school and a teacher plan their curriculum to have students experience what it means to live and learn in a supportive community:

- *Linda Samland's school emphasizes how humans share insights, gifts, and resources, and thus care for each other in community. Devotions and communal prayer begin each day. Cooperative classroom and assembly activities contribute to the school's being a caring community, as do special activities such as holding a cookie sale to buy Christmas gifts for poor people in the community. The choice of unit themes reflects this concern. A unit on building, for instance, explores how we work together to erect buildings, but more than that, how this shapes lives in community. The school helps students see how God calls them as persons with special gifts to be important "puzzle pieces" in the Body of Christ and in society. All units provide activities suited for diverse learning styles and for students with a spectrum of abilities.*

- *Hugo Vanderhoek uses a collaborative approach in his sixth-grade language arts/art unit on comics. He applies, for instance, the jigsaw technique by which students first learn the features of different types of comics in an expert group. They then report back to their home group. Each student has a specific role as he or she works in a group: checker for understanding, encourager, recorder, taskmaster, gatekeeper, reporter, or gofer. The students depend on each other but are also individually accountable for completing assignments. They are carefully taught the necessary skills for working effectively as a group. Vanderhoek also explains and monitors how to check for understanding and how to listen attentively. Each group gets cards with suggestions: make eye contact; ask questions such as, Will you explain? What does that mean? or What were your reasons? In the debriefing the teacher not only sums up the main content points but also reviews how the groups implemented these skills.*

Schools must help students realize how functioning as trustworthy individuals depends on being constructive community members. Indeed, it is self-worship to think that it is possible to be autonomous. God created us in relationship with Him and with other creatures. We are interdependent. We need each other. Communities function only if we strive to be responsible and respectful. We enrich (as well as bruise) each other's lives. We are part of communities that share common understandings and beliefs.

It is therefore important that schools function as communities that have a clear moral vision and that they adjust their structures and daily routines to reflect their values and goals. Schools also know that as "communities of memory," they need to tell the story of the community within its cultural setting. Retelling, together with honest assessment, leads to a common understanding. This, in turn, allows students to see themselves as cultural-social beings who realize that public good sometimes overrides personal short-term gain and may even require self-sacrifice (Bowers 1987, 138–43).

Christian school classrooms strive to function as covenant communities. That is, they "foster an environment in which students and teachers take delight in being with each other and build relationships based on a general desire to be with and for others" (Stronks and Blomberg 1993, 110). Such communities do not promote and celebrate individual accomplishment as the sole standard of success. Nor do they sacrifice individuality on the altar of the corporate good. Instead, their shared vision charts a framework within which students are free to carry out their personal role by unwrapping their individual gifts. Teachers and students accept and support each other in their respective tasks. Classroom communities with an atmosphere of mutual concern and trust are ones where children learn to accept and use their abilities in relation to themselves and others. There they experience the joys and difficulties of working unitedly toward common goals. There they encourage each other to exhibit the fruit of the Spirit: love, joy, peace, patience, kindness, goodness, faithfulness, gentleness, and self-control. There students and teachers share their gifts so that others may be blessed.

We will never reach this ideal, of course. But we can work toward it as we plan curriculum. Christian schools will make learning-focused classroom devotions, chapel, and assemblies an integral part of their curriculum. They will plan activities in which students help each other. They will plan to include cooperative learning on a regular basis. They will plan ways to include challenged or minority students so that all students feel enriched by their presence.

They will avoid ability grouping and streaming that destroys community. Instead, classroom groups will be, as much as possible, heterogeneous and flexible. They will design units for classes with a wide spectrum of abilities so that all students learn a basic core but also have optional activities that cater to differences in abilities. They will also choose unit topics that shed special light on what it means to live in community.

Footstep 5-7

Consider the following situations:

- A city has to decide where to put a new garbage dump.
- A family has to decide whether to buy a larger home. To do so, they would have to cut back on leisure spending and charitable donations.
- A government has to decide whether to spend two million dollars on advanced hospital equipment that will save twenty lives per year, or use the funds to launch a preventive health program that, in the long run, will save tens of millions of dollars.
- A friendship breaks up because of petty jealousies.
- A musician has to decide whether to earn a living from music by playing in bars and at dances, or to get an office job and use his music talent mainly as a volunteer in church.
- A school has to decide whether to put all its athletic resources into selected teams that will compete in a league, or into an extensive intramural program in which most students would participate.

Do you think each situation is a legitimate curriculum topic? Why or why not?

For one of the situations, discuss some problems and issues students could pose and explore. How would you actively engage the students in their learning? Can you suggest some learning activities for setting the stage? disclosure? reformulation? transcendence? How could students respond personally and yet build a sense of community as they study the topic? What means could you include to encourage students to use metacognitive strategies? What are some ways in which they could display the results of their learning?

Engaging the Head and the Heart

Effective learning engages both the head and the heart. Effective disciples of Jesus Christ are not only knowledgeable but also passionate about what they believe. They develop their insights and abilities in a context in which their unique gifts are recognized. Their learning fosters a sense of awe and wonder. It engenders purposeful enthusiasm about the possibilities of God's creation as well as sorrow about the effects of sin. It nurtures a committed, principled way of life made possible through the saving grace of Jesus Christ.

A curriculum that plans for this type of learning will include coherent thematic units that deal with big ideas and significant issues. Certainly the school will do everything possible to ensure that, in the early grades, every child learns to read, write, listen, speak, and compute. Without such basic skills, children will be unable to cope with further learning. But the curriculum

needs to go beyond such skills. Thematic units can be designed not only to deal with salient and relevant topics, but to also incorporate strategies suggested in this chapter:

- Accommodate different learning styles within the rhythm described by the four phases of learning.
- Provide for the developmental layers of understanding, teaching students about basic values and principles in ways suitable for their age (e.g., using the story format for younger children).
- Differentiate learning for students with varied aptitudes and interests, and preferred ways of knowing.
- Encourage personal response through open-ended and thought-provoking discussions and through activities and assignments in which students extend their own thought and work in original ways.
- Cultivate metacognitive strategies for intentional, thoughtful learning.
- Allow students to exhibit and explain their learning products.
- Establish a sense of community within and beyond the school through, for example, building personal connections with students about their personal thoughts, activities, and beliefs, as well as planning service opportunities as an inherent part of the curriculum.

The next two chapters will discuss the specifics of planning programs that engage students' heads and hearts, using such strategies.

Footstep 5-8

Choose a topic that could be taught, say, both at the second- and sixth-grade levels. How you would teach it according to Egan's recommendations for the primary and romantic layers of understanding? How would you plan the unit to take into account different learning styles? personal response? metacognition? service opportunities? exhibiting learning?

Reviewing the Main Points

- **Pedagogy and curriculum are closely intertwined.** Not only will curriculum implementation be ineffective if we neglect pedagogy, but our decisions about pedagogy will affect the content and structure of our curriculum. As Lee Shulman puts it, "Pedagogical content knowledge is of special interest because ... it represents the blending of content and pedagogy into an understanding of how particular topics, problems, or issues are organized, represented, and adapted to the diverse interests and abilities of learners, and presented for instruction" (Shulman 1987, 8). Pedagogical content knowledge is the specialty of teachers and makes meaningful classroom learning possible.

- **Most meaningful learning takes place in classroom learning communities with an atmosphere of openness, trust, and security.** Such communities recognize children as responsible and unique images of God, yet who need structure and guidance because of sin. They provide activities to suit different learning styles. As they do so, they recognize the rhythm of learning:
  1. Experience-based exploration and investigation
  2. Formal, precise presentation and instruction
  3. Rephrasing and practice
  4. Open-ended application and transcendence

- **Teachers need to take into account Egan's cumulative developmental layers of understanding:**
  1. Primary understanding where children can learn much about life and its values through story settings
  2. Romantic understanding where students enjoy mastering detailed content and skills within a value-based narrative context
  3. Philosophic understanding where students search for their place in society and for general causal networks relating to the purpose and meaning of life

  In all these layers, students' learning is enhanced through activities that cultivate genuine personal response and service opportunities.

- **The curriculum should incorporate learning strategies that reflect a biblical view of knowledge and of the person.** These include (but are not limited to) differentiated learning, personal response, metacognitive strategies, exhibiting learning, service learning, and forging authentic classroom community contexts for learning.

References

Bolt, J. 1993. *The Christian story and the Christian school*. Grand Rapids: Christian Schools International.

Bowers, C. 1987. *Toward a post-liberal theory of education*. New York: Teachers College Press.

Brandt, R., ed. 2000. *Education in a new era*. ASCD yearbook 2000. Alexandria, VA: Association for Supervision and Curriculum Development.

Bruer, J. 1998. Brain science, brain fiction. *Educational Leadership* 56 (3): 14–18.

Cotton, K. 1999. *Research you can use to improve results*. Alexandria, VA: Association for Supervision and Curriculum Development.

Diamond, D. 1993. How to develop volunteerism in students. In *Tips for Principals*, Reston, VA: National Association of Secondary School Principals (April).

Egan, K. 1986. *Teaching as story telling*. London, ON: Althouse Press.

———. 1988. *Primary understanding: Education in early childhood*. New York: Routledge.

———. 1990. *Romantic understanding: The development of rationality and imagination, ages 8–15*. New York: Routledge.

———. 1992. *Imagination in teaching and learning: The middle school years*. London, ON: Althouse Press.

———. 1997. *The educated mind: How cognitive tools shape our understanding*. Chicago: University of Chicago Press.

Fogarty, R. 1994. *How to teach for metacognitive reflection*. Palatine, IL: IRI Skylight.

Good, T., and J. Brophy. 1994. *Looking in classrooms*. 6th ed. New York: HarperCollins.

Groome, T. 1980. *Christian religious education*. San Francisco: Harper & Row.

Guild, P. Burke, and S. Garger. 1998. *Marching to different drummers*. 2d ed. Alexandria, VA: Association for Supervision and Curriculum Development.

Harris, M. 1987. *Teaching and religious imagination*. San Francisco: Harper & Row.

Healy, J. 2000. The I-generation—from toddlers to teenagers: A conversation with Jane M. Healy. *Educational Leadership* 58 (2): 8–13.

Issler, K., and R. Habermas. 1994. *How we learn: A Christian teacher's guide to educational psychology*. Grand Rapids: Baker Books.

Jackson, P., ed. 1992. *Handbook of research on curriculum*. New York: Macmillan.

Marzano, R., D. Pickering, and J. Pollock. 2001. *Classroom instruction that works: Research-based strategies for increasing student achievement*. Alexandria, VA: Association for Supervision and Curriculum Development.

McCarthy, B. 1996. *About learning*. Barrington, IL: Excel.

———. 1997. A tale of four learners: 4Mat's learning styles. *Educational Leadership* 54 (6): 46–51.

Ontario Alliance of Christian Schools. 1994. *Thy will be done: Old Testament studies*, Unit one. Draft edition. Ancaster, ON.

Parkay, F., and G. Hass. 2000. *Curriculum planning: A contemporary approach*. 7th ed. Boston: Allyn and Bacon.

Pinar, W. 1988. *Contemporary curriculum discourses*. Scottsdale, AZ: Gorsuch Scarisbrick.

Shulman, L. 1987. Knowledge and teaching: Foundations of the new reform. *Harvard Educational Review* 57 (1): 1–22.

Silver, H., R. Strong, and M. Perini. 2000. *So each may learn: Integrating learning styles and multiple intelligences*.

Alexandria, VA: Association for Supervision and Curriculum Development.

Sizer, T. 1992. *Horace's school: Redesigning the American high school.* Boston: Houghton-Mifflin.

Stronks, G., and D. Blomberg, eds. 1993. *A vision with a task: Christian schooling for responsive discipleship.* Grand Rapids: Baker Books.

Tomlinson, C. 1999. *The differentiated classroom: Responding to the needs of all learners.* Alexandria, VA: Association for Supervision and Curriculum Development.

Van Brummelen, H. 1998. *Walking with God in the classroom.* 2d ed. Seattle: Alta Vista College Press.

Whitehead, A. 1929. *The aims of education and other essays.* New York: Macmillan.

Willis, S. 1993. Learning through service. *Association for Supervision and Curriculum Development Update* 35 (6): 1–8.

Woehrle, T. 1993. Growing up responsible. *Educational Leadership* 51 (3): 40–43.

Steppingstone 6

School-Based Curriculum Planning

W ilma Van Brummelen's yearly *Kindergarten Course Outline* lists nine thematic units: creation, harvest, God made me special, conifer trees, transportation, Japan, farms, honeybees, and water all around. For each, she includes a time span, a field trip, a thematic statement, and intended learning outcomes.

For instance, she schedules her Japan unit for five weeks starting in early February. She includes a field trip where students experience Japanese dining in a restaurant. The unit reflects Kieran Egan's claim that even young children can learn a great deal about people and their values from studying a culture and context that is quite different from their own, particularly through stories. Her thematic statement for the unit is as follows:

> When God created the earth, He commanded people, as His images, to discover, explore, develop, and care for this world. God gave us a good creation, but sin distorted our ability to act as God's images in love for Him and each other. God scattered the nations because of our disobedience to Him at the time of the Tower of Babel. God's redeeming love in Jesus Christ gave us another chance to reflect God's love for us to people around us and in other cultures.
>
> People have formed cultures on the basis of their beliefs, languages, social interactions, economic contexts, and physical environments. In this unit the students will learn where and how the Japanese, our global neighbors, live and have developed their culture. They will learn that because of sin, people have not always treated each other justly. They will explore how to carry out God's Great Commandment and His Great Commission with respect to people from other cultural backgrounds. They will celebrate both their own uniqueness and gifts in Christ as well as those of people in a culture such as the Japanese. The unit's main focus will be on what it means to love God above all and to love our neighbors as ourselves as we interact with people from cultural backgrounds other than our own.

Besides listing her thematic units, Van Brummelen's yearly plan includes special celebrations such as a Christmas pageant produced for parents and grandparents. She describes the conflict resolution process and the playground behavior she will teach as part of the school's KIDS program (*Kids in Discipleship and Training*). She specifies her mathematics topics (e.g., sorting and classifying during four weeks in November). She gives her monthly literary themes as well as nine general and twelve specific language development emphases (e.g., becoming involved in emerging reading and writing, letter recognition and recording). She details the nineteen types of learning centers she uses at various times of the year (e.g., computer, water table, painting). She notes that science will be included in all thematic units, and that the government's curriculum guide will be used to monitor science skills. She also describes her "kindercooking" and buddy programs, and lists her major resources. Finally, she indicates eight personal development areas she emphasizes throughout: faith, moral, social, intellectual, language, aesthetic, emotional, and physical development.

This teacher did not make her course outline, of course, in isolation from those of the rest of the school. In fact, as a result of joint planning, she substituted the unit on conifers for one on food and nutrition. This led to a better balance of topics in kindergarten and enabled second-grade teachers to teach their unit on nutrition without undue repetition. Each year the teachers supply the principal with a schedule for each day, a curriculum map of the basic subjects, and unit plans that indicate thematic statements, goals and objectives, key learning activities, assessment and evaluation of student learning, and how the unit relates to learning outcomes required by the government (see figure 6.8 for the Japan unit example).

As they plan, teachers retain their individuality and professional responsibility. But they are also part of a school community for learning. Therefore, they also plan and work together to provide a focused, coherent, and balanced curriculum that reflects the school's mission and vision.

On the basis of what is given here about this teacher's curriculum plans, consider:

- What are the implied mission and vision of this particular school?
- What kind of deliberations should groups of teachers be involved in as they plan a school's curriculum?
- What tasks do teachers have to carry out individually to plan their classroom curriculum?
- What are the roles of the principal and others who have curriculum responsibilities (e.g., a primary curriculum coordinator, a high school department chair)?

Planning curriculum for your classroom is a complex task. To do so responsibly, you try to incorporate the contours of a biblical worldview and its values. You keep in mind that knowledge reflects created reality but is not static; it includes personal response. You set priorities as you plan and justify your content and pedagogy. You include various modes of knowing and provide for diverse learners. You keep the aspects of reality in balance while also having students experience the integrality of knowledge.

As a teacher you cannot consider directly all the elements that affect curriculum as you plan your classroom learning. But you should stand back regularly to reflect on key questions such as:

- What do I want my curriculum to accomplish? What evidence will show that I have accomplished my purposes?
- How does my guiding vision of life affect my planning?
- Which types of learning activities and resources fit my curriculum orientation?
- How will I monitor the effects of the implementation of my plans?

Figure 6.1 repeats figure 2.2, but it also shows the main curriculum players who affect classroom learning. Before a more detailed discussion of the roles of such planners, consider briefly what the diagram shows as **contextual frame factors**.

The Societal Context of Curriculum

We have already thought about our curriculum groundings: the aims of the curriculum, our worldview and value perspectives,

Figure 6.1 Key Players in Curriculum Planning

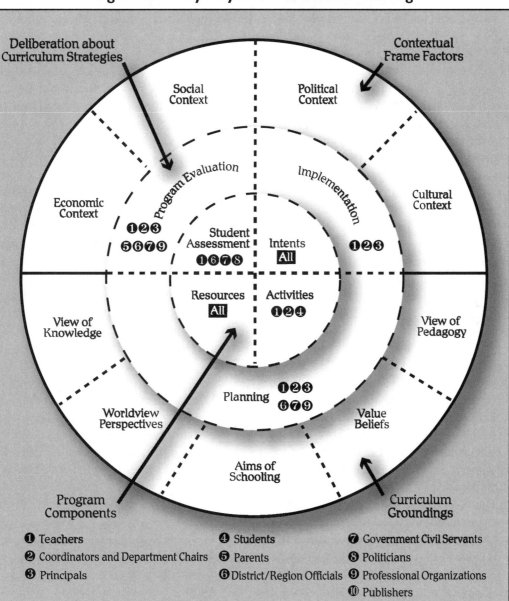

❶ Teachers ❹ Students ❼ Government Civil Servants
❷ Coordinators and Department Chairs ❺ Parents ❽ Politicians
❸ Principals ❻ District/Region Officials ❾ Professional Organizations
❿ Publishers

and our view of knowledge, the learner, and learning. Basic beliefs about these building blocks, even when unexpressed, guide curriculum planning. Besides these underpinnings, schools and teachers also need to take into account the economic, social, political, and cultural contexts. National or regional projects can consider only the broad strokes of such contexts. Individual schools and teachers use their local contexts to adapt general guidelines and plan programs that suit their own circumstances.

For example, in my province some public and Christian schools have large proportions of students of Chinese and Japanese ancestry, while others have many aboriginal Indian students. While all schools try to meet basic literacy and numeracy standards, parents in the former schools may demand a rigorous academic curriculum with a great deal of homework so that students are well prepared for a university career. In the latter schools, what becomes more important is a thorough understanding of what in Canada we call "First Nations traditions and culture." The second or third languages offered in the curriculum and the type of art experienced may also reflect students' cultural background. Moreover, the teachers' pedagogical strategies may also differ, with more emphasis on collaborative learning in First Nations settings.

Schools and teachers need to take into account at least four societal frame factors: the school's economic, social, political, and cultural contexts.

- **The economic context.** Both a school's financial resources and the students' economic background affect curriculum. For instance, a school board may require that children with special needs attend regular classrooms. If the board does not provide sufficient specialized help, how-

ever, teachers may cope by cutting special activities, including those that call for personal exploration and response (setting the stage and transcendence). It is well known that schools with less affluent clientele generally include more mechanical rote learning, while schools in more affluent communities tend to put more emphasis on creativity and individual initiative. While such differences are regrettable, the socioeconomic backgrounds of students do affect classroom curriculum and pedagogy. Nevertheless, each class is unique, and teachers are wise to avoid preconceptions.

- **The social context.** A school's social context also affects curriculum. A large number of dysfunctional families or a widespread pursuit of dual careers may mean that parents spend little time with their children. In such cases teachers may give more time to some functions traditionally carried out by parents (e.g., discussing everyday problems and values). They may also modify the curriculum to provide more time for reading readiness in early grades. Similarly, in racially diverse communities, teachers may put more emphasis on units dealing with multiculturalism.

- **The political context.** Politicians are swayed by public opinion. Public concern for higher standards may lead politicians to set competency exams at certain grade levels (although these often affect only minimum and not general standards). They may bow to public pressure on contentious issues (e.g., textbooks, high school leaving exams). Politicians may also have their personal agendas (e.g., the introduction of a compulsory course in consumer education because of a politician's personal belief of its importance).

- **The cultural context.** North American society places a strong emphasis on individualism. The notion that persons should look out mainly for themselves without regard for others affects how parents evaluate their students' progress in school—and what pressures they put on schools. People put less value on a shared ethos or a sense of a community where people support and care for each other. Curriculum guides and textbooks also often promote the concept that persons can and should decide their own values. School-based planning must counter such general trends by emphasizing respect, caring, responsibility, trustworthiness, fairness, and civic virtue. A school's cultural context may also have positive consequences for the curriculum. For instance, school programs today promote racial harmony and environmental stewardship. Also, the unified mission and ethos of a Christian school makes it possible for their programs to reflect their basis and purpose.

Of course, the economic, social, political, and cultural influences interact and overlap as they affect a school's curriculum. The main point of this section is that schools are a part of and reflection of what is going on in society as well as their local community. That is why schools and teachers adapt general curriculum guidelines to fit their own situation.

Footstep 6-1

Suppose your principal has appointed you to chair a curriculum task force that will review and make recommendations about your school's science program. At your first meeting the group agrees that learning about the applications of science and technology should be an important part of the science program. It also reaches a consensus that science education should involve, as much as possible, a problem-based approach.

A lively discussion takes place on how much of this will actually be possible. One person points out that elementary teachers often have little training in science—and little time to prepare for hands-on activities. The expectations of colleges, another says, force secondary teachers to teach theoretical rather than practical science. Moreover, adds a third, parents and school board members seem more concerned about language and math basics than about science. Therefore, they are reluctant to make enough funds available for science materials.

The group decides to ask the school's teachers to find out their views and constraints. You agree to draft the questions dealing with the context of teaching science.

List the relevant contextual factors, the ways in which each might affect the science program, and the questions you will ask the school's teachers. Which other sources of information should your committee consider? Who are the curriculum players behind such sources?

Players in the Curriculum Field

Curriculum planning takes place at many levels. Curriculum players exercise authority and influence in different ways. For example:

- **Teachers** adapt, plan, and implement classroom programs.
- **Government agencies and umbrella organizations** develop policies, publish

curriculum guides, authorize resources, prescribe standards, and administer testing programs.

- **Networks of schools, school districts, and local schools** set up curriculum committees. Such teams assess programs and recommend or develop more suitable ones.
- **Outside interest groups** share their insights with those charged with planning and implementing curriculum.

Usually the primary motive of all players is to help students become more insightful, capable, and responsible persons. However, the interpretations of these terms may differ a great deal!

Figure 6.1 shows how some key curriculum players directly affect different components of the curriculum. Since figure 6.1 is not exhaustive, you may be able to think of other ways these players influence the curriculum, or you may want to add other players. Note that the teacher is the only person involved in all aspects of planning. But the teacher does have to take into account the roles, beliefs and values, policies, and curriculum guidelines of other curriculum players.

The Teacher as Curriculum Planner

Teachers are professionals who make many curriculum decisions behind their classroom doors. They wield much power in deciding their pedagogy, content choice, activities, and resources. They give students a sense of ownership in their progress by being sensitive to student reaction and input (How did you feel about ...? What would you like to know about ...?). Teachers control the extent to which the curriculum that students experience will correspond with top-down directives.

As a teacher you are the crucial curriculum planner for your classroom. You are much more than a technician who follows a textbook or a curriculum guide. As a teacher-curriculum planner you gradually develop your own curriculum repertoire. As you plan your program, you should:

- Take into account your view of knowledge, learning, and the meaning of life. Develop your own framework and goals, but do so in consultation with the rest of your staff.
- Recognize and incorporate the content, skills, and values that your school and education system expect you to teach.
- Respond to the needs of your students and class(es).
- Use available resources in ways that advance your intended learning outcomes.
- Plan some units jointly with other teachers so that you gain from their insights.
- Use your grade coordinator's, department chair's, and/or principal's feedback and assistance to improve your yearly and unit plans.

As a teacher you have much freedom to fashion your own units and approaches on the basis of your beliefs, context, and personal characteristics. Of course, you do not design your whole program yourself. You are not an expert in all subjects or topics. You need time before and after school not only for planning but also for setting up your room, evaluating student work, contacting parents, copying materials, and attending meetings. So most often you adapt what others have developed. Yet your decisions about what you teach and how you teach it are important; they affect your students' lives. Thus curriculum planning is one of your most important tasks.

Footstep 6-2

Talk with some teachers about their class-room curriculum planning. How much and what kind do they do? Is there anything they would like to do but don't have time for? In what ways have they found such planning rewarding? frustrating?

The Role of Coordinators, Department Chairs, and Principals

At the school building level, curriculum players also include coordinators, department heads, and principals. They work with teachers to set schoolwide curriculum guidelines and choose resources. They help their teachers set priorities for schoolwide and classroom curriculum. Sometimes they are the catalysts for jointly planned units. They request and respond to teachers' yearly overviews and unit plans. The effectiveness of a school's curriculum often depends on their ability to be catalysts for curriculum improvement. Schools implement and maintain their educational focus and quality only as long as internal leaders with a compelling educational mission and vision shared by the school community act as effective change agents.

Interacting with Parents and Community Groups

The Bible assigns first responsibility for educating children to parents. Over time, governments have become the agencies that raise and distribute school tax funds. They have also taken on a prescriptive role in setting curriculum policies. It is neither necessary nor desirable, however, for governments to do more than ensure that schools enable children to function well in society. Their task is to set minimum standards and see to it that all schools provide a safe and secure environment.

Parents have the responsibility to choose the type and direction of their children's education. When parents agree with a school's vision and keep closely involved, the resulting esprit de corps usually fosters a good educational climate. This is one reason why Christian schools as well as charter and other alternative schools often provide effective educational programs. Parents who together with teachers build a unified vision for a school affect curriculum quality more than do top-down regulations. Schools may use parent advisory committees or education committees with parent members to seek input on major curriculum decisions.

Wise school leaders listen carefully to community concerns expressed by parents and other interest groups. They try to build a consensus before making important decisions. Some groups may want to raise reading and writing standards. Others may have concerns or suggestions about resources or electives. School principals work with their boards, teachers, and parent groups to develop and implement a coherent, balanced curriculum that takes into account the legitimate interests of such groups. At the same time, they ensure that teachers are able to exercise their professional judgment and expertise within the guidelines established by the school community.

Footstep 6-3

When the sixth-grade teachers of Pacific Christian Academy taught John Steinbeck's novel *The Pearl,* they sent home a letter that read, in part:

> The content of the novel deals with the constant struggle between good and evil, and the effect of the choices one makes. The author uses greed and prejudice as a representation of evil, to show readers the results of sin. Near the end, a child is unintentionally shot dead as a result of greed. We feel that you should be informed of this. To properly deal with this death, the students will be composing a letter of condolence to the parents of the deceased child.
>
> In choosing this novel, it is our hope that students will grasp the concept that joy does not come from riches but from Jesus Christ ... the greatest Pearl in the world.

What would be the effects of this letter? In what situations is it wise for a school to send parents an explanatory letter? To what extent should parents be able to influence the resources used in a school?

The Role of Students

Involving students in curriculum planning helps them take ownership of their learning and encourages them to become responsible. You may, for instance, use the K-W-L approach at the beginning of a unit and have students suggest some of the specific topics they would like to have included, either with the whole class or as individual explorations (see page 123). Also, you may offer students choices or alternatives. At the kindergarten level, students can already choose learning centers themselves. You may have a few rules so that all students regularly attend certain centers and do not attend the same center two days in a row. At higher levels, you may give students a choice of assignments or

major projects. By giving such choices (including and perhaps especially at the middle and high school levels), you foster responsible decision making about learning and provide for the range of learning styles, abilities, developmental levels, and interests in your class.

Students also affect your curriculum through their response to learning activities. Because of student response, you may sometimes have to forego the breadth you had planned in order that students learn the central concepts well. Or your students may benefit so much from a certain type of activity that you plan similar ones even when that means you go off on a bit of a tangent. Good teachers adapt their curriculum to student response and learning success.

School Boards and Regional Officials as Curriculum Players

School boards set policies that affect curriculum. They approve statements of philosophy. They suggest new curriculum initiatives. They make program decisions (e.g., to expand or reduce the music program). They choose standardized testing programs. They select major resources. At the same time, school boards may be limited in their authority. Public school boards must, by law, implement state directives. Even Christian school boards, in order for their students to achieve high school graduation, must often follow provincial or state curriculum guidelines. Public school boards and regional organizations of Christian schools may employ curriculum coordinators. Such consultants stimulate local and regional curriculum planning and related professional development.

Government Officials as Curriculum Players

Central provincial, state, and national education agencies often have the following curriculum roles:

- **Developing and mandating curriculum guides for different subjects.** Curriculum guides may contain a bare listing of content and skill requirements—or be very detailed. They may or may not provide conceptual maps for big ideas and approaches. They may or may not include assessment suggestions. Evidence suggests that teachers typically interpret the guides to justify their current practices. As a result, the influence of curriculum guides is seldom strong (Andrew Porter, John Smithson, and Eric Osthoff in Elmore and Fuhrman 1994, 161). Nevertheless, the documents may provide a helpful starting point for both newer teachers and school curriculum committees.
- **Setting policies such as mandatory course requirements and minimum time allocations for different subjects.** In my jurisdiction, for instance, students in all accredited schools must take French in grades five through eight, social studies from kindergarten through eleventh grade, and one sixty-hour fine arts course in either eleventh or twelfth grade.
- **Establishing mandatory assessment and testing programs based on pre-specified standards.** Regional testing programs have an impact on curriculum, mainly when tests are "high stake," i.e., when they have a direct bearing on the future of students and the status of schools and teachers. Research suggests that standards-based assessment tests raise student achievement in what is tested. At the same time, they may result in narrowing the curriculum, with a great deal of preparation for specific types of test questions (Fuhrman 2001, 7, 277). The tests influence the curriculum. They may also have unexpected consequences. High school graduation tests, for instance, have resulted in more students taking remedial rather than advanced mathematics courses (Elmore and Fuhrman 1994, 157). James Spillane (in Fuhrman 2001, 236) concludes that teachers become preoccupied with ensuring that disadvantaged students are up to speed on basic skills, and as a result, never manage to get to more challenging content.
- **Providing financial incentives** to encourage, for instance, teaching English as a second language, offering full-day kindergarten programs, or piloting new programs. Local schools generally adopt curriculum changes that benefit them financially.

Politicians as Curriculum Players

Politicians set policies that affect the curriculum. They may cut back or increase funding for technology in the curriculum. They may implement changes in high school graduation requirements, initiate tests, or launch new programs. However, general policies intended to set a direction for educational programs seldom live up to politicians' advance billing. To be successful, they need to be compatible with the structures and modi operandi of schools. They must be workable and must not raise undue negative reaction. They must call for incremental rather than wholesale change. They must be implemented in a climate of accommodation in which both teachers and the public are willing to give their support (Walker 1990, 420–30). It is uncommon for all these conditions to occur simultaneously, and many politically mandated changes do not last. A possible exception is the widespread introduction of student assessment programs.

Other Curriculum Players

- **Professional organizations**, such as the National Council of Teachers of Mathematics. Their resources and recommendations affect the thinking of curriculum planners. Their journals and professional development programs affect how teachers teach their subject.
- **Publishers** provide textbooks, test banks, audiovisual materials, and computer software for classrooms. Textbooks are often geared to state requirements in large states like Texas and California that have central textbook adoption. Textbooks have a significant impact on the day-to-day classroom curriculum.
- **Curriculum specialists** in college faculties of education serve regularly as consultants to curriculum planning and assessment teams.
- **Courts** may make decisions that affect, for instance, choice of resources or the inclusiveness of education.
- **Foundations** may influence curriculum by funding certain education projects.
- **The media** not only reports but also sways public opinion and student attitudes and behavior. It thus indirectly affects curriculum policies and practices. For instance, the largest newspaper in our area championed whole language in the early 1990s and ten years later is touting the advantages of phonics-based reading programs. The paper develops a mind-set that encourages parents to put pressure on their schools.

While teachers and schools are part and parcel of an education scene that has many curriculum players, they usually have much flexibility to implement a unique vision. Indeed, the history of Christian schools suggests that often they have not made effective use of their ability to plan a distinctly Christian curriculum. Despite government expectations, Christian schools "are free to develop a curriculum that fulfills our school's mission and our biblical mandate. We are free to develop curriculum that honors God as our Creator and Sustainer, Jesus Christ as Redeemer, and the Spirit as Comforter and Renewer ... to let the gospel's light shine through in every lesson, every unit, every course, every school activity" (Koole 2000, 1).

Footstep 6-4

The Council of Ministers of Education, Canada (1997, 26–30), released a 261-page document, *Common Framework of Science Learning Outcomes*. By the end of sixth grade, for instance, it is expected that students will:

- Describe positive and negative effects that result from applications of science and technology in their own lives, the lives of others, and the environment (a general learning outcome).
- Interpret findings from investigations using appropriate methods (a general skills outcome).
- Describe and predict causes, effects, and patterns related to change in living and nonliving things (a general knowledge outcome).
- Demonstrate perseverance and a desire to understand (a general attitude outcome).

Each general outcome has a set of specific learning outcomes. For instance, the general knowledge outcome above has twenty-one specific outcomes. Two of these are included in a fourth-grade unit on habitats and communities:

- Predict how the removal of a plant or animal population affects the rest of the community.
- Relate habitat loss to the endangerment or extinction of plants and animals. (CMEC 1997, 143)

The document goes on to give illustrative examples of activities, one of which is:

- Students explore the link between meeting basic needs and habitat:
  □ They observe animals within a local habitat or in the classroom to determine how various organisms satisfy their needs in the habitats in which they are typically found.
  □ They recognize that structural and behavioral adaptations make organisms well suited to a particular habitat but not to another.
  □ They use multimedia resources to expand the area of study in order to see the great diversity of life in different habitats.

The above exploration may lead to the following question: How do changes in a habitat affect the living things within that habitat? (CMEC 1997, 143)

What is the intent of this document when the responsibility for education in Canada rests with the provinces and not with the national government? How might other curriculum players described in this section use this document? How might the school curriculum committee described in footstep 6-1 use it? Would you as a teacher make use of it? Why or why not?

Note also the implied evolutionistic belief: "structural ... adaptations make organisms well suited to a particular habitat." Interestingly, the authors do not appear to believe their own statement. If they really did, they would not only have the students "clean up a local stream area to enhance habitat" but would also have the students observe (either directly or indirectly) how organisms change structurally to adapt to what initially is a less desirable habitat.

As a Christian teacher, how would you adapt these outcomes and activities to make them suitable for your classroom?

Seven Steps in Classroom Curriculum Planning

Classroom curriculum planning involves at least seven steps (see figure 6.2). You might think of them as seven steppingstones placed in various parts of the circular figure 6.1. I will discuss them in a specific order, but as a teacher you usually will not follow them in that exact order. You'll jump back and forth among them. Sometimes you may skip a stone or two; at other times you may slip and go back to previous steps. Curriculum planning is not a neat and clean process!

1. Remember Your Aims and Intents

Chapter 1 gave one set of general aims for a Christian school curriculum. Following is another set developed by the Society of Christian Schools in British Columbia (1998, I-15):

The central purpose of Christian schooling is to help students explore and experience what it means to be disciples of the Lord

Jesus Christ in all of life. The following goals form the basis for the design and development of curriculum in Christian schools:

- *To nurture students to stand in awe of the Creator and develop a sense of awe and wonder for God's creation*
- *To lead students to recognize and understand the interdependence and interrelatedness of everything in God's creation*
- *To help students recognize that sin has totally distorted reality, our experience in it, and our understanding of it*
- *To guide student exploration of what it means to be stewards of all God has made and to be and become Christ's agents of healing in a broken world, being enabled by the Spirit*

- *To assist students in discovering and developing their God-given gifts and abilities*

If you made a set of aims to guide your curriculum planning in chapter 1, take another look at it now and revise it on the basis of newly developed insights. If you have not made a set of aims, this would be a good point to stop and jot down your personal curriculum aims.

Your set of aims does not embrace all your intents. For instance, you want learning to be enjoyable for your students, on the whole—and teaching to be satisfying for yourself. You want learning to take place in an atmosphere of mutual trust and respect. You want to model a biblically responsible lifestyle to your students. You want to estab-

Fig. 6.2   Steps in Classroom Curriculum Planning

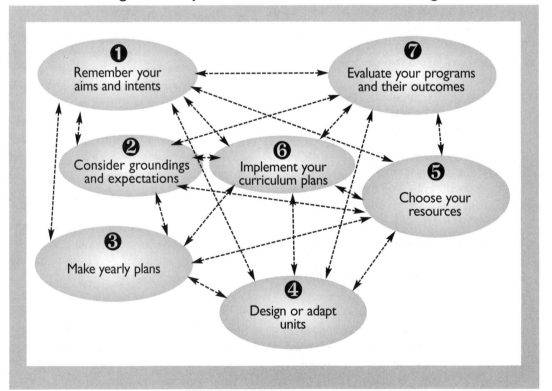

lish routines that help you keep things moving efficiently. Such intents are honorable; they will improve learning effectiveness. Jot down some of your personal intents not encompassed by your aims. Keep them in mind as you plan your classroom curriculum.

2. Consider Your Groundings and External Expectations

Without repeating what this book has already considered about curriculum groundings and contextual frame factors, here are some key questions to ask yourself:

How do my curriculum plans:
- *Reflect my school's vision and aims?*
- *Promote a biblical worldview and values?*
- *Foster responsive and responsible discipleship?*
- *Employ effective and varied learning strategies?*
- *Take into account the unique abilities, needs, and experiential background of my students?*
- *Consider the cultural and socioeconomic context of my school?*
- *Meet external requirements, standards, and recommendations as stated in official documents and policies?*

Christian schools may not be bound by government program guidelines. However, those policies and standards may reflect societal expectations for schooling that Christian schools should heed. They also need to recognize the role of external accreditation or assessment programs. Each school develops its own policies and practices to ensure that its curriculum maintains its vision while it also meets applicable external expectations.

Footstep 6-5

Government curriculum documents vary a great deal. Some specify detailed factual content; others, only broad concepts. Some structure sets of specific learning outcomes under more general goals; others list a seemingly haphazard collection of specific outcomes under a topic.

Obtain and examine a representative government curriculum guide or list of standards for your jurisdiction. Many are available on websites (e.g., <www.educ.gov.bc.ca/>). After reviewing the document, discuss:

- What are some of the features you like about the document? dislike?
- Which curriculum orientation(s) are represented most strongly in the document? What is your evidence?
- A curriculum document is never neutral. In what ways does the document promote certain points of view? Whose viewpoint is seen or heard? from what angle or perspective? What big ideas or enduring understandings are considered important?
- In what ways can you use the document in your curriculum planning while still maintaining your curriculum aims and perspective?
- How would a curriculum committee like the school science task force of footstep 6-1 use the document to align the school's science program with that of the document?
- Look at a particular topic in a document that you have taught or with which you are familiar. What are the strengths and weaknesses of the document as a resource for planning a unit on that topic?

- Ask some educators to what extent and how they use such curriculum documents. In what ways have they found them to be useful? Or why have they found them to be irrelevant?

3. Make Yearly Plans

Most schools provide you with a curriculum map that lists topics and skills to be taught at various grade levels. For instance, the school's curriculum grid may show that your fourth-grade science program must include units on habitats and communities of living things; light; sound; rocks, minerals, and erosion; and maintaining a healthy body. Schools also frame your program by supplying certain class resources and textbooks. For instance, for tenth-grade English, you may have to choose novels from those available in your school. You may sometimes consider some directives to be too limiting or inappropriate. In such cases you can seek individual exemption from them or try to change them for the whole school. However, your professional responsibility is to implement an effective learning program within the school's established curriculum framework.

When you know the external frames for your program, you can prepare a yearly curriculum overview. Figure 6.3 shows Wilma Van Brummelen's 2000–2001 kindergarten overview grid. She expands on this overview in her accompanying course outline described in the introduction to this chapter. She has also developed a more detailed curriculum map for mathematics and language arts (figure 6.4 gives a sample page). She also supplies her principal with each day's schedule (figure 6.5).

At the secondary level, teachers develop yearly overviews for each course that they teach. Again, different formats are possible. Heidi Hayes Jacobs shows a high school physics map that consists of four columns: month, content, skills, and assessment. In March, the unit on sound and light waves includes skills such as "Predict the result of wave interactions." The assessment column includes written lab reports, lab performance, a design project, and tests (Jacobs 1997, map Q). Derek Keenan shows a twelfth-grade biblical studies course that has five columns: unit title, concepts/principles, skills, text sections, and materials/media (Keenan 1998, 25). Figure 6.6 shows an excerpt of a twelfth-grade English course outline with a distinctive Christian approach that, at the same time, prepares students for a government final examination.

In order to incorporate your school's mission and vision in the yearly overview, Elaine Brouwer (2000, 8) suggests listing not only topics but also concepts, understandings, and essential questions. For the topic wetlands, for instance, she lists:

Main concept: Interdependence

Understandings: Wetlands are complex systems full of wonder. Their worth or importance is not first of all defined by their human or economic or recreational uses. They are not expendable wastelands but are a vital part of the planetary ecosystem, created to serve as nurseries, homes, reservoirs, and kidneys.

Essential questions: What is a wetland? How are wetlands formed? How do wetlands change over time? What is the role of wetlands in the ecosystem? What threatens wetlands? How can we steward wetlands?

Figure 6.7 shows an adaptation of Elaine Brouwer's basic grid.

In short, different overview formats are possible. If your school does not suggest a particular format, design one that will help your more detailed planning. Include:

- The topics and principal content, both within specific subjects and ones that span several aspects of reality
- Basic concepts, goals, understandings, and/or essential questions
- The main skills to be learned
- Main assessment strategies
- Topic sequence and approximately how much time to be spent on each

Some teachers also like to include their main resources, projects, and field trips. In designing your yearly overview, ask:

1. How will each major topic contribute to my basic aims and my school's mission and vision?
2. Does the plan account for my school and community expectations? Does it fit students' previous school experiences and prepare them for what follows, with no undue repetition?
3. Does topic choice and time allotment reflect a balanced consideration of all subjects and topics? Do I provide for learning appropriate content and skills that foster desired values, dispositions, and responses?

Footstep 6-6

Most principals require teachers to hand in yearly overviews at the beginning of the school year. Examine several yearly overviews, if available. What are their strengths and weaknesses?

Now choose a grade level and subject for which you have a school or government curriculum document available. Make a grid design for a yearly overview and complete it for two or three of the course topics.

4. Design or Adapt a Unit Plan

As you designed your yearly overview, you likely already thought of many worthwhile classroom activities for your topics. But you need to do more intermediate planning to ensure that you will meet your goals. Jumping directly from yearly outlines to daily planning leaves out the crucial step of developing detailed unit plans. Such plans usually include at least a rationale or thematic statement, objectives or learning outcomes, classroom activities, resources to be used, a time schedule, and a plan for evaluating student learning.

This part of your planning is so crucial that the entire next chapter is devoted to unit planning. Here I give only the outline of a unit plan on Japan for Wilma Van Brummelen's kindergarten class (figure 6.8). This gives you a preview sample of how the unit's thematic statement given in this chapter's introduction can be worked into a teachable unit.

5. Select Suitable Resources

Resources are valuable learning tools. The availability of resources will affect your choice of activities. You cannot teach a sixth-grade unit on famous Christian leaders unless you have multiple copies of several biographies. You cannot effectively teach a unit on the use and misuse of statistics unless you have collected a number of case studies. You are more likely to teach research skills in a unit if your library or classroom has diverse relevant resources.

Often textbook resources almost solely determine classroom learning experiences.

Fig. 6.3 Sample Yearly Overview Grid for a Kindergarten Class
(Wilma Van Brummelen; Langley Christian School)

Kindergarten 2000–01	SEPT	OCT	NOV	DEC	JAN	FEB	MAR	APR	MAY	JUNE
Theme/Unit/Topic	Creation	Harvest	God Made Me Special	Conifers, Christmas pageant	Tranportation—2 weeks, Space—2 weeks	Japan	Farms		Honeybees	Water
Realm of Study	Four realms: People, Animals, Plants, Nonliving things	God's gifts of fruits, vegetables, deciduous trees	God's gift of people, Grandparents	Evergreens, God's Son's birthday celebrated	Nonliving things as gifts of God for service	Different cultures, Tolerance, All creatures are created for His glory and enjoyment	God's gift for our provision—dairy cows, chickens	God's way of providing us with bees that pollinate, make honey	Discovering God's laws in creation and how they are used for His glory	
Responsive Discipleship, Spirituality, Love, and Aesthetic Beauty woven throughout	Stewardship, Service	Aesthetics, Balanced living, Stewardship	Individuality, Community, Ethics	Global Community, Stewardship	Vocation, Service	Justice for all people	Vocation, Service, Stewardship	Communication, Stewardship	Deliberation, Stewardship	
Biblical Studies	Garden of Eden		Psalm 139	Trees of the Field	Compare travel then and now	Matthew 22; Love neighbor	First farm: Garden of Eden	Honey references in Bible	Symbolic use of water in Bible	Stewardship

Bible Stories   Starting at Creation to Revelations in a sequential time frame. Overviews. God's covenantal golden thread. Creation, Fall, Redemption, Service, Stewardship.

L.A./Phonics/Spelling Listening, Speaking

- learn ABC names (upper- and lowercase)
- sounds and letters
- phonemic awareness
- beginning sounds (ending, middle)
- emergent writing and reading
- risk taking in journals in a safe environment
- show and tell, speaking loud and clear

- articulation (speech)
- learn to read quietly
- communal prayer
- chart writing/reading
- tracking
- modeling emergent writing (reading)
- interactive writing

- what is a question? a comment?
- critical thinking skills
- learn Japanese songs
- talk everyday Japanese language
- listen for correct sentence structure
- understand language
- increase vocabulary

Literature/Novels Read Aloud, Literary Strategies

- participate in stories
- enjoy stories
- act out stories
- read along in big books (pictorial or words)
- predicting
- change ending
- write stories
- beginning, middle, end

- poems, songs, rhyming
- interactive writing
- sounds book
- sign language
- attention span, concentration
- comprehension
- higher level thinking
- comparing (size of books, hard- and soft-bound spine, staples)

- collect objects regarding story, guess what the story is about
- Japanese literature
- nonfiction books in 4 realms
- fiction
- repetitive books
- circular stories
- phonemic awareness strategies (play with poems)

Author of the Month	SEPT	OCT	NOV	DEC	JAN	FEB	MAR	APR	MAY	JUNE
	Robert Munsch	Robert Munsch	Paulette Bourgeois Brenda Clark	Paulette Bourgeois Brenda Clark	Donald Crews	Tana Hoban	Brian Wildsmith	Dr. Seuss	Frank Asch	Bill Peet

149

Fig. 6.3 continued

Kindergarten 2000–01	SEPT	OCT	NOV	DEC	JAN	FEB	MAR	APR	MAY	JUNE
Writing Process, Types of Publication	Uses pictures, scribing; L/R Progression; Booklets on themes		Sign in names; Beginning, ending sounds; Journal writing		Labeling, Making books, Risk taking in safe environment		If developmentally ready, write stories and research			
Math, Math Their Way and Quest 2000 combined	Learning numbers; Counting to 10, 20, … 100; 1:1 correspondence; Tubbing free exploration		Calendar activities, Free exploration, Patterning all year			Classifying; Count by 2's, 5's, 10's; Comparing		Equations $(+,-)$ up to 10 or higher; More or less Half, whole Measuring all year		Tubbing all year
Science: concepts, experiments, gerbils, water/rice table, plants, and people all year	World in space, Gravity, God's miraculous power	Lifecycle of plants, Water content, Parts of apples and plants, Plants as food	Stethoscope, Heartbeat, Skeletal system, How to care for skin	Parts of tree, O_2/CO_2, Water, Seeds	Movement of air, land, water; Gravity; Outer space	Rice table measurement, Fishing, Bullet train movement, Volcanoes, Earthquakes	Reproduction, Mammals, Birds, Food Production and methods	Insect parts, Honey making, Pollination, Apiary methods	Making honey, Nectar to honey	Sink/float; Water affecting people, animals, plants, things; Properties of water
Aesthetics: art/music, listening to classical music, music appreciation, background music	Singing God's praises, Action songs, Music classes	Arts — craft activities are integrated with themes. Students will experience a variety of art projects, e.g. free drawing (learning detail), directed drawing, cut/paste, play dough, collage, fabric art, stenciling, coloring, painting, printing, finger painting, explore primary colors, paper bag puppets, cat making paper folding crayon resist, making musical instruments, and many, many others								
Physical Education	Taught by physical education teacher									
Field Trips/Speakers	William's Park	Dave's Orchard	Senior citizen homes	Derby Reach, My house	Lonsdale Quay	Japanese visitors	Dairy farm, Chicken farm	Apiary display, Teddy bear picnic		Water Park, Anderson Pool
Kids in Discipleship Training	2nd Step program every week until completed; apply these skills in classroom all year									

Fig. 6.4 Sample Page from a Mathematics Curriculum Map

MATH CURRICULUM MAP—GRADE: KINDERGARTEN   (Wilma Van Brummelen; Langley Christian School)

Time Frame	Content	Processes and Skills	Assessment	Gov't Outcomes Links
5 weeks Sept—Oct Reinforced throughout the year	Free Exploration: -make creative designs -work with others for developing new ideas	-using junk boxes, pattern blocks, mirrors, popsicle sticks, unifix cubes, beans, clothing pins, colored macaroni, etc.	Observation Participation	
4 weeks October Reinforced throughout the year	Patterning: -identify, reproduce, extend, create, and compare patterns -environmental/creational patterns -calendar patterns	-pattern cards, tubbing, pattern blocks, geoboards, junk boxes, macaroni necklaces, paper chains, unifix cubes, *Math Their Way* activities -observing and recording patterns in God's creation, calendar activities, rhythmic clapping, pattern block wall, snap clap patterns, dot charts, music, tubbing	Observation Recording Evaluating Listening	Identify, create, and compare patterns that arise from their experiences Identify, reproduce, extend, create, and compare patterns using action, manipulatives, diagrams, and the spoken terms Recognize patterns in the environment
4 weeks November Reinforced throughout the year	Sorting and Classifying: -by color, shapes, male/female, adult/child, numbers, animals, money, texture, other properties, etc.	-using materials collected in the classroom to facilitate these activities -people sorting, using pictures, tubbing	Observation Collecting information on each student Recording Evaluating progress	Explore, sort, and classify real world and 3-D objects according to their properties Explore and describe real-world and three-dimensional objects using descriptive attributes such as big, little, like a box, like a can Identify and describe two-dimensional shapes such as circles, squares, triangles, or rectangles Compare, sort, classify, and pattern two-dimensional shapes Sort objects to one attribute chosen by themselves or the teacher

Fig. 6.5 Sample Daily Schedule for Kindergarten—Tuesdays

(Wilma Van Brummelen; Langley Christian School)

8:45	Opening: attendance, singing, and communal prayer
9:00	Sharing: show and tell
9:10	Movement education: e.g., action songs
9:20	Calendar activities: e.g., mathematics, language arts, weather
9:35	Bible
9:45	Booklets related to the theme
10:10	Snack
10:20	Recess
10:40	Music listening
10:50	Center time
11:20	Mathematics: e.g., whole group, small group, graphing, measurement
11:40	Mathematics: e.g., tubbing, follow-up
12:00	Story time
12:15	Lunch
12:30	Outside recess
1:00	Quiet time: e.g., resting, reading, conferencing, testing
1:28	Music
1:56	Language arts: e.g., phonemic awareness, ABC book, sign language, journals
2:25	KIDS: Second step conflict resolution
2:40	Story time
2:50	Closing, prayer

Fig. 6.6 Grade 12 English Course Outline Excerpts: Reflections on the Nature of Truth
(Rick Rauser; Pacific Academy)

OBJECTIVES	CONTENT	ASSESSMENT
Our goal in English 12 is to wrestle with the questions that human beings have wrestled with since time began. These questions deal with issues such as the nature of humanity, the role of faith and belief in human life, the meaning and nature of thought and knowledge, and the ultimate purpose for human existence—or if such a purpose even exists. We will explore these questions from a variety of perspectives and become critically aware of the perspectives themselves, including Christianity, Hinduism, Buddhism, secularism and materialism, and various ideological viewpoints within philosophy and religious studies. To be a Christian means to believe in the existence of absolute, universal truth, applicable at all times, in all places, and to all human beings. Christ is seen as the locus of this truth, the eternal Word who embodied and reveals God the Father. The theme of the nature and reality of truth will dominate our course and will be the guiding principle behind the three major units on belief, thought, and spirituality. As with all English courses, we will not study these themes in isolation or without context. English 12 is a university preparation course that involves the intense study of various works of literature, both poetry and prose, fiction and nonfiction. These literary works, supplemented by several films, will be the vehicle through which we will address the themes of the course. Critical thinking, analytical and expository writing, and reflective reading are all essential skills that will be developed.	***The Human Need to Believe and the Nature of Belief*** **Week 1:** Chet Raymo, *Skeptics and True Believers* (Introduction); Augustine, "On Truth in Pagan Beliefs"; Bertrand Russell, "Why I Am Not a Christian" **Week 2:** "Why I Am Not a Christian"; Frances Bacon, "Of Atheism" **Week 3:** Stephen Dunn, "At the Smithville Methodist Church"; John Updike, "Pigeon Feathers"; Film: *Contact* **Week 4:** *Rig Veda* (Book 10, Hymn 129); *Upanishads* (selections) **Weeks 5 and 6:** C. S. Lewis, *Mere Christianity* ***Cultural Forms and the Death of Thought*** **Week 7:** Matt Taibbi, "The Day the TV Died"; Neil Postman, *Amusing Ourselves to Death* (selections); Charles Colson, "Does the Devil Have All the Good Music?" **Weeks 8, 9, 10, and 11:** Ray Bradbury, "The Concrete Mixer"; Aldous Huxley, *Brave New World*; Ted Child, "I Have Memories of the Sky" ***Spirituality and Meaning: The Levels of Value*** **Week 12:** *Digha* (selections); Yoshida Kenko, "Essays in Idleness" (selections) **Week 13:** Wordsworth, "The World Is Too Much with Us"; Thoreau, "Where I Lived, and What I Lived For" **Week 14:** Anonymous, "Moderation in Food"; Thomas Merton, *Thoughts in Solitude* (selections); Platon of Kostromo, "Rules of the Pious Life"	Quizzes, short in-class and out-of-class writing assignments: 25% Daily preparation, homework checks, and participation: 25% Essays and exams: 50% The course will consist of two terms, each worth 30% of the final grade. The provincial exam is worth 40% (the latter is a policy for all accredited high schools in British Columbia-HVB)
Guiding questions: The course outline adds a "beginning" activity that introduces some of the guiding questions of the course: What is the relationship between faith and intellect? Are there "levels of truth"? Is there a higher level of knowledge (than objective scientific knowing)? Are there ways of knowing that transcend the mind? To be a Christian is not merely to seek after illumination—it is to strive for transformation. Can we find this transformation by approaching truth through secular models of knowing? Or is the place of a Christian outside of "worldly wisdom"?	The remaining four weeks include selections from Mother Teresa, the Catechism of the Catholic Church, John Donne, Augustine, John Henry Newman, 1 John 1–2, and Thomas à Kempis. Films shown are *Religions of the World: Catholicism*; *Mother Teresa: A Life of Devotion*; and *Tammy Faye: Faith and Flamboyance*. The last week of the course is used to prepare students for the provincial government examination.	

Fig. 6.7 Sample Curriculum Overview Grid
(Elaine Brouwer, Alta Vista College)

Month	Concept	Understandings	Essential Questions	Skills	Assessments	Integration Possibilities	State Standards
September							
October							
November							

Fig. 6.8 Japan Integral Unit Plan (Kindergarten)
(Wilma Van Brummelen; Langley Christian School)

Intended Learning Outcomes	Key Learning Activities	Assessment and Evaluation	Gov't Learning Outcomes
To gain a sense of God's love for diversity and races as He created all people in the world	Discussions; have Japanese person(s) as guests in the classroom; read Bible stories and books about Japan	Observation; listen to feedback as the unit progresses	
To develop an interest in and appreciation for Japanese culture	Discover Japan's richness of culture through reading books and seeing videos; learning centers about Japanese customs	Listen to students talk about the Japanese facts studied, and observe their activities in learning centers	Demonstrate awareness of natural and human-built environments
To recognize that God has created every human creature in His image and that we are to love the Japanese as ourselves, regardless of differences between our ways of life	Discussions; practice our loving to Japanese people in the classroom and in a Japanese restaurant	Ask individual students for their views; observe behavior in the classroom and in the restaurant	Identify connections between students' thoughts and feelings and their reading, viewing, or listening experiences
To realize the importance of bringing the gospel of Jesus Christ to the ends of the earth including Japan	Discuss missions programs organized by the churches and schools	Observe student feedback during discussions	Identify connections between works that they have read, viewed, or heard
To enjoy and use Japanese language and culture through songs, poems, and familiar words used in everyday Japanese life	Sing Japanese songs; read poems; count in Japanese; use familiar words (e.g., thank you, hello, teacher, goodbye) in Japanese	Listen to individual students	
To compare and contrast the physical features and climate of Japan with our own community, and to recognize that Japan exists in a different time zone	Use maps and pictures to explain the different physical features and books to tell about different time zones	Student responses and feedback about these features	Infer the relationship between the position of an object, its shadow, and the sun
To investigate the people and the culture of Japan: its people, food, transportation, houses and buildings, what people do, and animals	Use picture charts, books, and Japanese articles; have Japanese persons as guests; eat Japanese food; draw pictures every day to reflect what has been taught; have daily class discussions	Student responses; evaluate drawings; listen to feedback as students participate in events	Collect information from a variety of sources and experiences Identify some characteristics of the communities
To examine the similarities and differences between Japanese and Canadian families	Discussions; use pictures, books, and videos on Japanese families and outline how they compare	Oral, visual, and journal feedback	Present information using oral, visual, or written representation
To learn about Japanese arts, crafts, traditions, and how they give expression to the unique nature of that culture	Use centers to practice origami, calligraphy, making kokeshi dolls, carp kites, etc.; fourth-grade buddies cooperate with their kindergarten buddies; draw and make collages to learn about the culture	Evaluate art works done either as a class or in centers	Describe how families can be similar and different

Fig. 6.9   Questions for Evaluating Curriculum Resources

Questions About the Content of Curriculum Resources

1. What commitments, values, priorities, and goals does the resource state or assume? What does it portray as important in the way we live and view the world? Does it promote biblical norms for ethical, economic, aesthetic, and family life? If not, what is the underlying point of view?

2. Which themes does the resource emphasize? Which topics does it consider significant? Do the choices of priorities and goals match those of your program? To what extent are the resource's topics and issues meaningful and relevant for your context?

3. Do the authors deal fairly with issues? Are there any overt or subtle biases in content or graphics? How will students and parents react to the resource?

4. If the perspective of the resource differs from yours, can you still use it? in what way(s)? How can you help students question the content and the inadequacies of the resource?

5. If the perspective of the resource is similar to your own, does the resource stimulate thought and not give glib answers to difficult issues? Can the resource foster intellectual, social, aesthetic, moral, and/or spiritual growth in your students?

Questions About the Pedagogical Use of Resources

1. What are the author's assumptions about teaching and learning? What does the resource imply about the students' role?

2. How does the resource expect (or allow) learning to take place? Does it assume that memorization or reproduction of material is the main focus of learning? Or does it encourage interpretation, analysis, evaluation, and application?

3. Does the resource allow for different types of learning activities, with students able to take responsibility for learning? Does it lead to active involvement in learning? Will it motivate and encourage thoughtfulness, problem posing and solving, personal response, and creativity?

4. Does the resource give suitably difficult content? Is it organized effectively? Does it relate to student experience and background? Is it practical and usable for your program and your students?

5. What other resources would you require? Which would be desirable? Are those available? Do you want to use a class set of the resource or just a few copies? In either case, how can you use the resource effectively with your class?

As such, they play an important role in transmitting the economic, social, and moral views of political and educational leaders. To gain market acceptance, today's textbook authors (as well as producers of audiovisual materials and software) try to be objective and avoid controversy. However, as shown in a study of Canadian elementary textbooks (Van Brummelen 1991, 1994), authors generally promote the worldview and values currently held by persons responsible for making decisions about textbooks. Those perspectives in turn influence both teachers' and students' beliefs, values, and attitudes (Klein 1985, 14).

Therefore, avoid using textbooks and other resources to frame the content and structure of your curriculum. Choose your own direction, scope, and learning outcomes within the contours of the expectations of your school and school community. Ponder and establish how you will help your students gain meaningful content, useful abilities, and positive values and attitudes. Only then decide which resources you will use as tools to help attain your objectives.

What values do textbooks commonly promote? Values bias in individual selections is often easy to discern. One story in the widely used *Impressions* reader describes a girl wondering about Christmas. Since a wise woman did not want to tell her, she goes out to search for it. Eventually, she finds a green glass bottle that she fills with branches of red berries and pine: "And lo! it was Christmas!" The last line in the script is: "Christmas is not only where you find it; it's what you make of it" (Trina Schart Hyman in Booth 1985, 170–84).

This selection fosters several values. First, wise adults do not tell you about important things in life. It is best to find out values and meaning yourself through experience and exploration. Second, whatever value you assign to an object or event, that will be its value for you. You alone choose and assign meaning. Community or cultural values are unimportant. Third, it is up to you alone to make something of whatever you face in life. Here the individualistic and existential values are clear.

In my study of Canadian texts, I went beyond identifying biases of specific selections, however. I teased out underlying values that pervade textbooks as a group. I described, for instance, how science authors promote the idea that technology guarantees continued progress. Such progress centers on an ever-improving consumer lifestyle, not on social justice or moral integrity. Reading anthologies foster the notion that personal courage and persistence are the basic ingredients of success and happiness. In social studies books families are arbitrary groups of people who band together for common advantage. Although authors avoid obvious sexism and racism, they neglect the existence of unjust social structures and barriers. Overtly they favor multiculturalism. Yet throughout the books they give the implicit message that to be content, all citizens should fit into the dominant individualistic and materialistic Western way of life.

Textbook authors do foster certain traditional moral values. Do unto others what you would have them do to you. Avoid personal dishonesty, theft, and greed. Hard work and ingenuity lead to personal gain. Yet the authors give students few opportunities to consider moral value problems. They do not deal with the need for making long-term value commitments. Nor do they give any rationale or ethical basis for what the founders of Canada, for instance, called "peace, order, and good government." As such, they do not consider or analyze communally held values that undergird life in a democracy. By the almost universal absence of faith and religion except when discussing aboriginal cultures, the authors also imply that those are irrelevant.

In short, textbook authors attempt to conform students to a narrow, consumer-oriented, individualistic autonomy: "Everything is possible when I am me." We can conclude that:

- Textbooks and resources do influence students.
- Impartiality in texts is notably absent.
- Most public school texts and resources promote values at odds with those of Christianity.

Such influence goes beyond textbooks. Channel One in Canada shows daily ten-minute news programs in many schools that include two minutes of commercials. Research indicates that students who watch the program regularly are more likely to agree than those who do not that money is everything and that wealthy people are happier than the poor. They also say more often that designer labels make a difference and that they want what they see advertised (Greenberg and Brand 1993, 57).

Other researchers also give reasons why textbooks should not determine the curriculum. Some of these complement my study, while others add other reasons:

- **Most textbooks give a simplified and skewed view of reality (Boyer 1983, 143; Loewen 1995). They bulge with detail without emphasizing basic understandings and generalizations. They often present views that are distorted through startling errors of omission and fact.** A two-year study of twelve science textbooks used by 85 per-

cent of American middle school students showed that they are riddled with errors. John Hubisz, a physicist who led the research project, said, "The books have a very large number of errors, many irrelevant photographs, complicated illustrations, experiments that could not possibly work, and drawings that represented impossible situations." Researchers compiled 500 pages of errors, most of which, Hubisz added, are basic errors, "stuff that anyone who had taken a science class would be able to catch" (*Curriculum Administrator 2001*).

The problems go beyond science. James W. Loewen (1995, 4) describes one American history text that gives no fewer than 444 main ideas and 624 key terms. He also points out that the same text makes numerous factual errors: Columbus' ships, for example, were not storm battered, nor did his crew threaten to throw their stubborn captain overboard (48–50). Samuel Wineberg (1991) presented a description of a well-known event from eight different American history textbooks to groups of historians and students. Significantly, the students judged the excerpt that was ranked as least trustworthy by the historians to be the most trustworthy account. The students failed to read the subtext bias.

- **When textbooks control the curriculum, the intent often becomes to move from cover to cover, with no clear overarching purpose.** Yet the "packaged" knowledge of textbooks gives students little insight into how we get to know, how we interpret, and how knowledge is often incomplete and contentious. Textbooks tend to cover rather than uncover. Assessment becomes testing based on memorizing the factual material of the text (Wiggins and McTighe 1998, 106–7, 131).

- **Textbooks do not make their philosophy explicit, yet they promote a particular point of view.** Gilbert Sewall, director of the American Textbook Council writes:

  > Publishers cater to pressure groups for whom textbook content is an extension of a broader political or cultural cause. They make books whose content is meant to suit the sensitivities of groups and causes more interested in self-promotion than in fact, scholarly appraisal, or balance. (Sewall 2000, 52)

  Sewall adds that in history texts, editors search for heroes who have advanced today's politically correct agendas, minimizing the roles of persons such as Julius Caesar, Augustine, Luther and Calvin, Copernicus, and Napoleon: "The result is bad history and an incomplete understanding of the origins of the nation and the world today" (p. 36).

- **While history textbooks have improved the amount of coverage of religion during the 1990s, they seldom explain its role in shaping human thought, motives, and action. Many social studies texts are insensitive or adversarial to traditional Judeo-Christian values.** History texts tend to equate the work of missionaries with cultural imperialism, and contemporary religion is shown in scant and unsympathetic ways. They portray Jesus as a social worker rather than as the Son of God (Sewall 1995, 32–34). A recent popular Canadian history textbook (Cranny 1998) makes many startling and false claims about Christianity (e.g., the Romans killed Jesus because they were afraid of Jesus leading an uprising against

them; the earliest known convert to Christianity in Africa was an Ethiopian king who lived in the fourth century; Luther rather than Calvin promoted predestination; many French business families became Calvinists in the century before Calvin was born).

More worrisome is Cranny's general and rather negative portrayal of Christianity. For instance, Cranny repeatedly harps on the negative view Christians had of women through the centuries. Then in the section on Islam, he extensively quotes an eighth-century Persian who wrote that "women are superior to men in certain respects." What he fails to point out is that the Persian's reasons show that he was a Christian, not a Muslim. Islam "fostered a wonderful civilization within a short space of time" (1998, 131), while Christianity just "helped build a common identity for western Europeans" (p. 68). The text shows only Islam as favoring tolerance. It neglects the fact that the concept of tolerance arose in and was coined by proponents of the Scottish Protestant Reformation.

- **Many math and science texts have shifted to the view that knowledge is created (not discovered).** Often students are asked to resolve problems for themselves, not using any particular solution method (McNeil 1995, 139–40). This is not only very time consuming when practiced consistently, but it also leaves the impression that effort counts for more than achievement.

- **The expository material in textbooks often fails to recognize the features of meaningful learning** (Shutes and Peterson 1994, 11–20). If used as a sole or primary source, a textbook may well cater mainly to the analytic learner and be unsuitable for students' developmental levels. Usually teachers need to design a much broader range of learning than those implied by the text. Yet research suggests that the structure of textbooks does affect teaching strategies (Fan and Kaeley 2000).

Just because texts have shortcomings or because you disagree with some of their values does not necessarily mean that you cannot use them to reach your goals. Indeed, at higher grade levels students may well benefit from considering, analyzing, and evaluating resources with perspectives that differ from their own or their teacher's. One Christian school deliberately used a Christian biology textbook for eleventh-grade biology, and an openly evolutionistic text in twelfth grade. It asked the students to critique both texts as they grew in their understanding of biology.

When you are aware of the strengths and weaknesses of resources, you can use them selectively and judiciously, without letting them dictate an agenda at odds with your goals. Assess the worldview, values, and pedagogy promoted by print, audiovisual, and computer resources. Make responsible decisions about your choice of resources and how you use them in your classroom. Many teachers use multiple resources rather than a single textbook, particularly at the elementary level. Then such evaluation may become time consuming.

No matter how you use resources, be alert to opportunities to discuss the underlying worldviews of key print and other resources with your students. Regularly explore the underlying value perspectives. Help students evaluate rather than blindly accept what they read and see. Ask frequent questions and give commentaries on textual content:

- How do you react to this paragraph? Do you think the author has presented a fair point of view? Are there important things that have been overlooked?
- What is the evidence for this claim? How could you check its validity? Are other conclusions or interpretations possible?
- What views does the author promote? Do you agree? Why or why not?

Ask older students to respond to textbook content in a journal, not just to write summaries in their notes. Use two textbooks with different slants, if available. Discourage the feeling that "the textbook knows best." Even second language teachers can on occasion discuss how a text portrays a view of life in its descriptive passages and illustrations.

Teachers usually do not make major textbook adoptions by themselves, of course. Use your position as a member of the school staff to be involved in evaluating and choosing new resource adoptions. Figure 6.9 gives some questions you should ask, particularly for the most promising textbooks being considered. It is important to ask these questions of resources published by both Christian and secular publishers. It is quite possible, for instance, that a Christian textbook may present a Christian worldview, but misses the mark pedagogically. I have seen some excellent resources developed specifically for Christian schools, but, regrettably, also ones whose worldview was little more than enlightenment modernism sweetened with a little Christian icing. In short, assess and choose all your potential resources with care.

Footstep 6-7

Examine some textbooks and use the questions in figure 6.9 to determine their suitability and how you might make use of them in your class.

Alternately, with two or three other people, choose a topic in a text. Before looking at those chapter(s), determine and list what you feel are four or five significant student learning outcomes for the topic. Then read the text and individually make a list of the strengths and weaknesses that you perceive. Share your observations with the others and then discuss:

- What values, commitments, priorities, and goals does the text state or assume? What does that mean for your use of the text for this topic?
- What view of teaching and learning does the text imply? What steps would you take to make effective use of it? Or, if you decide not to use the text, why not? What type of resources would you look for instead?

6. Implement Your Curriculum Plans

As you implement your curriculum plans, you want to sustain progress toward your intended learning outcomes. You want to keep your students interested, responsive, and responsible, while maintaining high standards of work. For this, you need to reflect on the learning and response of your students, and modify your plans accordingly.

Your unit plans guide your daily planning, but they are not formulas cast in stone. Feel free to make desirable revisions. Try to find the causes for student learning struggles, lack of interest, or classroom discontent. Your pacing may be too fast or too slow. If some activities drag on, shorten or delete others. Use teachable moments and student reaction or input to explore some unexpected tangents. Consider the school's day-to-day

rhythm. Some activities may not be suitable for late in the day or for the day before a long weekend. Special programs, unexpected events, hot weather, or restlessness before vacations may force you to alter your plans. Also, sometimes your plans or resources do not fit the nature of your class or its general aptitude. Even when you are meeting your goals, learning activities may have other unintended effects that you need to review. Responsive teachers constantly reflect on the effectiveness of their classroom learning and adjust accordingly, even while activities are going on.

I remember teaching two tenth-grade classes a mathematics unit while at the same time using an innovative collaborative learning approach. With one class this was a resounding success. They taught themselves a surprising amount of mathematics. Excitedly, they tackled difficult, open-ended exploration and application activities. Students in the other class had similar mathematical aptitudes. Nevertheless, my approach floundered with them. Soon the students begged me to go back to my more standard methods. While I didn't abandon the innovation completely, I had to modify it substantially with the second class. To this day, I do not know why I had such dissimilar reactions. But I do know that my pedagogy in the two classes had to differ to attain the same objectives.

Sometimes curriculum adjustments cannot overcome more basic problems that need to be addressed: lack of order in the class or school, frequent external distractions, or poor student attitudes toward learning. But often you can bring about positive change by modifying your pedagogical strategies, changing your sequence or time allocation, adding or deleting learning activities, or just inserting some unexpected excitement in learning.

For a more detailed discussion of the dynamics of curriculum implementation, see chapter nine.

7. Evaluate Your Programs and Their Outcomes

Curriculum evaluation assesses the value or worth of a program, a course, a unit, a pedagogical approach, or the intents of any of these. It does so in terms of the school's mission and aims. Curriculum evaluation should consider the actual effects of a program, whether intended or not. Its purpose is to use findings to make decisions. Such decisions take into account the beliefs held about curriculum groundings, the goals of a school, and the implementation context.

Curriculum evaluation differs from but overlaps with student evaluation. Its focus is on the general impact of a program rather than on the outcome for individual learners. Teachers may use the results of a test to help students overcome personal weaknesses (student evaluation) but also to find out the success of a particular approach (curriculum evaluation). They may also use systematic observation to be able to help a student's individual progress during conferences (student evaluation). However, an analysis of the observations as a whole also may lead to curriculum revisions to improve overall learning (curriculum evaluation). This section will focus on curriculum evaluation; the next chapter will briefly consider student evaluation.

No easy formulas exist to evaluate educational programs. Evaluation takes place before, during, and after planning and implementation processes. Evaluators question, observe, and analyze each of the following:

- Program groundings, intents, and contexts
- Planned and actual student learning
- Impact of resources

- Effects of the program on individual students and on the class

What makes evaluation even more complex is that evaluators (whether teachers or program planners) have a personal stake in the success of a program. They may find it difficult to take distance and be impartial. Yet they are the most familiar with and in the best position to evaluate a program in a particular setting. External assessments such as those designed by departments of education are more impartial but draw only general conclusions. They may, for instance, assess the abilities of seventh-grade students to solve math problems. Their conclusions may lead them to recommend general program revisions. They do not, however, know the best way to teach problem solving to a particular student or class.

The type of curriculum evaluation used depends on the curriculum orientation of the evaluators. Traditionalists use the results of content and skill-based tests to decide whether groups of students are making satisfactory progress with a certain curriculum. Evaluators of the process/mastery orientation devise instruments that include tests, inventories, and checklists. Then they gather and analyze data using suitable statistical methods. They interpret the data in terms of the specified learning outcomes. They base their advice on the discrepancy between the intended learning outcomes and the actual results. Once their recommendations are implemented, the cycle is repeated.

Note that both the traditional and process/mastery evaluations emphasize quantitative data. The data sheds light on student success in learning specific content or skills. Such evaluations, while useful, are limited in scope. They do not concern themselves with how the program affects the type of person the student is becoming.

Evaluators in the experiential orientation, on the other hand, believe that qualitative evaluation is essential for a complete picture. Elliot Eisner, for instance, recommends a process of educational critique that yields a rich subjective description of how students experience curriculum. Evaluators observe school life, the tone of learning, the quality of student work, how events arise and affect the participants, and the subtleties of individual situations (1979, 190ff). This type of evaluation has four interrelated steps (Doll 1989, 269):

1. Consider the question, What is happening here?
2. Describe the situation as accurately as you can.
3. Interpret what you observe in terms of worldview and contextual criteria.
4. Draw conclusions about the quality and merit of what you observe.

The advantage of the latter approach to evaluation is that it sheds light on a curriculum's overall impact. It addresses more basic educational concerns than would a purely quantitative appraisal. Disadvantages are that the criteria are subjective and the evaluation can be very time consuming. In fact, sometimes the resulting reports say as much about the evaluators as about the programs they evaluated.

When a school does a thorough evaluation of a program (e.g., its language arts program), it is important to use both internal and external assessments. Evaluation strategies include informal and formal observation, interviews, checklists and rating scales, teacher and student self reports, and achievement tests. For external evaluations some Christian schools use teams of teacher-leaders from neighboring schools as well as the results of government standardized tests.

To evaluate programs, schools ask questions such as the following:

- What keys to understanding the world does the curriculum use? What does the curriculum assume and endorse about truth and basic values? Is the program in harmony with the school's mission and vision?
- Do the content, recommended resources, and pedagogical strategies match the aims of the school? Do they match the context in which teachers will implement the program?
- Are the intents of the program clear for teachers and students?
- Can the teachers successfully implement the program? Why or why not? Is there sufficient in-service support for the teachers?
- How does the program affect classroom climate, teaching and learning strategies, distribution and use of resources, student learning, and student involvement and interest (including those with special needs)? What effects does the program have, not only in terms of cognitive knowledge and skills, but also in terms of values, dispositions, and commitments? What impact does the implicit curriculum have on the program?
- What are the program's strengths and weaknesses? Does the program meet quality and quantity standards? Do the results justify the cost in time, emotional investment, and money? How do results compare with those of similar and other programs in other schools?

Most program evaluation takes place internally and informally. It is formative; that is, its aim is improvement. It goes on continuously while schools and teachers plan, implement, and conclude units and programs. Teachers may ask their principal or colleagues to give feedback on a course or unit plan. They constantly assess the effects of their strategies and resources as they teach.

Schools also use the results of external evaluations. These may be the reports of external accreditation or evaluation teams (usually accompanied by internal self studies). They also include the results of externally designed tests. In both cases, schools must first ask in what ways the evaluators' beliefs about education match their own. They may disagree with advice because of a different perspective about the aims of education. Some years ago, for instance, a government-sponsored evaluation in my jurisdiction showed that the attitudes of Christian school students to science were less positive than those of their public school counterparts. A closer analysis revealed, however, that the problem was not the students' attitude but the bias of the test questions. Christian school students had been discernibly negative in their reaction to statements that claimed, for instance, that science is key to solving the world's problems. Nevertheless, while test results need to be interpreted in terms of the overall aptitude of students at that grade level, test results can be used to identify aspects of the curriculum that need attention and improvement.

Footstep 6-8

A school science curriculum committee is sent the results of a major science program evaluation conducted in your province or state. While it concluded that science education is generally satisfactory, it also points to some problems that it asks schools to address:

1. A decrease over the last five years in student performance in science, most noticeably at the third-grade level (from 65 percent to 61 percent correct overall, and from 69 percent to 63 percent in your school)
2. Marginal general scientific knowledge at the third- and sixth-grade levels, and a weakness in rational thinking skills in science
3. A pattern in many classrooms of science teaching not engaging learners
4. Few students wanting to pursue science careers
5. Schools spending insufficient time in science at the primary levels

How would the availability of this report affect your committee's planning? How would you make use of the above results? What additional evaluation of your school's program would you do in order to develop defensible recommendations?

Footstep 6-9

If someone asked you to list the three or four key questions you would ask when evaluating a school program, which ones would you list? Which questions would you ask after you had taught a unit?

Reviewing the Main Points

- As they plan the curriculum, schools and teachers must take into account the economic, social, political, cultural, and religious context of their supporting community.

- **Many curriculum players affect the nature and scope of the curriculum of a school.** Teachers are ultimately responsible for classroom curriculum planning and implementation. Their planning leads to day-to-day lesson plans that keep in mind the needs of their students and class dynamics. They use their beliefs and insights but work within the framework established by government agencies, professional organizations, school systems, their local school, and their parent community.

- **Steps in curriculum planning** include the need to:
  - Bear in mind your aims, intents, groundings, and external expectations throughout your planning.
  - Make yearly plans that identify the principal content, concepts, understandings, essential questions, and/or skills; a timeline; and assessment strategies.
  - Design or adapt a unit plan.
  - Evaluate and choose suitable resources. Identify basic perspectives and biases in resources, and encourage and help students to do so as well.
  - Implement your curriculum plans.
  - Develop strategies to evaluate your program, its outcomes and effects, on an ongoing basis. Ask yourself how you can make learning more effective the next time you teach a unit.

References

Booth, J., ed. 1985. *Over the mountain.* The first of two grade 3 reading anthologies in the *Impressions* readers. Toronto: Holt, Rinehart, and Winston.

Boyer, E. 1983. *High school: A report on secondary education in America by the Carnegie Foundation for the Advancement of Teaching.* New York: Harper & Row.

Brouwer, E. 2000. Mapping your curriculum: using the mapping process to promote ongoing dialogue about biblical perspective. *InSearch,* Seattle: Alta Vista College (September/October).

Council of Ministers of Education, Canada (CMEC). 1997. *Common framework of science learning outcomes K–12: Pan-Canadian protocol for collaboration on school curriculum.* Toronto, ON: CMEC Secretariat.

Curriculum Administrator. 2001. It's third period … Do you know where your science textbooks have been? *Curriculum Administrator* 37 (3): 20.

Cranny, M. 1998. *Pathways: Civilizations through time.* Scarborough, ON: Prentice Hall Ginn.

Doll, R. 1989. *Curriculum improvement: Decision making and process.* 7th ed. Boston: Allyn and Bacon.

Eisner, E. 1979. *The educational imagination: On the design and evaluation of school programs.* New York: Macmillan.

Elmore, R., and S. Fuhrman, eds. 1994. *The governance of curriculum.* Alexandria, VA: Association for Supervision and Curriculum Development.

Fan, L., and G. Kaeley. 2000. The influence of textbooks on teaching strategies: An empirical study. *Mid-Western Educational Researcher* 13 (4): 2–9.

Fuhrman, S., ed. 2001. *From the Capitol to the classroom: Standards-based reform in the states.* 100th yearbook of the National Society for the Study of Education. Chicago: NSSE.

Greenberg, B., and J. Brand. 1993. Channel One: But what about the advertising? *Educational Leadership* 51 (4): 56–58.

Jacobs, H. 1997. *Mapping the big picture: Integrating curriculum and assessment K–12.* Alexandria, VA: Association for Supervision and Curriculum Development.

Keenan, D. 1998. *Curriculum development for Christian schools.* Colorado Springs: Association of Christian Schools International.

Klein, G. 1985. *Reading into racism: Bias in children's literature and learning materials.* London: Routledge, and Kegan Paul.

Koole, Robert. 2000. Do you feel that your hands are tied? *Curriculum Link,* Langley, BC: Society of Christian Schools in British Columbia (November).

Loewen, J. 1995. *Lies my teacher told me: Everything your American history textbook got wrong.* New York: The New Press.

McNeil, J. 1995. *Curriculum: The teacher's initiative.* Englewood Cliffs, NJ: Merrill.

Sewall, G. 1995. Textbooks and religion. *The American School Board Journal* 182 (9): 32–34.

————. 2000. History 2000: Why the older textbooks may be better than the new. *Education Week* 31 May, pp. 36, 52.

Shutes, R., and S. Peterson. 1994. Seven reasons why textbooks cannot make a curriculum. *NASSP Bulletin* 78 (565): 11–20.

Society of Christian Schools in British Columbia (SCSBC). 1998. *Christian pathways for schooling: Curriculum planning.* Langley, BC.

Van Brummelen, H. 1991. The world portrayed in texts: An analysis of the content of elementary school text-books. *The Journal of Educational Thought* 25 (3): 202–21.

———. 1994. Faith on the wane: A documentary analysis of shifting worldviews in Canadian textbooks. *Journal of Research on Christian Education* 3 (1): 51–77.

Walker, D. 1990. *Fundamentals of curriculum*. San Diego: Harcourt Brace Jovanovich.

Wiggins, G., and J. McTighe. 1998. *Understanding by design*. Alexandria, VA: Association for Supervision and Curriculum Development.

Wineberg, S. 1991. On the reading of historical texts: Notes on the breach between school and academy. *American Educational Research Journal* 28 (3): 495–519.

*S*teppingstone *7*

Planning Classroom Units

Principal Lloyd Den Boer had in mind at least three goals when he proposed to his staff a schoolwide integral unit. First, he wanted to give his 400 elementary students a meaningful learning experience, one that would bind them into a closer community. Second, he wanted to improve his teachers' curriculum-planning skills. Those skills included choosing significant curriculum themes, enduring understandings, and modes of knowing; and designing activities for various learning styles. Third, he hoped the joint planning would bring primary and intermediate teachers in closer contact so they would share their insights and skills.

Den Boer and a consultant drew up a proposal for a one-week unit, with an open house celebration to follow one week later. From 10:30 to 12:20 each day, cross-age groups of students would investigate one of five topic strands. Students would return to their own classrooms in the afternoons. Each would serve as an "expert" in one strand, teaching the others about that strand. Den Boer's staff agreed with the proposal and chose Oceans as the main topic.

The consultant came in for a professional development day in mid-November. He showed how the unit could help students explore and experience Christian discipleship. He stressed that it must be Christ centered, teacher directed, student oriented, and community connected. He helped teachers develop a thematic statement:

> The ocean is a large part of our created world, teeming with life. It reflects God's power and the diversity of His creation. He made it good, for our use and enjoyment. As stewards, we have a responsibility to care for the ocean. Where greedy people have misused and squandered this gift, we can influence decisions made about its restoration and maintenance. We base our hope in its ultimate renewal on our belief that eventually all things, including the ocean, will be made new when Christ returns.

Staff discussions led to five different unit strands: creatures of the sea, physical aspects of the ocean, using the sea, effects of the ocean, and exploration and transportation. After the professional development day, some teachers had misgivings about the "jigsaw" approach. They preferred students to spend one day on each strand in rotation. Others felt that the strands were too abstract for young children. The principal called a meeting in late November where a discussion of the two approaches led to an 8 to 8 tie vote. After giving the staff the opportunity for more input, he decided to go with the original plan, but the topics for the five strands would be more concrete. That's how "using the sea" became "fishing."

Den Boer gave the five planning groups a timeline. In the second week of December, all five groups were to report on their general direction. In mid-January they were to share their objectives; two weeks later, their activities. Den Boer also put out a short report on how to meet the needs of diverse learners, including special needs students. Also, he gave out a planning chart on living things in oceans prepared by another school. The chart gave suggested activities in five developmental areas. The learning assistance teacher provided lists of reading and writing activities suitable for different levels.

Next, teachers developing the five strands set out to gather resources. They planned learning activities and assessment to fit the thematic statement. They assigned about sixty students from grades one through seven to each strand. The school launched the unit in late February.

The students in the "fishing" strand visited a fishing village and saw a film on salmon fishing. In small groups, they made charts on what they knew about oceans. Den Boer told them the sad story of the demise of the Atlantic cod fishery and its effects on the people of Newfoundland. He emphasized that God gave us resources that were decimated by international as well as local overfishing. Divided into four groups, students completed a handout on this story with their partner from another grade level. The students also worked on one of five projects, ending with a fish-tasting party prepared by some mothers.

In general, activities geared to lower grade levels were successful. Students, for instance, appreciated picture books read by the teacher, even if the books were written for children several years younger than their own age. Older and younger buddies collaborated well on activities such as writing stories together using "ocean words." They had one pencil between them and were instructed to include setting, characters, a problem, a solution, and an ending. Art and craft activities were effective because teachers geared them to a spectrum of age groups.

The unit was not without glitches. Some first- and second-graders felt overwhelmed, particularly if their group met in a sixth- or seventh-grade classroom. They grasped concepts primarily when they were taught in the context of story settings, and were perplexed when some more abstract activities did not relate directly to fish. Some homeroom teachers just asked their students to share what they had learned in the morning session instead of using the jigsaw approach. Nonetheless, the unit created a real sense of community in the school, with younger and older students helping each other and feeling good about their interaction. The unit was one of the highlights of the year for most teachers and students.

What do you see as the pros and cons of planning a unit like this with a whole school? Consider how the teachers worked together, the cross-age groupings, the thoroughness and complexity of planning, and the jigsaw approach. In what ways can the principal claim that "everything in curriculum that needs attention came out" because of this unit? Make a list of the steps needed to design a unit. Compare your list with the one you will read in the next section.

Designing and adapting units is probably the most significant component of your curriculum planning. Even more than in yearly or daily planning, you must consider your intents carefully and establish how you will go about accomplishing them. When you are developing units, it is especially important that your general goals and views of content and pedagogy play a crucial role. You must keep asking yourself, Where am I taking my students?

A unit is a portion of the curriculum that focuses on a particular theme. The theme could center on a topic and its concepts, or on an issue or problem that requires investigation to find a desirable solution. I have seen effective units as short as one week and as long as twelve, although most tend to be between three and five weeks. Some units concentrate on one subject or aspect of reality. Others are fully integrated: they deal with a theme that involves many aspects of reality. Some units may be taught in three 45-minute class sessions per week; others may be organized in half-day blocks of time. In short, units come in all shapes and sizes.

Students can experience the advantages of both integrated and subject-focused curriculums if teachers plan their units to be *integral units*. I use the term *integral* rather than the more common *integrated* deliberately. *Integral* means that the unit forms a unity with a clearly focused theme. While this is also true for integrated units, the term *integrated* also implies that the unit is a multidisciplinary one. It is possible to have effective integral units whose content embraces one, two, or many subject fields.

For example, the unit on oceans described at the beginning of this chapter is both an integral and an integrated one. The thematic statement gave the unit a clear focus. At the same time, it included science, social studies, language arts, and art content. However, a fifth-grade teacher could also design an integral unit on oceans that centers mainly on science but brings in other aspects of reality only occasionally. The latter makes limited use of the "pizza" model of integration and avoids the "soup" model (see chapter 4).

An integral unit, in short, can be fully integrated in the "soup" sense of the term or have very little content integration. An integral unit is defined as follows:

An **integral unit** is a portion of a course or program that has a clear thematic focus and that:

1. Has internal unity
2. Has external consistency
3. Includes pertinent and meaningful aspects of reality that are related to, and may even go beyond, the main discipline focus of the unit

---

First, an integral unit is internally unified. That is, as a teacher you direct all thought and activity toward a unifying theme. Such a theme focus is more than a natural phenomenon, an event, or an issue. It does not just list a topic such as *To Kill a Mockingbird,* Explorers, Light, or Statistics (all topics with good potential). Rather, it contains the key idea(s) and concepts, the values, and the dispositions that you want to foster in the unit. You capture the central purpose when you formulate your thematic statement. This statement provides the framework for the unit's objectives or intended learning outcomes, content, activities, and structure. Themes often soar beyond the particular topic or subject discipline, contributing to the personal development of students and encouraging them to commit themselves to live by what they learn.

Second, an integral unit is externally consistent. That is, it explicitly intends to attain some of the overall aims of the school and, where applicable, the goals of subject discipline(s). Further, the unit is planned on the basis of a well-defined curriculum orientation, and it promotes a defensible and coherent set of values, attitudes, and dispositions. Two curricular consequences may result if teachers do not plan for external consistency. The unit may be internally unified but may address issues or use approaches that the school considers insignificant or that detract from its basic aims. Also, the unit may have interesting content but fail to nurture values and commitments considered crucial for the well-being of students and society.

The third characteristic of an integral unit is that it includes significant, natural interrelations that exist between its central concepts and aspects of reality that may go beyond its main focus. In this way students experience how the aspects of reality interrelate. They begin to understand the unity of knowledge and life that exists within the diversity of our experiences. Many unforced, meaningful relationships exist for almost any topic. A history unit on revolution may consider, for instance, how the arms industry affected the Iranian revolution and its consequences, how art posters are used to maintain internal support for a revolution, how both emotions and economics play a role in the cause of revolutions, whether armed revolution is ever ethically justifiable, and how religious and worldview beliefs affect revolutions. Including meaningful interrelationships that go beyond the unit's main subject focus encourages students to address significant, multifaceted problems and phenomena.

Good integral units have other features, of course. They provide carefully designed activities for students with diverse learning styles and different aptitudes, engaging a spectrum of modes of knowing. They include activities that foster understanding, skill development, problem solving, and creativity. They use assessment and evaluation to promote their aims. An integral unit with these characteristics could be a unit taught within a particular subject area. It could also be one, however, with the features of any of the four types of integration described in chapter four. A teacher can plan worthwhile integral units regardless of a school's curriculum organization.

Footstep 7-1

Donna Ferguson taught a unit on trees and forests to her fourth-grade students. The topic was particularly relevant since her community's economy depends mainly on the forest industry. Her theme was that, as stewards of God's earth, people must be concerned about natural habitats and must therefore develop a new approach to forestry, one that replaces immediate greed with long-term care and responsible harvesting of trees.

She planned all activities to relate to her theme. The class made a "giving tree" showing all the things that God provides through trees. She discussed God's righteous anger at ecological abuse. The students made scrapbooks about trees and forests that included much personal response. Six field trips—to a forest company logging operation, a wood veneer plant, a tree sanctuary, a forest museum, an original growth forest, and a forest tour organized by an environmental group—provided the basis for structured activities and student response. The teacher kept in mind her general goal of discipleship not only for students in these learning activities but also for those planning and directing a fund-raising effort for tree planting in Ethiopia. She emphasized that responsible stewardship can lead to hope for the future. She designed the unit so that students not only were learning about science but also were involved in some language arts, geography, and art activities.

Does this unit meet the criteria of an integral unit? Why or why not? What changes would you make if you taught the unit? Explain your reasons.

Nine Steps in Planning Classroom Units

The following pages detail the steps for planning integral units. Often you may not follow these steps in strict order; in fact, steps 4 through 8 are best done simultaneously. Also, the suggested steps are not intended to be a rigid formula. Many teachers use these steps effectively, but others plan successfully in different ways. Reflect on the examples given from units designed by classroom and preservice teachers. It is also worthwhile, as you read, to perform the steps, at least in outline form, for a unit that you plan to teach at some point.

NINE STEPS IN DESIGNING A UNIT

1. Consider the suitability of a proposed topic.
2. Brainstorm ideas, possibly using a planning chart or web diagram.
3. Formulate your unit focus (e.g., a thematic statement, guiding questions, and intended learning outcomes; or Egan's narrative structure with binary opposites or transcendent values).
4. Design, balance, and sequence learning activities. Include a motivational introductory activity and a culminating summative one.
5. Review linkages with state or provincial standards and/or curriculum guides, adding or revising learning activities accordingly.
6. Plan a schedule.
7. Select your resources.
8. Plan student assessment. Throughout the unit, consider what evidence will show that you have met your intents.
9. Review the effectiveness of your unit.

1. Consider the Significance and Relevance of a Topic

Often a school will begin by determining what unit topics are to be taught at various grade levels. It may base such decisions on recommendations in curriculum guides or the availability of appropriate resources. There are also occasions when teachers themselves choose unit topics or adapt them from general recommendations. If, in first grade, you need to teach something about mammals, for instance, you could teach a unit on whales or one on farm animals. If you teach seventh- or eighth-grade history, you could decide to include a unit on the Middle Ages, or to jump quickly from a unit on ancient Rome to one on the Renaissance. You may well choose the novel(s) to include in your tenth-grade English course. In the introduction to this chapter, the teachers chose the topic Oceans. But before making the decision, they considered fifteen other topics, including Democracy, The Desert, Food, Forgiveness, Handicapped People, The Media, and Water.

Whether or not you choose your own topics, it is a worthwhile exercise to consider in what ways a topic can be made significant to your students. Your school can also consider the significance of each topic when you plan, for instance, a complete topical grid for the social studies or science curriculum. In it, you can use questions similar to those given for curriculum justification in footstep 1-10:

DETERMINING THE SIGNIFICANCE AND RELEVANCE OF A TOPIC

1. **How can the topic advance understandings needed for responsible and responsive discipleship?**
   - How can the topic introduce students to a Christian worldview, biblically based values, and our Christian and cultural heritage?
2. **How is the topic relevant for your students?**
   - How can the topic expand previous knowledge and deal with significant issues?
   - Is the topic too general, without a clear focus? or too narrow, restricting substantive learning?
3. **Can the topic meet students' learning needs?**
   - Is it suitable for diverse backgrounds, learning styles, aptitudes, and developmental phases?
   - Can it engender interest and encourage personal, meaningful response?
   - Can it include skill development in different modes of knowing?
   - Are sufficient resources available?

Topics can focus on themes with important concepts, problems, or issues:

- A unit on light may highlight wave theory as an important concept.

- A unit on government may emphasize justice as its key concept.
- A unit on World War II may focus on the problem of how to prevent war and its related atrocities.
- A unit on Africa may highlight issues such as poverty and malnutrition, the devastation caused by AIDS, or the persecution of Christians in a country like Sudan.
- A unit on contemporary music may involve concepts such as rhythm, tempo, and dynamics while also underscoring how music both reflects and shapes culture and its values.
- A unit on geometry may stress the concepts of axioms, postulates, and proof, and, at the same time, have students investigate problems that require non-Euclidean geometry.

Teachers sometimes choose topics that are interesting and accessible but superficial. At the primary level, for instance, I have seen topics like The Circus or Balloons. The Circus has little cultural relevance when compared with a topic such as Life on a Farm. The topic Balloons lends itself to many interesting experiments but is unduly narrow. Changing the topic to something like Our Atmosphere would allow students to investigate broader concepts and issues while still learning from the same balloon experiments. On the other hand, topics such as Change, and Ecology are so general and rich that the resulting units may cover much ground but lack depth and coherence.

A topic has to be suitable for a particular grade level. A topic like Whales is suitable for six-year-olds. Eleven-year-olds would still be interested in this topic; however, they would benefit more from learning about groups of living beings interacting in a certain setting rather than considering just one species. So a study of how whales function could be one part of a more general unit on ocean ecosystems. Some topics that fascinate students at one age will not appeal to different levels. It would be difficult to interest kindergartners in a full unit on the solar system or revolution. And high school students would balk at a unit that looks at neighborhood helpers or at apples and fall.

Of course, you can teach many topics meaningfully at various levels. Transportation is an example (see chapter 5). Similarly, a unit on families is significant at the first grade as well as at the high school level. Six-year-olds would learn how God intends families to be settings where people find love and security. That is not always the case, but families can work at restoring broken relationships. Concrete activities would bring out the fact that unconditional love should be the foundation of all families, no matter what kind. Students would also explore how to use their gifts to show love and empathy for other family members. The children might investigate their family ancestry. Making a family scrapbook might be an ongoing activity throughout the unit (Rau, Roseboom, and Zazitko 1993).

A high school unit on the family could have a similar theme. But now students can analyze the family and family roles in much more depth. They can consider how interdependent family members are bound by loving authority and mutual submission. They can examine biblical standards for marriage and family life, comparing them with current practices. They may also investigate the joys and sorrows of family life (and of singleness), the changes families undergo over time, and the causes and effects of family breakdown. One major activity might be a formal debate on the following statement:

"The present social problems relating to the breakdown of the family are the result of people discounting scriptural norms for the family" (Maggs 1988).

Footstep 7-2

For three or four topics shown below, answer the questions about the significance and relevance of a topic. On that basis, decide whether or not you would choose to teach the topic as a unit, and, if so, at what grade level(s):

- Polar Bears
- Kites
- Progress
- The Arctic
- Poetry
- Geometry
- The Computer
- The Impact of Technology
- Wind and Weather
- Shakespeare's Sonnets
- Rectangles
- Two-Dimensional Figures

2. Brainstorm Ideas

Once you know your unit topic, you want to generate some ideas about its scope, focus, basic understandings, content, skills to be learned, structure, and so on. If other teachers will also be teaching the unit, you may want to brainstorm individually first and then share ideas with your colleagues.

Make a web: Some teachers like to begin by making a web diagram of the concepts and subtopics of the theme. Figure 7.1 shows the start of such a web diagram for a primary unit on gardens. A web is a way to show relationships among relevant ideas and topics. During brainstorming, you can change the web until you feel that the set of subtopics and concepts forms a manageable and unified whole. Most often a web indicates subtopics, sometimes arranged under two or three main concepts. As such, a web gives a topical overview but does not help much in working out a worldview-based approach.

Work out your worldview for the topic: In order to develop a line of action based on a Christian worldview, you can use figures 7.2 and 7.4 as templates, perhaps in enlarged format on a double sheet. Figure 7.2 is based on the key questions directly preceding footstep 3-1. They may help you find a meaningful theme in which to frame your topic. Figures 7.3 and 7.7 show how teachers answered these questions and used them in their unit design.

Consider which aspects of reality are part of the topic and issues: Figure 7.4 lists aspects of reality, with a few key values listed. (Read this chart by moving down the left side and then up the right). Use figure 7.4 as follows:

- Think about your *unit focus.* This could be a theme that incorporates enduring understandings or Egan's narrative structure together with binary opposites or transcendent values. Some teachers like to add some open-ended guiding questions that they want their students to answer as a result of the unit's learning.
- Use the chart's suggested *key values* as a starting point for considering which values to emphasize in your unit.
- Look at the types of *skills* you want students to learn, and indicate them in the appropriate categories.
- Insert some *sample activities* in the appropriate cells.

Figures 7.3 and 7.5 illustrate how such initial planning charts might have looked for a primary unit on gardening, "*How Does My Garden Grow? ... God Makes It So!*" (Chin-nery et al. 1993). Your completed chart will provide a basis for:

- Recognizing the significance of the topic for your students, and what enduring understandings you want them to grasp
- Identifying the values that you can weave into the unit
- Determining which aspects of reality are relevant and can be an integral part of the unit
- Getting some ideas on how to help students learn through different modes of knowing (multiple intelligences)
- Choosing the skills that students can learn in a meaningful setting as part of the unit
- Seeing what types of activities are possible that would fit your topic and theme

The gardening unit centers on science. Where meaningful, the authors have incorporated other aspects of reality. Note that you do not have to try to include every aspect; for instance, figure 7.5 leaves empty the ethical/moral and political/legal aspects. That is not to say that these aspects have no bearing on gardening (e.g., discussing the legality and morality of watering a garden when there is a ban due to a water shortage). The unit's authors, however, decided that other values and activities were more important for the children at this age level and in their context.

Completing such charts will also set the stage for writing your thematic statement and intended learning outcomes. In short, use them for some initial brainstorming and planning.

175

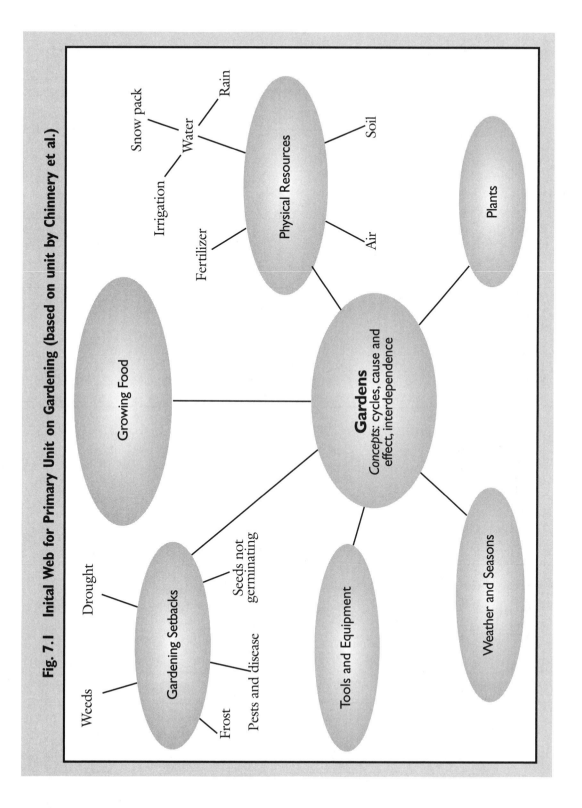

Fig. 7.1 Inital Web for Primary Unit on Gardening (based on unit by Chinnery et al.)

176

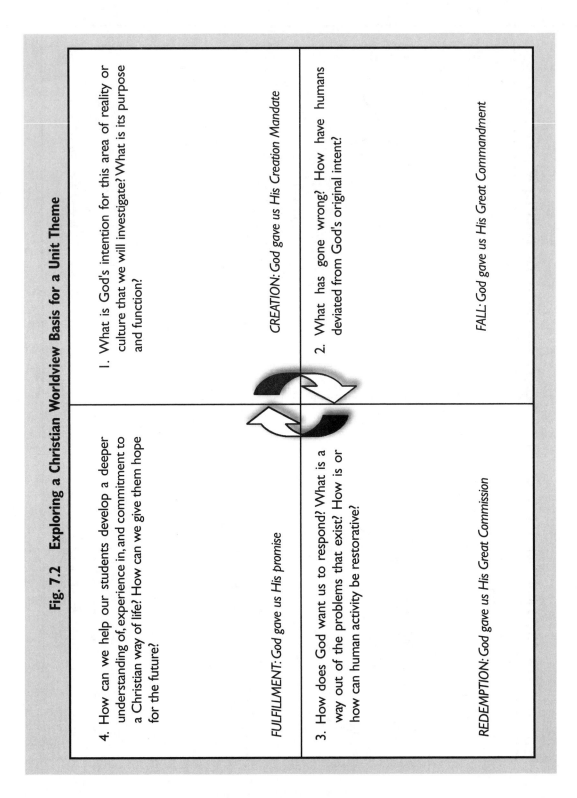

Fig. 7.2 Exploring a Christian Worldview Basis for a Unit Theme

1. What is God's intention for this area of reality or culture that we will investigate? What is its purpose and function?

CREATION: God gave us His Creation Mandate

2. What has gone wrong? How have humans deviated from God's original intent?

FALL: God gave us His Great Commandment

4. How can we help our students develop a deeper understanding of, experience in, and commitment to a Christian way of life? How can we give them hope for the future?

FULFILLMENT: God gave us His promise

3. How does God want us to respond? What is a way out of the problems that exist? How is or how can human activity be restorative?

REDEMPTION: God gave us His Great Commission

Fig. 7.3 Exploring a Christian Worldview Basis for a Primary Unit on Gardening (based on Chinnery et al.)

1. What is God's intention for this area of reality or culture that we will investigate? What is its purpose and function?

⇨ We are to enjoy God's garden, the earth, and the fullness He provides.
⇨ We are to take care of God's garden (keep it holy for His intended purpose that the earth be a beautiful and bountiful home for all creatures).

CREATION: God gave us His Creation Mandate

2. What has gone wrong? How have humans deviated from God's original intent?

⇨ Because of sin, growing food became more difficult (Genesis 3). Also, humans have not always cared for the earth and plants in a way that sustains food production (e.g., soil erosion, lack of composting, use of pesticides that harmed other life).

FALL: God gave us His Great Commandment

4. How can we help our students develop a deeper understanding of, experience in, and commitment to a Christian way of life? How can we give them hope for the future?

⇨ We are to understand that the growing of living things is part of the human praise response to God.
⇨ We are to be living lives of thankfulness for God's provisions for life.

FULFILLMENT: God gave us His promise

3. How does God want us to respond? What is a way out of the problems that exist? How is or how can human activity be restorative?

⇨ We can be good stewards in growing food and flowers, being faithful workers, preventing erosion, being careful with fertilizers, and preserving the earth for future generations.

REDEMPTION: God gave us His Great Commission

Fig. 7.4 Template for Brainstorming Integral Unit Ideas

MATHEMATICAL:
accuracy, precision, responsible use of numbers and space

PHYSICAL AND BIOLOGICAL:
respect for physical things and life, good judgment in observation and interpretation

PHYSICAL HEALTH:
physical wellness, vitality, coordination

PSYCHOLOGICAL/EMOTIONAL:
emotional balance, sensitivity to others, self-control, perseverance

AESTHETIC:
creativity, expressiveness, beauty

ANALYTICAL/LOGICAL:
validity, discernment, respect for the life of the mind

UNIT FOCUS
Theme, major concepts, enduring understandings, guiding questions and/or narrative with transcendent values

CULTURAL FORMATION
(includes history and human geography)

individual and communal responsibility,
love for neighbor

CONFESSIONAL/SPIRITUAL:
faith, devotion, piety

ETHICAL/MORAL:
honesty, integrity, respect for truth, fidelity

POLITICAL/LEGAL:
respect for authority, justice, peace, rights, and responsibilities

ECONOMIC:
stewardship, compassion for the poor and disadvantaged

SOCIAL:
respect for others, cooperation, trustworthiness, humility, kindness

LANGUAGE/COMMUNICATION:
authenticity, meaningfulness, clarity

Fig. 7.5 Ideas for an Integral Unit on Gardening (based on Chinnery et al.)

UNIT FOCUS:
Theme and enduring understandings

How Does My Garden Grow? ...God Makes It So!

- interrelationships and interdependence of physical and living things as they pertain to gardens
- role of people as food producers and as stewards of the "garden"
- pattern and order found in God's creation as it is revealed in garden-related activities

Guiding questions:
Who makes gardens grow?
What makes gardens grow?
How do gardens grow?

CULTURAL FORMATION
(incl. history and human geography)
individual and communal responsibility, love for neighbor

- maintaining the garden
- building and using a composting bin

☑ Values emphasized in unit
⇧ Skills to be learned
🖉 Sample activities

MATHEMATICAL:
accuracy, precision, responsible use of numbers and space
🖉 graphing, estimating, patterning, adding estimating, counting, classifying, and graphing different fruits and vegetables and their seeds

PHYSICAL AND BIOLOGICAL:
respect for physical things and life, good judgment in observation and interpretation
☑ thankfulness for God's provision for plant growth and the large variety of plants we have for food
⇧ observing and recording, designing, planting and growing, weighing using a simple balance scale
🖉 designing and planting a garden
investigating effects of light and water on plant growth

PHYSICAL HEALTH:
physical wellness, vitality, coordination
⇧ motor skills for gardening
parachute game with vegetable names

PSYCHOLOGICAL/EMOTIONAL:
emotional balance, sensitivity to others, self-control, perseverance
☑⇧ persevering over time

AESTHETIC:
creativity, expressiveness, beauty
☑ expressiveness and creativity in use of language, drama, art, music, and technical design

CONFESSIONAL/SPIRITUAL:
faith, devotion, piety
🖉 prayer and praise

ETHICAL/MORAL:
honesty, integrity, respect for truth, fidelity

POLITICAL/LEGAL:
respect for authority, justice, peace, rights, and responsibilities

ECONOMIC:
stewardship, compassion for the poor and disadvantaged
☑ careful and diligent workmanship, responsible stewardship of plants and related physical resources

SOCIAL:
respect for others, cooperation, trustworthiness, humility, kindness
⇧ cooperation

LANGUAGE/COMMUNICATION:
authenticity, meaningfulness, clarity
⇧ listening, speaking, writing, learning vocabulary
🖉 choral reading of student psalms

ANALYTICAL/LOGICAL:
validity, discernment, respect for the life of the mind
⇧ alphabetizing, categorizing, inferring

AESTHETIC, cont.
⇧ singing, illustrating, drama
🖉 dramatizing songs and story books about gardening cycles
🖉 creating a new garden tool

3. Formulate Your Unit Focus

There are several ways to give focus and direction to your unit. One way is to use Kieran Egan's planning frameworks described in chapter 5. Egan's story or narrative format provides a unifying thread that holds a unit together. For the garden unit, for example, a story line could have been, "How the bean got to my plate: The story of a seed." Possible binary opposites could be "plenty versus scarcity" or "success versus failure." Stories within the overall story could include the Bible stories of the Garden of Eden and the Fall, Joseph, and the parable of the sower.

You can use a thematic statement, intended learning outcomes, and guiding questions to provide a clear focus for your unit.

Thematic Statement

A **thematic statement** describes the overall approach that will frame your unit's teaching and learning. It describes your overall goals. In particular, the statement includes:

- The basic values, dispositions, and commitments that you want to foster
- The enduring understandings, major concepts, and key skills that you want students to acquire

---

Sometimes teachers first state some general themes that reflect their school's vision. Then they denote more specifically what they expect their students to learn in the unit, including the important concepts and skills. For a fifth-grade unit on the polar regions, you might include concepts such as cause/effect and interdependence. Skills might include map construction, use of the Internet for researching, and the writing of coherent and clear paragraphs.

Enduring understandings go beyond describing content to be learned. They put content learning in perspective. They help students make sense of what they have learned and enable them to explain, interpret, and apply the key concepts. Enduring understandings are the linchpin ideas that we want students to grasp and retain long after they've forgotten much of the specific content (Wiggins and McTighe 1998, 10). For instance, a fourth-grade unit on the polar regions might include these enduring understandings:

- The earth's polar regions are marked by stark beauty, extreme weather conditions, and delicate ecosystems.
- All living things of the polar regions were created by God to fit a particular niche in that environment.
- The fragility of the polar regions underscores the interdependence of various forms of life as well as the need to take special care of these parts of the earth.

Some curriculum planners write a rationale for a unit rather than a thematic statement. A **rationale** is a thematic statement that begins by giving a justification for a unit. For instance, the rationale for the unit on the polar regions might begin by stating that the unit is important because the impact of humans on the environment is having some alarming effects on these ecosystems.

To develop your thematic statement, use what you said about the suitability and significance of your unit as well as the results of your brainstorming activity. You may find that it takes some practice to write an effective thematic statement. Keep your statement fairly short; you want to reduce the scope of your unit to its essentials. Here is a possible thematic statement for the polar region unit (for other examples see figures 7.6–7.9):

> The polar regions are large areas of the earth marked by stark beauty, harsh conditions, and delicate ecosystems. In this unit students will investigate the fragile nature of the polar regions. They will explore how the living things of the polar regions exist in an extreme climate, are interdependent, and were created by God to fit a particular niche in that environment. They will also study how Inuit communities existed in the past and how they have changed with the intrusion of Western culture and technology. They will consider how human activity has led to some deterioration in the polar region ecosystem and how this will affect life not only in the Arctic and Antarctic but throughout the rest of the world. They will reflect on how people can make and influence decisions that help us make good use of the resources of the polar regions while preserving and restoring its environment. They will recognize that God calls us to take special care of all parts of the earth, including the polar regions. The students will also develop their research and paragraph writing skills in this unit.

Guiding Questions

You may also want to identify three or four guiding questions that will help students focus on the enduring understandings. Some teachers discuss these questions with their students at the beginning of the unit in order to draw them into the unit and help them see the unit's central points. Open-ended why and how questions can help students look for patterns and meaning, think about what they learn at higher levels, and call for personal response (Erickson 2001, 91). For the polar regions unit, the questions might be:

- How do living things depend on each other for survival in the harsh conditions of the polar regions?
- How has human activity affected the polar regions?
- Why is it important for humans to take special care of these regions of the earth? How can this be done?

Some teachers base their guiding questions on the four worldview questions in chapter 3. For instance, the Valley Christian School in Morwell, Australia, asked these questions in planning a grade one/two unit on trees and forests (Brown 1994):

- How do humans depend on trees?
- How have humans negatively affected trees and forests?
- How can humans become better guardians and act responsibly in using forest resources so that the earth can continue to sustain human life?

Try to make guiding questions engaging (e.g., Can human life exist without trees?). Wiggins and McTighe suggest writing the questions at the students' own level, making sure that they understand the questions, posting them in the classroom, and helping students personalize them (1998, 28).

Intended Learning Outcomes (ILOs)

Learning outcomes (the current term for what used to be called objectives) specify and extend your thematic statement. They have not been without controversy in education. At one pole are process/mastery proponents who list detailed learning outcomes or objectives not only for units but for each lesson. They insist on precise, prespecified standards by which you measure whether students have attained each outcome. They may reduce education to learning tidbits of information and skill fragments. Their mechanistic view of the person easily leads to mechanical learning. Little sense may remain of overall aims. They often neglect learning goals that are difficult to measure, important as they may be. Teachers object to the time it takes to develop such very specific learning outcomes. They point out that their activities themselves make clear their goals.

Educators at the other pole argue that learning outcomes are superfluous. They hold that listing the values you want students to learn and outlining an overall approach is all you need to do to choose appropriate and well-focused content and skills. If a school system requires certain learning outcomes, these educators may show that the unit they designed covered those outcomes.

I recommend an approach somewhere between these two extremes. Your thematic statement captures the direction and essential understandings of your unit. It is helpful to develop a set of intended learning outcomes (ILOs) that flow out of your thematic statement but are more specific. I use the term *intended* deliberately. First, all learning includes outcomes that were unplanned and inadvertent. ILOs describe only those that are part of the planned curriculum. Second, we cannot predict or guarantee learning outcomes for all students. Our intent and hope is that students will learn certain understandings and skills.

A set of ILOs provides direction and balance for your choice of learning activities, your selection of resources, and your means of student assessment. When written in terms of student outcomes, ILOs identify the desired results of classroom learning. You reconsider and alter your ILOs as planning progresses. Nevertheless, if the thematic statement provides the compass direction, the ILOs help you see and work toward your

destination. Remember, however, that curriculum planning is not a linear process, and that as your thinking progresses, you will come back to and revise both your thematic statement and your ILOs.

It is often helpful to organize ILOs so that each of three or four major outcomes is achieved through a number of related ones that are smaller and more specific. However, long lists of minute outcomes are unnecessary. Teachers may either neglect them or lose themselves and their students in detail. The danger is that they then overlook the general issues raised by the guiding questions.

Learning outcomes have different emphases. Try to include some ILOs from each category:

- **Content outcomes** set out the subject matter and concepts that students need to learn in order to adequately understand the part of God's creation dealt with in the unit.

- **Ability outcomes** indicate the abilities and skills students learn and develop in the unit. These include processes such as problem posing and problem solving, analyzing and evaluating issues and situations, literacy and numeracy skills, psychomotor abilities, and so on.

- **Value and disposition outcomes** express how you want the unit's purpose and worth to affect your students' attitudes and responses. These outcomes specify what you hope your students will learn to value and how they will act on what they learn.

- **Expressive-creative outcomes** tend to be indefinite and yet important. They allow for creative personal responses and are therefore somewhat unpredictable. Worthwhile learning can take place during expressive-creative experiences even when you cannot stipulate or anticipate precisely what each student will learn.

Outcomes in each category can be at different levels of complexity. Content outcomes, for instance, may involve recall and interpretation, simple application and analysis, or complex application and evaluation. For each ILO, ask yourself why you believe the outcome is important in terms of your thematic statement.

The best way to begin an ILO is with an infinitive that specifies what you expect students to do as a result of their learning. You can preface a set of ILOs with a statement such as "It is intended that students will ..." to emphasize that this is the intent for which you will strive. Below are some descriptors of what students can be expected to do, arranged by approximate levels of difficulty

Least complex level:

define	describe	discuss
enjoy	examine	experience
identify	illustrate	observe
practice	read	recite
select	state	trace

Level of medium complexity:

classify	compare	construct
contrast	critique	demon-
differentiate	distinguish	strate
present	reason	investigate
review	solve	reflect
		write

Most complex level:

analyze	apply	appreciate
assess	create	design
evaluate	explain	generalize
hypothesize	imagine	interpret
justify	pose problems	predict

(although the level depends on the specific performance expectation and its context).

Figures 7.6 through 7.9 give four examples of thematic statements and their related ILOs at various grade levels and for different subjects. The credit for the ideas goes to the teachers who developed these units. I take responsibility for minor editing of the originals for space considerations.

4. Design and Choose Learning Activities

Steps four through eight for designing a unit are best done at the same time. For instance, once you have written a thematic statement and your intended learning outcomes, you have identified your desired results for your unit. So step 8, student assessment, takes place throughout the unit as you consider what evidence will show you that you have attained those results.

Grant Wiggins and Jay McTighe (1998) suggest that you should determine acceptable evidence for meeting your intents *before* planning learning activities. You could begin by asking, for instance, "What would be sufficient and revealing evidence of understanding? What performance tasks must anchor the unit and focus the instructional work?" (p. 68) The authors call this the "backward design" process of planning curriculum (pp. 9ff).

While I appreciate Wiggins and McTighe's motives, it is not always necessary or even feasible to plan assessment evidence prior to designing learning activities. But what is important is that student assessment be planned alongside the design of all key learning activities and not left to the end. Considering assessment at that point will help you see whether the activity can be used to meet your learning outcome(s), or will show you that you need to revise the activity.

Fig. 7.6 Grade I Unit: Trees

Kim Franklin, Arlene Paluch, and Melinda Tegart (Pacific Academy)

Thematic Statement: First-grade children have had many everyday experiences with trees. They view trees as a natural part of their environment and have learned to appreciate the seasonal changes in trees, to enjoy the playful aspect of trees, and to be thankful for some of the gifts trees can give. However, a first-grade child's experience with forests is usually not as broad and may be limited for some of the forest in mystery and fear. A forest theme allows first-grade children to positively experience the natural cathedral-like beauty of forests and to learn about trees in a unique way. They can begin to develop an understanding of the interdependence of living things in a forest ecosystem. They can also observe trees in every stage of their life cycle and marvel at the importance of each stage. By examining the amazing variety of forest trees and their uses, the children can broaden their awareness of the many gifts trees give to both animals and people and will naturally be inspired to respond thankfully to our God who created such an incredible, renewable resource. Finally, the children can consider the impact of taking from trees without caring for trees. They can begin to make responsible decisions as caretakers of this aspect of God's creation.

Learning Outcomes:	Learning Outcomes:	Instructional Strategies and Resources:
Content-focus (facts, concepts, principles) It is expected that students will: √understand that God created an inter-dependence of all living things √acknowledge our responsibility to take care of trees in our environment √understand God's purpose in creating trees, air, shelter, beauty, fruit, shade, nuts, and seeds √understand the symbolic use of trees in the Bible (e.g., tree of life, burning bush, cross)	*Skill- and strategy-focus* It is expected that students will: √memorize and illustrate an understanding of John 15:5 √participate in class discussions √participate in caring for trees and forests in God's creation √retell and illustrate the Creation story √participate in daily prayer, particularly prayers of thankfulness √develop one-to-one letter/sound concept √develop fine motor skills	*Affective and Expressive* √appreciate the beauty and wonder of our environment as God created it √display a heart of thankfulness **Assessment:** √discussion √oral testing √illustration of Creation story and memory verse √notes on students' drama and art √recite and read memory verse √tell story of Creation, *Tale of Three Stories*, *Johnny Appleseed* √songs: "I Shall Not Be Moved," "The Apple Song," "Trees of the Field," "The Old Rugged Cross" √*Adam Raccoon* series

Science Aspect

(the unit has eight aspects, e.g., reading, writing, math)

Learning Outcomes:	Learning Outcomes:	Instructional Strategies and Resources:
Content-focus (facts, concepts, principles) It is expected that students will: √identify seasonal changes of a tree and understand the importance of those changes √identify the stages in the life cycle of a tree in the growth cycle of a tree √develop an awareness of the inter-dependence of all things √discover how trees help and are used by people and animals √identify the parts of the tree and their function	*Skill- and strategy-focus* It is expected that students will: √describe the characteristics of a variety of trees, and compare and contrast the different trees and their parts √determine the requirements of a healthy tree √observe and record their findings when performing simple scientific experiments involving trees and parts of trees √demonstrate the ability to use a magnifying loupe	*Observation* √models, drawings, booklets about trees and forests, labeling and naming parts of trees *Discussion* √student use of vocabulary, comparing and contrasting different trees and their parts *Knowledge* √orally check understanding of concepts, review illustrations and poster, written work, oral presentations √*Private Eye* √thematic books, videos, computer software, posters √student theme booklets √trees and their parts √drama about environment √*The Voice of the Wood* √field trip to forest

Fig. 7.7   Grade 6 Unit: Nutrition—Food for Life   Cindy Halvorson (Trinity Western University)

Biblical Worldview Questions

What is God's purpose for this particular area of creation or culture we are studying?	How has God's purpose been distorted by the effects of human disobedience?	How does God want us to respond?	How can students develop a deeper understanding of and commitment to a biblical way of life?
God provides enough food in creation to meet the physical needs of everyone. The intricacy of our bodies, which require food for life, shows the wisdom of their Creator. From the time of Adam and Eve, God has given people choice in the foods they choose to eat. God's purpose is that all will enjoy physical nourishment through food in creation, and spiritual nourishment through the written Word, the Bible, and the Living Word, Jesus Christ.	Individuals in countries with plentiful food choices can choose whether or not to eat foods that provide nourishment to their bodies. Thus, they can treat them as temples of the Holy Spirit. While there is enough food in creation to feed the entire world, many people are hungry because of human disobedience in the forms of selfishness and corruption. There is enough food to feed all, but not the will to share among those who have much more than they need.	As those who have access to plentiful nutrition, God wants us to respond with gratitude and humility. As stewards of creation, our role is not to be wasteful, and to share with those who are hungry, both in our own country and throughout the world. While the issue of world hunger may seem too complex or immense to deal with, individuals who take action can provide significant help. In addition to sharing physical sustenance, Christians are also called to meet spiritual hunger.	Students should be given knowledge of their bodies' own nutritional needs and challenged to commit to treating their bodies as temples of the Holy Spirit. Through exposure to foods and food-related traditions from other cultures, students can consider the ways in which various cultures are alike and different. Also, through increased awareness of the problem of global hunger, students can be challenged to respond with compassionate generosity, as God calls them to do.

Thematic Statement

Nutrition is a requirement for life. An important aspect of healthy living is to treat the amazing bodies God designed for us with respect by choosing to eat well. Proper nutrition has many benefits to the body, from an increased energy level to prevention of diet-related diseases. Eating well is part of living well.

In this unit, students will deepen their understanding of their own nutritional needs and will appreciate the benefits of adequate nutrition. They will examine why people choose to eat the food they do and the impact of these choices. Also, students will critically examine advertising messages about food. Through personal reflection, they will be encouraged to incorporate nutritional knowledge into lifelong nutritional practice.

A global perspective will broaden this study, as students will experience foods eaten in different regions of the world, foods that vary because of geographical features and cultural traditions. It is hoped that students will develop an appreciation for the abundance of food that God has provided in creation, as well as an awareness of the prevalence of hunger in our world, the result of human sinfulness. Students will be challenged to respond with compassionate generosity.

Intended Learning Outcomes

TO KNOW	TO DO	TO VALUE
It is expected that students will:	It is expected that students will:	It is expected that students will:
K1 Become aware of their own eating habits	D5 Analyze advertising messages relating to food	V9 Experience and respect foods and food-related traditions from other cultures and geographical regions
K2 Understand their bodies' nutritional needs	D6 Respond practically to the global problem of hunger	V10 Marvel at the intricacy of our bodies as designed by the Creator in His great wisdom
K3 Recognize the many benefits of adequate nutrition	D7 Construct a personal vision of healthy living that includes but extends beyond nutrition	
K4 Examine biblical themes that point to Jesus Christ as the answer to our deepest kind of hunger	D8 Explore and present the information learned in a variety of creative ways, according to students' interests and abilities	

Fig. 7.8 Grade 8 Unit: Cells—The Wonder of Life Chiang et. al. (Ontario Alliance of Christian Schools, 2001)

Thematic Statement	Intended Learning Outcomes		
	TENDENCY (ATTITUDE)	COGNITIVE	SKILLS
The fear and wonder of being created includes our awe of one cell multiplying and growing to become a complexity of countless cells working together as tissues, organs, and systems of organs. We are "knit ... and ... woven together" (Psalm 139:13–15): the created being is made up of intricately designed single units woven together to serve particular functions in the whole as God intended. All creatures reflect the order that is found in the basic unit of living things. In Genesis God declares the final, unified product to be good. *Cells: The Wonder of Life* is a study of the cell as the basic unit of living things. The characteristics of living things and the organization of cells into organ systems will set the stage for students examining the cell and its organelles through microscopic exploration. They will investigate osmosis and diffusion—cell processes that have application in their lives. They will give attention to understanding the differences between multicellular and unicellular organisms. They will focus particularly on understanding plant structures: cells functioning as tissue, organs, and organ systems. The creation exhibits God's purposeful and willful design. God's awesome demonstration of this design is evident in the adaptations in plants for a variety of environments. Students will also reflect on the effects of sin found at the cellular level, and be reminded of and challenged to be aware of their communal and individual responsibilities as stewards of God's creation.	It is expected that students will: 1. Appreciate the intricacies of the cell 2. Respect the diversity and order in creation as represented by cells 3. Marvel at the organization of cells to work together and serve the entire organism 4. Care for the microscope 5. Make personal connections between the application of their cell knowledge and their lives 6. Recognize the effects of the "cloak of sin" that affects all of creation (including cells) 7. Be aware of the restorative gifts of God that overpower the effects of sin	It is expected that students will: 8. Know what characterizes living things 9. Explain the concept of the cell theory 10. List the differences between plant and animal cells 11. Recognize the differences between multicellular and unicellular organisms 12. Know the parts and functions of cells 13. Explain osmosis and diffusion 14. Become familiar with the organization of cells into tissue, organs, and systems in plants	It is expected that students will: 15. Demonstrate the proper use and care of a microscope 16. Prepare and stain wet mounts 17. Develop lab reporting and communication skills 18. Learn self-evaluation and cooperative learning skills 19. Make proper biological drawings 20. Practice making qualitative and quantitative observations

Fig. 7.9 Grade 8 Unit: Novel Study—*The Outsiders*   Jodaye St. Cyr (Trinity Western University)

Thematic Statement	Intended Learning Outcomes		
	KNOWLEDGE It is expected that students will:	**SKILLS** It is expected that students will:	**DISPOSITIONS** It is expected that students will:
Literature is a way of conveying meaning to students, providing them with the means to interact with the world. Studying a novel provides opportunity to explore the language, themes, imagery, structure, point of view, literary devices used, different levels of meaning, and interpretation. Furthermore, it is through stories (novels) that we struggle to discover what we have been, who we are, and what we ought to be. S.E. Hinton's *The Outsiders* is a novel that can help students as they attempt to understand and act in God's world. Through adolescence, the need for belonging is an ongoing concern for teens. They begin to move away from relying on their parents and toward the need for acceptance from their peers. God created each unique student to learn how to accept and love each other in order to build healthy friendships and relations. *The Outsiders* is a novel containing several themes that will affect eighth-grade students in many areas of their lives, including social, language, emotional, aesthetic, ethical, and moral. The novel centers on friends and family relationships, making it possible for the students to personally engage with the themes of the text. They will think about and respond to what it means to belong; the significance of friendship and family, loyalty and acceptance; the role of responsibility and accountability; and the meaning behind life and death. In this unit, students will deepen their understanding of literary analysis and their appreciation for literature, while providing much opportunity for listening, speaking, writing, dramatizing, expressing points of view, and valuing. Students will compare the values in the novel with their own experience and beliefs, explore who they themselves are, and learn to value life in the way God intended.	1. Define new, challenging vocabulary words found in *The Outsiders* 2. Identify the author's purpose for writing 3. Name the character traits of the antagonist and protagonist in *The Outsiders* 4. State the central themes in the novel 5. Identify three levels of conflict: man vs. man, man vs. self, and man vs. environment 6. Explain how Ponyboy develops and matures throughout the novel 7. Recognize stereotypes in the novel and in students' own experience 8. Draw conclusions about the themes in the novel 9. Assess the meaning of the symbols used in the novel 10. Analyze the significance of the important events in the novel	11. Formulate their own ideas and concepts, and effectively communicate them to the rest of the class 12. Make critical judgments about actions and consequences in *The Outsiders* and in their own lives 13. Use brainstorming, group discussion, and reading to generate ideas for writing 14. Interpret meaning behind characters' actions and words in *The Outsiders* 15. Compare and contrast the conflicts in the novel to those in present-day society 16. Communicate effectively in both oral and written assignments 17. Display divergent thinking in creative exercises 18. Work cooperatively and productively in a group of their peers 19. Use punctuation correctly 20. Correctly format written documents	21. Value God's creation by developing an increased awareness, appreciation, and respect for life 22. Relate literary experience to personal experience, making connections between the events of the novel and events in their own lives 23. Explore values, morals, and ideals both collectively and personally 24. Appreciate the significance of looking at situations from different perspectives 25. Respond personally to the themes of friendship, belonging, peer pressure, family relationships, violence, death, and the value of life through discussion, writing, and individual pursuit 26. Develop an enjoyment and desire for future reading and literary analysis

That is why the Japan unit for kindergarten (figure 6.8) included an "Assessment and Evaluation" column right beside the "Key Learning Activities" column. In short, even though steps 4 through 8 are described in turn, keep in mind that you will carry out the steps concurrently.

Every year I am delighted with the inventiveness of preservice teachers in my curriculum planning course. They have all observed classrooms in action, but most have not yet taught. Working in small groups, they are able to come up with a wealth of possible learning activities on almost any topic. Some of these activities have to be modified to fit particular age levels, and others may need to be structured more tightly. Nevertheless, these future teachers are able to come up with many worthwhile and useful learning experiences.

What is more difficult is to ensure that the activities fit the intents of a thematic statement and the detailed learning outcomes. They must also suit the intended audience and form a balanced unity. To do so, keep the following questions in mind:

Questions to Guide Your Thinking About Learning Activities

1. Does each learning activity contribute to your unit's **thematic statement and ILOs**? Does the set of activities do justice to your overall theme?
2. Will the activities help **meaningful learning** to take place? (e.g., students have the prerequisite knowledge and aptitudes; the level of difficulty is suitable; activities are adaptable for special needs)
3. Do the activities include a **range of pedagogical strategies**? Is there a suitable balance of the four phases of learning? learning styles? the modes of knowing or multiple intelligences? Do the activities include varied student products so that students can demonstrate their understanding in different ways? Is there adequate involvement and response?
4. Do the activities encourage the learning of enduring understandings, worthwhile skills, important values, and higher level thinking skills at a **high but attainable level of achievement**?
5. Are there motivational **introductory activities** based on students' experiences that set the stage for the unit? Are there **culminating activities** that review and pull together the main themes?
6. Will the necessary **resources** be available?

You also need to decide a convenient format for describing your activities. Some teachers use a grid with four or five columns (for a condensed example, see figure 6.8):

- *First column:* Intended learning outcomes
- *Second column:* Learning activities
- *Third column:* Assessment
- *Fourth column:* Resources
- *Fifth column (depending on state or provincial requirements):* Linkages with government performance standards or outcomes

Other teachers prefer to list the activities, indicating the ILOs, resources, and assessment in the day-to-day descriptions (see figure 7.10 for two different formats for the same activity). The advantage of this is that often a learning activity will achieve more than one learning outcome and, conversely, more than one activity may be needed to attain and reinforce one learning outcome.

Use a format that will help your day-to-day planning. List activities that are ongoing throughout the unit or that are done in learning centers separately either at the beginning or end of a unit. Check that you have an appropriate balance of activities in the four phases of learning and modes of knowing. You do not need all phases or multiple modes for each time block, but you do need to take into account both the rhythm of learning and the learning needs of individual students.

You set the stage for your unit by planning an introductory activity that kindles students' interest, links the unit's content to something in their experience, and points to some of the guiding questions or basic concepts that the students will explore in the unit.

Let me give an example of how ninth-grade social studies teacher Sophia Kraeling introduces a unit on early North American inhabitants. The class first reads some information on the Bering Strait Land Bridge theory (still presented as a fact in her resources). She asks her students to investigate whether the estimated dates of remains found support the theory. She then switches to something that is seemingly unrelated: a video about the Shroud of Turin that shows the great variance of carbon-dating results by different scientific teams. The teacher asks her students to identify the problems with this type of testing and why this information might be useful to them. She gives the students a newspaper article about the popular captain of the local professional ice hockey team. He says that he experienced an epiphany while watching the same video and that it caused him to reexamine his own faith. The students discuss how the article relates to their topic of study. They discuss how historians draw conclusions—sometimes ones that decades later are called into question. They learn that textbooks must be read critically. They see how historians influence people to believe certain claims

and theories even when the supporting evidence is scant or even contradictory. This activity, then, provides a good springboard for analyzing the claims that texts make about early aboriginal life in North America.

The unit ends with one or two concluding activities in which students:

- Consider a final overview of the unit's main themes.
- Give a thoughtful personal response to the unit's themes and guiding questions.
- Complete a task that enables you to make a final assessment of how well they understand the major ideas of the unit and what they are able to do with their new insights and abilities.

Again, let me give an example. At the end of a tenth-grade unit on the novel *To Kill a Mockingbird*, Sandra Paetkau wants her students to show that they understand the novel's basic concepts (e.g., empathy, forgiveness) and how those relate to their own lives. She allows students to choose one of three small-group assignments:

- Create a performance-based documentary chronicling the life of one of the main characters, with interviews of friends, family, and outsiders. The performance (live or video) reflects on what it is like to be that individual.
- The second choice is similar to the foregoing, but the product is a bound book that includes original drawings, paintings, black and white photographs, and written commentary.
- Produce a multimedia presentation on a theme from the novel, accompanied by suitable music as well as a 750-word response to the production.

The students also have the opportunity to propose individual projects if they prefer not to be involved in a small-group activity.

Fig. 7.10 Grade 4: Body Systems Unit Activity   Rachel Pruim (Trinity Western University)

Format #1: Becoming Royalty (50 minutes)

Key concept: Viewing our bodies as temples of the Holy Spirit.

Learning outcome: To recognize the superiority of internal characteristics to external appearance.

Learning activity: Display pictures of two people on a projection screen and ask students whom they would choose for a king or queen. Project diagrams of the insides of people and ask the students to choose again. Play the song "Shepherd Boy" by Ray Boltz. Tell the Bible story of David being anointed as king. Discuss the intricacies of the inner body. Discuss answers to the worksheet and then give students time to write down the key verse in their Bible notebook and draw a picture to illustrate that verse. Have students share their verse and picture. Write 1 Samuel 16:7b inside a key drawn on the board.

Assessment: Class discussion to verify that students have understood the key concept (God values the inside of a person more than a person's outward appearance); learning log entries of key verse, picture, and one or two sentences of personal response.

Format #2: Becoming Royalty (50 minutes)

Key Concept: Viewing our bodies as temples of the Holy Spirit

Learning outcomes: It is expected that students will:
- recognize the necessity and intricacy of body systems
- reflect on and appreciate the superiority of internal characteristics to external appearance
- *read, listen, and view for specific purposes
- *use strategies, including asking and developing questions, rereading and reading further to develop understanding

[* government-mandated learning outcomes]

Guided learning steps:

<u>Setting the stage:</u> Display pictures of two people on a projection screen and ask students whom they would choose for a king or queen. Show pictures of body systems of two people and ask students to choose once more. Discuss the intricacy and beauty of the insides of our bodies.

<u>Disclosure:</u> Have students sit in a circle as teacher tells the story of David's anointing as king. Students work in pairs to answer questions on the worksheet. Discuss students' responses.

<u>Guided/independent practice:</u> Have students enact the scene while playing the song "Shepherd Boy" by Ray Boltz.

<u>Transcendence:</u> Have students look in the Bible for the key verse. Write 1 Samuel 16:7b inside a key on the board. Ask students to write down the verse in their notebook and illustrate it. Ask them to write one or two sentences about their personal conclusions.

Materials:
Overhead projector
CD player
Ray Boltz CD
Bible
Story Bible
Worksheets
Bible notebooks

Preparation:
Prepare overhead transparencies.

Know the Bible story well enough to tell it with accuracy and excitement. Prepare the worksheet for students. Set up the CD player.

Ensure every student has a Bible. Draw a key on the chalkboard so that the key verse can be recorded in a prominent place in the classroom.

Assessment: Analyze the group discussion to verify that students have understood the key concept and have answered the worksheet questions appropriately; give brief comments on the drawings and concluding personal responses.

191

Fig. 7.11   Unit Time Chart

	Monday	Tuesday	Wednesday	Thursday	Friday
Week 1					
Week 2					
Week 3					
Week 4					

5. Incorporate Government Standards

Many states and provinces require schools to participate in testing programs that are based on specified standards, or to show that they cover the learning outcomes specified in curriculum guides. Figure 6.8 shows how one school adds a column to all unit plans to ensure that these requirements are met. Format 2 of figure 7.10 shows how a teacher includes such government outcomes in the description of each unit activity.

6. Plan a Schedule

You need to plan a schedule for your unit. Decide how much time you will spend on the unit each day of the week. Then examine your yearly overview to decide how many weeks you can spend on the unit. The length of units depends on a number of factors. A first-grade teacher may teach a one-week unit on Christmas around the world, but devote large blocks of time to it each day. A fourth-grade teacher may alternate science- and social studies-focused units in double time blocks, giving two weeks to a unit on sound but six weeks to a unit on their state or province. A teacher who has a music class twice a week may take eight weeks to teach a recorder unit. Schools usually schedule cross-graded units such as the one on oceans for no more than one or two weeks; they demand much planning and day-to-day organization. In short, there are no hard and fast rules.

Many teachers find it helpful to develop an overall time chart or one for each week of the unit. Such charts give a planned schedule of activities (see figure 7.11 for a template). Other teachers just indicate, for instance, Week 2, Day 4, when they describe a unit activity.

You will likely find you have to deviate from your planned schedule at times. Some activities take longer (or shorter) than expected. Sometimes you change your unit because an activity did not work as well as you had anticipated or the class needs a change of pace. Also, you will face unexpected events such as school photographs or a special assembly. However, if you have a schedule in place, you can then make a reasoned decision about desirable adjustments—for example, whether to lengthen the time spent on a topic or to delete some activities. Without a planned timeline, units tend to take more time than you intended. You may then be forced to shortchange other important aspects of your program.

7. Select Resources

Chapter 6 describes in detail the criteria for selecting resources. The questions of figure 6.9 apply both to choosing major textbook series for a school and to choosing text and media resources for particular units.

The Internet provides a wealth of resources for students. However, the quality of such resources varies greatly, and many websites have inherent biases. It is worthwhile to discuss with your students from time to time how they can use Internet-based sources responsibly in their research.

8. Plan Student Assessment

You assess student learning by gathering information about your students' learning. You then evaluate the effectiveness of your teaching-learning strategies, drawing conclusions and making decisions about future approaches, perhaps for tomorrow, or possibly for the next time you teach a unit. How to use assessment so that you help students to improve their learning is a complex issue. Following are some key points, an example, and some pertinent questions:

- **Make assessment of student learning an integral part of your unit design.** Elaine Brouwer puts it this way:

  Because assessment and evaluation practices determine curricular priorities, influence student and teacher decisions about what tasks are allotted the most time and energy, and set the tone for the relationships in and around schooling, our practices must grow out of and be directed by our foundational beliefs and commitments. Assessment, curriculum, instruction, and the structures we use to house them should be woven together like a seamless garment. (Brouwer 2001, 2)

  Assessment attaches value to the types of learning that you assess and the evidence you emphasize. Since the results of assessment affect students personally and often acutely, it teaches them values and influences their attitudes to school and to life. Therefore, use your assessment methods and strategies to promote the intents of your unit. Encourage standards that are high but related to students' individual abilities. Use evaluation to help students apply their God-given gifts responsively and responsibly. However, always stress that their inherent personhood and worth do not depend on how well they can do a learning task.

- **Emphasize formative assessment feedback.** That is, evaluate student products and behavior in order to nurture and support them. The intent of evaluation is, first of all, to improve performance and encourage growth in different developmental areas. Students need correction, but it must be accompanied by encouragement, patience, and careful instruction (2 Timothy 4:2). Ask students to assess their own learning and use

that to set goals. Use the evidence you collect to discuss progress with your students and make responsible decisions and choices about future learning. Remember—the primary purpose of assessment is to identify progress and guide improvement.

- **As much as possible, align learning outcomes, learning activities, student products, and assessment strategies.** Sometimes there is one-to-one correspondence between two learning outcomes, activities, and assessment strategies, but that is not always true. You may have a series of learning activities that relate to several outcomes. In that case, ask yourself what task(s) you want students to be able to perform that will demonstrate to your satisfaction that they have accomplished your intents. Your answer will determine your assessment; in turn, your assessment may lead to a revision of your learning activities to ensure that students can give you suitable evidence of their learning.

- **Use varied assessment strategies.** Assess frequently, in various settings, using a range of methods. Observe and reflect informally as students learn. Assess daily learning tasks as well as longer projects, exhibits of student products, student portfolios, and tests. Include definite student responses as well as open-ended responses. Use rubrics as scoring guides that set criteria work at different levels of competence. Remember that tests are only one of many assessment methods. Even on tests, include diverse types of questions. Multiple choice questions check mainly recall of information and a basic understanding of concepts. Open-ended essay-type questions check this as well as the ability of students to process, organize, apply, and present their understanding and thinking.

- **Use state standardized tests as only one of a broad array of assessment strategies.** These tests may have their place to ascertain whether our students meet minimum performance standards. However, the tests usually do not match a school's mission and overall goals. They are usually narrow in scope. Test results have been called "false positives." That is, you can teach toward such tests and increase students' scores, but you then limit your students' educational experiences and encourage rote learning. A better approach is to plan your units so that you incorporate the standards into your units—and assess students broadly. Many educational leaders claim that such an approach is just as effective in bringing up test scores but has far greater educational value (Franklin 2001).

- **Remember that not all intended learning outcomes can be assessed immediately. Also, learning activities may have outcomes that are unintended.** Some of the most important intended outcomes are positive internal responses. We can assess these only partially and usually not immediately. One of our intended outcomes may be that students use statistics responsibly. They may do so in a project—but will they do so when they become politicians and use polling results? The results of our discussions on the misuse of statistics may also have the unintended consequence of encouraging some students to "cook" results on a science experiment. When we assess, we also try to unearth the unintended results of our teaching/learning situation.

Let me give an example. Sharon van Dijk's grade two/three unit on reptiles includes whole-class activities such as reading nonfiction and fiction books about reptiles, responding to slides, making charts of reptile characteristics, teaching research skills, and dramatizing ways reptiles move. She also uses reading buddies and organizes a small-group reptile project. Students keep an ongoing personal journal/chart and make a poster on how they can be good caretakers of a chosen reptile. The six learning centers include research, composing, museum, computer, pattern and design, and creativity. Children complete at least one activity from each center. Examples include completing open-ended activity sheets (e.g., If I were a ...), composing reptile résumés, examining slides, creating reptile pictures on the computer, and painting reptile habitats.

The teacher's multifaceted evaluation includes:

- Checklists to assess language arts skills
- Conferences with several children each day to check comprehension and other items on the teacher's checklist, and to discuss students' personal goals and achievements
- Written feedback to two or three children each day about their goals and progress
- Anecdotal written comments on the daily learning and "post-it notes" (later put into files) about social and emotional growth as children work at learning centers
- Assessment of students' audiotaped readings to check choice and difficulty of reading material and fluency

- Weekly evaluation of children's work portfolios
- Group project assessment on the basis of criteria developed for research skills, presentation, cooperative skills, quality of report, habitat mural, and creativity

Sharon van Dijk also involves her students and parents in her assessment and evaluation strategies:

- The students keep a goals booklet and complete "What I learned/what I did" sheets.
- The whole class completes "What I know/What I want to learn/What I learned" charts at the beginning and end of the unit.
- Each term, all children prepare a large envelope with sample work. They use these to self-evaluate and to recall and celebrate all they have learned over the past three months. Then, with the teacher, the students set new goals for the coming term.
- The work portfolio/envelope is sent home or used in student-led conferences. When sent home, it includes a sheet that states, "Please encourage _____ to discuss his/her work folder with you. Please write three positive things you have learned about your child from the enclosed work." The teacher asks parents to return the folder and completed note. She discusses these with the parents at parent/teacher interviews.

At higher grade levels, teacher-made tests play a more prominent role than in a grade two/three unit. Tests serve a purpose in encouraging students to review and understand course material. Some of the questions can also be learning activities in themselves as students apply and evaluate what they have

learned. Indicate in your unit what types of questions you will give and what weighting you give tests in your total student evaluation.

Ask yourself the following questions as you design student assessment for a unit:

Do your planned assessment strategies:

- Evaluate the realization of your intents at a level appropriate for your students?
- Enable students to show what they know and can do with respect to key understandings, concepts, principles, abilities, and values and dispositions?
- Reflect task and quality expectations required for the unit's learning activities?
- Allow for a range and balance of student tasks?
- Include criteria for scoring?
- Require a reasonable amount of time and scoring effort?
- Motivate students to do their best?
- Provide information that helps to improve learning?

9. Review the Effectiveness of Your Unit

After each unit or major topic, it is also important to evaluate your unit's success. You don't need high-powered techniques. Some informal but honest reflection will help you to improve the unit. Some teachers use a photocopied sheet with questions such as the ones in the following box to guide their thoughts. Then they jot down their observations so that they can review what changes are desirable before they teach the topic again.

HOW EFFECTIVE WAS THIS UNIT?

- Did I realize the unit's intended learning outcomes?
- Were the concepts, skills, and values appropriate? Did the students grasp the key themes and enduring understandings?
- Which learning strategies were successful? Which did not work well? Was there enough variety? Were the students interested in their learning?
- Were the resources relevant and suitable?
- Was the student assessment balanced, fair, and helpful for improving learning?
- What things were particularly successful? Which would I change next time?

Adapting Units for Your Classroom

You will develop a totally new unit, particularly when you plan a new topic for which few suitable references are available or when you work with colleagues on a unit. For example, you may develop a second-grade unit on rocks and geology since this is one of your interests but no teaching materials are available. Or you may want to teach a collection of short stories particularly suitable for your class, combining this with creative writing. Or a major world event takes place that you want to study with your class.

More often, however, you will adapt other units to fit your goals and purposes. You may even have two or three units available on a topic, some commercial educational materials, and a class set of textbooks with a teacher's guide that contains a section for your topic. In such cases, first decide your theme, main concepts, enduring understandings, learning outcomes, scope of the

unit, and general approach. Once this is done, then use other units and resources to design and choose suitable learning activities, resources, and assessment strategies. Keep in mind the make-up and dynamics of your class and your special needs students.

Suppose you teach a grade four/five class in a school that is located on the Canadian prairies. The social studies curriculum indicates that you are expected to teach a unit on early prairie settlement. You find two units on Canadian pioneers. One deals with Ontario, while the other focuses on homesteading on the prairies.

To plan a unit that is relevant for your students, you want to look at a pioneer community in your area around 1900. Initially, you decide on the enduring understandings that you want students to grasp:

- A vision for a better economic future motivated most pioneers to emigrate and build farming communities in a new land.
- Times and cultures may change, but human nature does not: human life is guided by basic commitments to faith and values, and is affected by the power of sin.
- The gifts of hard work and perseverance helped many pioneers overcome great hardships.
- God's provision for family and church was the basis for stable pioneer communities.

You also come up with some guiding questions to help students focus on these understandings:

- Why did early settlers come to the Canadian prairie provinces one hundred years ago?
- How did the pioneers manage to carve out a living in the face of harsh conditions?

- What were the roles of faith and family life in early prairie communities?

You then consider the key values that you want to foster during the unit: perseverance and patience in adversity, cooperation, compassion for those who suffer loss, honesty and loyalty (as opposed to greed and lust for power), and devotion to God.

You think that this unit would benefit from a narrative development. So you go to your bookshelf and find the true story of eighteen-year-old Irishman Ivan Crossley (this took less than fifteen minutes of looking; it is from Berton's *Promised Land: Settling the West 1896–1914*, 1984, 114ff).

The story is as follows: Ivan Crossley was taken in by the promises of the Reverend Isaac Barr. Reverend Barr falsely claimed that settlers who joined him could look forward to an easy farming life in a new colony around what is now Lloydminster on the border of Alberta and Saskatchewan. Timber would be readily available, and fruit trees would grow. In the spring of 1903, Crossley and the other 2,000 people who accompanied Barr had a long, difficult voyage in a converted troop ship from England to New Brunswick. A five-day train trip to Saskatoon and a 200-mile wagon trek to the new colony followed.

Crossley, along with a few friends, paid his ten dollars and claimed his 640-acre (260 *ha*) homestead. For a house, he built a sod hovel without windows. His first crop of vegetables withered and died; like most other colonists, he lacked farming experience. He did everything by trial and error. He alternately broke ground, farmed, and took temporary jobs plowing for others and delivering winter mail. Yet despite inept leadership, lack of know-how, and a refusal to learn from non-British immigrants, Crossley and his fellow colonists succeeded. They persevered as they muddled through, although they knew how to run their Anglican church and their literary and music societies better than their farms! Crossley's family prospered. Some of his descendants still live in Lloydminster.

Crossley's story provides an intriguing and rich lode for a narrative approach to this unit. You can develop the unit along the lines of the narrative (conditions in Great Britain, the sea/train/wagon voyage, initial challenges, building a farm, and establishing a community). You can then go to the two units, and choose and adapt their learning outcomes, activities, and assessment strategies. For instance, you can use an outcome such as "to assess ways in which supportive family units were a gift and blessing in settlement communities," and "to compare and contrast family life of the pioneers to family life in our society." If you change the context from Ontario to the prairies, you can fit many of the unit's activities into your unit. As in the unit, the class can set up and operate a general store (as first set up by Barr as a cooperative venture). They can have a pioneer family and a pioneer school day. They can do research, and analyze and make maps at centers. They can investigate the treatment of native Indian people and other immigrant groups. They can survey their own family background to see if there were pioneer experiences in their families. They can consider why the role of the church was not as strong here as in some other colonies. Throughout, Barr's quest for power and profit can be contrasted with Crossley's reported honesty, perseverance, and loyalty.

The point here is that if you adapt a unit (or use a text as the main source for a unit), it is important to first determine your own framework and direction. Only later should you look at other units and resources, for instance, for ideas for activities. You can still follow the remaining steps for designing a unit. With other units available, you may be able to do so fairly quickly. Some topics and units lend themselves to adaptation more easily than others. You will always find, however, that you need to make some revisions to make the unit one you can teach comfortably and successfully.

One final note: If you are a new teacher or a teacher who has not used a unit approach before, you will find that developing a unit is time-consuming. Therefore, plan to design two or three per year, and gradually build up your "repertoire" of classroom units. You will find that the rewards are great: it is especially through unit planning and adaptation

that you can implement a curriculum that reflects a thoroughly Christian worldview.

Footstep 7-3

This is only the third footstep in this chapter. The reason is that I hope you will follow the suggested unit design steps and construct or adapt a classroom unit that you will be able to teach within the foreseeable future. Completing that will be a major steppingstone on your curriculum journey—all the best!

Reviewing the Main Points

- **An integral unit has a clear thematic focus with internal unity, external consistency, and meaningful links to related subject disciplines.** Your personal curriculum orientation and aims find expression particularly in the design of integral units.
- **You can plan (or adapt) effective units in various ways. One such way uses the following steps** (not always in sequential order):

  1. Determine the significance and relevance of a topic.
  2. Brainstorm ideas, possibly using a planning chart.
  3. Formulate a unit focus and intents. A thematic statement describes the overall approach and main thrust of a unit. It includes the basic values, enduring understandings, key concepts, and main skills you want students to acquire. Intended learning outcomes (ILOs) specify and extend the thematic statement.
  4. Design and choose suitable learning activities.
  5. Review and incorporate linkages with government-mandated standards and outcomes.
  6. Plan a schedule.
  7. Select your resources.
  8. Plan student assessment.
  9. Review the effectiveness of your unit.

- **To adapt a unit from other source(s), first determine your own focus and intents,** and only then, use and adjust ideas from the source(s) that are available.

References

Berton, P. 1984. *The promised land: Settling the West 1896–1914.* Toronto: McClelland and Stewart.

Brouwer, E. 2001. Assessment as a gift. *In Search,* Seattle: Alta Vista College (January): 1–15.

Brown, P., ed. 1994. Trees and forests. Unpublished grade 1/2 resource unit. Morwell, Australia: Valley Christian School.

Chiang, J. et al. 2001. *Cells: the wonder of life.* A grade 8 resource unit. Ancaster, ON: Ontario Alliance of Christian Schools.

Chinnery, J. et al. 1993. *How does my garden grow? ... God makes it so!* A primary unit. Langley, BC: Society of Christian Schools in British Columbia.

Erickson, H. L. 2001. *Stirring the heart, heart and soul: Redefining curriculum and instruction.* 2d ed. Thousand Oaks, CA: Corwin Press.

Franklin, J. 2001. Trying too hard? How accountability and testing are affecting constructivist teaching. *ASCD Education Update* 43 (3): 1–8.

Maggs, D. 1988. The family. Unpublished grade 11/12 unit.

Rau, S., L. Roseboom, and M. Zazitko. 1993. *The role of the family.* A primary resource unit. Langley, BC: Society of Christian Schools in British Columbia.

Wiggins, G., and J. McTighe. 1998. *Understanding by design.* Alexandria, VA: Association for Supervision and Curriculum Development.

Steppingstone 8

The Subjects of the Curriculum

"A Christian worldview encompasses all my teaching," says high school English teacher Margaret Barlow. "Everything about my classroom must demonstrate that worldview. The physical environment is rich. I have art prints and poems around the room that say something about God's world. My classroom ambience stresses that it is better to give than to receive—just look at the photographs I've taken of the class and posted on the bulletin board. I also constantly try to instill a sense of wonder and playfulness. After all, the child in us is the best learner."

I ask, "What would that mean for teaching grammar?"

"Well," Barlow responds, "I start with spidergramming to see how much the students know. They all contribute. Usually they're excited about how much they already know. Then, to learn the parts of speech, they stand in a circle. As they throw a ball to someone else they call out a part of speech. That student has to give an example and then repeat the process. This teaches them to listen. They're moving around a bit as they learn. That's important for adolescents. Later they imagine that they are a specific part of speech and write a short story that shows their function. Then they share each other's stories. Other ideas emerge from the classroom situation. For instance, I may ask them to write different types of sentences about my art reproductions, making their sentences as creative as possible."

This teacher realizes that learning about grammar is an important tool in understanding language. She uses diverse modes of knowing to teach grammar, including the psychomotor and aesthetic ones. Moreover, she has the students learn grammar within the context of various aspects of reality, and then use what they learn in practicing and developing their grammar and communication skills with reference to those aspects, both orally and in writing. She may relate their oral reports and their story writing, for example, to the history of art or to science (e.g., to write a story about how our muscles interact). Yet clearly English is the one school subject that she teaches.

In chapter 4, we discussed a categorization of reality into thirteen aspects, each with its own key meanings and structures. A balanced curriculum, I concluded, should take into account all these aspects as well as a more comprehensive area of thought called cultural formation. We do not always organize learning into subjects that correspond to one particular aspect, however:

- Many important phenomena and issues in life cut across several aspects of reality.
- New learning is most effective when based on students' own experiences, which are often multifaceted.
- Several aspects of reality may be taught and learned well as a combined subject (e.g., mathematics involves both the numerical and the spatial aspects).
- Some school subjects do not relate directly to just one or two aspects of reality (e.g., information technology).

Nevertheless, many school subjects relate closely to one or several aspects of reality. In this chapter I consider some basic goals and key issues for common school subjects, roughly arranged according to the increasing complexity of the aspects of reality. The intent of these short discussions is to provide you with one more steppingstone for planning a classroom program. I therefore emphasize what a biblical worldview means for teaching the subject. Each section begins with an example and ends with a footstep that asks you to consider one or two issues for that subject.

The basic subject goals have changed little since Geraldine Steensma and I co-edited *Shaping School Curriculum: A Biblical View* (1977), and often this chapter reflects its thinking. However, knowledge about the subjects and about learning does not stand still. As the previous example of Margaret Barlow's class indicates, today we are more aware of different modes of knowing and of the need to teach basic skills in meaningful contexts even if that involves situations and phenomena that cut across traditional subject divisions.

Mathematics

➤ *In its discussion of standard notation of numbers, the book series* Charis Mathematics *asks students to work with numbers representing very large sizes and distances in the solar system, the Milky Way, and the universe, as well as very small ones describing cells, viruses, molecules, and atoms. It also quotes physicist Paul Davies' observation that the universe is "full of stunning surprises" and that "it is difficult not to be struck by some surprisingly fortuitous accidents without which our existence would be impossible." It then asks students to consider, as part of their work on extreme numbers, whether our presence on Earth could be a cosmic accident or whether there is design behind the universe. The authors intend students not only to learn standard notation but also to gain a sense of wonder about the universe and to reflect on its origins and their place in it. (Shortt 1996, 11–21, 69–77)*

Mathematics is more than a construction of the mind. It is not just a series of pure formalisms that we manipulate using rules of logic. It originated from human experience and activity with two aspects of God's created reality: the quantitative and the spatial. It takes faith in the continuing validity of mathematical laws to do and use mathematics. Thus, the study of mathematics brings out a sense of awe and wonder in the design and order of God's creation, as well as pointing to the faithfulness, immanence, and transcendence of God (MacKenzie et al. 1997, 136ff). Once people discovered mathematical results through observation and informal reasoning, they developed symbols to represent their conclusions. Those symbols stand for real and changeless created entities.

Only after using the results for many years or even centuries do mathematicians prove results logically, using self-evident axioms. Such self-evident assumptions may not always hold. Rejecting a postulate that held only for geometry on a flat surface led, for instance, to non-Euclidean geometry. Moreover, in 1931 the German mathematician Gödel proved that it is impossible to design a mathematical system that is both complete and consistent. That means that mathematicians must live with some inexplicable paradoxes. They can do so because they have faith in the basic order and law structure that God embedded in the universe.

The first key meaning in mathematics is *discrete numbers*. Numbers function according to laws that we discover from experience. People have named numbers and gradually improved their designation. Our present system is probably too firmly entrenched to make further advancements, even though some argue that changing from a base ten to a base twelve number system would make our mathematical lives easier. Even when human descriptions of the underlying structures change, basic mathematical laws stay constant.

The second key meaning in mathematics is *continuous space*. This concept cannot be reduced to or explained in terms of discrete numbers. We have no way to designate all numbers on the number line as fractions or as terminating or repeating decimals, even though there are infinite amounts of each of these. Yet we need numbers to describe space and figures in space: a plane has two dimensions; a quadrilateral, four sides. In other words, we use numbers to think about geometry, but numbers or numerical descriptions will never do full justice to geometry. Mathematicians may, however, develop understanding of the numerical and spatial aspects concurrently, as in coordinate geometry.

Mathematics plays an essential but limited role in other knowledge. It points beyond itself to the other aspects of reality. Mathematical models are useful tools in physics, psychology, and economics, for instance, but never fully describe the meaning of a situation. Physicists, psychologists, and politicians must consider other aspects of reality besides the mathematical ones to analyze situations and make responsible decisions. Note also that mathematics cannot be equated with logic or analytic reasoning. The content of mathematics involves the two simplest aspects of reality. Therefore, we can prove mathematical propositions with deductive logic more clearly and more convincingly than theses in other areas of knowledge—but the basic principles of logic apply there just as much.

Mathematics intends to deepen students' understanding of God's creation and how that understanding helps them fulfill their calling. Students can abstract the mathematical aspects of real-life situations, analyze them, and use the results of their learning in applications. They can explore how we use math in science (e.g., leaf surface area and water loss). However, applications go beyond science. Mathematics is part and parcel of human culture.

Through the study of mathematics, it is expected that students will:

1. **Recognize that God is faithful and reliable in upholding the world through orderly mathematical patterns, laws,**

and structures that He embedded in His creation.

2. **Gain understandings of the concepts of number and space and their inter-relationships.**

3. **Deepen awareness of mathematics as a functional tool in solving everyday problems in diverse settings.**

4. **Experience mathematics as a developing science.** Mathematics is not a fixed body of knowledge but grows as cultures develop—and is fallible. For instance, the Babylonians for years used an incorrect formula for the area of quadrilateral fields, using the results to levy taxes.

These goals suggest that we base classroom mathematics on everyday situations. We give students time to explore situations, pursue hunches, and draw conclusions from their observations. Such situations may involve experiences from students' lives outside school or classroom explorations with manipulatives, science activities, human geography, or business settings.

We also give students more formal instruction and practice to ensure that they gain a clear grasp of math concepts and how to apply them. It is helpful to relate such direct instruction to situations in which students have tried to solve problems using a variety of strategies.

With the use of calculators, the scope and nature of numerical practice has changed, but students still need dexterity with basic number skills and estimation. Mental mathematics still has a place in grades two through six. Some teachers report that it can add elements of accomplishment, fun, and joy to learning. Besides, students need drill to reinforce concepts and algorithms.

Students should experience the use of mathematics in various relevant contexts.

They should apply math results from one situation to a variety of settings. The broad scope of math applications lends itself to meaningful problem solving. Mathematics is not an isolated, self-sufficient body of knowledge but an indispensable tool in most areas of life.

Textbook problems tend to ask students to apply only one math algorithm at a time. This promotes convergent thinking. Students look for one pattern and apply it mechanically. Real problem-solving ability depends on critical and creative thinking. That is why the National Council for Teachers of Mathematics (2000), in its standards document, promotes both conceptual understanding and procedural competence, with an emphasis on conjecturing, inventing, reasoning, and solving mathematical problems in various settings. This approach requires active involvement in transforming and simplifying given problems, writing different versions, modifying problems to yield different solutions, and constructing original problems (J. Kilpatrick in Lewy 1991, 848). Students need this type of experience with everyday graphical, statistical, and financial data, using calculators and computers when appropriate.

Leaders in society today often base economic and political decisions mainly on the numerical aspects of a situation. They use polls and look at the short-term balance sheet. Students should learn that we cannot reduce complex situations and decisions to mathematical ones only, even when quantitative aspects provide useful insights. Even a decision to buy skis should involve deeper questions than their price. What should be our financial priorities? Why? If we neglect those aspects in math class, students get a skewed view of life's priorities.

The history of mathematics should also be part of the curriculum. Students should see how mathematicians unfold new concepts and techniques, often in informal, intuitive, and creative ways. They learn that mathematics is an important but limited part of culture, and that intuition and value judgments affect its development (A. M. White in Lewy 1991, 892). Historical approaches can make clear how mathematical problem posing and solving has contributed to cultural development (e.g., Hamming, Van Brummelen, and Boonstra 1984).

Teaching and learning mathematics is not a neutral activity. Textbook examples and problems often promote an individualistic, materialistic way of life. According to Paul Ernest, current mathematics learning values individual, reproductive, and formal approaches rather than cooperative, creative, exploratory, and applied work. For a better balance, he suggests using approaches that involve students in doing cooperative projects, discussing problems, studying the origins of numbers and geometry, pursuing some open-ended investigations, and exploring value-rich issues such as misleading uses of statistics (Ernest 1991, 265–73).

In short, to support their aims, teachers may need to design alternate examples and learning strategies. The Christian *Charis Mathematics Project* (Shortt 1996, 1997) includes good examples:

- **How much is your gift worth?** (giving to churches and charities in relation to one's means: calculations with percentages)
- **Fractals** (the complexity of the universe: ratios, perimeters, and accurate constructions)
- **The moment of truth** (respect for reasoning and truth based on the history of prime numbers)

- **But can you afford it?** (personal and ethical responsibility when making financial decisions; calculating interest)

Footstep 8-1

- At the primary level, many teachers stress exploration of mathematical meaning and results using a variety of manipulatives. They claim that these approaches give children a better understanding of basic concepts. Primary teachers also develop creativity as they design problems and find alternative solutions. A criticism of this approach is that students do not learn basic math facts and skills well enough. Is it possible to combine an exploratory approach with reinforcement and drill? In an age of calculators and computers, how important is a thorough knowledge of addition and multiplication facts?

- Traditionally, mathematics books available to teachers often lack diverse, open-ended, life-related problems. That means that teachers may gradually have to develop a bank of suitable problem situations. First-graders can operate a supermarket using play money. Fifth-graders can draw conclusions from statistical data about countries in the world and present them in graphical ways. Seventh-grade students can consider how a contractor figures out the length of the diagonal to see whether his building footings are at right angles, or estimate the cost of a building that they design. Ninth-graders can investigate how architects and engineers use geometry. Can you think of other learning activities that require students to learn and apply mathematics in meaningful contexts?

The Physical and Biological Sciences

> ➤ *You teach the concept of gravity. You hold a marble between two fingers. You ask your students what would happen if you opened your fingers. They predict that the marble will fall, and it does. You do it a second, a third, a fourth, a fifth time. Each time you have the same result. You ask, "Why?" "Gravity," says one of your students. But what is gravity? Why does it always work? You draw out that we can describe it as a force and predict its effects, also mathematically. But we don't really know what it is or why it works. You discuss the law structure of the universe established by the Law Giver. You then have your students experiment to discover some results (e.g., a large and small marble will accelerate equally because of the pull of gravity). Your students are actively involved. They respond by seeing how faith in created, unfailing laws makes science possible, but that what they discover is but a pale reflection of those laws. They learn how science results, even if tentative and approximate, help us fulfill God's Creation Mandate if we apply them responsively and responsibly.*

The key meaning in physical science is energy; in biology, life. The physical sciences (physics, astronomy, geology, physical geography, and chemistry) make much use of numbers and space. Mathematical descriptions and models, however, do not exhaust the meaning of, nor fully describe, physical concepts such as motion and gravity. Similarly, a full understanding of biology requires some knowledge of chemistry. But life cannot be explained in terms of physical or chemical attributes. Rather, something that is alive has been created with life or vital

functions that enable, for instance, growth and reproduction to take place.

Scientists examine the physical and biological aspects of phenomena. They hypothesize and try to replicate evidence in order to construct theories and scientific laws. However, repeating an experiment several hundred times, even if the results are consistent, still does not prove a conclusion. Yet two or three instances with conflicting results may disprove a theory (although proponents of firmly believed theories usually find ways to account for contradictory data!). Nevertheless, results cannot be "scientifically proven."

Assumptions and commitments color scientists' findings. In 1850 French physicist Jean Foucault "proved" the wave theory of light on the basis of an experiment with mirrors. The scientific world accepted this conclusion until a 1927 experiment endorsed an alternate theory based on Einstein's thinking. What scientists expect to see affects what they see and how they interpret what they see (M. Poole in Francis and Thatcher 1990, 373–74). Therefore, school science programs should show scientists at work, struggling with uncertainties and the effects of their presuppositions.

Scientific knowledge is much more tentative than most school science programs imply. Scientific theorizing is not neutral. Thomas Kuhn (1970, 185) described how scientists work within certain paradigms based on cultural beliefs and values. Such models influence what scientists investigate, how they go about their investigation, and what kinds of results they reject. This, in turn, affects curriculum. A deeply held value of scientists today, for instance, is that quantitative predictions are preferable to qualitative ones. This colors both research and high school science curricula.

Another example illustrating the fact that science is not neutral is that the basic faith and interpretative framework for most biologists is evolutionism. They hold that organisms emerged from adaptation of other organisms to the environment and by a process of natural selection, which operates by chance. The acceptance of this belief raises an unanswered question. Adaptation must be based on underlying structural laws. A fish develops gills to be able to take in oxygen from its water environment. But what caused the fish to know that to live it needed oxygen? The fish itself cannot have developed the structural laws for its existence as it developed. The evolutionistic concept of adaptation fails to consider the origin and nature of the structural laws of reality (Uko Zylstra in Steensma and Van Brummelen 1977, 125–26).

As is true for proponents of evolutionism, my basic interpretive framework for biology rests on faith assumptions. My starting point is that biology is possible only because God created and sustains a law order. Biologists, like physical scientists, discover God's creation order. The first chapters of Genesis make clear that God is the origin of all reality, including its structural laws. Thus, God created fish with gills to enable them to live in a water environment, taking into account His laws for the physical and biological aspects of reality. God created each living being with a particular fitness for a specific niche where He put it. Evolutionists have no choice but to find the meaning of life in nonliving matter. Christian scientists, on the other hand, find it in God's faithfulness in creating and upholding reality, and calling humans to be stewards of the earth.

Curricula often implicitly promote a dogmatic reliance on science. Yet such reliance "leads to elitism, to an excessively techno-cratic philosophy, to authoritarianism and antidemocratic behavior, attributes that in turn provoke indifference and even disenchantment" (Nadeau and Desautels 1984, 56). Science textbooks assert that science is objective and that its methods can provide solutions to society's problems. They often lead students to accept unquestioningly that all scientific research leads to truth and progress. Yet science continually raises philosophical questions that go beyond science (Price, Wiester, and Hearn 1986, 23).

Scientific laws, theories, and conclusions reflect current understandings of scientific phenomena. They are not truth, however. They are compelling but incomplete explanations. Each new discovery brings about more questions and reveals new complexities. Scientific theories and laws are useful approximations of God's law structures. Newton's laws of motion are apt representations but break down when applied at high speeds. Einstein's theory of relativity gives more insight about what happens at high velocities and about the relationship between energy and motion. But even Einstein's theory fails to account for some phenomena. As scientists go about their work, they continue to be surprised!

The scientific mode of knowing involves drawing reasoned conclusions from experimental data. Most textbooks, however, overplay the role of the scientific method. The method seldom results in new discoveries in science. Scientists more often use mathematical analysis, deductive and inductive logical reasoning, creative hunches, intuition, and accidental discoveries (e.g., penicillin). Scientists do use the five steps of the scientific method to strengthen or weaken support for a conclusion. Even then, however, scientists' observations are necessarily informed and guided by some theoretical presuppositions

(M. Degenhardt in Francis and Thatcher 1990, 238). The scientific method, in other words, is not the final arbiter of truth. We therefore need a more reflective and critical approach to science education. Incorporating topics from the history of science may dispel the mystique of the scientific method.

Pamela MacKenzie and others (1997, 155) list misconceptions about the nature of science that we need to counter as we teach science. They include:

- The belief that science is superior to all other kinds of knowledge
- The idea that scientific discoveries have disproved Christianity
- The belief that there is a single scientific method that is an assured path to scientific knowledge and, therefore, to truth
- The belief that science deals with infallibly proven facts while other subjects such as religion and art deal only with subjective values
- The belief that all aspects of reality are equally open to scientific inquiry (a scientific analysis of a work of art would not have any aesthetic meaning, for instance)

Students do learn much about science through hands-on activities. They benefit from reconsidering everyday phenomena through experimentation with simple science materials and equipment. Direct experiences enhance the meaning of the more formal instruction that follows. Good science programs focus on investigating questions and problems that learners can relate to their everyday lives. Each step of such workshop or lab activities requires students to ask appropriate questions, find and synthesize information, design and implement explorations, and draw valid conclusions. It is easy, however, for students to do experiments in which inadequate evidence is used to draw conclusions. Also, the experiments lead simply to finishing a task but not to expanding previous scientific understandings. Students are given few strategies for determining the quality or validity of their observations. Teachers have to work at helping students to perform inquiry-based tasks heedfully and reflectively (J. Krajcik, R. Mamlok, and B. Hug in Corno 2001, 224–28).

Too often curricula treat science in isolated fashion with little reference to the rest of life. Nearly 85 percent of high school graduates enrolling as physics and engineering majors in the United States cannot relate science concepts and processes to real situations (NASSP 1993, 1). David Layton (in Tomlinson and Quinton 1986, 161–63) gives examples to show why this happens. The usual theoretical account of the bonding of hydrogen and oxygen atoms in water deals only with objective abstract information. A very different approach would be to teach the make-up of water in the context of removing impurities from the water supply of a poor third world community. Introductory chemistry courses describe the electrolysis of brine without any mention of the effects of mercury losses on ecosystems. Similarly, textbooks seldom make explicit the moral dimensions of statistical data such as risk from nuclear waste. In such ways, chemistry promotes technical efficiency and excludes concern for environmental or social impact.

Science and technology courses benefit from a problem-based approach. Examples might include the problems in copper mining, the effects of fertilizers used in farming, or the health risks of X-rays or food additives. Such problems often involve more than the purely scientific aspect. Suppose someone has a choice of buying natural or genetically modified canola oil for baking. Students can investigate the (often limited) information about long-term effects on such crops. They can also consider the economic aspect (How much does each cost?), the social-political aspect (What are potential social disruptions caused by the new technology? What government regulations are in place?), and the ethical aspect (Should I support a product that calls for manipulating gene pools with unknown long-term results?). Whenever possible, a problem-based approach should begin with situations well known to students. They should investigate both the science and technology involved in the social relevance of the issue. This type of approach leads to different content choices than teaching theoretical science topics and simply adding some applications.

Physical phenomena and living things exist in environments that affect human life and culture. We may apply science-related technologies only after we have tried to understand their impact on our environment and on human life. New reproductive technologies, for instance, have serious ethical and social implications. Similarly, the automobile is not just a technical means of transportation. The number sold is a barometer of our economic health. Cars affect our social interaction, our environment, the way we lay out our cities, how we shop, and how much money we can spend on longer-lasting things. Science curricula need to deal with such impacts of science and technology.

Recent science materials do put more emphasis on these issues. This fact stems in part from the paradox that most authors see science and technology not only as a cause of problems but as the solution of those same problems. This new emphasis also stems from concerns in society. For example, indiscriminate use of technology has led to health risks (e.g., pollution caused by unacceptably high sulfur content in gasoline). Thus research findings can be used for harmful ends as well as beneficial ones. Finally, most science materials impose on us an incontestable way of looking at life (e.g., progress without limits, technology without cost).

Summing up, the goals of teaching and learning science include (Van Brummelen et al. 1985; MacKenzie et al. 1997, 152–53):

- **Investigate physical and living things as part of God's plan**

  - To examine the physical and biological aspects of daily phenomena in experiential, hands-on ways
  - To survey the basic concepts, structures, and theories of science
  - To investigate the complexity and unity of the scientific aspects of reality with wonder and delight, as well as with perseverance and humility
  - To recognize that (1) the world is an ordered and consistent creation reflecting God's laws, and (2) science is not religiously neutral—scientific activity is directed by scientists' worldviews and values

- **To identify and experience God's unique calling for humans to develop science and technology as cultural activities that honor God and His creation**

  - To understand and use science and its applications responsibly
  - To recognize the important but limited place of science in society and develop a critical understanding of issues related to science
  - To consider how brokenness in the world can be restored, at least in part, because through His grace, God allows us to develop and use scientific investigation and application responsibly

Footstep 8-2

□ North American surveys show that elementary teachers spend an average of only thirty minutes per day on teaching science. They use mainly textbook readings and discussions—and few hands-on activities. Reasons include lack of confidence in their own scientific know-how, a tightly packed curriculum, time demands to prepare, lack of equipment, and the need to prepare students for standardized tests (Willis 1995, 1–6).

Choose a primary- or intermediate-level science topic. Suggest some meaningful learning approaches and activities. What would keep you from implementing such activities? What can you do to improve the teaching of science in your classroom?

□ Scientists genetically engineer tomatoes that will not rot and salmon that grow ten times faster than normal. They also apply such research to genetic cures for diseases. But this technology gives rise to troublesome questions:

- Is it right for human genes to be inserted into animals?
- Can virus genes stitched into plants to increase disease resistance lead to the creation of "superviruses"?
- What happens when genetically engineered salmon in salmon farms escape and breed with wild ones?
- Should parents be able to pay to have genetically superior babies?
- How should governments regulate genetic engineering and its products?

The late Nobel Prize winner Michael Smith said that he did not have enough expertise to make ethical judgments about his research. Other scientists claim, however, that unwillingness to face the implications means that the commercialization of genetic research is already out of control.

Should you deal with these momentous issues in your science classroom? If so, at what age levels? Can you think of creative approaches that would help students explore the underlying issues? To what extent should school science deal with the consequences of technology rather than with just scientific concepts and theories? Do you agree with Margaret Somerville (2000), who says that science has moved so far ahead of ethics that it is time to slow down science and technology, and let ethics catch up? Do you think this would be possible, if it is desirable?

Physical Education and Health Education

➤ *Physical education teaches not only motor skills but also cooperation and leadership skills. "A typical cooperative activity, for example, is the Spider Web. To successfully complete this low-rope element, each team has to get its members through the web without touching any of its sides. To make it even more challenging, students can pass through each hole in the web once. Students who can't work together can't finish the exercise, claims [Cathy] Thornton. 'Students learn that they really need to work together, and we hope they also learn that there are peaceful solutions to problems,' she explains."* (Checkley 1996, 8)

Physical health and fitness affect all of life, including emotional well-being and intellectual success. Therefore physical education and health education are important. Physical education involves movement of the body to perform tasks, to maintain physical fitness, and to express and communicate creatively in and through motion. Health education focuses on maintaining bodily and emotional health: care of the body, nutrition, substance abuse, disease prevention and care, coping with stress and loss, and so on. Schools may teach some of these topics in science or in personal development courses.

Our physical bodies are an integral part of our humanity. The Bible indicates that we must glorify God with our bodies as with the rest of our being (1 Corinthians 6:20). A responsible lifestyle includes participating in physical activities and looking after our bodies. Physical fitness and health, at the same time, should not glorify personal prowess or beauty. Instead, we must help students see that maintaining good health and fitness is a way to serve God and those around us.

The goals for physical education and health education include (based on Zuidema 1995, 11ff; and NASPE 1995):

- **To use our physical health to praise God by serving Him and our neighbors**

  □ To use health knowledge to achieve and maintain optimal health in order to serve God and others meaningfully and obediently
  □ To behave in ways that are personally and socially responsible in physical activity and health care settings
  □ To respect differences among people with respect to physical and health attributes

- **To maintain physical fitness, lead a physically active lifestyle, and enjoy movement in order to vigorously serve God, others, and self**

  □ To recognize that physical activity can provide health-enhancing enjoyment, challenge, self-expression, social interaction, and service to others
  □ To apply movement concepts and principles in developing motor proficiency
  □ To practice and use motor skills in a variety of settings and activities

The Bible says little about athletics. It does, however, promote cooperation and self-sacrifice rather than competition. I conclude from this that competition in sports and physical education is desirable only when students strive together to develop their physical potential, and when they try to better others as well as themselves as they participate. We can promote those outcomes by measuring success in terms of participation, effort, and improvement rather than just in terms of winning. Some schools have "houses" that gather points mainly for participation and improvement of individual skills. It also helps to have students compete with those whose abilities are similar. To build the type of Christian community of which Paul speaks in Ephesians 4, participants must be joyful and supportive team members who help each other strive for excellence.

To encourage students to include physical activity in their lifestyles, schools can offer various activities that can be done individually or with partners: hiking, jogging, table tennis, bicycling, weight training, swimming, cross-country skiing, and so on. Through these we try to foster individual growth. Sometimes that is not easy. Teachers may be frustrated because they fall short of their goals. Common reasons include student apathy toward participation, teachers' needs to maintain order, oversized classes, and lack of suitable facilities. As a result, the latent function of many physical education classes becomes keeping students busy and happy rather than developing skills and attitudes (Steinhardt in Jackson 1992, 975, 988).

To encourage participation, some teachers allow students with poor coordination or low skill levels to practice in nonthreatening settings, giving frequent encouraging (but honest) feedback. They help students not to feel totally defeated or intimidated by allowing them some choice, involving them in designing games to develop certain muscles or skills, and planning some units such as basketball around the theme of cooperation. Some of these students may be able to take some leadership in using their bodies in aesthetic expression in creative movement. Developing positive attitudes to physical activity is the most important single effect on adult physical activity patterns.

Health education deals with physical and emotional health. Often we do not teach it as a separate subject. Kindergarten and first-grade teachers teach integral units such as God Made Me Special or families. Elementary teachers also teach units on friendship, nutrition, our bodies, and health and disease. At higher levels core courses may include units on substance abuse, understanding oneself as an adolescent, or courtship and marriage. Schools may include health-related topics in their physical education, personal planning, or guidance programs.

Schools should avoid two pitfalls. First, it is easy to neglect health topics, particularly when no formal health curriculum exists. Yet many parents spend little time with their children on health-related issues. Therefore, schools are often the only place where students can receive guidance about the consequences of health-related decisions they make and habits they establish.

Schools should plan a year-by-year health education program, even if they do not teach health as a separate subject—and obtain parental support.

A second pitfall is that in order to sidestep controversy, schools teach only the biological aspects of health issues. For instance, a school may teach only the physical aspects of sex. Schools shirk their responsibility if they do not concurrently teach about the emotional, social, economic, and ethical consequences of sexual relationships. By dealing only with physical aspects, schools mislead students into believing that sex is a purely physical act. It is much more responsible to include a biblical understanding of family life, friendship, marriage, and sexuality, including how God allows us to find joy and meaning in such relationships. Parents can be involved in planning the program and encouraged to discuss topics with their children as they arise in school. For such programs, see De Moor (1994) or Ezell (1993).

Footstep 8-3

- Think about some physical and health education issues that have been contentious. Should physical education be compulsory at all grade levels? If so, should it be taught every day? Should it emphasize team sports or individual skills? Why? What is the role of creative movement and dance in physical education? Should we include emotional health in health education? How much should we teach children about sexuality? at what levels?

- North America values egocentric competition: "Winning isn't everything; it's the only thing." In sports, players see what they can get away with in order to win. Yet some cultures play games (and keep fit) without keeping score. Games, in a sense, are laboratories for value experiments, ranging from winning at all costs to practicing fair play to valuing cooperation (or a combination of these). Design some games that develop fitness and skills while emphasizing cooperation and care for others, sensitivity to the feelings of classmates, and reflection on personal involvement.

▫ The topic of sexuality has been a controversial one, especially in public schools, where parents have widely diverging views about the related values. What content about sexuality would you include in a Christian school curriculum? How would you justify your position? In what ways would you involve parents? What precautions would you take so that your teaching would not lead to parental or student resistance?

The Fine Arts

➤ *John Zuidema spends three weeks of his seventh-grade music course on contemporary music. His students explore standards for good music. They suggest that it should be original, have unity as well as variety, be wholesome, have balanced instrumentation and voice, and be understandable. The students bring a recording they own to class, with a written transcription of the lyrics. Zuidema plays the music. "If you haven't heard it before," he asks, "did you like it? Why or why not? If you like it right away, is it really good? How would you evaluate the music in terms of our standards for good music?"*

Aesthetics is an integral part of life, not something that happens only in museums and concert halls. Artistic gifts are gifts of God's Spirit, both to Christians and non-Christians. God Himself wants to be glorified through artistic and musical expression. The Bible includes poetry and song. God gave explicit instructions for the artwork in His tabernacle and endowed the artisans with His Spirit. The Bible encourages people to dance to express their joy and thankfulness for God's blessings. God wants us to use the arts—visual, musical, dance, film, and drama—in responsive and creative ways. The arts enrich our daily lives. Regrettably, the arts are vulnerable in a technological, profit-driven society. They are often the first to be cut when budget shortfalls loom.

Yet the arts often affect our personal lives more directly than scientific formulas or economic theories. They enrich life through joy, delight, playfulness, and creativity. They can change and enhance the way we see and understand ourselves, others, our society, and the purpose and meaning of life. They affect our perspectives by symbolically presenting points of view in aesthetically striking ways. They stimulate us to investigate the perspectives and values of others. We discover some of life's possibilities through the arts. They may lead to the surprise and wonder that enrich life.

The fine arts can be used to serve God and one's neighbor, but they can also serve one's idols. The dominant aesthetic images of our society become "a crystallized version of what is true, good, or proper—a representation of society, personal relationships, or political practices" (L. Beyer in Pinar 1988, 395). Thus schools should critique society's prevalent images with their students. They should also help students explore how a biblical vision of shalom that incorporates compassion, justice, and peace provides a wholesome foundation for aesthetic activity.

Christian artists serve God through their art. They may be agents of reconciliation as they manifest shalom. Their art may witness to God's redemptive grace and love as well as to the distortion and despair of sin. The work of Christian artists should not be superficial propaganda for the Christian faith, nor should it reflect an innocuous view of life. Bland, moralizing images misrepresent the meaning of living as Christians in today's world. Instead, Christian art should represent real life, including experiences of fear, sin, guilt, and joy (Deborah Kellogg Kropp in Steensma and Van Brummelen 1977, 89).

What makes an aesthetic work "art"? Basically, the answer would be its imagery and symbolism. In other words, it presents some aspect of life visually or audibly (or both) while suggesting other meanings. We can therefore experience and feel works of art in different ways and at different levels. Often the images "appropriately and surprisingly articulate those tensions and resolutions of feelings which we experience in reality" (Dengerink 1987, 27). Works of art evoke and refer.

Of all school subjects, only the arts (including creative writing and film production) make developing creativity the main focus. Within this context, the arts have at least three goals:

- To become critically aware of the role of aesthetics in society, both past and present
- To enjoy and appreciate aesthetic products through experience and performance
- To unfold aesthetic potential through creating and composing works of art

These three goals are interrelated. For instance, performance and composition enhance critical awareness, and critical awareness can give new insights for the creation of new works of art. What is clear is that a range of aesthetic experiences, experimentation, and thoughtful instruction are all necessary components of arts education.

Schools foster critical awareness through a wide range of aesthetic experiences. Such experiences should include various aesthetic forms in familiar and unknown cultural settings. Students should unwrap works of art to appreciate and understand them. Initial encounters should be open-ended, asking questions like, What do you notice? How do you react? What surprises you? Why? The students observe imagination, beauty, and striking symbolism. They share multiple perspectives and meanings. They give their interpretations of what the artist is communicating. Our intent is to help students see the world around them with new understanding based on fresh insights about visual and aural qualities.

Good artists balance aesthetic surface, symbolism, and worldview perspective to create works with an integrated unity. Students respond quickly to the aesthetic surface, to the form or composition of images or sounds. They may also respond to the artists' symbolism, to the imagery used to portray elements of life. Finally, while students usually cannot identify underlying worldviews from single works, teachers can help them recognize and respond to the life perspective that underlies an artist's total body of work (Dengerink 1987, 30–31). An understanding of oft-implicit worldviews paves the way for students to be aware of the suggestive qualities and driving forces behind their own compositions. This awareness helps them consider how image and value interact and how art can address issues such as cruelty and love or despair and hope. They then become more conscious that art products embody social, political, economic, ethical, and religious values and functions.

To give worshipful praise to God through the arts, it is not enough to just analyze and respond. Students must also perform music, dance, and drama; and create and compose works of visual and aural art. They explore, experiment, invent, and shape as they express their perceptions. They also learn in a more formal way about the principles of composition and style. They begin to perceive how form is part of a work's content and meaning. They evaluate their own work, learning from their successes and mistakes. Gradually they learn to base their work on their own sense of values. Schools support them by providing frequent opportunity for exhibitions and performances. In this way they encourage students to make the arts an integral part of their lives.

Schools give sequential instruction in visual arts without inhibiting self-expression. Besides exploring freely with a variety of media, students receive instruction in specific techniques. Crafts such as pottery, weaving, stitchery, and quilting may not involve as much allusiveness as painting or sculpture. However, many students use them more easily in gratifying vocational and leisure settings.

Music captures and presents purposefully organized sounds and silences in an aesthetic manner. Today, music has become so pervasive that it not only expresses but also shapes our culture. This pervasiveness spurs us to teach students what excellence and aesthetic richness mean in a diversity of styles, including rock, rap, jazz, and others. As students are taught effectively, they learn to express themselves personally through music as they manipulate, explore, create, and compose. They play simple percussion, string, and wind instruments (e.g., ukuleles and recorders), and in this way they learn to "sing to the Lord a new song" (Psalm 98:1).

As a side benefit, music education promotes overall mental and physical health, as well as nurturing "soft" skills such as teamwork, adaptability, and presentation confidence (Jones 2001, A18).

Drama, literature, and filmmaking portray and communicate a vision of human existence in an aesthetic way. Here students interpret and assess life experience through involvement with situations that may be challenging, unpredictable, or full of tension. Performing and creating such works can sharpen students' imagination and deepen their insight into life-related issues and values.

It is particularly at the middle and high school levels that students can begin to understand the place of aesthetics in culture. How aesthetics has interacted with culture becomes clear, in part, through the study of history. Such diverse activities as reading poetry and studying patterns in math may enhance aesthetic sensitivity. Yet to do justice to the goals of aesthetics education, we also need separate courses in the arts for all students. Usually, only high school students with particular studio talents take such courses. However, if we believe that aesthetic knowledge adds an important dimension to life, all students should choose and take some courses in the fine arts. Otherwise, too often students do little more than ape popular culture in their aesthetic attitudes and behavior.

Footstep 8-4

□ John F. Alexander (1993, 28–29) tells the story of going to the Rodin Museum in Philadelphia with his daughter's class. He thought the students would discuss beauty, how the sculptures made them feel, and which ones were the most beautiful. But the teacher dealt only with details of Rodin's life and the methods of bronze casting. Alexander concluded that the crucial things in life such as awe, beauty, and holiness have been replaced in the curriculum with things that fit on multiple-choice tests. Schools, he added, leave out everything that might fill our hollowness and the emptiness of our culture.

Is Alexander right? Is this how the fine arts are generally taught in schools? What values do the fine arts foster? What values should they foster? How would you plan a trip to an art museum or a concert?

❏ In his sixth-grade unit on comics mentioned in chapter 5, Hugo Vanderhoek combines aesthetics, language, and media studies. He considers comic strips an important genre since they influence people's values. His students analyze different types of comics. They consider the underlying values and how cartoonists portray them. They develop their own comics using the cultural, moral, and artistic standards that they have formulated. The class publishes a collection of these cartoons for the community.

Are comics significant enough to warrant an integral unit? Why or why not? How does this unit meet the three goals of aesthetic education? In what ways does it meet the overall goals of a Christian approach to curriculum?

Language and Literature Studies

➤ *David Wu teaches a unit on John Bunyan's* Pilgrim's Progress *to his seventh-grade class. His theme is that God calls Christians to travel the road of discipleship with the promise of eternal life. He starts by asking students to consider characteristics of the Christian life. Students first work in pairs. They then design a questionnaire that they use to interview adults. The class examines the themes of suffering, despair, and temptation, finding modern-life parallels to the allegorical situations. Later, small groups of students write about how Bunyan contrasts good and evil, hope and despair, truth and deceit. At the end, students may choose their final mode of response. They may create and present a modern drama illustrating or comparing themes or characters from the novel. They may also create a mural of a modern Christian life. Other possibilities include writing an essay or song about the Christian life, or a pamphlet to explain the Christian life to non-Christians.*

Teaching and Learning Language

"In the beginning was the Word, and the Word was with God, and the Word was God.... Through him all things were made ..." (John 1:1, 3). Here, the Bible uses a powerful metaphor for Jesus Christ: God's love and communication reach us through the Word that is Christ. Through that Word all things were made. Therefore, God's gift of language also comes to us through God's love in Jesus Christ. God speaks to create. He speaks to rule and inform. He speaks to bless and to curse. God expects us as His image bearers to respond by speaking responsibly (Smith 1991, 4–5).

Language communication is an incredibly significant and beautiful gift of God. We therefore nurture respect for language and a concern for integrity in its use. The Bible decries language that violates love, truth, or justice. The apostle Paul warns against unwholesome talk, adding that we should use language to benefit others and build them up (Ephesians 4:29). The Bible gives us norms for language use: truthfulness, considerateness, fairness, appropriateness, clarity, conciseness, and aesthetic vitality. These norms provide a framework of responsibility and freedom within which we unfold and use language with gratitude and wonder (Smith 1992, 11–12). Regrettably, sin and ignorance often cause people to use language to remake the world in their own image, for their own self-interest.

Language learning is intended to help students:

- To use language with integrity, both functionally and creatively, in order to praise God and serve others: to listen thoughtfully, speak clearly, read critically, and write imaginatively
- To develop communication skills that clarify thought and feeling, and thus contribute to building relationships in community
- To realize and experience how to use language to deepen personal and communal perceptions and insights, and thus to become constructive and reconciling agents in their communities

Language learning takes place across the curriculum. It is a tool that is sharpened not just in the language arts time slot but in all subject areas. The main goal of language studies, to learn to communicate effectively with others, is so broad that it almost defies description. Through speaking, writing, reading, and listening, students learn to conceptualize and respond to feelings and attitudes. They articulate and shape their experiences in their environments. They become committed to certain values. Language studies contribute to critical discernment and foster creative abilities.

Language learning is fraught with controversy. This stems as much from differences in philosophical orientations as from knowledge of what works. Some things are clear however. Students learn language incrementally through interactive experiences in listening, speaking, writing, and reading. They learn more from using language for varied purposes and audiences than from specific skills taught out of context. The teaching of skills such as writing, vocabulary study, and spelling are more effective within a meaningful setting. As students process language actively, they also develop and extend interpretations and meanings.

Teaching and Learning Reading

The whole language approach holds that language is learned from whole to part. It emphasizes the meaning being communicated rather than specific skills. Teachers who use a whole language approach provide a range of meaningful and appealing reading materials. These materials may include selections that contribute to a Christian worldview. Teachers encourage students to communicate their insights and discoveries both orally and in writing. Kindergartners become excited about their ability to communicate through writing when they can experiment with emergent writing without at first adhering to "adult" spelling and grammar conventions.

Using only whole language, however, results in many students in higher grades who lack phonetic word attack skills and are still inventing their own spelling. Especially students who have reading problems or whose parents have low levels of literacy have need for a special structured approach in teaching reading. Kindergarten teachers begin to provide this structure by teaching phonemic awareness as they also provide rich reading and writing experiences. They teach word attack skills methodically, but often in playful ways. They recognize that different children benefit from different approaches. Therefore, they complement informal exploration with specific instruction, including word recognition skills, comprehension strategies, and, when the children have made good progress, "adult" spelling.

Whatever methods are used, teachers should foster critically reflective reading to complement decoding and comprehension skills. As early as kindergarten and first grade, teachers can ask, What do you think will happen next? or, What could this person have done differently? Later they can ask more probing questions, not only in language arts but across the curriculum. Helping students develop and apply strategies for critical discernment encourages them to evaluate the worth and validity of what they read. They learn to distinguish between fact and opinion, detect false claims and contradictions, identify the assumptions and biases of authors, and develop their own value commitments (R. Parker and L. Unsworth in Lewy 1991, 522).

Teaching and Learning Writing

Writing as process has become popular in classrooms, using a cycle of prewriting, drafting, editing, publishing, and presenting. A danger is that students may practice writing without receiving any direct instruction. As long as teachers provide structured writing instruction, the workshop or process approach helps students learn to think about and express their ideas well and often (see footstep 8-5). Such instruction happens more in elementary schools than in high schools, where the amount of writing often declines sharply. Using self- and peer-evaluation may help high school teachers keep their marking time at a reasonable level while still having students consider and express their views in longer writing assignments.

Teaching and Learning About Literature

Literature uses the lingual and aesthetic aspects of reality to catch and present the meaning of a slice of life. It is a human, imaginative, and symbolic response that expresses some vision of life's meaning. It affords the opportunity to interact with great characters and interpreters of human life. Christian teachers allow students to enjoy the beauty, wonder, and vicarious adventure of literature. They also use it to shape their students' view of and responses to life. They help students discern the vision of literary works, understand it in terms of a biblical worldview, and respond in a considered, personal way. To achieve these results often requires a thorough consideration of a literary work's aesthetic and lingual characteristics as well as how it deals with its confessional and ethical questions.

Students can consider questions that explore the beliefs, values, attitudes, and behaviors portrayed in literature (based on MacKenzie et al. 1997):

- How is human nature portrayed? Are people basically good, or are they born with a bias toward sin?
- Are people locked in deterministic patterns, or are they shown to be able to change?
- What is the cause of evil or injustice?
- Is there ultimately hope or meaning? If so, what is its source?

Choosing what literature to teach is not always easy. Christian teachers should teach some literature written by Christian authors. If it is of good quality and sensitive to biblical mandates, such literature nurtures a Christian vision of life. Teachers should also include significant literature written by others, though it may sometimes contain language or situations that offend Christians. The basic criterion for its inclusion should be whether teaching it can affirm God's Kingdom and His righteousness, including an ethically and socially responsible world. Non-Christian works taught in a Christian classroom can extend students' vision of reality and their understanding of and sensitivity to other people and other cultures. As Barbara Pell put it:

> Let us view these portrayals of human suffering and doubt—of positive values and of values that show the poverty of a world without God—with compassion, sensitivity, and a larger Christian perspective that realistically recognizes the depths of man's sinfulness but also the tremendous potential of God's grace. For remember, if God is the answer, we don't have to be afraid of the question. (Pell 1989, 7)

Teaching and Learning Foreign Languages

Foreign language study helps students develop an understanding of how people in other cultures live and express themselves. Students become less insular and ethnocentric, and they see how language and culture are interrelated. They gain insight into the factors that have shaped how we speak, think, and live, and how languages obey certain laws. Sometimes economic competitiveness is stressed as a goal for foreign language study. While acquaintance with their language is helpful when dealing with people, a more basic reason for learning a language is that it enriches our perception, understanding, and discernment of other cultures as well as of our own. Therefore, foreign language teaching should include a critical awareness of the associated cultures. Foreign language knowledge helps Christians serve and work with people in other cultures, and, of course, acquaint them with the gospel.

David Smith and Barbara Carvill (2000) argue that the study of foreign languages is particularly important to help students explore new cultures or "the world of the stranger." They learn new forms of personal interaction and new norms for conversation. Within this context Smith and Carvill decry foreign language textbooks, not so much for what is included as for what is missing: the influence of faith on the culture, the interconnections between faith and life, sensitive praise for cultural differences, and a context of mutual giving and receiving. They suggest asking questions such as the following when assessing foreign language texts (p. 16):

- How does the text present the humanity of members of the culture? Do they fear, doubt, suffer, sin, hope, pray, or celebrate as well as work, shop, play, and eat?
- Do the people portrayed ever face significant decisions involving more than issues of personal preference? How do they approach these decisions, and by what criteria do they make them?
- Do the teaching materials include any spiritual or religious dimension of the target culture?
- Does the resource incorporate any voice of lament for the broken aspects of that culture?

Foreign language teachers may have to compensate for shortcomings in their textbooks that are suggested by these questions.

Footstep 8-5

Joan Konynenbelt usually begins her middle school language arts block with a brief lesson on a topic that needs attention (e.g., punctuation, formal essay writing). Then she asks her students about their progress. She arranges individual conferences where she gives students personal attention, and they then become responsible for their own work. Normally they themselves choose what they read and write. They keep a reflective reading log. In peer conferences they help each other as they go through the prewriting, composing, revising, and publishing cycle. About once a week, students share their work with the whole group. They write for each other and become considerate of each other's learning space. Since students make their own choices, they relate their learning to their concerns in life, especially in and through their reading response journals. The teacher complements her workshop approach with novel studies that frequently relate to social studies themes. In this way, the class as a whole also analyzes issues that are significant for Christians.

Do you think this language arts program is a balanced one that meets the aims of a Christian curriculum? Why or why not? If you taught middle school language arts, how would you alter this program?

Social Studies

➢ *Gwen Wray's tenth-grade social studies class includes several aboriginal Indian students. The class explores the roots of the problems currently facing Indian people.*

Students take a critical look at a range of materials: historical and recent articles, textbooks, tapes and videos, and parts of Michener's Centennial. *They begin to see the complexity of the issues. They no longer simply blame problems on native people's own abuse and idleness, nor, on the other hand, just on white male oppression. Wray asks what society can offer Indian people today. She has her students investigate how we can balance justice and responsibility, as seen from a biblical perspective, in particular situations.*

The heartbeat of social studies is cultural formation. Social structures depend on religious, ethical, political, legal, economic, and social beliefs. Social studies therefore includes content from history and geography and often also from anthropology, sociology, economics, law, and political science. Social studies sheds light on how the motivating ideas of groups of people have affected the development of communities and cultures. It explores how the dominant worldview of a culture—its beliefs, commitments, values, and dispositions—has framed and guided human endeavors.

The concept of cultural formation is therefore central in the main aim of social studies:

• **To understand and respond to the process of cultural formation, both past and present**

Social studies explores the elements that shape cultures, countries, communities, and individuals. Thus, it involves all aspects of reality from the mathematical to the confessional. Accordingly, it helps students understand their physical, aesthetic, social, economic, institutional, and religious environments and how they came about.

How do human ideals, movements, and structures affect cultural formation? How has the spirit of cultures resulted in diverse patterns of human activity? What are the basic beliefs, commitments, and values that shape nations and civilizations? Interdisciplinary integral units often are good vehicles for teaching social studies.

Clearly, a social studies curriculum does more than impart information. It helps students consider the values that guide society and encourages them to act on biblically based ones. Such social values include human dignity, responsibility, economic fairness, and environmental integrity. For instance, human dignity means that all persons and their communities have the right to be treated with justice, love, compassion, and respect—and have the responsibility to treat others likewise. Mutual responsibility includes the principles that persons respect the law and that governments implement fair laws that make provisions, for instance, for stable family life.

The whole curriculum should foster an active interest in the affairs of society and should ingrain commitment to basic values, rights, and responsibilities. The particular role of social studies is to have students consider human actions in social settings and, especially, in social institutions such as governments. Social studies in Christian schools prepares students for biblically based citizenship: they learn to recognize the dead ends in our world and work for real change by demonstrating that God's justice can bring peace, well-being, and fulfillment (Koole 1990, 7).

The North American elementary social studies curriculum is usually an expanding horizons curriculum. Kindergartners and first-graders look at their personal environment (e.g., My Family, My Neighborhood,

God Made Me Special). Successive grades branch out to neighborhoods, communities, states or provinces, the nation, and the world. This pattern, however, is not well grounded. For instance, what fascinates young children are things foreign to their experience. They learn a great deal from units about Japan or Mexico if the content is concrete and embedded in stories. By contrasting life in such countries with their own, they learn to appreciate different cultures. And at higher levels, adolescents would benefit from taking an in-depth look at their own community and how it functions.

Teaching and Learning Geography

Geography considers how people use their physical environment to shape communities and society. It involves both environmental and social issues. The values of individuals and societies are important in explaining landscapes. Where, for instance, do communities build churches, parks, shopping areas, and industries? Why and how do they grow? There have been two main interpretations to such questions. The capitalist one is that entrepreneurship and the accumulation of personal wealth drive the economic engine. The Marxist one is that workers will be oppressed until the state on their behalf takes over the means of production and rewards all citizens equally.

A Christian interpretative framework holds that God created the world to enable humans to unfold reality's potential. The fall into sin led to selfish and sinful developments, including capitalist excesses and Marxist oppression. Those who live in Christ resist such patterns of self-interest. They work toward justice and compassion, balancing rights and responsibilities. This interpretative framework does not give simple answers to complex problems. Nevertheless, it does shed light on issues in environmental studies, urban planning, and economic development at home and abroad (M. Bradshaw in Francis and Thatcher 1990, 377–81).

The goals of teaching geography include (see also MacKenzie et al. 1997, 228–31):

- To recognize that people have a responsibility to care for God's earth physically, environmentally, aesthetically, economically, socially, and ethically
- To investigate the possibilities and limitations of different geographical settings as people develop their lives and lifestyles
- To examine how societies have used physical and human conditions on the earth's surface to shape their environments, in both responsible and irresponsible ways
- To understand that poor geographical stewardship has led to environmental problems
- To bring geographical knowledge to bear on current issues in a God-honoring manner, and to explore ways of restoring our environment both locally and globally

Teaching and Learning History

History investigates how humans have responded to God's call to care for and unfold the earth. Often, it tells a lamentable story. Yet its focal point, Christ's cross and resurrection, brings meaning and hope. In history, students learn how ideals and ideologies have shaped people and their institutions. They explore how beliefs, physical and social conditions, and institutions have interacted. They begin to recognize that history is never neutral. Historians usually choose and interpret events to fit their guiding perspective. In high school, students may be asked to compare different versions of his-

torical events and begin to use biblical norms to interpret such events.

The aims of learning history include:

- To recognize that God acts providentially in history, and continues His redemptive work through His Holy Spirit until Christ returns
- To explore open-mindedly, interpret fairly, and evaluate discerningly how humans have unfolded aspects of life as they fashioned various cultures and made consequential decisions
- To understand how cultural values rooted in worldview beliefs have shaped societies
- To acquire skills such as the ability to locate, evaluate, and interpret information; to detect bias; to understand cause and effect; and to draw valid conclusions concerning human activity in the past

Regrettably, many students find history unrelated to their experience and boring because of rote learning of much detail. Yet history lends itself to diverse and active learning strategies:

- **Analyses of primary materials** for deeper and more balanced insight into historical events and issues. Students can access many primary sources on the Internet, but you need to limit the number of sites and give a list of criteria to verify a website's reliability (e.g., <http://memory.loc.gov>; <www.teachtci.com/default.asp>).
- **Case studies** with follow-up discussions and debriefing (for an example, see footstep 8-6).
- **Jigsaw techniques** (e.g., each student investigates how a knight or lady, a free tenant, a serf, or a monk or nun lived in the Middle Ages. Then they teach this to

each other in groups of four, with each group having one representative of each role).

- **Simulations, role-plays, and games** about historical situations (e.g., reenactment of trench warfare in World War I or of a newscast about Luther's Ninety-five Theses at Wittenberg).
- **Debates** (e.g., whether it was justified to use the atomic bomb to end World War II).
- **Historical narrative and fiction.** Stories based on historical events can make history more vibrant: they can give insight into personal as well as communal motives and aspirations.
- **Boxes of artifacts** from a particular time in history (e.g., items dealing with the depression of the 1930s).
- **Biographies** of influential Christians in history. Michael Clarke's *Canada: Portraits of Faith* (1998) gives more than fifty biographies of Christians who made an impact in Canadian history—including their strengths as well as their shortcomings.

Knowledge, Commitment, and Action

To deal adequately with cultural formation, social studies includes more than geography and history. It also considers the roles of governments and citizens. It looks at how our economic system works and the increasing disparity between rich and poor. Christian teachers help students see that material prosperity does not define the quality of life. What are Christian responses to resource abuse, armed conflicts, poverty, and the population explosion? How can students contribute, even if in small ways, to restoring brokenness and despair?

Some years ago Chuck Chamberlin wrote a chapter on teaching social studies entitled "Knowledge + Commitment = Action" (Parsons, Milburn, and van Manen 1983, 321ff). Chamberlin described how primary students have influenced decisions of parks departments, how middle school students persuaded a city to condemn and remove dangerous buildings, and how high school classes participated in the hearings for a low-rent housing proposal. Such commitment and action requires students to investigate problems, plan cooperatively, and extend their oral and written communication skills. This type of activity may be time-consuming but is necessary if students are to become strongly committed to acting on their convictions and to taking an active hand in cultural formation.

Footstep 8-6

Selma Wassermann (1992, 793–95, 800) describes how Rich Chambers uses the internment of Japanese-Canadians during World War II as a case study. The study deals with three "big ideas": society's paranoia and racist attitudes, government's discriminatory policies, and the gutting of civil rights. Students read the narrative and, in small groups, discuss five provocative questions. After forty minutes of heated discussion, Chambers debriefs the case with the whole class, listening to and paraphrasing students' comments while zeroing in on the main issues. He avoids making value judgments, even about clearly racist attitudes. Over the next week, he introduces print and visual materials that supplement the original narrative. Students openly and freely express their feelings and insights. This allows the teacher to help them reevaluate their views.

Think of an event or phenomenon in social studies for which you could write a case. What would be its "big ideas"? How would you teach the case so that the students would remain involved and yet address issues that deal with important values?

Religious Studies and Ethics

➤ *To make the Bible speak to their own experience, Curt Gesch's eleventh-grade students paraphrased passages in Isaiah using modern examples. An excerpt from Raymond's work for Isaiah 11:1–9:*

> *[God] will create a new earth where all is good,*
>   *and he will be happy with his people.*
>
> *It will be a place where*
>   *the ivory hunter will live with the rhino,*
>   *the Iraqi and the American will be neighbors,*
>   *the Serbs and Croatians will live side by side,*
>   *and all will be brought together by a child....*
>
> *A child will play alone in the park and be safe,*
>   *and a child will not find needles in the grass ...*
>   *for the earth will be filled with the knowledge of the Lord.*

Gesch helps his students to understand the redemptive nature of Scripture and how to interpret it so that the implications for themselves and our culture become more understandable. Further, he teaches the Bible as a metanarrative, as the "big story" of Creation, the Fall, Redemption, and the forthcoming Fulfillment, with God calling students to be part of God's Kingdom through Christ's work of redemption and the Holy Spirit's work of sanctification.

The Bible functions in three ways in Christian schools:

- **As the Word of God the Bible gives basic perspectives for life, and there-** fore also for schooling. Our understanding of Scripture undergirds our views of curriculum aims and content.

- **In devotions and chapels the Bible's message gives spiritual direction for being a committed and discipling learning community.**

- **The Bible serves as the main resource for biblical studies as a subject.** Here students analyze and interpret its textual meaning, explore its cultural context, trace its themes, and discuss its implications for everyday life.

Faith affects all of life and the entire curriculum. That is why an important goal of social studies is to explore how basic faith commitments affect cultural formation. Religious studies and ethics focus more specifically on the confessional and ethical aspects of reality. They may include courses or units in world religions and church history as well as biblical studies. Some high schools also offer a course or units in ethics.

A course in biblical studies uses the Bible as its main text even as teachers and students submit to its authority as the trustworthy Word of God. The Bible is the story of a loving, faithful, and just God acting to redeem His people, a story that culminated in the death and resurrection of His Son Jesus Christ. It is also the story of God interacting with His people and calling them to faith response. God calls those renewed in Jesus Christ to be coheirs and coworkers in planting signposts to God's Kingdom of truth and justice. The biblical studies course deals directly with such biblical themes and helps students explore and deepen their faith and commitment.

The goals of biblical studies include:

- **To experience the biblical narrative as God's revelation of His plan of**

redemption. Through hearing and retelling the Bible narratives, students begin to experience God's power, anger, and mercy. They understand the Bible as the history of salvation in Jesus Christ, a history through which God calls them to repentance, faith, and discipleship.

- **To understand and interpret the Bible.** Students investigate the Bible's literary forms, its cultural contexts, and its origins and translations. They tease out significant biblical themes and practice techniques of Bible interpretation.

- **To apply the biblical message to one's personal life and to situations in our culture.** The Bible is a light for our path (Psalm 119:105) and teaches us to do what is right (2 Timothy 3:16).

Children should experience the Bible as the big story of Creation, the Fall, Redemption, and Fulfillment—not just as disjointed stories used to illustrate moral truths while missing God's good news and His comprehensive call. Let me give an example. A teacher could tell the story of Jacob by stressing that while Jacob did a wicked thing in lying to his father, afterward he became a good man who served God. Another may emphasize that despite human wrongdoing, God remains faithful to His promises and that God uses even sinful situations to further His plan of salvation. The first teacher falls into the trap of reducing the richness of Scripture to the moral aspect of reality. The second acknowledges that the moral dimension is important, but the story of God's redemption in the face of human failure is the confessional crux of this event.

With respect to applying the biblical message to life, Rosemary Cox (2001) makes two important points. First, the Bible as an object of study will not prove life-giving apart from a relationship with Christ. Therefore (and this is my conclusion), we need to confront students with the need for such a relationship at appropriate times. Second, the Bible is not a prescriptive rulebook for Christian living that can always be applied directly and immediately to our life and culture. Often it is a shaper of our presuppositions, thought, and action. Passages such as Proverbs and Jesus' parables are more indirectly and yet profoundly influential in developing godly wisdom and transforming the way we think and act:

> The model of the Bible as "shaper" is theologically satisfying. It is, though, too, practically useful when thinking about communicating the biblical content to children. It relieves me of the burden of having to find a "right" meaning for every text, and it opens the way for me to be able to study the text together with the children, allowing children to bring creative insights of their own. (Cox 2001, 44)

One danger of teaching biblical studies in Christian schools is that we force faith and spirituality onto students. Students, particularly as adolescents, need to come to their own commitment. Teachers can help students read and interpret the Bible in more meaningful ways, but they cannot force them to believe that it is the Word of God. Here as elsewhere, teachers need to foster an atmosphere of trust and care where students feel free to express their personal views. At the same time, teachers need to model how they base their whole life on their faith. Prayers and faith insight mean little to students if teachers fail to apply biblical holiness, compassion, and justice in their classroom dealings and everyday life.

While only Christian schools can teach biblical studies in the way described above, schools in general need to pay attention to the spiritual and ethical dimensions of human life, which are significant for life and, therefore, also for the curriculum. A good example is a program of the Quebec English-speaking public schools. It includes a module on knowledge of the Bible since "the Bible is not only the source of the moral and spiritual values of the Protestant tradition, but it is also the foundation of many values found in Western culture and civilization" (Commité Protestant, 1992a, 14). The program includes an understanding of both Christian and other religious traditions. It views topics such as human sexuality, the environment, peaceful solutions to conflict, and concern for the poor and vulnerable from the perspective of religious and spiritual values (Commité Protestant, 1992b).

This type of approach is much more sound than the superficial ways of nurturing spirituality often suggested today, such as inner and extrasensory experiences, communing with nature, and emphasizing ritual (e.g., Suhor 1998/1999). At the same time, it is encouraging that many educators once again realize, as Dwayne Huebner put it, that "everything that is done in the schools, and in preparation for school activity, is already infused with the spiritual ... the problem is—the schools are not places where the moral and spiritual life is lived with any kind of intentionality" (Huebner 1999, 414–15).

The ethical aspect of reality is dealt with to some degree in all subjects, of course. But at the senior secondary level it may be worthwhile to offer a separate ethics course, as suggested by the Quebec committee, especially in a time of ethical uncertainty and superficiality. The meaninglessness of our culture is the most serious disease of our times, and schools must do what they can to counter this hollowness.

Footstep 8-7

A pastor claimed that biblical studies should not be included in the curriculum of a new Christian school. He gave three reasons. First, teaching the subject is the task of the church, not the school. Also, it would lead to controversies about doctrine in an interdenominational school. Most importantly, the school's Christian nature should be evident in its whole program. He did not want teachers to be complacent and assume that biblical studies gives the school its Christian character.

However, most Christian schools have argued that church education programs are too limited to do justice to biblical-theological analysis and reflection. They use biblical studies to explore basic biblical motifs and themes. Should biblical studies be part of a Christian school's curriculum? Why or why not? If so, what components other than biblical studies should be part of the school's religious studies program?

Subjects with Application Emphases

> *"So what makes your information technology (IT) courses special?" I ask Tom Pankratz, a high school computer specialist. He hands me an article by art educator Elliot Eisner and says, "If you now substitute 'God' for 'art,' you'll know what I want to do in my courses." Pankratz, like Eisner, wants to transform students' ideas, images, and feelings by seeing the connections between content and form, by imagining possibilities, and by exploring ambiguities. Pankratz has obviously given*

this much thought and makes the following points:

- *I teach students to be critical: technology will not make us better. In fact, technology may prevent people from seeing the big picture. I want my students to walk away with a sense of something beyond technology, with a sense of hope in God.*

- *My students must become computer literate but also see and deal with the ethical dimensions of technology (e.g., illegal downloading), how computers have made life more difficult (e.g., more thinking and less repetitive work, higher expectations of work quantity and quality), and that programs should often be seen not as an end-all but as a basis for open and honest discussions (e.g., career path programs).*

- *My students create and maintain a website for a Christian sports association. This service activity not only develops skills but also raises questions about significant and effective content. A crucial activity in my senior IT class is students' creation of a mission statement for their own lives and their later reflection on how IT fits into their lives and how they can glorify God using IT. There are no pat answers: each student has to respond personally. Unless my courses lead students to more faith, more hope, and more love, my IT courses have failed.*

We often refer to school subjects with direct work applications as practical or vocational subjects. This may set up a false dichotomy, for what is more practical than being able to read and write? Or can we really say that learning woodworking skills is more practical than learning interpersonal and moral decision-making skills in a classroom debate about capital punishment? Conversely, what is as rooted in a thorough understanding of the dynamics of our culture and its values as learning about family management in home economics?

All school subjects contain—or should contain—a mixture of more theoretical and more practical aspects. Some subjects have more direct application than others, of course. Those include, for example, technology education, home economics, information technology studies, and business education. The importance of these is not specific vocational training, however. That would be counterproductive in our rapidly changing technology and work settings. Instead, such studies should include general social, technical, and business skills that benefit students no matter what their future careers will be. Students should receive some insight into the world of work, career possibilities, and their inclination and aptitude for certain fields.

Elementary students might experience how using simple tools and processes in creative ways can enrich their lives. Students can recycle materials such as aluminum, or make birdhouses or ceramic pottery. First-grade students can design and build an electric alarm system on a board. They can also explore alternative ways of heating buildings. They can make some items in an assembly line, then in small groups, and then by themselves, comparing the advantages of each. Through this, they get an intuitive feel for technology. They can begin to talk about how technology relates to work and lifestyle values.

In the middle grades many schools offer a wide range of short electives, or exploratories, sometimes taught by parents or other volunteers. The range of courses depends on the expertise of teachers and volunteers. Many are work or hobby related and may include, for instance, various crafts, car and small appliance repair, food and nutrition, first aid, and webpage design. A wide range of such experiences broadens students' horizons, shows how they can use their gifts in practical and creative ways in obedience to God, and raises questions about a stewardly lifestyle.

High school courses with a practical emphasis may include family living, career planning, business education, technological education, and work experience. Some schools require all students to take a course, or at least some units, in family living and career planning. Family living includes home management but also allows students to explore, within the framework of God's Word, the effect of redefined sex roles, two-career families, divorce, and so on. Work experience, even of short duration, enables students to analyze and discuss the nature of work and life on the job.

Throughout all such experiences, students should begin to reflect critically on the values that shape our technological world, investigate the impact of technology on culture, and understand that the development and use of technology reveals our commitments and visions (MacKenzie et al. 1997, 173). God's gifts of wisdom and imagination have led to the technological age. While technology can be a powerful tool to advance God's Kingdom of righteousness and justice, it can also enslave us and be used in ways that undermine a just and peaceful society. Any new technology poses new opportunities as well as new moral, social, political, and legal challenges.

Computers have become such an integral part of life that computer studies or information studies as separate subjects may well become less important over time. Students need to learn how to use computers effectively for accessing information, word pro-

cessing, and creating multimedia documents. But computer-related technology has limitations. Access to more information or more efficient mastery of skills does not always cause social progress. According to C. A. Bowers, computer studies also contribute to students' belief that they are autonomous, self-directing individuals. The technological-computer mind-set assumes that all problems can be technologically fixed. Further, computers easily lead students to reduce knowledge, meaning, and wisdom to objective bits of information that can be recovered efficiently (1988, 6–8, 33, 77).

Computer technology has changed how we view what is good for our society and how we go about making personal and societal decisions. There is evidence that computers have had a major impact in changing the foundation of economic and political decisions from a moral to a statistical one (Anderson 2000, 4). We have incredibly easy and broad access to information. What our students need help with is to deal with such information in a meaningful context, recognize its significance, and use it responsibly. Computer studies should also include a healthy dose of skepticism about the limitations and dangers of this technology. It has a tendency, for instance, to idolize technical efficiency for self-interest—with little or no commitment or responsibility.

Footstep 8-8

List topics with an application emphasis that you believe should be included in the curriculum at elementary, middle, or high school levels. Which of these are currently not taught in schools with which you are familiar? If these topics were introduced, what parts of the curriculum would they replace? How do you respond to the argument that with the workplace and technology changing so rapidly, schools should use their limited time to provide a basic general education and leave it to employers to teach vocational skills? What should schools do to help students use computer-related technology in a responsible way?

Footstep 8-9

In terms of the personal curriculum orientation you have developed as you have read and interacted with the content of this book, which subjects currently in the curriculum do you consider most important? least important? How would the age level of students influence your answer?

Reviewing the Main Points

A balanced curriculum includes content that deals with all aspects of reality, ranging from the numerical in mathematics to the confessional in religious or biblical studies. To determine what content to include is difficult. Schools, therefore, need to set priorities on the basis of what they consider the basic aims and issues of each subject. This will enable them to develop a responsible Christian approach in each subject area.

References

Alexander, J. 1993. *The secular squeeze: Reclaiming Christian depth in a shallow world.* Downers Grove, IL: InterVarsity.

Anderson, K. 2000. Computers and the information revolution. Richardson, TX: Probe Ministries. Available at <www.leaderu.com/orgs/probe/docs/computer.html>.

Bowers, C. 1988. *The cultural dimensions of educational computing.* New York: Teachers College Press.

Checkley, K. 1996. Physical education: Preparing students to be active for life. *Curriculum Update,* Alexandria, VA: Association for Supervision and Curriculum Development (fall): 1–3, 6–8.

Clarke, M., ed. 1998. *Canada: Portraits of faith.* Chilliwack: Reel to Real.

Commité Protestant. 1992. *Protestant educational values.* Sainte Foy, Quebec: Gouvernement du Quebec.

———. 1992. *Protestant moral and religious education program: Advice to the minister.* Sainte Foy, Quebec: Gouvernement du Quebec.

Corno, L., ed. 2001. *Education across a century: The centennial volume.* One hundredth yearbook of the National Society for the Study of Education. Chicago: NSSE.

Cox, R. 2001. Using the Bible with children. *Journal of Education and Christian Belief* 5 (1): 41–49.

De Moor, S., ed. 1994. *Now you are the body of Christ.* Edmonton, AB: CSI District 12.

Dengerink, A. 1987. *Reflections on the arts: A study guide.* Toronto, ON: Institute for Christian Studies.

Ernest, P. 1991. *The philosophy of mathematics education.* London: Falmer.

Ezell, G. et al. 1993. *Healthy living.* A series of textbooks and teacher guides for teaching health. Grand Rapids: Christian Schools International.

Francis, L., and A. Thatcher, eds. 1990. *Christian perspectives for education.* Leominster, UK: Gracewing.

Hamming, C., H. Van Brummelen, and P. Boonstra. 1984. *The story of numbers and numerals.* Grand Rapids: Christian Schools International.

Huebner, D. 1999. *The life of the transcendent.* Mahwah, NJ: Lawrence Erlbaum.

Jackson, P., ed. 1992. *Handbook of research on curriculum.* New York: Macmillan.

Jones, A., ed. 1998. *Science in faith: A Christian perspective on teaching science.* Romford, UK: Christian Schools' Trust.

Jones, D. 2001. Music in education: Putting a price on it. *Vancouver Sun,* 15 March, sec. A, pp. 18–19.

Koole, R. 1990. *Christian perspective for teaching social studies.* Edmonton: CSI District 11.

Kuhn, T. 1970 [1962]. *The structure of scientific revolutions.* 2d ed. Chicago: University of Chicago Press.

Lewy, A., ed. 1991. *The international encyclopedia of curriculum.* Oxford: Pergamon.

MacKenzie, P. et al. 1997. *Entry points for Christian reflection within education.* London, UK: Christian Action Research and Education.

Nadeau, R., and J. Desautels. 1984. *Epistemology and the teaching of science.* Ottawa: Science Council of Canada.

National Association for Sport and Physical Education (NASPE). 1995. *Moving into the future: National standards for physical education.* Reston, VA: NASPE.

National Association of Secondary School Principals (NASSP). 1993. Science/technology/society-addressing the real problems in science education. *Curriculum Report* 22 (3): 1–4.

National Council for Teachers of Mathematics. 2000. *Principles and standards for school mathematics.* Reston, VA: NCTM.

Parsons, J., G. Milburn, and M. van Manen, eds. 1983. *A Canadian social studies.* Edmonton: University of Alberta.

Pell, B. 1989. Should Christians read "dirty books"? *Christian Educators Journal* 28 (3): 6–7.

Pinar, W. 1988. *Contemporary curriculum discourses.* Scottsdale, AZ: Gorsuch Scarisbrick.

Price, D., J. Wiester, and W. Hearn. 1986. *Teaching science in a climate of controversy.* Ipswich, MA: American Scientific Affiliation.

Shortt, J., ed. 1996. *Charis mathematics units 1–9.* Nottingham, UK: The Stapleford Centre.

———. 1997. *Charis mathematics units 10–19.* Nottingham, UK: The Stapleford Centre.

Smith, D. 1991. Language, God, and man. *Language matters.* No. 1: 3–5.

———. 1992. Language, God, and man. *Language matters.* No. 3: 10–12.

Smith, D., and B. Carvill. 2000. The right book. *Christian School Teacher* 2 (1): 12–16. Excerpted from Smith, D., and B. Carvill. 2000. *The gift of the stranger: Faith, hospitality, and foreign language learning.* Grand Rapids: Eerdmans.

Somerville, M. 2000. *The ethical canary.* Toronto: Penguin.

Steensma, G., and H. Van Brummelen, eds. 1977. *Shaping school curriculum: A biblical view.* Terre Haute, IN: Signal.

Suhor, C. 1998/1999. Spirituality-letting it grow in the classroom. *Educational Leadership* 56 (4): 12–16.

Tomlinson, P., and M. Quinton, eds. 1986. *Values across the curriculum.* London: Falmer.

Van Brummelen, H. et al. 1985. *Science.* A component of the SCS-BC *Curriculum handbook.* Surrey, BC: Society of Christian Schools in British Columbia.

Wassermann, S. 1992. A case for social studies. *Phi Delta Kappan* 73 (10): 793–801.

Willis, S. 1995. Reinventing science education. *Curriculum Update,* Alexandria, VA: Association for Supervision and Curriculum Development (summer): 1–8.

Zuidema, M., ed. 1995. *Physical education 3–5.* 3d ed. Grand Rapids: Christian Schools International.

Steppingstone 9

Curriculum Leadership

As I dream about the future, I see Christian schools that are truly Christ-centered communities of learning. The stakeholders in such communities learn through modeling Christlikeness, reflection, dialogue, inquiry, and action. These communities help students and teachers explore and experience what it means to be disciples of the Lord Jesus Christ and stewards of God's creation.

Peter Senge (1990) suggests that building a learning community requires an ecology of leadership in which everyone is involved. This includes not only administrators but also teachers, students, and parents. In an ideal Christian school, all stakeholders strive to implement a clear, focused biblical vision. They are mission-driven, acting within a well-defined set of core values. They ensure that their policies, processes, and organizational structures support a community where all activities lead to Christ-centered learning and growth. They know that rhetoric about collaboration and vision is not the same as the real thing. They avoid cynicism and disengagement that degenerates into a pseudo-community. They encourage and exhort each other to avoid slipping into a negative "shadow culture."

As I dream I ask, "How can we strengthen leadership in a Christ-centered learning community?" First of all we must outline its framework and vision. It must have a transformational impact on culture, be faithful to the authority of Scripture, provide for solid biblical integration in every subject area, and have Christian personnel that model servant leadership at every level (board, administration, teachers, and support staff). Learning experiences actively engage students, challenging them to responsible discipleship.

As I dream, I envision schools that, as Parker Palmer put it, create space for students in which obedience to truth is practiced—in order that Truth can ultimately capture them (1983, 69). We construct teaching and learning space in which our vision can be realized. Before responsible curriculum and instructional leadership can be given, whether in the classroom or in a larger venue, we consider how to create and sustain nourishing, invigorating, and truth-seeking space for learning. As I dream, I focus on the leadership required to do this. Effective leaders in Christ-centered learning communities persuade others to pursue a common goal and unleash a shared, collaborative, and dynamic leadership structure and process. Administrators, teachers, parents, and other supporters willingly and appropriately participate in goal-setting, planning, curricular decisions, budgeting, and staffing activities. Many of these were previously the sole domains of administrators. With shared leadership, some duties now shift to other members of the school community.

As I dream, I ask, "What should our leaders look like? And what should they do?" I envision *transformational* leaders. They must, first of all, model Christlikeness and humility as they serve their communities in the complex context of today's leadership. According to Leithwood and others (1998, 1999), transformational leaders will:

- Identify, articulate, and build toward a shared vision and the acceptance of group goals
- Structure the school organization to permit broad participation in decision making
- Keep groups focused, check for consensus, and hold high performance expectations
- Stimulate members of the learning community to think reflectively and critically about their practices, and plan follow-up discussion and action
- Provide appropriate models of the practices and values considered central to a school
- Provide individualized support for staff members
- Anticipate and handle constraints and obstacles flexibly, seeing these as opportunities to learn from experience
- Be knowledgeable and yet willing and able to be learners as well as leaders, using new information and the insights of teachers and other community members

Transformational leaders in Christian schools develop a Christ-centered collaborative culture using team-building activities. They provide teachers space where they together examine the relational world of the classroom, engage in meaningful discourse about their personal practical knowledge, and make sense of their practice within the context of the school and community. They welcome teachers' voices and encourage authentic relationships. They help to overcome teacher isolation by providing time within the timetable for dialogue and joint planning. They also continually assess where the school is at, where it hopes to be, and what steps must be taken to continue in that direction.

In an ideal Christ-centered learning community, the teachers will also be leaders as they create nourishing learning spaces for their students:

- **They understand the mission, vision, and values of the school and live them out as they plan and teach.** They affirm that biblical faith and values affect every part of the school. They are sacrificially committed to applying and teaching a biblical worldview based on the themes of creation, fall, redemption, and restoration.
- **Their orientation to learning reflects a biblical view that knowledge is acquired through personal relationship with God, His creation, and His created beings.** They tailor their lessons to effect life-changing growth. They model and teach love, care, and acceptance for all; conflict resolution and forgiveness; and

fairness and justice. They provide students opportunities to serve others and to reflect on the value of making positive contributions to the community.

- **They create nourishing learning spaces by engaging and supporting all students in learning.** They build on students' prior knowledge, life experience, interest, and spiritual insight. They use diverse strategies and resources. They actively involve students in their own learning and each other's learning, setting boundaries that provide some room for student responsibility and choice. They engage them in problem solving and critical thinking within and across subjects. They teach them concepts and skills in ways that encourage their application in meaningful and real-life contexts. They challenge all students to become self-directed learners who seek truth and are able to demonstrate, articulate, and evaluate what they learn.
- **They are lifelong learners whose professional and spiritual growth are closely linked.** They present their bodies as living and holy sacrifices, seeking to be acceptable to God through the transformation and renewing of their minds. They promote a communal working environment characterized by love, unity, and mutual support. They are reflective practitioners as well as risk takers who try new curriculum initiatives—and help colleagues to do so.

I have a dream. I dream that Christian schools will nurture students to become proficient and reflective thinkers whose minds and hearts are devoted to Jesus Christ. I dream that they will acquire a significant understanding of Christianity as a culturally relevant worldview. I dream that they will know how to deal responsibly with the injustices they see. I dream that they will be ready to serve Christ in home, church, and society. I dream that they (together with other members of the community) will counteract the materialism and radical individualism of the larger culture. I dream that Christ will be honored in every school subject and service program so that when students are asked what makes their schools distinctive, they will answer, "A biblical view of life and reality, and how it is practiced." I dream that teachers and students will translate the schools' stated missions into systematic and purposeful student action—action that translates into significant student ownership of the mission.

I dream that school administrators will be transformational leaders who cultivate Christ-centered communities of learning. I dream that they are visionaries who will help community members understand and enact a transformational Christian mission for their schools. I dream that the schools' written outcomes will express what the schools seek to accomplish spiritually, academically, and socially. I dream that the schools' leaders will actively involve all faculty and parents in determining those outcomes and how they are to be realized. I dream that schools live out their mission, vision, and values in observable thought and behavior.

I have a dream!

The foregoing introduction was originally written for one of my graduate courses by Anne Rauser, director of the Western Canada Region of the Association of Christian Schools International. Anne presents a powerful vision for Christian school education, as well as indicating the essentials of curriculum and instructional leadership. In chapter 6 we saw the various steps that different players must take with respect to curriculum planning. In this chapter we look more closely at the nature of curriculum leadership and the dynamics of change within the framework that Anne Rauser describes.

A Vision for Curriculum Renewal

➢ *Vision for ministry is a clear mental image of a preferred future imparted by God to His chosen servants and is based upon an accurate understanding of God, self, and circumstances.* (Barna 1992, 28)

Without a vision of what we want our curricula to achieve, our schools flounder. The meaning of Proverbs 29:18 is that if people do not base their vision on God's guidance, they will stumble. A lack of a common curriculum vision, or aims, is a major cause of school ineffectiveness. In short, curriculum leaders ought to have a clear vision that is based on God's Word. They then work toward achieving that vision in their particular context—and assess their school's curriculum accomplishments in terms of that vision. Note that Anne Rauser, like Martin Luther King, begins with a vision ("I have a dream!"), not with a strategic plan or a process flowchart. It is the vision that galvanizes, motivates, and provides a compass for the curriculum journey.

This book describes one possible vision for curriculum. Anne Rauser sums up a similar vision in this chapter's introduction. Not all Christians share this particular vision. Some Christians promote a vision of a Christian classical education (e.g., Wilson 1991). Kevin Ryan sees schools in terms of becoming communities of virtue and character development (Ryan and Bohlin in *Jossey-Bass Reader* 1999, 309–17). Barry Kanpol (1998, 116ff) lauds Christians who use

schools as avenues to fight injustice, alienation, oppression, and competition. Stephen Holtrop, as we saw in chapter 2, has a vision of using the curriculum to foster responsibility perspectives. While these visions are not all mutually exclusive, they do lead to curricula with distinctive emphases.

The point here is that curriculum leaders—whether they are teachers, grade level or subject coordinators, principals, superintendents, or school board members—must have a very clear idea of what they want the curriculum to achieve. Not only that, but they must also help the rest of the school community to own the vision and work toward the same curriculum goals. That does not mean that teachers lose their individuality. Rather, it means that they use their insights and gifts to contribute in their own unique way to the accomplishment of the overall vision.

Transformational leaders mobilize their communities to develop a shared vision. Then they support their teachers in implementing that consensus in their classrooms. Specifically, they will:

- **Work with the school community's stakeholders to develop a shared conception of what the school's programs should achieve.** The vision should be clearly focused but not inflexible. It should be developed collaboratively by the school community, perhaps with the help of an outside facilitator. Without such participation, "our visions become mandates without meaning. Our stakeholders feel marginalized. The result is lack of understanding and commitment from those whose support we need most" (Brown and Moffett 1999, 87).

A leader could introduce a vision-forming session by reviewing the school's raison d'etre, its historical ethos, and the expectations for the process. Glatthorn suggests that the participants then work in small groups. They first complete the statement "I have a dream of a curriculum that is...." They insert ten adjectives that capture their vision, and write one or two sentences about each before sharing their ideas with the rest of the group. After discussions, they vote on each adjective, possibly by using fifteen pennies with which they give weight to the adjectives they favor (1997, 44–45). Afterward, someone pulls together the results into a coherent document rooted in the school's mission. This document goes back to all stakeholders, including the board, for further response and input. Remember that collaboration means that everyone listens to conflicting voices and tries to find a consensus. Leaders strive to create ownership, not buy-in.

- **Build a sense of community centered on the vision.** Transformational leaders want to maintain a shared purpose while allowing diversity within the overall vision. Therefore, they articulate and communicate the shared vision regularly and consistently. They demonstrate their commitment to learning that implements the vision. A culture of positive collaboration is a basic building block for successfully implementing a curriculum vision. Teachers must not only own the vision but also be committed to work with others to implement it. So leaders must work with teachers, including the informal leaders among them, to foster mutual trust, respect, honesty, and openness with students, with colleagues, and with the administrators. Too often, a sense of isolation among teachers limits their desire and capacity to change. Yet research sug-

gests that teachers who work together on shared vision and goals also have better student achievement and conduct.

- **Continue to work with teachers on interim improvements while the vision is being developed or renewed.** If their leader doesn't do so, the school may lose motivation and momentum to work on improving the curriculum.

Without a common vision and a united school community, curriculum change will be inconsistent or even incompatible with the school's mission, with teachers going off in different directions.

👣 Footstep 9-1

Do either (a) or (b).

(a) Suppose that you have been appointed principal of a new school that will open its doors on September 1. Since the school is new, the teachers have been hired as of August 1. List the steps you will take to develop a vision for the school. Include a timeline. What three points do you hold to be "nonnegotiables" that must be included in the vision statement?

(b) Suppose that your principal appoints you to lead a review of a subject discipline in which you have some expertise. This is the first in-depth review of this subject area in almost ten years. List the steps you will take to develop a vision for the subject area. Include a timeline. What three points about the subject will you hold to be "nonnegotiables" that must be included in the vision statement?

Fostering a School Culture That Supports Curriculum Change

➢ *In my experience there are four essential conditions for educational change:*

- *Shared vision of the goals of learning, good teaching, and assessment*
- *Understanding of the urgent need for change*
- *Relationships based on mutual respect and trust*
- *Engagement strategies that create commitment rather than mere compliance* (Wagner 2001, 380)

Sustained curriculum improvement happens only when a school has a culture that supports transformation. Effective school leaders engage teachers not only in setting a vision but also in examining how explicit and implicit beliefs, values, policies, and practices have affected their school's curriculum and learning. They then consciously go about building a positive school culture. Christian schools have an advantage: they usually have homogeneity about basic beliefs and values. However, there may still be surprising differences in views about curriculum aims and practices.

The following items summarize the responsibilities of those charged with curriculum change and development, including not only principals but grade coordinators, department chairs, and subject leaders as well. Some items may seem only indirectly related to curriculum change. However, they are essential elements of a school culture that facilitates curriculum improvement. The vital context for all these elements is a continuing commitment to a shared vision.

- **Foster collegiality and leadership capacity.** Pray for the school and all those involved in its operation. Commu-

nicate with honesty and feeling. Collaborate consistently. Develop caring relationships and a joyful atmosphere. Involve the staff in meaningful projects and decisions. Ask them to work in small teams on curriculum projects (e.g., cross-grade or department teams). They may well have new, helpful thoughts. Build their capacity to become active agents in reviewing, choosing, and creating programs and curriculum practices.

- **Cultivate your staff.** Encourage them regularly. Give tangible support and help where needed. Provide sufficient and useful professional development opportunities. Model integrity, evenhandedness, and, especially, trust. Nurture faith, hope, and love—especially love!

- **Be positive and confront negativity.** Be enthusiastic about the school and its potential in words and actions. Support and celebrate positive accomplishments, both ongoing and new. Compliment a commitment and willingness to change. At the same time, deal with and try to overcome destructive pessimism.

- **Plan purposefully,** but allow for input from others and remain flexible. Keep in mind the vision as well as the needs of diverse students in your school. Help your staff evaluate the present situation, plan for change, and set implementation priorities. Address the problems of resources (e.g., time, support, finances). Nothing undermines new curriculum initiatives more quickly than lack of time or rising expectations without adequate resources.

- **Move forward with those who are ready,** but take time to get everyone "on board." Ensure that all those involved can see the benefits of the proposed changes. In any group of people, there will be some stragglers or initial opponents. It can sometimes be an uphill grind to gain commitment for change, especially from more experienced teachers. Listen carefully to their reasons. They may feel threatened. Remember that many of them have poured much energy and expertise into developing units and programs that work for them and their students. It takes time for everyone to own the problem and agree that changes need to be made. Some people will jump on board right away, while others need time to reflect and be convinced. Work with those who resist, to test the wisdom of the recommended changes. Inspire them with a vision of a considerably improved school that they can create. Encourage them to agree to help solve the problem. Whenever feasible, give them some responsibilities. And sometimes you may have to agree that their resistance is valid and that a search for other solutions is needed.

- **Involve all the stakeholders.** Not all parents or board members want to be involved in planning curriculum change. But you want to keep them fully informed of major contemplated changes and give them opportunity for meaningful input. You might, for instance, hold an evening forum on proposed changes to the school's social studies program. You might start by listing some of the pros and cons and then ask for input, possibly dividing the participants into small groups for maximum input.

- **Don't allow the "pull of the past" to draw the school back to old curriculum practices**. It is not uncommon for changes to be implemented for several years and then gradually disappear, even if everyone is officially on board. Even

when the change seems effective, monitor, evaluate, and review its implementation carefully. Ask teachers to report regularly on their progress and their frustrations.

- **Expect turbulence and setbacks—they're natural and inevitable**. Steven Gross (1998, 114ff) talks about different degrees of curriculum turbulence. The light level might be due to a staff, for instance, becoming overloaded with new curriculum initiatives. Severe turbulence involves a feeling of crisis when, perhaps, a school faces deep conflicts about curriculum values. In a time of turbulence or setback, have the courage to face reality. Actively seek out the cause(s), deal with them openly, and use staff and community suggestions to overcome the problems. Don't become defensive; admit your own failures. Work on the issues in an open and collaborative way as you implement specific solutions. With severe turbulence, protect the stability of your school and even be prepared for personnel changes. Do remember that conflict can be an impetus for creativity and motivation. In these situations take much time for prayer, asking for God's guidance.

Footstep 9-2

When looking at an aspect of a school's curriculum that needs review and possible improvement, it may be helpful to conduct

Strengths:	Weaknesses:
Opportunities:	Threats:

a SWOT analysis. That is, with a small group of people you complete a (large) chart as shown in the diagram.

Complete a chart for your school's mathematics or language arts program (or that of an imaginary school if you are not currently teaching), taking into account the results of recent standardized tests, how the needs of strong and weak students are being met, the goals of the subject given in chapter 8, the resources available, and the feeling about the program among students, teachers, school board members, and parents. On the basis of your work, answer:

- What are the most urgent and important things that need changing, replacing, or reinventing?
- What strategies would you put into place to make such changes in your school?

The Dynamics of Curriculum Implementation

> *To adopt a curriculum change is not necessarily to use it. Moreover, if an adopting school uses a curricular innovation, it is rarely assimilated into the school in the manner intended by the developer.* (Thomas Romberg and Gary Price in Early and Rehage 1999, 205)

Curriculum proposals imposed on schools from the top down have a poor record in improving education. But school-based curriculum reform has also seldom been sustainable over a period of time. Michael Fullan, a foremost researcher on educational change, has concluded that "in the mid to long run, there can be no district development without school development, or school development without district development" (Fullan in Elmore and Fuhrman 1994, 198). For Christian schools, the phrase "regional service organization" replaces "district." In other words, an ethos of curriculum collaboration must exist between central administrators and schools. Central coordinators provide essential stimuli and support for change. Schools that are part of a network that implements and supports new programs are more successful in maintaining effective change. Top-down and bottom-up strategies need to be coordinated (pp. 186–202).

The support of administrators is necessary (but not sufficient) for successful implementation. Wide-ranging consultation needs to establish a climate of trust and relate the innovation to the mission and vision of the school. Teachers, administrators, and parents must believe that the project will benefit students. They must understand fully the rationale, goals, and central features of the proposed change. The principal needs to support the initiative, as does, preferably, another effective in-school leader-facilitator. Change needs both district and local advocates.

Even when the above support exists, there are no simple formulas to bring about curriculum change. Indeed, curriculum plans, particularly those developed outside the school, often sit on shelves without being implemented. Reasons include:

- Grandiose plans clash with teachers' limited time or expertise. Teachers feel a perceived or real lack of time, knowledge, skills, or resources.
- Teachers are uncertain about the outcomes because of a lack of clarity about the intent and/or implementation of the new initiative.
- Curriculum change signals more work, strain, and fatigue. Teachers therefore feel

that personal costs outweigh the benefits, and they try to maintain the status quo.

- Schools do not want to open themselves to criticism from parents and public interest groups.

What is clear from this is that teachers are at the heart of any curriculum improvement. As John Brown and Cerylle Moffett put it:

> The literature of school reform constantly affirms the powerful role of the teacher as the heart of the reform process in schools today. External authority and wisdom figures, it turns out, have significantly less effect on the restructuring process than teacher leaders.... Such a transformation derives from trust, honor, teamwork, a receptiveness to the inevitability of change, respectful communication, and shared leadership. (Brown and Moffett 1999, 108, 115)

Curriculum leaders therefore need to identify and address any aspects of the teachers' role and work that may change as a result of a proposed curriculum innovation (e.g., patterns of work, views of knowledge and the student, classroom management, or student-teacher relationships). They must collaborate with teachers to develop implementation and monitoring plans. They want their teachers to:

- **Sense how the change matches their own curriculum platform** (if it doesn't, it is unlikely to succeed).
- **Become genuinely committed to take ownership of the planned change.**
- **Be involved in reviewing, exploring, and evaluating plans and recommended resources.**
- **Experience systematic training and support.** Without adequate knowledge or skills, or without adequate human and material resources, teachers seldom make the intended changes.
- **Participate in frequent formal and informal consultations and decision making.** Supportive feedback and help with unexpected problems need to be on hand.
- **Feel free to learn from their initiatives and possible failures, and to make revisions for their own situation.**
- **Convince their students that the change will benefit them, and get their cooperation.**

As we already saw, it takes time to convince people of the value of curriculum change. It takes even more time to orient teachers and get them ready to implement a new program. Don't rush major changes such as replacing or reinventing a program. You and your staff need ample time for careful deliberation, planning, problem solving, decision making, and carrying out collegial tasks. A lack of time impedes both collaboration and progress. We tend to underestimate the complexity of change and the fact that change, if it occurs too quickly, can be unsettling for those involved. Also, quality is more important than speed.

A major new initiative usually takes at least three years to implement: one year for discussion and planning, one year for having some teachers pilot parts of the new program, and one year (or more) for general implementation. Deliberation and assessment take place throughout the process. Leaders and staffs should together develop a workable timeline for a project. Don't ask teachers to address too much at once, or forget that effective and long-lasting curriculum change is usually limited in scope.

Curriculum planners should be aware of both the benefits and costs of curriculum initiatives for individual teachers. Decker

Walker (1990, 408) includes as benefits renewed enthusiasm, greater self-esteem and status, professional contact and involvement, and more teaching satisfaction. There also are costs, however. Curriculum change takes time and effort. It involves risk of failure and embarrassment. Also, less satisfaction in teaching may result if the proposed changes do not work out. Planners help overcome the inevitable initial resistance by giving first-hand information about the project, suggesting how teachers can implement programs to fit their individual styles, and facilitating early success (p. 410).

There is a dilemma embedded in the conditions for successful implementation. Teachers usually implement change only when they believe it to be worthwhile. But some will not try until convinced, and they will not be convinced until they themselves experience the benefits. If some teachers continue to strongly resist a change, it may be wise not to force them to make the change. If coerced, they are unlikely to implement it in the intended way. Glatthorn (1997, 86–87) suggests emphasizing mutual accomplishment, not total fidelity—while continuing to build a collaborative culture where teachers who cooperate are encouraged and rewarded. When others see their success and enthusiasm, they may follow later.

Footstep 9-3

Suppose you chair a committee to review your school's science program. You decide to recommend to your other colleagues that they introduce a new series of texts and place much more emphasis on hands-on activities that relate to everyday phenomena and situations. What steps would you take to convince your staff that the change (a) is important for the school, (b) will bring about desired results, and (c) will have payoffs for the teachers that outweigh the additional time required for implementation?

Teachers as Curriculum Leaders

➤ *Teachers who become leaders experience personal and professional satisfaction, a reduction in isolation, a sense of instrumentality, and new learnings—all of which spill over into their teaching. As school-based reformers, these teachers become owners and investors in the school, rather than mere tenants.... All teachers can lead! Most teachers want to lead. And schools badly need their ideas, invention, energy, and leadership.* (Barth 2001, 443, 449)

The first responsibility of teachers is good leadership within their classrooms. Nothing is more powerful for students, parents, and staff than to see teachers who love both God and their students, who relish both teaching and learning, who are well-informed and skilled, and who wholeheartedly support the school's vision.

Good leadership inside the classroom does not necessarily translate into leadership outside the classroom. Nevertheless, when we recognize teachers for their classroom leadership success, they are more willing to take on broader leadership roles. Principals depend on teacher leadership, both formal and informal. They cannot bring about a positive school culture and curriculum improvement by themselves. It is important to create leadership opportunities for teachers and a shared leadership ethos. Also, with broader leadership opportunities, teachers often regain enthusiasm and energy for their calling. James Kahrs claims that "change in our schools can only come about as a result of teacher leadership, with principals' support" (Moller and Katzenmeyer 1996, 20).

Here are some constructive curriculum leadership roles for teachers:

- **Subject leaders.** Subject leaders monitor and evaluate the effectiveness of teaching and learning in a subject, and plan for improvements. This may be a short-term appointment to head a committee of four or five teachers to review, for instance, one of the school's subject areas and make recommendations for future improvements. The committee collects, interprets, and disseminates data and recommends new programs and resources. In a large school, a long-term appointment may enable the subject leader to continue to help teachers implement programs and strategies in the subject. In high schools, department chairs usually function in this capacity.

- **Lead teachers.** Some schools appoint official teacher-leaders or curriculum coordinators, usually ones who have the respect of their colleagues. They are change agents who mentor, coach, and consult. Their role may include visiting classrooms to gain a schoolwide perspective on particular programs. They then give feedback to teachers, helping them improve their program implementation, and providing them with resources. To be effective, such teacher-leaders should use most of their time in classrooms and working with other teachers.

Lead teacher appointments are usually for one- or two-year periods. Schools

choose teachers who are able to meet a particular need, and at the end of the period appoint others who have other areas of strength that would benefit the school. Both subject leaders and lead teachers should be good teachers who themselves model the learning approaches that they recommend. They should also have a good grasp of the school's mission and the learning needs of the students (Feiler, Heritage, and Gallimore 2000; Judith Little in *Jossey-Bass Reader* 1999, 390–418; Field, Holden, and Lawlor 2000).

- **Leaders of curriculum committees or task forces.** The work of these groups may involve choosing a new textbook series or instructional materials for a subject, or reviewing one of the school's programs in the light of an external assessment.

- **Partners in developing new units or courses.** Partner teachers may cooperate in designing, for instance, a cross-grade unit or a program for a subject at a certain grade level.

- **Professional development leaders.** Teachers who have attended professional development workshops may be asked to share their experiences at grade or subject meetings. Some may design and organize a staff in-service program. They may also offer workshops to the staff at a school-based professional development day. Such in-house professional development is generally more effective than one-time external workshops, in part because it can be followed up. Schools can also put a committee of teachers in charge of allocating professional development funds.

- **Speakers to parents.** Teachers can introduce the school's curriculum plans to groups of parents.

Often teachers avoid taking risks, especially when the school culture favors the status quo. They may also be skeptical of bandwagons that have come and gone. They therefore need to be encouraged and coached to take on leadership functions. But they are often capable of effective leadership, and have insights and expertise that will enrich the school and its curriculum. And when principals share their leadership with their staff, as one administrator put it to me, contagious momentum often results. Teachers then see themselves as full partners in the enterprise. They enjoy working with other adults in contributing to the future of the whole school. A healthy school needs teacher leadership. Indeed, research suggests that schools with few discipline problems and high student achievement involve teachers in designing new materials and curricula (Barth 2001, 444–45).

Are there pitfalls to teacher leadership? One main one to avoid is asking teachers to do too much or adding to their responsibilities without giving them adequate time. Time is a valuable commodity, and teachers also have responsibilities outside of school. Another difficulty can be that one or two teachers dominate discussions and listen poorly. Their colleagues may resent or be intimidated by them. Progress may even grind to a halt. A principal may have to intervene and discuss this openly with such teachers. Another stumbling block to effective teacher leadership is lukewarm administrative support. Unless the principal wholeheartedly hands teachers the necessary authority, relinquishes specified responsibilities to them, and gives them support and credit for success, teachers will not long be willing to take on leadership tasks outside the classroom.

In short, if you are a principal, you should:

- **Continue to ask whether the school is operating in harmony with its purpose, vision, and values,** and work on establishing a shared sense of mission.
- **Organize your school for broad-based leadership.** Discuss with your teachers how they can have optimal input, interaction, and participation.
- **Use teachers in both formal and informal leadership capacities.** Support them as they take on the mantle of leaders, facilitators, coaches, and even mediators.
- **Keep a long-term perspective.** Build on teachers' strengths, and give them enough time and support. Anticipate setbacks and be prepared to deal with them, but celebrate successes.

👣 Footstep 9-4

Identify both the formal and informal teacher-leaders in your school (or, if you are not teaching, in a school with which you are familiar). In what ways can the school strengthen teacher leadership? Indicate the steps that would be required to plan and implement such leadership.

Being a Transformational Servant Leader

The Bible is clear that leaders are to be servants of God anointed to do various tasks. God therefore wants school leaders to listen to and execute His will faithfully. Servant-leader principals nurture and empower their teachers. Servant-leader teachers empower their students, their colleagues—and their administrators. All servant leaders show compassion toward and strengthen the weaker and the disadvantaged (Ezekial 34:2–10). The Greek word for leadership is *diakonia*. This literally means "serving at tables." For educational leaders, it means serving in between the chairs and desks!

Jesus Himself exemplified the type of leadership that Paul describes:

> Do nothing out of selfish ambition or vain conceit, but in humility consider others better than yourselves. Each of you should look not only to your own interests, but also to the interests of others. (Philippians 2:3–4)

Jesus explained and practiced that leadership was not to be modeled after that of the Gentiles and great men of the world: Whoever would be first among you must be servant of all (Mark 10:42–44, Matthew 20:25–28). What counts in God's sight is how faithfully we serve. That does not mean that we are to be doormats. A firm and demanding but loving structure is often needed. We invest in our teachers' and students' lives, especially in their professional and academic but also in their moral, social, and emotional lives. We stimulate them toward greater achievement as holistic beings. In this way we help them in turn become servant leaders.

The story of Jesus washing the feet of the disciples is the classic Christian model of how a leader must be a servant (John 13). But to get a fuller picture of such leadership, we also need to consider chapters 14 through 21 of the Gospel of John. The following are seven characteristics and strategies that Jesus uses in these chapters to implement servant leadership, along with suggestions of how they apply to curriculum leadership:

1. Have the Right Relationship with God the Father and Jesus Christ

Jesus spoke about and modeled the ultimate relationship: "I am in the Father, and … the Father is in me…. it is the Father, living in me, who is doing his work" (John 14:10). That's how Jesus could also give perfect obedience: "I do exactly what my Father has commanded me" (John 14:31). Even in His passion and death, "Not my will, but yours be done" (Luke 22:42).

Having the right relationship and the right attitude is the fundamental key to servant leadership. As principals and teachers we are not fit to lead unless we have given ourselves to leadership that is greater than our own. Only through an authentic relationship with our Servant Leader, Jesus Christ, can we put aside our own agenda and hold foremost God's agenda for our teachers and students. Jesus Christ is our source of strength, insight, and courage: "He who loves me will be loved by my Father, and I too will love him and show myself to him" (John 14:21). "No branch can bear fruit by itself; it must remain in the vine. Neither can you bear fruit unless you remain in me" (John 15:4). Engrafting ourselves in Jesus as our Vine is the starting point for being a godly curriculum leader.

2. Have a Strong Sense of Mission and Live Your Vision

Our relationship with God leads to a mandate: "As you sent me into the world, I have sent them into the world" (John 17:18). God does not leave curriculum leaders to fend for themselves: "The Counselor, the Holy Spirit … will teach you all things and will remind you of everything I have said to you" (John 14:26). Jesus adds, "I chose you and appointed you to go and bear fruit—fruit that will last…." (John 15:16) In other words, Jesus sends each one of us to proclaim God's truth and thus bear fruit in our schools and in our classrooms. God calls us to develop curricula that enable teachers to model and testify to God's love, grace, and truth. As curriculum leaders we encourage and enable teachers to develop, adapt, and implement programs that unfold the basis, framework, and implications of a Christian vision of life, that discern and confront the idols of our time, and that help students have a transformational impact on culture. Note that we have come full circle, back to the curriculum aims of chapter one!

As school leaders we do not seek positions of leadership so that we can do great things. Rather, we carry out this calling because we have a passion to serve God, our students, and our teachers. Such passion is energizing, enabling us to tap inner resources and to use strengths and talents of which we may have been unaware.

3. Pray for Your Teachers and Students

Servant leaders pray for those they equip. They know that their power comes from God, not from themselves. Listen to how Jesus prayed as an example of how we should pray for teachers and students: "I am not praying for the world, but for those you have given me, for they are yours…. they are still in the world … protect them by the power of your name…. My prayer is not that you take them out of the world but that you protect them from the evil one…. Sanctify them by the truth; your word is truth" (John 17:9–17). Such prayer is the source of vision, direction, and correction.

Some principals and teacher-leaders pray weekly or daily for each person with whom they work. Some teachers go to school early to pray at each desk for the students who will sit there an hour or so later. Pray particularly for those who are difficult to work with and may even undermine what we try to accom-

plish. They also are images of God that He has put in your way. Prayer helps both those being prayed for and those praying to fulfill their respective callings. It also leads to practicing love and forgiveness—hallmarks of the Christian faith. Within such a climate, we have the best opportunity to empower teachers and students to be what God intended them to be: creative, insightful, committed, and responsive human beings.

4. Invest in and Equip Teachers and Students: Share Responsibility and Authority Without Seeking Personal Reward

Servant leaders serve without seeking external rewards. Servant leadership may require giving up our rights or comfort or desires. We serve our teachers and students—and therefore God—before and over self. Humility, a concept almost totally foreign to our culture, is a necessary quality of a servant leader.

It is significant that in the night before His crucifixion Jesus put the focus not on Himself but on preparing the disciples for their calling. Throughout His ministry, Jesus challenged others to accept responsibility and authority. He sent out the seventy disciples long before we would have felt they were ready. He told the disciples to heal in God's name. He even left them at a crucial time when He ascended into heaven, giving them an awesome responsibility.

Servant leaders share and even deliberately give away responsibility and authority. The more teachers and students assume responsibility for various tasks, the more authority they should be given. Qualify your teachers and students by holding up high standards even while encouraging them. Be present to them: "You can do this!" Be a mentor who challenges them to take on responsibility and authority.

Let me give two personal examples, one as a teacher and one as a student. As a teacher with only two years of experience, I was given the responsibility of revamping a high school's mathematics program. I became so interested in finding out how children learned mathematics that it led me to take a master's degree in mathematics curriculum—something that benefited both that school and the next one where I taught. A second example: One of my most meaningful learning experiences in school was in eighth grade when the teachers put me in charge of the school's field day. I had to organize the cross-age groups and determine where and in what order the events would be held on the school playground, which students would supervise each station, and how statistics would be tallied and totaled. I think I rose to the challenge, for things went smoothly that day. Looking back, the teachers took quite a remarkable risk. But they displayed servant leadership. They equipped their students through a challenging learning experience in which they shared authority in order to develop student responsibility and student leadership.

5. Speak and Act Wisely but Forthrightly

God's Holy Spirit gives each of us gifts that enable us to be servant leaders in our schools. Teaching, leadership, administration (steersman or pilot), showing mercy, and encouragement—all these are listed as spiritual gifts by Paul, and all are important for our calling as curriculum leaders. At the same time, when there are shortcomings or problems, leaders will confront them, doing so lovingly but honestly. Remember that conflict, even about curriculum, can be a source of creativity and motivation when dealt with openly in a spirit of love.

Let Jesus be our example. He did not hide His views: "I said nothing in secret" (John 18:20). He spoke the truth in love, even to Pilate: "For this I came into the world, to testify to the truth. Everyone on the side of truth listens to me" (John 18:37). Jesus took risks throughout His life. He was a radical (that is, *rooted* in truth and justice!). He even turned the tables in the temple upside down both literally and figuratively—always keeping in mind His mission and obeying the will of His Father.

6. Invite and Encourage Teachers and Students to be Partners in Community

The essence of community is a shared experience of belonging and contributing to something larger than oneself. Jesus forged His twelve disciples into a unified, focused, and supportive group. Typical was how He helped the disciples catch fish and had breakfast with them after His resurrection (John 21:5–13). He gave them a calling and the responsibility to carry out that calling—even after Peter had denied Him three times.

Like Jesus, servant leaders create in their schools and classrooms a vibrant sense of togetherness, a sense of common purpose and values. They enable members to share ideas, plan together, give each other feedback, and support each other in new efforts. They show caring concern for all teachers and students. They give all teachers and students places of worth with meaningful and significant input and roles. They also demonstrate the importance of sometimes putting the common good of the school or classroom ahead of personal gain. Thus, they build a school with a shared sense of purpose, one that passionately advances the worth of teaching and learning, and where both formal and informal leaders communicate the school's deeper mission and core values in what they say and do.

7. Lead with Authority

Jesus taught with authority that reflected both His attitude and what He taught. Unlike the Pharisees He did not lord it over His followers. He was authoritative but not authoritarian. He did not impose His views on others. In fact, He encouraged personal consideration and response. But He did testify to the truth in word and deed, also in the last chapters of John when His life was in danger. He was knowledgeable but understanding, powerful but unpretentious, purposeful but patient, and ambitious for the Kingdom but not for Himself.

We may not think, first of all, of choosing or teaching curriculum content when we think of servant leadership. I believe that it is an important ingredient, however, just as the Sermon on the Mount, the parables, and Christ's teachings at the Last Supper were integral parts of Jesus' servant leadership. Choosing and teaching content carefully and wisely—and helping other teachers to do so—is essential if we are to help our students grow into the persons they can become.

Let's consider a final example, a unit on metals in science. Considering only the geological and chemical aspects of metals would, in my view, fall short of teaching the truth or leading with authority. If the world were perfect, we would use metals in a sustainable manner to help the quality of life in society, and without causing social or health problems. How have humans fallen short? To give a few examples, the greedy pursuit of gold by one mining company in West Papua in Indonesia some time ago took place without consulting or compensating the Amungme tribe. The company took their land and killed unarmed protesters in order to make a profit. The mining of aluminum has improved society but yet, at the same time, has left large areas of tropical and sub-tropical land damaged beyond recognition. Moreover, people suffering from Alzheimer's disease often have abnormally high levels of metal such as aluminum in their brain cells. Similarly, lead has been used in paint and gasoline and, currently, is still used in car batteries. It is a cumulative poison that has caused memory loss and reduced intelligence. And half the mercury mined each year is still lost in the environment, with partly unknown consequences (Shortt 1997, 73–84).

Servant-leader teachers who develop and implement this curriculum topic with authority will go beyond the purely scientific aspects. They will consider how humans have fallen short in promoting Kingdom values, even when such learning may be controversial. In this case, they will expose some of the problems and raise questions about what can be done to mine and use metals in positive ways. They will help students see that peoples and ways of life in third world countries are not just resources to be exploited (see, for instance, Ezekiel 22:12 where God condemns "unjust gain from your neighbors"). They will ask students to investigate how we can restore the earth to a safer, more just, and healthier state. They will relate this to Kingdom values and encourage (but not force) students to commit themselves to a way of life that reflects biblical norms. They will do so in an authoritative way, but also recognize that some problems are so complex that we do not have all the solutions. They will also point students beyond these particular issues and explore with them what it means to serve God in and through science and technology. Schoolwide curriculum leaders will challenge their teachers to find and develop real examples like this, and make them an integral part of their courses.

As a servant leader working with curriculum, whether you are a teacher, a teacher-leader, a department chair, a principal, a superintendent, or a curriculum consultant, remember that God has chosen and called you, and has given you a vision as well as the required insights and skills: "It is God who works in you to will and to act according to his good purpose" (Philippians 2:13).

Footstep 9-5

If you are an administrator, reflect on the ways in which you have exercised the foregoing seven aspects of curriculum servant leadership. How can you address some of your weaker areas?

If you currently teach in a school, in what ways have you contributed to curriculum leadership, either formally or informally? How can you be involved in meaningful ways in the future, taking into account the foregoing principles?

If you do not currently teach in a school, you may be a preservice teacher, a curriculum consultant, or someone with an interest in education. No matter what your position, reflect on how and to what extent the foregoing principles of leadership affect your current responsibilities.

Reviewing the Main Points

- **Anyone involved in curriculum leadership must develop a clear curriculum vision.** When such a vision is developed jointly with all stakeholders, the whole school community can own a shared vision and work to implement curriculum goals with a unified focus.

- **Sustained curriculum improvement happens only when a school has a school culture that supports transformation.** Such a school has a positive and trusting atmosphere, a staff willing to work together for the common good, and curriculum leaders who involve all those affected in meaningful ways and set realistic time demands.

- **No simple formulas exist to bring about curriculum change.** What is clear is that desirable conditions for curriculum improvement include the availability of outside consultants, full support of administrators, and teachers who are convinced that the benefits of proposed changes outweigh personal costs in time and effort.

- **Student learning benefits from teachers who serve as curriculum leaders in their schools.** Such teachers often become keen owners of the school's programs, and their teaching improves.

- **Jesus modeled what it means to be a transformational servant leader.** His leadership suggests that curriculum leaders needs to have a right relationship with God, forge a shared curriculum vision, pray for those they serve, equip teachers for responsibility and leadership, speak and act wisely but honestly, build a sense of community, and lead with insightful but compassionate authority.

References

Barna, G. 1992. *The power of vision.* Ventura, CA: Regal.

Barth, R. 2001. Teacher leader. *Phi Delta Kappan* 82 (6): 443–49.

Brown, J., and C. Moffett. 1999. *The hero's journey: How educators can transform schools and improve learning.* Alexandria, VA: Association for Supervision and Curriculum Development.

Early, M., and K. Rehage. 1999. *Issues in curriculum: A selection of chapters from past NSSE yearbooks.* Ninety-eighth yearbook of the National Society for the Study of Education. Chicago: NSSE.

Elmore, R., and S. Fuhrman, eds. 1994. *The governance of curriculum.* Alexandria, VA: Association for Supervision and Curriculum Development.

Feiler, R., M. Heritage, and R. Gallimore. 2000. Teachers leading teachers. *Educational Leadership* 57 (7): 66–69.

Field, K., P. Holden, and H. Lawlor. 2000. *Effective subject leadership.* London: Routledge.

Glatthorn, A. 1997. *The principal as curriculum leader.* Thousand Oaks, CA: Corwin Press.

Gross, S. 1998. *Staying centered: Curriculum leadership in a turbulent era.* Alexandria, VA: Association for Supervision and Curriculum Development.

Jossey-Bass reader on educational leadership. 1999. San Francisco: Jossey-Bass.

Kanpol, B. 1998. *Teachers talking back and breaking bread.* Cresskill, NJ: Hampton Press.

Leithwood, K., L. Leonard, and L. Sharratt. 1998. Conditions fostering organizational learning in schools. *Educational Administration Quarterly* 34 (2): 243–76.

Leithwood, K., D. Jantz, and R. Steinbach. 1999. *Changing leadership for changing times.* Philadelphia: Open University Press.

Moller, G., and M. Katzenmeyer, eds. 1996. *Every teacher as a leader.* San Francisco: Jossey-Bass.

Palmer, P. 1983. *To know as we are known: A spirituality of education.* San Francisco: Harper & Row.

Senge, P. 1990. *The fifth discipline: The art and practice of the learning organization.* New York: Doubleday/Currency.

Shortt, J., ed. 1997. *Charis science units 1–11.* Nottingham, UK: The Stapleford Centre.

Wagner, T. 2001. Leadership for learning: An action theory of school change. *Phi Delta Kappan* 82 (5): 378–83.

Walker, D. 1990. *Fundamentals of curriculum.* San Diego: Harcourt Brace Jovanovich.

Wilson, D. 1991. *Recovering the lost tools of learning: An approach to distinctively Christian education.* Wheaton, IL: Crossway Books.

Appendix I

Selected Christian Curriculum Resources

General Discussions of Curriculum in Christian Schools

Edlin, Richard J. *The Cause of Christian Education.* 3d ed. Colorado Springs: Association of Christian Schools International, 2000. Contains chapters on the foundations of curriculum in the Christian school, student evaluation, and resource selection.

Greene, Albert E. *Reclaiming the Future of Christian Education: A Transforming Vision.* Colorado Springs: Association of Christian Schools International, 1998. A book that deals with the foundations of Christian schooling. Part III deals with content in Christian schooling; Part IV, with methods.

MacKenzie, Pamela, Alison Farnell, Ann Holt, and David Smith. *Entry Points for Christian Reflection Within Education.* London: CARE for Education (53 Romney St, London, UK SW1P 3RF), 1997. This practical resource includes chapters on ten different subject disciplines, as well as models of curriculum development used by Christian schools.

Society of Christian Schools in British Columbia. *Christian Pathways in Schooling: Curriculum Planning.* Langley: SCSBC (7600 Glover Road, Langley, BC, Canada V2Y 1Y1), 1998. A guide for curriculum development for Christian schoolteachers including both vision and process as well as practical examples. Useful for in-service professional development.

Steensma, Geraldine, and Harro Van Brummelen. *Shaping School Curriculum: A Biblical View.* Terre Haute, IN: Signal, 1977. Out of print, but has a comprehensive discussion of Christian approaches to the different subject disciplines at the elementary and secondary level.

Stronks, Gloria, and Doug Blomberg, eds. *A Vision with a Task: Christian Schooling for Responsive Discipleship.* Grand Rapids, MI: Baker, 1993. Includes chapters on knowing, thinking about curriculum, and evaluating student learning. Out of print, but available free of charge online at <www.calvin.edu/academic/education>.

Stronks, Gloria, and Nancy Knol. *Reaching and Teaching Young Adolescents: Succeeding in Deeper Waters.* Colorado Springs: Association of Christian Schools International, 1999. Contains a chapter on middle school curriculum and one on teaching eighth-grade biblical studies.

Vander Ark, Daniel R. *From Mission to Measurement.* Grand Rapids, MI: Christian Schools International, 2000. A short discussion on how to organize the curriculum so that you test what you value.

Discussions of Approaches to Subject Disciplines

Barratt, D., R. Pooley, and L. Ryken, eds. *The Discerning Reader: Christian Perspectives on Literature and Theory.* Leicester, UK: InterVarsity Press; and Grand Rapids, MI: Baker Books, 1995.

Brand, H., and A. Chaplin. *Art and Soul: Signposts for Christians in the Arts.* Carlisle, UK: Solway/Paternoster, 1999. A resource for middle and high school art teachers.

Byl, J., and T. Viskers. *Physical Education, Sport, and Wellness: Looking to God As We See Ourselves.* Sioux Center, IA: Dordt College Press, 1999.

Harper & Row (now HarperCollins) in the late 1980s and early 1990s published a series of volumes for the Council of Christian Colleges and Universities on different subject disciplines. While intended as supplementary texts for first- or second-year university students, the following titles will also be of interest to middle and high school teachers: *Biology Through the Eyes of Faith; History Through the Eyes of Faith; Literature Through the Eyes of Faith; Music Through the Eyes of Faith;* and *Business Through the Eyes of Faith.*

Howell, Russell, and James Bradley, eds. *Mathematics in a Post-Modern Age: A Christian Perspective*. Grand Rapids, MI: Eerdmans, 2001. Contains chapters discussing pedagogy as well as the influence of worldviews on the development of mathematics.

Jones, Arthur, ed. *Science in Faith: A Christian Perspective on Teaching Science*. Romford, UK: The Christian Schools' Trust, Immanuel School (Havering Grange Centre, Havering Road North, Romford, Essex, UK RM1 4HR), 1998. General principles of science teaching as they relate to a Christian worldview, a discussion of evolution and creation, and some practical classroom examples.

Keenan, Derek. *Curriculum Development for Christian Schools*. Colorado Springs: Association of Christian Schools International, 1998. A brief introduction to curriculum design for Christian schools, with examples of outlines for different grades and subjects.

Poole, M. *A Guide to Science and Belief*. Oxford, UK: Lion Publishing, 1997. Suggestions for how to deal with issues such as belief and evidence, miracles, accident or design, and science and the Bible. You may not agree with all of Poole's conclusions, but its use will stimulate discussion and insight, and it's a book you can use with middle and high school students.

Roques, M. *Curriculum Unmasked: Toward a Christian Understanding of Education*. Eastbourne, UK: Monarch Publications, 1989. A discussion of British textbooks and a Christian response.

Schultze, Q. *Communicating for Life: Christian Stewardship in Community and Media*. Grand Rapids, MI: Baker Books, 2000.

Smith, David, and Barbara Carvill. *The Gift of the Stranger: Faith, Hospitality, and Foreign Language Learning*. Grand Rapids, MI: Eerdmans, 2000. An important book for Christian foreign language teachers.

The Stapleford Centre (Old Lace Mill, Frederick Road, Stapleford, Nottingham, UK NG9 8FN) has published *Charis Project* teacher resource guides in English, French, German, mathematics, and science. Each volume contains teacher notes and reproducible materials for middle and high school classroom use. These volumes include many practical ideas on teaching topics within a Christian framework without becoming didactic. Some samples are available at the Stapleford website <www.stapleford-centre.org>.

Van Dyke, F., D. Mahan, J. Sheldon, and R. Brand. *Redeeming Creation: The Biblical Basis for Environmental Stewardship*. Downers Grove, IL: InterVarsity Press, 1996.

Wells, R., ed. *History and the Christian Historian*. Grand Rapids, MI: Eerdmans, 1998.

Appendix 2

Using Internet Websites for Curriculum Planning

Websites on the Internet come and go—and if they stay, they may not be updated regularly. Moreover, the quality varies considerably, and usually it's left up to the user to determine the worldview perspective and curriculum orientation that guides a particular site. To find suitable sites can be time-consuming. Nevertheless, the Web does contain a vast multitude of useful resources—as long as you take care that whatever you use fits your own curriculum platform and vision. One good source for useful sites is the Association of Supervision and Curriculum Development, both in its electronic newsletter to members and in its journal *Educational Leadership*.

In the spring of 2001, students in the curriculum-planning course at Trinity Western University searched for and assessed various curriculum websites. Here is a selection of those found useful by these preservice teachers:

General:
www.cln.org/subjects.html
www.ericsp.org/
www.schoolnet.ca
www.ceris.schoolnet.ca/
www.sitesforteachers.com
www.proteacher.com
www.education-world.com
www.lessonplanspage.com
www.pbs.org/teachersource
www.education.com/teachspace/resources
www.yahooligans.com/tq/
www.resource.mediacentre.com/

Biology:
www.sc2000.net/~czaremba/
www.guilford.k12.ct.us/~faitschb/

Christian sites:
www.educationplanet.com
www.teacherhelp.org
www.cgocable.net

English:
www.lessonplanspage.cam/lajh.htm
http://falcon.jmu.edu/~williaps/english.html
www.cogeco.ca/~rayser/
http://members.aol.com/mezim/
www.youth.net/cec/ceclan/ceclang.high.html

History:
http://askeric.org.virtual/lessons/crossroads
www.teachtci.com/default.asp
www.history.org/nche

Mathematics:
www.allmath.com
www.tc.cornell.edu/edu/mathsci/
www.mathgoodies.com/
www.tqjunior.thinkquest.org/3797/index.html

Music:
www.education-world.com/a_curr/curr123.shtml#resources

Physical education:
www.education-world.com/pe_health/
www.pe-net.co.uk

Science:
www.school.discovery.com/teachers
www.teachervision.com
http://lessonplanz.com
http://nyelabs.kcts.org/opennyelabs.html
Key issues in science from a Christian perspective but no lesson plans: www.cis.org.uk

Social studies:
http://commtechlab.msu.edu/sites/letsnet/noframes/subjects/ss/index.html
www.teachnet.org
www.bc.sympatico.ca/socials
www.bcarchives.gov.bc.ca
www.usgs.gov/education/learnweb/wwmaps.html

Appendix 3

List of Persons Providing Curriculum Examples

The response of teachers and schools to my requests for curriculum examples was deeply gratifying. Indeed, for both the first and this second edition, I was able to use only some of the many good examples that both teachers and preservice teachers provided. My appreciation continues for the many capable, committed, and innovative classroom teachers in Christian schools! Below I list the persons who not only provided examples but also freely gave of their time to allow me to observe and/or discuss their classroom experiences. My thanks to them as well as all the others whose shared practices, while not used directly, contributed to my insight into what is going on in Christian schools and classrooms, especially in western Canada. Some of my examples were also based on the work of groups of teachers working for Christian school or Christian teacher associations; in such cases, I have provided references at the end of the pertinent chapter.

Abbotsford (BC) Christian Schools:	Rick Binder, Henry Contant, Lloyd Den Boer, Janet Hitchcock, Anna-May Taekema
Alta Vista College, Seattle, WA:	Elaine Brouwer
Bulkley Valley Christian School, Smithers, BC:	Curt Gesch
Calvin College, Grand Rapids, MI:	Arden Post
Credo Christian Elementary School, Langley, BC:	Hugo Vanderhoek
Duncan (BC) Christian School:	Susan Dick, Glenda MacPhee, John Zuidema
Edmonton (Alberta) Christian Schools:	Alisa Ketchum, Joan Konynenbelt, Doug Monsma Marian Piekema, Derk Van Eerden
Highroad Academy, Chilliwack, BC:	Wayne Lennea, Gwen Wray
Kelowna (BC) Christian School:	Bruce Hildebrandt, Paul Smith
Langley (BC) Christian School:	Paul Still, Wilma Van Brummelen
Nanaimo (BC) Christian School:	Donna Ferguson
Pacific Christian Academy, Surrey, BC:	Clayton Chalfour, Carina Drisner, Kim Franklin, Chat Ironmonger, Sophia Kraeling, Sandra Paetkau, Arlene Paluch, Tom Pankratz, Rick Rauser, Melinda Tegart
Pacific Christian School, Victoria, BC:	Margaret Barlow, Leigh Bradfield, Berta Den Haan, Inge Maier
Torbain Primary School, Scotland:	Emma Johnstone
Trinity Western University, Langley, BC:	Cindy Halvorson, Rachel Pruim, Jodaye St. Cyr
Vernon (BC) Christian School:	Linda Samland
Western Canada Region, ACSI:	Anne Rauser
White Rock (BC) Christian Academy:	David Wu

Bibliography

Airasian, P., and M. Walsh. 1997. Constructivist cautions. *Phi Delta Kappan* 78 (6): 444–49.

Alexander, J. 1993. *The secular squeeze: Reclaiming Christian depth in a shallow world.* Downers Grove, IL: InterVarsity.

Anderson, K. 2000. Computers and the information revolution. Richardson, TX: Probe Ministries. Available at <www.leaderu.com/orgs/probe/docs/computer.html>.

Anderson, L., and L. Sosniak. 1994. *Bloom's taxonomy: A forty-year retrospective.* Ninety-third yearbook of the National Society for the Study of Education, Part II. Chicago: NSSE.

ASCD Panel on Moral Education (ASCD). 1988. Moral education in the life of the school. *Educational Leadership* 45 (8): 5–7.

Baker, D., and M. Piburn. 1997. *Constructing science in middle and secondary school classrooms.* Boston: Allyn and Bacon.

Barna, G. 1992. *The power of vision.* Ventura, CA: Regal.

Barth, R. 2001. Teacher leader. *Phi Delta Kappan* 82 (6): 443–49.

Beisner, E. C. 1993. Justice and poverty: Two views contrasted. *Transformation* 10 (1): 16–22.

Berton, P. 1984. *The promised land: Settling the West 1896–1914.* Toronto: McClelland and Stewart.

Blomberg, D. 1991. The integral curriculum. *Christian Educators Journal* 31 (2): 6–13.

Bolt, J. 1993. *The Christian story and the Christian school.* Grand Rapids: Christian Schools International.

Booth, J., ed. 1985. *Over the mountain.* The first of two grade 3 reading anthologies in the *Impressions* readers. Toronto: Holt, Rinehart, and Winston.

Bowers, C. 1987. *Toward a post-liberal theory of education.* New York: Teachers College Press.

———. 1988. *The cultural dimensions of educational computing.* New York: Teachers College Press.

Boyer, E. 1983. *High school: A report on secondary education in America by the Carnegie Foundation for the Advancement of Teaching.* New York: Harper & Row.

Brandt, R., ed. 2000. *Education in a new era.* ASCD yearbook 2000. Alexandria, VA: Association for Supervision and Curriculum Development.

British Columbia Ministry of Education (BCME). 1977. *Guide to the core curriculum.* Victoria, BC: BCME.

———. 1990. *Intermediate program: Learning in British Columbia: Response draft.* Victoria, BC: BCME.

———. 1990. *Primary program: Foundation document.* Victoria, BC: BCME.

Brouwer, E. 2000. Mapping your curriculum: Using the mapping process to promote ongoing dialogue about biblical perspective. *In Search,* Seattle: Alta Vista College (September/October).

———. 2001. Assessment as a gift. *In Search,* Seattle: Alta Vista College (January): 1–15.

Brown, J., and C. Moffett. 1999. *The hero's journey: How educators can transform schools and improve learning.* Alexandria, VA: Association for Supervision and Curriculum Development.

Brown, P., ed. 1994. Trees and forests. Unpublished grade 1/2 resource unit. Morwell, Australia: Valley Christian School.

Bruer, J. 1998. Brain science, brain fiction. *Educational Leadership* 56 (3): 14–18.

Checkley, K. 1996. Physical education: Preparing students to be active for life. *Curriculum Update*, Alexandria, VA: Association for Supervision and Curriculum Development (fall): 1–3, 6–8.

Chiang, J. et al. 2001. *Cells: the wonder of life*. A grade 8 resource unit. Ancaster, ON: Ontario Alliance of Christian Schools.

Chinnery, J. et al. 1993. *How does my garden grow? ... God makes it so!* A primary unit. Langley, BC: Society of Christian Schools in British Columbia.

Clarke, M., ed. 1998. *Canada: Portraits of faith*. Chilliwack: Reel to Real.

Clouser, R. 1991. *The myth of religious neutrality*. Notre Dame: University of Notre Dame Press.

Comité Protestant. 1992. *Protestant educational values*. Sainte Foy, Quebec: Gouvernement du Quebec.

———. 1992. *Protestant moral and religious education program: Advice to the minister*. Sainte Foy, Quebec: Gouvernement du Quebec.

Corno, L., ed. 2001. *Education across a century: The centennial volume*. One-hundredth yearbook of the National Society for the Study of Education. Chicago: NSSE.

Cotton, K. 1999. *Research you can use to improve results*. Alexandria, VA: Association for Supervision and Curriculum Development.

Council for Basic Education. 1991. Standards: A vision for learning. *Perspective* 4 (1): 1–5 and enclosed chart.

Council of Ministers of Education, Canada (CMEC). 1997. *Common framework of science learning outcomes K–12: Pan-Canadian protocol for collaboration on school curriculum*. Toronto, ON: CMEC Secretariat.

Cox, R. 2001. Using the Bible with children. *Journal of Education and Christian Belief* 5 (1): 41–49.

Curriculum Administrator. 2001. It's third period ... Do you know where your science textbooks have been? *Curriculum Administrator* 37 (3): 20.

Cranny, M. 1998. *Pathways: Civilizations through time*. Scarborough, ON: Prentice Hall Ginn.

De Moor, A., ed. 1992. *Living in hope: Teacher resource manual*. Grand Rapids: Christian Schools International.

De Moor, S., ed. 1994. *Now you are the body of Christ*. Edmonton, AB: CSI District 12.

Dengerink, A. 1987. *Reflections on the arts: A study guide*. Toronto, ON: Institute for Christian Studies.

Diamond, D. 1993. How to develop volunteerism in students. *In Tips for Principals*, Reston, VA: National Association of Secondary School Principals (April).

Doll, R. 1989. *Curriculum improvement: Decision making and process*. 7th ed. Boston: Allyn and Bacon.

Early, M., and K. Rehage. 1999. *Issues in curriculum: A selection of chapters from past NSSE yearbooks*. Ninety-eighth yearbook of the National Society for the Study of Education. Chicago: NSSE.

Egan, K. 1986. *Teaching as story telling*. London, ON: Althouse Press.

———. 1988. *Primary understanding: Education in early childhood*. New York: Routledge.

———. 1990. *Romantic understanding: The development of rationality and imagination, ages 8–15*. New York: Routledge.

———. 1992. *Imagination in teaching and learning: The middle school years*. London, ON: Althouse Press.

———. 1997. *The educated mind: How cognitive tools shape our understanding*. Chicago: University of Chicago Press.

Eisner, E. 1979. *The educational imagination: On the design and evaluation of school programs*. New York:Macmillan.

Eisner, E., ed. 1985. *Learning and teaching the ways of knowing*. Eighty-fourth yearbook of the National Society for the Study of Education. Chicago: University of Chicago Press.

Eliot, T. S. 1952. Modern education and the class. *In Social criticism*. London: Penguin.

Ellul, J. 1981. *Perspectives on our age*. Toronto: Canadian Broadcasting Corporation.

Elmore, R., and S. Fuhrman, eds. 1994. *The governance of curriculum*. Alexandria, VA: Association for Supervision and Curriculum Development.

Erickson, H. L. 2001. *Stirring the heart, heart and soul: Redefining curriculum and instruction*. 2d ed. Thousand Oaks, CA: Corwin Press.

Ernest, P. 1991. *The philosophy of mathematics education*. London: Falmer.

Ezell, G. et al. 1993. *Healthy living*. A series of textbooks and teacher guides for teaching health. Grand Rapids: Christian Schools International.

Fan, L., and G. Kaeley. 2000. The influence of textbooks on teaching strategies: An empirical study. *Mid-Western Educational Researcher* 13 (4): 2–9.

Feiler, R., M. Heritage, and R. Gallimore. 2000. Teachers leading teachers. *Educational Leadership* 57 (7): 66–69.

Field, K., P. Holden, and H. Lawlor. 2000. *Effective subject leadership*. London: Routledge.

Fogarty, R. 1994. *How to teach for metacognitive reflection*. Palatine, IL: IRI Skylight.

Fosnot, C. 1996. *Constructivism: Theory, perspectives, and practice*. New York: Teachers College Press.

Fowler, S. 1991. *A Christian voice among students and scholars*. Potchefstroom, South Africa: Potchefstroom University for Christian Higher Education.

Francis, L., and A. Thatcher, eds. 1990. *Christian perspectives for education*. Leominster, UK: Gracewing.

Franklin, J. 2001. Trying too hard? How accountability and testing are affecting constructivist teaching. ASCD *Education Update* 43 (3): 1–8.

Fuhrman, S., ed. 2001. *From the Capitol to the classroom: Standards-based reform in the states*. One-hundredth yearbook of the National Society for the Study of Education. Chicago: NSSE.

Gardner, H. 1993. *Multiple intelligences: The theory in practice*. New York: Basic Books.

Gesch, C. 1993. Selections and highlights from English 10 and Bible 12 examinations. Distributed, respectively, as *Powerful stories, Sensitive readers*, and *Studying God's Word: Light for our path*. Smithers, BC: Bulkley Valley Christian School.

———. 1993. *Teaching aids for the conservation and outdoor recreation education course*. Telkwa, BC: Eskerhazy Publications.

Glatthorn, A. 1997. *The principal as curriculum leader*. Thousand Oaks, CA: Corwin Press.

Goleman, D. 1995. *Emotional intelligence*. New York: Bantam.

Good, T., and J. Brophy. 1994. *Looking in classrooms*. 6th ed. New York: HarperCollins.

Goudzwaard, B. 1984. *Idols of our time*. Downers Grove, IL: InterVarsity.

Greenberg, B., and J. Brand. 1993. Channel One: But what about the advertising? *Educational Leadership* 51 (4): 56–58.

Greene, A. 1984. Helps for preparing a statement of educational objectives for schools. Seven-page paper. Seattle: Alta Vista College.

———. 1998. *Reclaiming the future of Christian education: A transforming vision*. Colorado Springs: Association of Christian Schools International.

Greig, S., G. Pike, and D. Selby. 1989. *Greenprints for changing schools*. London: The World Wide Fund for Nature, and Kogan Page.

Groome, T. 1980. *Christian religious education*. San Francisco: Harper & Row.

Gross, S. 1998. *Staying centered: Curriculum leadership in a turbulent era*. Alexandria, VA: Association for Supervision and Curriculum Development.

Guild, P. Burke, and S. Garger. 1998. *Marching to different drummers*. 2d ed. Alexandria, VA: Association for Supervision and Curriculum Development.

Hamming, C., H. Van Brummelen, and P. Boonstra. 1984. *The story of numbers and numerals*. Grand Rapids: Christian Schools International.

Hare, W., and J. Portelli. 1988. *Philosophy of education: Introductory readings*. Calgary: Detselig.

Harmin, M., and T. Gregory. 1974. *Teaching is ...* Chicago: Science Research Associates.

Harris, M. 1987. *Teaching and religious imagination*. San Francisco: Harper & Row.

Haynes, C. 1993. Beyond the culture wars. *Educational Leadership* 51 (4): 30–34.

Healy, J. 2000. The I-generation-from toddlers to teenagers: A conversation with Jane M. Healy. *Educational Leadership* 58 (2): 8–13.

Holmes, M. 1992. *Educational policy for a pluralist democracy: The common school, choice, and diversity*. New York: Falmer.

Huebner, D. 1999. *The life of the transcendent*. Mahwah, NJ: Lawrence Erlbaum.

———. 1999. *The lure of the transcendent*. Mahwah, NJ: Lawrence Erlbaum.

Hytten, K. 1994. Pragmatism, postmodernism, and education. Paper presented at the American Educational Studies Association, November 1994. ERIC document ED378181.

Issler, K., and R. Habermas. 1994. *How we learn: A Christian teacher's guide to educational psychology*. Grand Rapids: Baker Books.

Jackson, P., ed. 1992. *Handbook of research on curriculum*. New York: Macmillan.

Jacobs, H. 1989. *Interdisciplinary curriculum: Design and implementation*. Alexandria, VA: Association for Supervision and Curriculum Development.

———. 1997. *Mapping the big picture: Integrating curriculum and assessment K–12*. Alexandria, VA: Association for Supervision and Curriculum Development.

Jones, A., ed. 1998. *Science in faith: A Christian perspective on teaching science*. Romford, UK: Christian Schools' Trust.

Jones, D. 2001. Music in education: Putting a price on it. *Vancouver Sun*, 15 March, sec. A, pp. 18–19.

Jossey-Bass reader on educational leadership. 1999. San Francisco: Jossey-Bass.

Kanpol, B. 1993. The pragmatic curriculum: Teacher reskilling as cultural politics. *The Journal of Educational Thought* 27 (2): 200–215.

———. 1998. *Teachers talking back and breaking bread*. Cresskill, NJ: Hampton Press.

Keenan, D. 1998. *Curriculum development for Christian schools*. Colorado Springs: Association of Christian Schools International.

Kilpatrick, W. 1992. *Why Johnny can't tell right from wrong*. New York: Simon and Schuster.

Klein, G. 1985. *Reading into racism: Bias in children's literature and learning materials*. London: Routledge, and Kegan Paul.

Kohlberg, L. 1971. Stages of moral development as a basis for moral education. In Beck, C., B. Crittenden, and E. Sullivan, *Moral education: Interdisciplinary approaches*. Toronto: University of Toronto.

Koole, R. 1990. *Christian perspective for teaching social studies.* Edmonton: CSI District 11.

———. 2000. Do you feel that your hands are tied? *Curriculum Link*, Langley, BC: Society of Christian Schools in British Columbia (November).

Kuhn, T. 1970 [1962]. *The structure of scientific revolutions.* 2d ed. Chicago: University of Chicago Press.

Lambert, I., and S. Mitchell, eds. 1997. *The crumbling walls of certainty: Toward a Christian critique of postmodernity and education.* Sydney, Australia: Centre for the Study of Australian Christianity.

Lasch, C. 1984. *The minimal self: Psychic survival in troubled times.* New York: Norton.

Leithwood, K., L. Leonard, and L. Sharratt. 1998. Conditions fostering organizational learning in schools. *Educational Administration Quarterly* 34 (2): 243–76.

Leithwood, K., D. Jantz, and R. Steinbach. 1999. *Changing leadership for changing times.* Philadelphia: Open University Press.

Lewy, A., ed. 1991. *The international encyclopedia of curriculum.* Oxford: Pergamon.

Lickona, T. 1991. *Educating for character: How our schools can teach respect and responsibility.* New York: Bantam.

———. 1993. The return of character education. *Educational Leadership* 51 (3): 6–11.

Loewen, J. 1995. *Lies my teacher told me: Everything your American history textbook got wrong.* New York: The New Press.

Luke, C., and J. Gore, eds. 1992. *Feminisms and critical pedagogy.* New York: Routledge, Chapman and Hall.

Macdonald, J., and D. Purpel. 1987. Curriculum and planning: Visions and metaphors. *Journal of Curriculum and Supervision* 2 (2): 178–92.

MacKenzie, P. et al. 1997. *Entry points for Christian reflection within education.* London, UK: Christian Action Research and Education.

Maggs, D. 1988. The family. Unpublished grade 11/12 unit.

Marzano, R., D. Pickering, and J. Pollock. 2001. *Classroom instruction that works: Research-based strategies for increasing student achievement.* Alexandria, VA: Association for Supervision and Curriculum Development.

Matthews, M. 1997. Introductory comments on philosophy and constructivism in science education. *Science and Education* 6: 5–14.

McCarthy, B. 1996. *About learning.* Barrington, IL: Excel.

———. 1997. A tale of four learners: 4Mat's learning styles. *Educational Leadership* 54 (6): 46–51.

McLaren, P. 1986. *Schooling as a ritual performance.* New York: Random House.

McNeil, J. 1995. *Curriculum: The teacher's initiative.* Englewood Cliffs, NJ: Merrill.

Moller, G., and M. Katzenmeyer, eds. 1996. *Every teacher as a leader.* San Francisco: Jossey-Bass.

Molnar, A. 1997. *The construction of children's character.* Ninety-sixth yearbook of the National Society for the Study of Education. Chicago: NSSE.

Nadeau, R., and J. Desautels. 1984. *Epistemology and the teaching of science.* Ottawa: Science Council of Canada.

National Association for Sport and Physical Education (NASPE). 1995. *Moving into the future: National standards for physical education.* Reston, VA: NASPE.

National Association of Secondary School Principals (NASSP). 1993. Science/technology/society-addressing the real problems in science education. *Curriculum Report* 22 (3): 1–4.

National Council for Teachers of Mathematics. 2000. *Principles and standards for school mathematics.* Reston, VA: NCTM.

Newbigin, L. 1983. *The other side of 1984.* Geneva: World Council of Churches.

———. 1989. *The gospel in a pluralist society.* Grand Rapids: Eerdmans.

Noebel, D. 1991. *Understanding the times: The religious worldviews of our day and the search for truth.* Eugene, OR: Harvest House.

Ontario Alliance of Christian Schools. 1994. *Thy will be done: Old Testament studies,* Unit One. Draft edition. Ancaster, ON.

Owens, V. 1983. *God spy: Faith, perception, and the new physics.* Seattle: Alta Vista College.

Palmer, P. 1983. *To know as we are known: A spirituality of education.* San Francisco: Harper & Row.

Parkay, F., and G. Hass. 2000. *Curriculum planning: A contemporary approach.* 7th ed. Boston: Allyn and Bacon.

Parsons, J., G. Milburn, and M. van Manen, eds. 1983. *A Canadian social studies.* Edmonton: University of Alberta.

Paul, R. 1988. Ethics without indoctrination. *Educational Leadership* 45 (8): 10–19.

Pell, B. 1989. Should Christians read "dirty books"? *Christian Educators Journal* 28 (3): 6–7.

Phillips, D. 2000. *Constructivism in education: Opinions and second opinions on controversial issues.* Ninety-ninth yearbook of the National Society for the Study of Education. Chicago: NSSE.

Pinar, W. 1988. *Contemporary curriculum discourses.* Scottsdale, AZ: Gorsuch Scarisbrick.

Pinar, W., W. Reynolds, P. Slattery, and P. Taubman. 1995. *Understanding curriculum: An introduction to the study of historical and contemporary curriculum discourses.* New York: Peter Lang.

Poincaré, H. 1956. Mathematical creation. In James R. Newman, *The World of Mathematics,* Vol. 4, pp. 2041–50. New York: Simon and Schuster.

Postman, N. 1993. *Technopoly: The surrender of culture to technology.* New York: Vintage.

Price, D., J. Wiester, and W. Hearn. 1986. *Teaching science in a climate of controversy.* Ipswich, MA: American Scientific Affiliation.

Purpel, D. 1989. *The moral and spiritual crisis in education.* Granby, MA: Bergin and Garvey.

Rau, S., L. Roseboom, and M. Zazitko. 1993. *The role of the family.* A primary resource unit. Langley, BC: Society of Christian Schools in British Columbia.

Senge, P. 1990. *The fifth discipline: The art and practice of the learning organization.* New York: Doubleday/Currency.

Sewall, G. 1995. Textbooks and religion. *The American School Board Journal* 182 (9): 32–34.

———. 2000. History 2000: Why the older textbooks may be better than the new. *Education Week* 31 May, pp. 52, 36.

Shapiro, B. 1993. Interpreting the world: Artistic and scientific ways of knowing. *English Quarterly* 26 (1): 26–29.

Shortt, J., ed. 1996. *Charis mathematics units 1–9.* Nottingham, UK: The Stapleford Centre.

———. 1997. *Charis mathematics units 10–19.* Nottingham, UK: The Stapleford Centre.

———. 1997. *Charis science units 1–11.* Nottingham, UK: The Stapleford Centre.

Shulman, L. 1987. Knowledge and teaching: Foundations of the new reform. *Harvard Educational Review* 57 (1): 1–22.

———. 2001. Appreciating good teaching: A conversation with Lee Shulman. *Educational Leadership* 58 (5): 6.

Shutes, R., and S. Peterson. 1994. Seven reasons why textbooks cannot make a curriculum. *NASSP Bulletin* 78 (565): 11–20.

Silver, H., R. Strong, and M. Perini. 2000. *So each may learn: Integrating learning styles and multiple intelligences.* Alexandria, VA: Association for Supervision and Curriculum Development.

Simon, S., L. Howe, and H. Kirschenbaum. 1972. *Values clarification: A handbook of practical strategies for teachers and students.* New York: A & W Publishers.

Sizer, T. 1992. *Horace's school: Redesigning the American high school.* Boston: Houghton-Mifflin.

Smith, D. 1991. Language, God, and man. *Language matters.* No. 1: 3–5.

———. 1992. Language, God, and man. *Language matters.* No. 3: 10–12.

Smith, D., and B. Carvill. 2000. The right book. Christian School Teacher 2 (1): 12–16. Excerpted from Smith, D., and B. Carvill. 2000. *The gift of the stranger: Faith, hospitality, and foreign language learning.* Grand Rapids: Eerdmans.

Society of Christian Schools in British Columbia (SCSBC). 1996. *Humanities 8: A resource guide.* Langley, BC.

———. 1998. *Christian pathways for schooling: Curriculum planning.* Langley, BC.

Somerville, M. 2000. *The ethical canary.* Toronto: Penguin.

Son, B. 1993. Uniqueness of Christ and social justice. *Evangelical Review of Theology* 17 (1): 93–109.

Spencer, H. 1911. *Essays on education.* London: J. M. Dent and Sons.

Steensma, G., and H. Van Brummelen, eds. 1977. *Shaping school curriculum: A biblical view.* Terre Haute, IN: Signal.

Steffe, L., and J. Gale, eds. 1995. *Constructivism in education.* Hillsdale, NJ: Lawrence Erlbaum.

Stott, J. 1978. *Christian counter-culture: The message of the Sermon on the Mount.* Downers Grove, IL: InterVarsity.

Stronks, G., and D. Blomberg, eds. 1993. *A vision with a task: Christian schooling for responsive discipleship.* Grand Rapids: Baker Books.

Suhor, C. 1998/1999. Spirituality-letting it grow in the classroom. *Educational Leadership* 56 (4): 12–16.

Thiessen, E. 1993. *Teaching for commitment: Liberal education, indoctrination, and Christian nurture.* Montreal: McGill-Queen's University Press.

Tomlinson, C. 1999. *The differentiated classroom: Responding to the needs of all learners.* Alexandria, VA: Association for Supervision and Curriculum Development.

Tomlinson, P., and M. Quinton, eds. 1986. *Values across the curriculum.* London: Falmer.

Tyler, R. 1950. *Basic principles of curriculum and instruction.* Chicago: University of Chicago Press.

Van Brummelen, H. 1991. The world portrayed in texts: An analysis of the content of elementary school textbooks. *The Journal of Educational Thought* 25 (3): 202–21.

———. 1994. Faith on the wane: A documentary analysis of shifting worldviews in Canadian textbooks. *Journal of Research on Christian Education* 3 (1): 51–77.

———. 1998. *Walking with God in the classroom.* 2d ed. Seattle: Alta Vista College Press.

Van Brummelen, H. et al. 1985. *Science.* A component of the SCS-BC Curriculum handbook. Surrey, BC: Society of Christian Schools in British Columbia.

Van Brummelen, H., and D. Elliott, eds. 1997. *Nurturing Christians as reflective educators.* San Dimas, CA: Learning Light Publishing.

Wagner, T. 2001. Leadership for learning: An action theory of school change. *Phi Delta Kappan* 82 (5): 378–83.

Walker, D. 1990. *Fundamentals of curriculum*. San Diego: Harcourt Brace Jovanovich.

Walsh, B., and J. Middleton. 1984. *The transforming vision: Shaping a Christian worldview*. Downers Grove, IL: InterVarsity.

Wassermann, S. 1992. A case for social studies. *Phi Delta Kappan* 73 (10): 793–801.

Werner, W., and T. Aoki. 1979. *Programs for people: Introducing program development, implementation, and evaluation*. Vancouver: Centre for the Study of Curriculum and Instruction (University of British Columbia).

Whitehead, A. 1929. *The aims of education and other essays*. New York: Macmillan.

Wiggins, G., and J. McTighe. 1998. *Understanding by design*. Alexandria, VA: Association for Supervision and Curriculum Development.

Willis, S. 1993. Learning through service. *Association for Supervision and Curriculum Development Update* 35 (6): 1–8.

———. 1995. Reinventing science education. *Curriculum Update*, Alexandria, VA: Association for Supervision and Curriculum Development (summer): 1–8.

Wilson, D. 1991. *Recovering the lost tools of learning: An approach to distinctively Christian education*. Wheaton, IL: Crossway Books.

Wineberg, S. 1991. On the reading of historical texts: Notes on the breach between school and academy. *American Educational Research Journal* 28 (3): 495–519.

Woehrle, T. 1993. Growing up responsible. *Educational Leadership* 51 (3): 40–43.

Wolters, A. 1985. *Creation regained: Biblical basics for a reformational worldview*. Grand Rapids: Eerdmans.

Wolterstorff, N. 1976. Reason within the bounds of religion. Grand Rapids: Eerdmans.

———. 1980. *Educating for responsible action*. Grand Rapids: Eerdmans.

Woods, J. 1982. *Looking at the consumer*. Toronto: Gage.

Zuidema, M., ed. 1995. *Physical education 3–5*. 3d ed. Grand Rapids: Christian Schools International.

Index